FROMMER'S

COMPREHENSIVE TRAVEL GUIDE
WASHINGTON, D.C. '95

by Rena Bulkin

MACMILLAN • USA

About the Author

Rena Bulkin began her travel-writing career when she set out for Europe in search of adventure. She found it writing about hotels and restaurants for the *New York Times* International Edition. She has since authored 15 travel guides to far-flung destinations.

FROMMER BOOKS

Macmillan Travel
A Prentice Hall Macmillan Company
15 Columbus Circle
New York, NY 10023

ISBN 0-671-88383-6
ISSN 0899-3246

Design by Robert Bull Design
Maps by Ortelius Design

SPECIAL SALES

Bulk purchases (10+ copies) of Frommer's Travel Guides are available to corporations at special discounts. The Special Sales Department can produce custom editions to be used as premiums and/or for sales promotion to suit individual needs. Existing editions can be produced with custom cover imprints such as corporate logos. For more information write to: Special Sales, Prentice Hall, 15 Columbus Circle, New York, NY 10023

Manufactured in the United States of America

CONTENTS

FOREWORD by Arthur Frommer

LIST OF MAPS

INVITATION TO THE READERS

In researching this book, I have come across many wonderful establishments, the best of which I have included here. I'm sure that many of you will also come across special hotels, inns, restaurants, guesthouses, shops, and attractions. Please don't keep them to yourself. Share your experiences, especially if you want to comment on the places that have been included in this edition that have changed for the worse. You can address your letters to:

Rena Bulkin
Frommer's Washington, D.C. '95
c/o Macmillan Travel
15 Columbus Circle
New York, NY 10023

By Arthur Frommer

Once a sleepy, southern-style town, Washington, D.C., has now become the communications capital of the nation, ousting New York from that position (to the dismay of New Yorkers like me). It's hard to admit that Washington, D.C., is now the publishing site of so many major U.S. newspapers, magazines, and books, that Dupont Circle has world-class salons and galleries, that great theatrical pageants open here before they come to Broadway, or that the city's Georgetown is as vital as Greenwich Village—but there it is. Washington, D.C., is now as cosmopolitan as any U.S. city (a sharp reversal of its previous status), and some visitors come here for recreation, leisure, and learning that have nothing at all to do with the federal government.

For that matter, several of its museums are today among the nation's greatest, and one of them—the new United States Holocaust Memorial Museum—is thoroughly unique and just as important. The magnificent Gothic National Cathedral has become a must-see, the restored Ford Theatre provides a touching moment, and a score of other nongovernment buildings, collections, and memorials—the Phillips Collection (European masters of the 19th and 20th centuries), Dumbarton Oaks (pre-Columbian art), the Corcoran Gallery of Art—would do credit to any city.

Still, it is Washington's status as capital of this country that provides its most essential sights. Although my own list of indispensable attractions won't differ much from anyone else's, it's important always to include such a recital at the outset of any guidebook to Washington, D.C., to prevent any highlight from being overlooked, either by inattention or because there is so much else to see here. My own unsurprising checklist is as follows:

(1) The Capitol, sessions of Congress, and meetings of Congressional committees. The latter can be attended by simply wandering into the appropriate committee rooms—without tickets or advance appointments; these meetings often provide insights into the workings of Congress as important as do the full sessions of the House or Senate (for which you'll need a ticket from your representative).

(2) The Supreme Court, especially on an "arguments-day" (for this information call 202/479-3030), and also courtroom lectures presented every half-hour on other weekdays.

(3) The Library of Congress, for such absorbing exhibits as the first rough drafts of the Declaration of Independence and the Gettysburg Address.

(4) The Washington, Lincoln, and Jefferson Memorials.

(5) The Folger Shakespeare Library, which the casual traveler will value for its important exhibits, if not for its research resources.

(6) The National Archives.

(7) Arlington National Cemetery, with its tomb of the Unknowns, the Kennedy gravesites, and Arlington House.

(8) The several museums of the Smithsonian Institution on the Mall, every one of them free of charge and together comprising the world's greatest array of artifacts and art.

(9) The new United States Holocaust Memorial Museum.

(10) The special tours of "working agencies" such as the Bureau of Engraving and Printing and the FBI.

And when you've completed the in-city sights, there are almost as many interesting trips to make to the outskirts and nearby: to the home of Washington at Mount Vernon some 20 miles away, to the U.S. Naval Academy at Annapolis about 30 miles away, and many more.

Of all the activities in Washington, D.C., the most rewarding to see may be a political gathering of citizens outside the Capitol, a "March on Washington" at the Mall, or a demonstration at Lafayette Square (opposite the White House) or elsewhere. Having participated in such weekend rallies myself for causes in which I believed, I can attest that nothing is more worthy of the capital city than these direct demonstrations of democracy by citizens who have come long distances to convey their views to their representatives. It is a glorious sight, whether or not you believe in the particular cause.

The reasons for coming to Washington, D.C., are fairly obvious, as can be confirmed from my short list above; no one can be at a loss for how to spend their time here—there are never enough hours in the day! But the best options for choosing lodgings and meals, in particular (selected from hundreds of alternatives and options)—have required months and months of research and repeated trips over the years. Rena Bulkin, our author, has been doing this book for nearly two decades, and having hired her initially for that task, I'm proud of her achievement. On these pages, you'll find the kind of skilled judgment and suitable choices made from long experience that are the hallmarks of a Frommer guide. And for added pleasure, I don't think you'll find another text that presents its information as lucidly and delightfully as Rena does.

Our very best wishes for your Washington, D.C., trip.

A DISCLAIMER

Readers are advised that prices fluctuate in the course of time and travel information changes under the impact of the varied and volatile factors that affect the travel industry. Neither the author nor the publisher can be held responsible for the experiences of readers while traveling. Readers are invited to write to the publisher with ideas, comments, and suggestions for future editions.

SAFETY ADVISORY

Whenever you're traveling in an unfamiliar city or country, stay alert. Be aware of your immediate surroundings. Wear a moneybelt and keep a close eye on your possessions. Be particularly careful with cameras, purses, and wallets, all favorite targets of thieves and pickpockets.

WHAT THE SYMBOLS MEAN

 FROMMER'S FAVORITES—hotels, restaurants, attractions, and entertainments you should not miss

 SUPER-SPECIAL VALUES—really exceptional values

 FROMMER'S SMART TRAVELER TIPS—hints on how to secure the best value for your money

IN HOTEL AND OTHER LISTINGS

The following symbols refer to the standard amenities available in all rooms:

A/C air conditioning   TEL telephone   TV television
MINIBAR refrigerator stocked with beverages and snacks

The following abbreviations are used for credit cards:

AE American Express   DISC Discover   MC MasterCard
CB Carte Blanche   JCB Card   V Visa
DC Diners Club

INTRODUCING WASHINGTON, D.C.

As home to one of the world's major powers, Washington, D.C., offers its own special brand of excitement. Here, visitors can linger in the halls and chambers where great leaders formulated the democratic process; listen to Senate debates; hear the Supreme Court in session; visit the National Archives, where the most cherished U.S. documents—the Declaration of Independence, the Constitution, and the Bill of Rights—are enshrined; find inspiration in magnificent monuments to the greatest American presidents and check out the palatial digs of the current chief executive; learn how the FBI works to thwart crime; and see dollar bills being churned out at the Bureau of Engraving and Printing. In short, visitors can experience firsthand just how the government of the United States works.

Edifices of gleaming marble are the background to Washington sightseeing. And surrounding the city's grand beaux arts buildings are spacious boulevards and tranquil tree-lined streets, grassy malls and parks, and circular plazas with splashing fountains and statuary at the focal points. This is a lushly verdant city. Millions of flowers create a dazzling riot of color in spring and summer, and every April the famous Japanese cherry trees burst into bloom along the Tidal Basin like a pink snowstorm. In almost every respect, the capital is a showplace, one of the most beautiful cities in the country. But that hasn't always been the case. . . .

1. CULTURE, HISTORY & BACKGROUND

Probably not an American alive thinks of Washington as a capital in the wilderness. But back in 1800, when Congress moved from its temporary home in Philadelphia to its new permanent seat of government on the Potomac, that's precisely what it was.

The Continental Congress had decided as early as 1783 that a federal city should be established as a permanent locale for its

WHAT'S SPECIAL ABOUT WASHINGTON, D.C.

Government Buildings

- ☐ The White House, the Capitol, two of America's most-visited shrines.
- ☐ The Supreme Court, Cass Gilbert's marble-columned temple.
- ☐ The National Archives, displaying original parchments of the Constitution, Declaration of Independence, and Bill of Rights.

Monuments

- ☐ Monuments to Presidents Washington, Lincoln, and Jefferson.
- ☐ The Vietnam Veterans Memorial, a poignant tribute.

After Dark

- ☐ The John F. Kennedy Center for the Performing Arts—our national cultural facility.
- ☐ The Arena Stage, repertory theater at its very best.
- ☐ Wolf Trap Farm Park, bucolic setting for a prestigious summer performing-arts festival.

Zoo

- ☐ National Zoo, home to more than 5,000 animals.

Architectural Highlights

- ☐ Library of Congress—the ornate Italian Renaissance-style Thomas Jefferson Building (1897).
- ☐ Smithsonian "Castle" (1849), Victorian red-turreted and towered James Renwick building, the first in the famed museum complex.
- ☐ Union Station (1907), modeled after Rome's Baths of Diocletian and Arch of Constantine.
- ☐ Old Post Office Pavilion (1899), in Romanesque style, crowned by a 315-foot clock tower.
- ☐ Old Stone House (1765), probably the city's oldest surviving pre-Revolutionary building.
- ☐ The Renwick Gallery (1859), a landmark building of the French Second Empire style.

Parks and Gardens

- ☐ West Potomac Park, site of the famous cherry trees.
- ☐ C&O Canal, built in the 1800s when inland water routes were vital to transportation; today a major D.C. recreational area.
- ☐ The National Arboretum, containing the National Bonsai Collection.
- ☐ Rock Creek Park, a 1,754-acre playground in the heart of the city.

For Kids

- ☐ The National Air & Space Museum, where exhibits range from the 1903 Wright Brothers' plane to the *Apollo 11* command module.
- ☐ The Museum of Natural History Discovery Room, for a hands-on learning experience.
- ☐ The FBI building, where exhibits range from the DNA lab to weapons used by notorious 1930s gangsters.

meetings. But even then, the question of slavery created a gap between the North and the South. The northern states insisted that the new capital be in the North, while southerners championed a national seat of government in their precincts.

Wrangling about a location for the capital continued until 1790, when New Yorker Alexander Hamilton and Virginian Thomas Jefferson resolved the dispute (over dinner in a Manhattan restaurant) with a compromise. In return for the South's agreement to pay the national Revolutionary War debts, the capital would be located in the South. Furthermore, it would be named Washington after the first U.S. president and (probably more important) a resident of the Commonwealth of Virginia.

By Act of Congress, George Washington was given full authority to choose a site "not exceeding ten miles square on the River Potomac . . . for the permanent seat of the Government of the United States."

ENTER PIERRE L'ENFANT

Virginia and Maryland, by agreement, ceded land for the new capital. It was to be known as the Federal District and to include Georgetown in Maryland and Alexandria in Virginia. In 1791 Pierre Charles L'Enfant was employed by George Washington to survey the land and plan the city. L'Enfant, a Frenchman, had distinguished himself as an engineer in the Revolutionary Army. He had also remodeled New York's City Hall to serve as the first seat for our federal government.

L'Enfant's master plan (which you can see in the Library of Congress) proposed a "presidential palace" linked to the "home of Congress" by a vast green mall. Asked how he happened to choose the hill at the west end of Jenkins Heights as the site for the Capitol, he responded, "It stands as a pedestal waiting for a monument."

Assisting L'Enfant in laying out the design was Benjamin Banneker, an African-American surveyor, inventor, and mathematician. He was specifically responsible for drawing up the District boundary that affected the state of Maryland.

DATELINE

- **1608** Capt. John Smith sails up Potomac River from Jamestown; for the next 100 years Irish-Scotch settlers colonize the area.
- **1783** Continental Congress proposes new "Federal Town"; North and South vie for it.
- **1790** A compromise is reached: If South pays off North's Revolutionary War debts, new capital will be situated in its region.
- **1791** French engineer Pierre Charles L'Enfant designs capital city but is fired within year.
- **1792** Cornerstone is laid for Executive Mansion.
- **1793** Construction begins on Capitol.
- **1800** First wing of Capitol completed; Congress moves from Philadelphia; Pres. John Adams moves into Executive Mansion.
- **1801** Library of Congress established.
- **1812** War with England.
- **1814** British burn Washington.
- **1817** Executive Mansion rebuilt, its charred walls painted white; becomes *(continues)*

DATELINE

known as White House.

1822 Population reaches 15,000.

1829 Smithsonian Institution founded for "increase and diffusion of knowledge."

1847 Cornerstone laid for first Smithsonian museum building.

1861 Civil War; Washington becomes North's major supply depot.

1865 Capitol dome completed; Lee surrenders to Grant April 8; Lincoln assassinated at Ford's Theatre April 14.

1871 Alexander "Boss" Shepherd turns Washington into a showplace, using many L'Enfant plans.

1889 National Zoo established.

1900 Population reaches about 300,000.

1901 McMillan Commission plans development of Mall from Capitol to Lincoln Memorial.

1907 Union Station opens, largest train station in country.

1908 Federal Bureau of Investigation (FBI) created.

1912 Cherry trees, a gift from Japan, planted in Tidal Basin.

1914 World War I begins.

1922 Lincoln Memorial completed.

(continues)

L'Enfant, though a genius, was also temperamental. He had no patience for practical politics and refused to cooperate with building commissioners or Washington's appointed surveyor, Andrew Ellicott. And he ignored Washington's repeated requests to produce a preliminary blueprint so that fundraising could begin. His situation became increasingly difficult, and in 1792 he was fired. For the next few decades, the embittered L'Enfant was often seen "haunting the lobbies of the Capitol . . . pacing the newly marked avenues"—keeping a jaundiced eye on the developing city. Architect Benjamin Latrobe wrote in his diary: "Daily through the city stalks the picture of famine, L'Enfant and his dog."

When L'Enfant died in 1825, the fact that he had designed Washington had been practically forgotten. His superb plans were gathering dust; the city that had begun with such grandiose vision muddled along as a nondescript small town. L'Enfant was buried without fanfare, and it wasn't until 1909 that his grave was moved to Arlington National Cemetery to rest on a hill looking out over the city that owes him so much.

LAYING THE FOUNDATION

Back in 1792, a nationwide competition was held for the design of the Capitol Building to be erected on the hill L'Enfant had designated. The winner was a young physician, an amateur architect named William Thornton, who later founded the Patent Office. (Architects in those days had little professional standing.) In the words of Thomas Jefferson, another "amateur" architect, the Capitol plan "captivated the eye and judgment of all." George Washington noted that "grandeur, simplicity, and convenience appear to be . . . well combined in this plan." The cornerstone for the Capitol was laid September 18, 1793, beside the banks of what the Native Americans called "The River of Swans," the Potomac.

The competition to design the "presidential palace" was won by an Irishman, James Hoban, who received $500 for his plan. (Other entrants included Thomas Jefferson, who submitted his design anonymously.) Hoban hailed from North Carolina, where he had designed that state's capitol building. Because the White House cornerstone was laid in 1792, it holds the distinction of being the oldest public building in Washington. George Washington, however, never occupied the mansion and is, in fact, the only American president never to have resided there. John Adams, the second president, became the first tenant on November 1, 1800—before the house was fully completed.

A CITY RISES

In the considerable period before the public buildings were finished, it was suggested that Congress meet alternately in Trenton, New Jersey, and Annapolis, Maryland—that is, part of the time in the North, part of the time in the South. This idea of shifting meetings was rejected when Francis Hopkinson suggested, sardonically, that a federal town be built on a platform on wheels and rolled back and forth between two places of residence.

By 1800 one wing of the Capitol Building was ready for the legislators. They moved down from Philadelphia, the last temporary capital, in the fall of that year.

As the first occupants of the White House, President and Mrs. Adams headed from Baltimore cross country, and they got so hopelessly lost that they "wandered for two hours without finding a guide or path." When they finally arrived, however, Abigail Adams pronounced her new home "a beautiful spot, capable of any improvement." Mrs. Adams, a Yankee woman of grit and gumption, finding "not the least fence, yard, or other convenience," took it upon herself to hang the laundry out to dry in the East Room.

Pennsylvania Avenue, on paper the principal boulevard between the Capitol

DATELINE

- **1941** National Gallery of Art opens; U.S. declares war on Japan.
- **1943** Pantheon-inspired Jefferson Memorial and Pentagon completed.
- **1949** Interior of White House rebuilt.
- **1957** Helicopters first seen on White House lawn.
- **1960** Population reaches almost 800,000
- **1961** John F. Kennedy becomes first Catholic president.
- **1971** John F. Kennedy Center for Performing Arts opens.
- **1976** Metro, city's first subway system, opens in time for Bicentennial.
- **1982** Vietnam Veterans Memorial erected in Constitution Gardens.
- **1987** Arthur M. Sackler Gallery, a new Smithsonian facility focusing on Asian art, opens on Mall; expanded Museum of African Art, also part of Smithsonian, moves to Mall.
- **1991** Population exceeds 3 million.
- 1993 U.S. Holocaust Memorial Museum, documenting the horror and tragedy of Nazi era, opens near Mall.

and the presidential palace, was then a muddy morass of a pathway covered with alder bushes. Where the path reached Georgetown, "houses had been erected, which bore the name of *The Six Buildings*," a put-down of those who harbored ideas that it was a blossoming megalopolis

Never mind. The new federal capital was in business. And John Adams wasted no time in delivering his presidential address to the first joint session of Congress. Yet the grumbling continued.

John Cotton, a congressman from Connecticut, complained: "A sidewalk was attempted in one instance by a covering formed of the chips hewed from the Capitol. It extended but a little way and was of little value, for in dry weather the sharp fragments cut our shoes, and in wet weather covered them with white mortar."

Newspapers all over the country quipped about "the palace in the wilderness" and referred to Pennsylvania Avenue as "the great Serbonian bog." Georgetown was called "a city of houses without streets" and Washington "a city of streets without houses."

Speculation escalated land prices in the capital. Congress had agreed to purchase land for public building sites. Land surrounding these sites was to be sold, with half the proceeds from the sale of lots to go to the landowners, half to the government for the erection of government buildings.

But as land prices soared around the Capitol Building, those who would have liked to live in the area were forced to buy elsewhere. As a result, settlement shifted toward the northwest, and, even today, the most fashionable town houses and embassies are found in the Northwest section. The area along Pennsylvania Avenue remained a soggy swamp. And when the land speculation syndicate fell apart in 1796, financial support for constructing government buildings went down the drain, too.

Jefferson, when he assumed the presidency in 1801, had to secure money from Congress for public buildings. He planted poplar trees along Pennsylvania Avenue, doing what he could to make the "Appian Way of the Republic" something better than a "slough of despond " The Library of Congress was also established at this time

Thomas Moore, Ireland s national lyricist, on a visit in 1804 cracked

> *And what was Goose Creek once is Tiber now*
> *This fam'd metropolis, where fancy sees,*
> *Squares in morasses, obelisks in trees,*
> *Which second-sighted seers e'en now adorn,*
> *With shrines unbuilt and heroes yet unborn*

Building went on slowly, but no sooner had the youthful Congress seen James and Dolley Madison installed in the White House than it became necessary to declare war England had been impressing American seamen, and disputes over western land worsened the situation The War of 1812 had begun

A CITY BURNS

On August 24, 1814, the British fleet sailed into Chesapeake Bay and marched on the capital. Admiral George Cockburn (pronounced Co-burn by the British) was in charge of the attack.

Fortunately, everybody knew that they were coming. Dolley Madison stubbornly stayed on in the White House, determined to save all she could. She hustled important documents off to Lewisburg, 35 miles northwest of Washington, for protection. When friends insisted that she leave for her own safety, at the last minute she cut Gilbert Stuart's portrait of George Washington out of its frame, rolled it up, and hied off to a nearby army camp where she spent the night in a tent, a soldier guarding the entrance. This famous portrait, probably the oldest original possession in the White House, hangs today in the East Room. Dolley Madison knew George Washington well—her younger sister, Lucy, was married to Washington's nephew—and she considered the portrait a remarkable likeness. Dolley saved another painting, too—a portrait of herself—which also hangs in the White House.

Luckily for the budding nation, the rains came on that fateful night. A torrential storm halted the flames that might have destroyed the city completely.

When the Madisons moved back into town, they set up housekeeping at Octagon House, on the corner of 18th Street and New York Avenue. The gala parties Dolley threw helped relieve the pall over Washington left by the war.

The Madisons remained at Octagon House until 1815, when they moved to the northwest corner of Pennsylvania Avenue and 19th Street, to a place known simply as "The Seven Buildings," early housing for the Department of State. There they stayed until the executive mansion was rebuilt, its charred walls painted white in March 1817 Ever since, the "president's palace" has been called the White House

A CITY REBUILDS

After the British withdrew, Congress first met in the Blodgett Hotel, then moved into a brick building across from the burned-out Capitol James Monroe took the presidential oath on the porch of what became known as the "Brick Capitol," which stood where the Supreme Court now stands, beginning the tradition of taking the presidential oath in open air, sometimes a chilly event in January

Monroe also refurnished the burned-out White House with some $15,000 worth of French-designed furniture Jefferson, Madison, and Monroe all had a taste for things French, and it's still reflected throughout the White House More recently, First Lady Jacqueline Kennedy also a Francophile, was responsible for refurnishing and redecorating the White House to reveal its original French character

Repair work on the Capitol Building was directed by Benjamin Latrobe, an Englishman who had taken over responsibility for its construction in 1803 Slowly he replaced the gutted wood with marble, brick, and metal. It was reoccupied by Congress in 1819.

By 1822, only 22 years after its founding and eight years after being burned, the capital city boasted a population of nearly 15,000 people.

In 1829 the Smithsonian Institution was created when an Englishman, James Smithson, left half a million dollars "to found at Washington, under the name of the Smithsonian Institution, an establishment for the increase and diffusion of knowledge. . . ." Smithson never visited the United States, but the cornerstone for his great legacy, the now-sprawling Smithsonian, was laid in 1847. The first building in the complex is a red sandstone castle of Norman inspiration. That original building is located on the Mall, and it was reopened to the public after undergoing considerable restoration in 1972. Today it serves as a visitor information center for the Smithsonian complex.

Government building continued to boom. By 1842 the present Treasury Building—blocking the vista from the White House to the Capitol and spoiling L'Enfant's original plan—was completed. Andrew Jackson had tired of waiting for the appointed Commission to choose a Treasury site, so he marched out of the White House one day, pointed to a spot, and said that the Treasury cornerstone would be laid there. His will was done . . plunk in the middle of Pennsylvania Avenue!

MID-19TH-CENTURY WASHINGTON

From all this, you might assume that Washington was well on its way from villagehood to cityhood. Gas lights were lit on the Capitol grounds in 1847. But by 1860 no more than Pennsylvania Avenue had been lit. "Pigs roamed the principal thoroughfares, pavements but for a few patches were lacking, and open sewers carried off refuse" Visiting author Anthony Trollope declared Washington "as melancholy and miserable a town as the mind of man could conceive" Soon things would get even worse.

The Civil War turned the capital into an armed camp. It was the principal supply depot of the North and an important medical center. The rotunda of the Capitol Building—its 9-million-pound cast-iron dome completed in 1865—was used as a barracks, referred to by the soldiers as "the big tent" Later it became a troop hospital, and here the American poet Walt Whitman wandered among the wounded, helping where he could Altogether, 3,000 troops were billeted in the Capitol, and basement committee rooms were converted into bakeries

The Civil War ended when Lee surrendered to Grant on April 8, 1865 The greatest parade in the capital's history celebrated this event To the tune of fife and drums, troops marched down Pennsylvania Avenue for two full days and nights. Less than a week later, on April 14, Pres. Abraham Lincoln was shot at Ford's Theatre by John Wilkes Booth, and the city went into mourning.

The war's legacy was poverty, unemployment, and disease Washington's population swelled with uneducated, agrarian

IMPRESSIONS

I know of no other capital in the world which stands on so wide and splendid a river. But the people and the mode of life are enough to take your hair off!
—HENRY ADAMS

My God! What have I done to be condemned to reside in such a city!
—A French diplomat in the early days

The whole aspect of Washington is light, cheerful, and airy; it reminds me of our fashionable watering places.
—MRS. FRANCES TROLLOPE

Washington . . . enormous spaces, hundreds of miles of asphalt, a charming climate, and the most entertaining society in America.
—HENRY JAMES

ex-slaves, and tenement slums arose within a stone's throw of the Capitol

SUDDEN EXPANSION

In 1870 several factions attempted to transfer the national capital to another city. St. Louis bid several million dollars for the honor, and Horace Greeley suggested that the capital go west. But the move never got seriously under way, and Congress went ahead and voted $500,000 to build the Departments of State and War and the Navy Building.

Enter "Boss" Shepherd and a new era. Gov. Alexander R. Shepherd was chosen to head a territorial government established in the District of Columbia from 1871 to 1874. Shepherd was a handsome, strapping man with blustery charm. He'd been a successful plumber, an alderman, a newspaper owner, and president of the City Reform Association. He was a natural to become leader of the territorial government. Once installed in office, though, he ignored budgets and followed a bankruptcy course to beautify his domain. Under his guidance, the L'Enfant plan was finally executed in earnest. Three hundred miles of half-laid streets were improved. Nearly every thickly populated thoroughfare was paved with wood, concrete, or macadam. Some 128 miles of sidewalks were built, and 3,000 gas lamps and a system of sewers were installed. Old Tiber Creek was filled in. Scores of new parks were graded and beautified with fountains. A special park commission planted 6,000 trees.

Soon there were more paved streets in Washington than in any other city in the country. And Pres. Ulysses S. Grant declared in a message to Congress, "Washington is rapidly becoming a city worthy of the nation's capital." Grant temporarily swept a few facts about the grand public works under the rug—like the whopping $20-million bill for the improvements.

Before long Congress reacted, and Shepherd was nearly booed out of town. In 1874 the territorial form of government gave way to a trio of commissioners. Shepherd took his family to Mexico.

But when he returned to the United States in 1887, he was acclaimed as the man who had made Washington a showplace. And he certainly had.

The nation's Centennial Celebration of 1876 in Philadelphia and the Chicago Exposition of 1893 brought about a cultural awakening throughout the country. Following that period, the Corcoran Art Gallery was built in Washington, the Metropolitan Museum in New York, and the Museum of Fine Arts in Boston. In 1884 the Washington Monument was completed. And in 1897 the Library of Congress, which took 11 years to build, was completed. During the following year, 1898, L'Enfant's plan was dusted off again, and adjustments were made to tailor the District to the motor age.

But the capital of the United States was 100 years old and home to 300,000 before the plan for development and improvement drawn up by the McMillan Commission was enacted in 1901. At his own expense, James McMillan, a senator from Michigan, sent an illustrious committee—New York's Central Park landscapist Frederick Law Olmsted, sculptor Augustus Saint-Gaudens, and noted architects Daniel Burnham and Charles McKim—to Europe on a seven-week study tour to observe the architecture and landscaping of the world's great capitals. It was a committee worthy of L'Enfant's vision and backed by the necessary political clout to get the job done

The principal thrust of the commission's plan was to develop the Mall, which, at the turn of the century, was little more than a pasture traversed by the tracks of the Pennsylvania Rail Road. The company agreed to remove its tracks in return for funding to construct Union Station.

The Mall, in addition to housing the National Gallery of Art and the Smithsonian Institution, was to become the site for the Department of Agriculture and other important structures. When finished, it would extend 1 mile in length, 300 feet in width, from the Capitol through the Washington Monument, beyond to the Lincoln Memorial. Projected plans also included several public buildings—office buildings for members of the House, Senate, and the Supreme Court (which had met in the Capitol until then).

Aesthetics came into play in 1910, when the National Commission of Fine Arts was created by President Taft. Its duty was to advise on fountains, statues, and monuments in public squares, streets, and parks throughout the District of Columbia. Thanks to Mrs. Taft, the famous cherry trees presented to the United States by the Japanese in 1912 were planted in the Tidal Basin. And thanks to Taft's commission, neoclassic architecture and uniform building height became the order of the day. The commission fixed a 110-foot maximum rooftop height for buildings in the downtown district, so that the Capitol dome might be seen from miles around.

WASHINGTON TODAY

During the Great Depression in the 1930s, FDR's Works Progress Administration—WPA, *We Do Our Part*—put the unemployed to work erecting public buildings and artists to work beautifying them

More recently (1971), the John F. Kennedy Center for the Performing Arts, on the Potomac's east bank, filled a longtime need for a cultural haven.

In 1974 the opening of the new Hirshhorn Museum and Sculpture Garden on the Mall met the need for a major museum of modern art. Another storehouse of art treasures is the magnificent East Building of the National Gallery of Art, which opened in 1978. It was designed to handle the overflow of the gallery's burgeoning collection and to accommodate traveling exhibits of major importance.

In time for the Bicentennial, the National Air and Space Museum opened in splendid new quarters, and the first leg of the capital's much-needed subway system, Metro, was completed. The 45 acres between the Washington Monument and the Lincoln Memorial were transformed into Constitution Gardens, and in 1982 the park became the site of the Vietnam Veterans Memorial.

In 1987 Washington got a new $75-million Smithsonian complex on the Mall; it houses the Arthur M. Sackler Gallery of Art, the relocated National Museum of African Art, the International Center, and the Enid A. Haupt Garden. In 1989 renovation of the city's magnificent Union Station (inspired by the Baths of Diocletian) was completed. And 1993 saw the opening of the United States Holocaust Memorial Museum, adjoining the Mall.

Over the years, the capital has changed for the better, and the people are changing too. Washingtonians are becoming much more sophisticated and much more demanding. Today, D.C. can hold its own as a great town for theater, dining, shopping, concert-going, and other metropolitan pleasures.

So it's no wonder Washington attracts more than 20 million tourists each year. History and heritage, art and politics, cuisine and culture combine to make this a vital and beautiful city—a fitting capital for a great nation.

2. FAMOUS WASHINGTONIANS

Benjamin Banneker (1731–1806) When Pierre L'Enfant left Washington in 1792, Banneker, a black mathematician, astronomer, and surveyor, re-created his maps and city plans from memory.

Art Buchwald (b. 1925) Pulitzer Prize–winning syndicated columnist and political satirist.

Frederick Douglass (1818–95) Born in slavery, he escaped and fled north to become a driving force in the abolitionist movement and its most impassioned voice.

Edward [Duke] Ellington (1899–1974) Native Washingtonian, bandleader, pianist, and songwriter, he composed "Mood Indigo," "Sophisticated Lady," and "Take the 'A' Train."

Helen Hayes (1900–93) The First Lady of the American Theater was well known for her roles in *Long Day's Journey into Night* and *The Glass Menagerie*

Pierre Charles L'Enfant (1754–1825) Brilliant French military engineer who, invited by George Washington, laid out plans for the national capital in 1791.

Dolley Madison (1769–1849) President Madison's wife and capital society's first queen, she rescued Gilbert Stuart's famous portrait of George Washington from the British in the War of 1812.

Perle Mesta (1891–1975) Official Washington's "hostess with the mostest," especially during the Truman years. She was the inspiration for the musical *Call Me Madam.*

James Smithson (1765–1829) Although he never set foot in the United States, he should be considered an honorary Washingtonian because he left his fortune to this country for the museum complex that, bearing his name, has become the largest in the world.

John Philip Sousa (1854–1932) America's bandmaster, known as "The March King," composer of "Semper Fidelis," "Stars and Stripes Forever," and "The Washington Post."

Walt Whitman (1819–92) American poet, author of *Leaves of Grass* and "O Captain, My Captain," the latter a tribute to Lincoln, whom he greatly admired

3. RECOMMENDED BOOKS & FILMS

BOOKS

As the capital of the United States, Washington probably is better documented than any other American city. The following list is a good starting point for further reading

ECONOMIC, POLITICAL & SOCIAL HISTORY

Adler, Bill. *Washington, a Reader.* Meredith Press, 1967.

Arnebeck, Bob, *Through a Fiery Trial: Building Washington, 1790–1800.* Madison, 1991.

Bishop, Jim. *The Day Lincoln Was Shot.* Harper & Row, 1955.

Cooke, Alistair. *One Man's America.* Knopf, 1952.

Duncan, Don. *Washington: The First One Hundred Years.* Seattle Times, 1989.

Kite, Elizabeth S. *L'Enfant and Washington, 1791–92* Ayer Co., 1970.

Loftin, T. L. *Contest for a Capital.* TL Loftin, 1989.

Schlesinger, Arthur M., Jr. *The Birth of the Nation.* Houghton Mifflin, 1968.

Terrell, John Upton. *The Key to Washington.* JB Lippincott, 1962.

ARCHITECTURE & THE ARTS

Aylesworth, Thomas, and Virginia Aylesworth. *Washington, the*

Nation's Capital. Gallery Books, a division of WH Smith, 1986.

Carter, Edward C., et al. *Latrobe's View of America, 1795–1820* (Selections from the Watercolors and Sketches). Yale University Press, 1985.

Reed, Robert. *Old Washington, D.C., in Early Photographs.* Dover, 1980.

FICTION & MYSTERY

Drury, Allen. *Advise and Consent.* Doubleday, 1959.

McCarthy, Abigail. *Circles, a Washington Story.* Doubleday, 1977.

Roosevelt, Elliott. *The White House Pantry Murder* and others in the Eleanor Roosevelt as sleuth series. St. Martin's Press, 1987.

Truman, Margaret. *Murder at the Smithsonian, . . . at the FBI, . . . at the CIA, . . . in Georgetown*; and six others in the Capital Crimes Series. Fawcett, 1985–1990.

HUMOR

Adler, Bill. *The Washington Wits.* Macmillan, 1967.

Pitch, Anthony S. *Exclusively Washington Trivia.* Mino, 1989.

Rash, Bryson B. *Footnote Washington.* EPM, 1983.

FOR KIDS

Krementz, Jill. *A Visit to Washington, D.C.* Scholastic, 1987.

Loewen, N. *Washington, D.C.* Rourke, 1989.

Petersen, Anne. *Kidding Around Washington, D.C.: A Young Person's Guide to the City.* John Muir, 1989.

Weston, Marti, and Florri DeCell. *Washington! Adventures for Kids.* Vandemeer, 1989.

FILMS

Hundreds of film companies have used the streets and famous interiors of Washington, D.C., as a setting for films for some 80 years. Some of the more memorable include *Birth of a Nation* (1915), *Mr. Smith Goes to Washington* (1939), *Born Yesterday* and *Magnificent Yankee* (1950), *The FBI Story* (1959), *Advise and Consent* (1962), *Seven Days in May* (1964), *The Last Detail* (1974), *All the President's Men* (1976), *The Seduction of Joe Tynan* (1978), *Heartburn* (1985), *No Way Out* (1986), and *Broadcast News* (1987).

CHAPTER 2

PLANNING A TRIP TO WASHINGTON, D.C.

A lot of what you'll want to see and do in the capital can be arranged after you arrive, but some things should be planned in advance, while you're still home.

1. BEFORE YOU GO

Before you leave, contact the **Washington, D.C., Convention and Visitors Association,** 1212 New York Ave. NW, Washington, DC 20005 (tel. 202/789-7000), and ask for free maps, a calendar of events, and a copy of the *Washington, D.C., Guide,* which details hotels, restaurants, sights, shops, and more. They'll also be happy to answer specific questions.

Also write or call the **D.C. Committee to Promote Washington,** P.O. Box 27489, Washington, DC 20038-7489 (tel. 202/724-4091, or toll-free 800/422-8644), and request a copy of *Washington Weekends.* It lists low weekend rates at dozens of Washington hotels.

SPECIAL PASSES FOR VIP TOURS

Senators and/or congressional representatives can provide their constituents with passes for VIP tours of the Capitol, the White House, the FBI, the Bureau of Engraving and Printing, and the Kennedy Center. This is no secret. Thousands of people know about it and do write, so make your request as far in advance as possible—even six months ahead is not too early—specifying the dates you plan to visit and the number of tickets you need. Their allotment of tickets for each sight is limited, so there's no guarantee you'll secure tickets, but it's worth a try. At the very least you can get some general information about Washington.

Address requests to representatives to: U.S. House of Representatives, Washington, DC 20515; and to senators to: U.S. Senate, Washington, DC 20510. Don't forget to include the exact dates of your Washington trip. When you write, also request tourist information and literature.

Note: Before writing, you might try calling a senator or congressperson's local office; in some states you can obtain passes by phone.

THE CAPITOL There are special, more comprehensive, tours of the Capitol given between 8 and 9am, Monday to Friday, for those with passes.

THE WHITE HOUSE Between 8 and 8:45am the doors of the White House are open for special VIP tours to those with tickets. Once again, write far, far in advance, because each senator receives only 15 tickets a week to distribute, and each representative only 10. These early tours ensure your entrance in the busy tourist season when thousands line up during the two hours daily that the White House is open to the public. They're also more extensive than later tours, with guides providing explanatory commentary as you go; on later tours, docents are on hand to answer questions but don't give formal talks in each room.

THE FBI The line for this very popular tour can be extremely long. One way to beat the system is to ask a senator or representative to make a reservation for you for a scheduled time.

BUREAU OF ENGRAVING & PRINTING Guided VIP tours are offered weekdays at 8am, except on holidays and the days after holidays. Later, non-VIP tours are self-guided.

THE KENNEDY CENTER The VIP tour offered Monday through Saturday at 9:30am allows you to avoid a long wait with the masses who did not take the trouble to write to a senator or representative.

WHAT THINGS COST IN WASHINGTON U.S. $	
Taxi from National Airport to downtown	10.00–12.00
Bus from National Airport to downtown	8.00 (14.00 round-trip)
Local telephone call	.25
Double at the Jefferson Hotel (very expensive)	235.00–275.00
Double at the Barceló Washington Hotel (expensive)	155.00–180.00
Double at the Channel Inn (moderate)	110.00–135.00
Double at the Days Inn Downtown (inexpensive)	87.00–97.00
Double at the Hostelling International (budget)	20.00
Three-course dinner at the Willard Room (very expensive)	55.00
Three course dinner at Petitto's (expensive)	35.00
Three-course dinner at Clyde's (moderate)	18.00–22.00

	U.S. $
Three-course dinner at Scholl's Cafeteria (budget)	7.00–8.00
Bottle of beer (restaurant)	2.75
Coca-Cola (restaurant)	1.50
Cup of coffee (restaurant)	1.25
Roll of ASA 100 Kodacolor film, 36 exposures	4.50
Admission to all Smithsonian museums	Free
Theater ticket at the National	22.50–60.00

2. WHEN TO GO—CLIMATE & EVENTS

THE CLIMATE

Probably you'll visit when you have vacation time or when the kids are out of school, but assuming you have the luxury of choice I'd recommend the fall. The weather is lovely, Washington's scenery is awash in fall foliage colors, and the tourists have thinned out.

If you really hate crowds and want to get the most out of Washington sights, winter is your season. It's not that cold (see chart below), there are no long lines or early-morning dashes to avoid them, and hotel prices are lower.

Spring weather is delightful, and of course there are those cherry blossoms. Along with autumn, it's the nicest time to enjoy D.C.'s outdoor attractions, to get around to museums in comfort, to laze away an afternoon or evening at the ubiquitous Washington street cafés. But the city is also crowded with millions of tourists.

The throngs remain in summer, and anyone who's ever spent a summer in D.C. will tell you how hot and steamy it is. Though there's occasional relief, those 90° days do seem to arrive with amazing frequency. The advantage: This is the season to enjoy hundreds of outdoor events—free concerts, festivals, parades, Revolutionary War reenactments, and more. There's something doing almost every night and day. And, of course, Independence Day (July 4) in the capital is a spectacular celebration. But no matter when you visit, you can be sure there's plenty going on around town.

Average Temperatures [°F] in Washington, D.C.

	Jan	Feb	Mar	Apr	May	June	July	Aug	Sept	Oct	Nov	Dec
High	44	44	53	64	75	83	87	84	78	68	55	45
Low	24	28	35	44	55	64	68	66	60	48	38	30

WASHINGTON CALENDAR OF EVENTS

The District is the scene of numerous daily special events, fairs, and celebrations. Listed below are the major annual events. When in town, check the *Washington Post,* especially the Friday "Weekend" section, and pick up an events calendar at the Washington Visitor Information Center, 1455 Pennsylvania Ave. (tel. 789-7038). The Smithsonian Information Center, 1000 Jefferson Dr. SW (tel. 357-2700), is another good source. For annual events in Alexandria, see Chapter 10.

JANUARY

☐ **Washington Antique Show,** Omni Shoreham Hotel, 2500 Calvert St. NW, at Connecticut Avenue (tel. 234-0700). About 50 outstanding East Coast dealers display their wares. Admission is charged, and profits go to charities. This is an impressive show, with displays of artifacts relating to the annual theme (for example, historical preservation). Catalogs include articles by scholars and museum curators, and there are guest speakers—for example, George Plimpton, J. Carter Brown, and Henry Kissinger. Early in January.

☐ **Presidential Inauguration,** on the Capitol steps. After the swearing-in, the crowd follows the new president down Pennsylvania Avenue to the White House. The event is heralded by parades, concerts, parties, plays, and other festivities. For details, call 789-7038. January 20 in years following a national election.

☐ **Martin Luther King, Jr.'s, Birthday.** Events include speeches by prominent civil-rights leaders and politicians; readings; dance, theater, and choral performances; prayer vigils; a wreath laying at the Lincoln Memorial; and concerts. Many events take place at the Martin Luther King Memorial Library, 901 G St. NW (tel. 727-1186). Call 789-7000 for further details. Third Monday in January.

FEBRUARY

☐ **Chinese New Year celebration,** in Washington's small Chinatown. A friendship archway, topped by 300 painted dragons and lighted at night, marks Chinatown's entrance at 7th and H Streets NW. The celebration begins on the day of the Chinese New Year and goes on for 10 or more days, with traditional firecrackers, dragon dancers, and colorful street parades. Some area restaurants offer special menus. For details, call 789-7000 or 724-4093. Late January or early to mid-February.

☐ **Black History Month.** Features numerous events, museum exhibits, and cultural programs celebrating contributions of African Americans to American life. For details check the *Washington Post* or call 357-2700 or 789-7000.

☐ **Abraham Lincoln's Birthday,** Lincoln Memorial. Marked by the laying of a wreath and a reading of the Gettysburg Address at noon. Call 426-6895. February 12.

☐ **George Washington's Birthday,** Washington Monument. Similar celebratory events. Call 426-6841 for details. Both presidents' birthdays also bring annual citywide sales. February 22 (celebrated the third Monday in February as Presidents Day).

MARCH

☐ **Spring Antiques Show,** D.C. Armory, 2001 E. Capitol St. Features close to 200 dealers from the United States, Canada, and Europe. Admission is charged. Call 301/738-1966 for details. Usually the first week in March.

☐ **St. Patrick's Day,** on Constitution Avenue NW from 7th to 17th Streets. A big parade that's all you'd expect—floats, bagpipes, marching bands, and the wearin' o' the green. Past grand marshals have included Tip O'Neill, Redskins' "player of the decade" John Riggins, and political comic Mark Russell. For parade information, call 703/379-1125 or 789-7000. The Sunday before March 17 (unless March 17 falls on a Sunday).

✪ *SMITHSONIAN KITE FESTIVAL A delightful event if the weather cooperates—an occasion for a trip in itself. Throngs of kite enthusiasts fly their unique creations and compete for ribbons and prizes.*

  Where: On the Washington Monument grounds. When: A Saturday in mid- or late March. How: If you want to compete, just show up with your kite and register between 10am and noon. Call 357-2700 for details.

✪ *CHERRY BLOSSOM EVENTS Washington's best-known annual event—the blossoming of the famous Japanese cherry trees. Festivities include a major parade with princesses, floats, and celebrity guests, not to mention bands, clowns, fireworks, fashion shows, concerts, a Japanese lantern-lighting ceremony, a ball, and a marathon race.*

  Where: The trees bloom by the Tidal Basin in Potomac Park. Related events take place all around town. When: Late March or early April (national news programs monitor the budding). How: For parade and ball information, call the DC Downtown Jaycees (tel. 728-1135). For other cherry-blossom events, check the Washington Post or call 789-7038.

APRIL

Cherry blossom events continue (see above).

☐ **Easter Sunrise Services,** Memorial Amphitheater at Arlington National Cemetery. There are free shuttle buses to the site from the visitor center parking lot. Call 475-0856 or 789-7000 for details. Date varies.

✪ *WHITE HOUSE EASTER EGG ROLL The biggie for*

little kids. In past years, entertainment has included clog dancers, clowns, storytellers, Easter bunnies, Ukrainian egg-decorating exhibitions, puppet and magic shows, military drill teams, an egg-rolling contest, and a hunt for 1,000 or so hidden wooden eggs, many of them signed by celebrities (e.g., Tom Hanks and Barbra Streisand), astronauts, or the Clintons. Note: *Only children ages 3 to 6 can participate in the egg hunt, but older kids will enjoy the other activities.*

Where: *The White House South Lawn and the Ellipse; enter at the southeast gate on East Executive Avenue.* **When:** *Easter Monday between 10am and 2pm; arrive early.* **How:** *Just show up. Call 456-2200 for details.*

□ **Filmfest DC,** at theaters throughout the city. Premiers dozens of international and American films. Check the *Washington Post* for film schedules and locations, or call 727-2396. April and May.

□ **Thomas Jefferson's Birthday,** Jefferson Memorial. Celebrated with a wreath-laying, speeches, and a military ceremony. Call 462-6822 for time and details. April 13.

□ **The Imagination Celebration,** Kennedy Center for the Performing Arts. At this two-week festival of performing arts for young people, events are free or moderately priced. Call 467-4600 for details. Mid-April.

□ **White House Gardens.** These beautifully landscaped creations are open to the public for special free tours between 2 and 5pm. Call 456-2200 for details. Two days only, in mid-April.

□ **Georgetown Garden Tour.** View the remarkable private gardens of one of the city's loveliest neighborhoods. Admission is charged, but high tea is included. Call 333-4953 for details. Mid- or late April (or early to mid-May).

□ **Georgetown House Tour.** The interiors of beautiful old Georgetown homes can be seen. Admission is charged, and includes high tea at St. John's Georgetown Parish Church. Call 338-1796 for details. Late April.

□ **Justice Douglas Reunion Hike,** C&O Canal. If you love hiking, don't miss this event. Douglas, bless him, once walked the entire 184½-mile towpath in protest against a plan to build a scenic parkway along the canal. The annual hike covers about 12 miles, on a different section each year. A buffet banquet wraps up the day's activities, and there's a bus to take you back to town. For details and tickets (there's a charge for the bus and buffet), contact the C&O Canal Association, P.O. Box 366, Glen Echo, MD 20812 (tel. 703/356-1809 for reservations). Usually the last Saturday in April.

MAY

□ **Washington National Cathedral Annual Flower Mart,** on the cathedral grounds. Includes displays of flowering plants and herbs, decorating demonstrations, ethnic food booths, children's rides and activities (including an old-fashioned carousel), costumed characters, puppet shows, and other entertainments. Call 537-6200 for details. First Friday and Saturday in May.

■ **Asian Pacific American Heritage Festival,** Freedom Plaza, on Pennsylvania Avenue between 13th and 14th Streets NW. Honors the contributions of Asian Americans to this country and presents their varied cultural heritages. All of Washington's Asian communities participate. There are cultural displays, crafts booths, ethnic foods, dragon dances, and martial arts exhibitions. For information, call 703/354-5036. Weekend day early in May.

■ **Memorial Day.** At 11am, a wreath-laying ceremony takes place at the Tomb of the Unknowns in Arlington National Cemetery, followed by military band music, a service, and an address by a high-ranking government official (sometimes the president); call 475-0856 for details. There's also a ceremony at 1pm at the Vietnam Veterans Memorial—wreath-laying, speakers, and the playing of taps; call 619-7222 for details. In the evening the National Symphony Orchestra performs a free concert at 8pm on the West Lawn of the Capitol; call 619-7222 for details. Last Monday in May.

JUNE

■ **Spirit of America Pageant,** USAir Arena, Landover, Maryland. Programs tracing the history of America in music and skits. The concerts are given by the Third U.S. Infantry and the U.S. Army Band. Call 475-0685 for details. Mid-June.

✪ *SMITHSONIAN FESTIVAL OF AMERICAN FOLKLIFE* *A major event with traditional American music, crafts, foods, games, concerts, and exhibits. Past performances have ranged from Appalachian fiddling to Native American dancing, and demonstrations from quilting to coal mining. All events are free.*

Where: Most events take place on the Mall. When: For 5 to 10 days, always including July Fourth weekend. How: Call 357-2700, or check the listings in the Washington Post, *for details.*

JULY

✪ *INDEPENDENCE DAY* *There's no better place to be on the Fourth of July than Washington, D.C. The festivities include a massive National Independence Day Parade down Constitution Avenue, complete with lavish floats, princesses, marching groups, and military bands. Other events include baseball games, a jazz festival, dances, arts and crafts exhibits, celebrity entertainers, concerts, and food booths. A Revolutionary War encampment is set up on Constitution Avenue in front of the*

National Archives, where a program includes military demonstrations, period music, and a reading of the Declaration of Independence. In the evening the National Symphony Orchestra plays on the west steps of the Capitol with guest artists (for example, Leontyne Price). And big-name entertainment also precedes the fabulous fireworks display over the Washington Monument.

  Where: Most events take place on the Washington Monument grounds. **When:** July 4, all day. **How:** Just show up. Check the Washington Post or call 789-7000 for details.

___

□ **Men's Tennis Classic,** Rock Creek Park at 16th and Kennedy Streets NW. Top-seeded players compete. Call 703/276-3030 for details, 432-SEAT for tickets. Mid- or late July.

AUGUST

□ **Tchaikovsky's *1812* Overture,** Sylvan Theatre on the Washington Monument grounds. The U.S. Army Band gives a free performance of this famous work, complete with roaring cannons. For details, call 703/696-3718. Sometime during the month.

SEPTEMBER

□ **National Frisbee Festival,** on the Mall near the Air and Space Museum. See world-class Frisbee champions and their disc-catching dogs at this noncompetitive event. For details, call 301/645-5043. First weekend in September (some years, in late August).

□ **International Children's Festival,** Wolf Trap Farm Park in Vienna, Virginia. At this three-day arts celebration, the entertainment—all of it outdoors—includes clowns, musicians, mimes, puppet shows, and creative workshops from 10am to 4pm each day. Admission is charged. For details, call 703/642-0862. Late September

□ **Washington National Cathedral's Open House.** Celebrates the anniversary of the laying of the foundation stone in 1907. Events include demonstrations of stone carving and other crafts utilized in building the cathedral, carillon and organ demonstrations, and performances by dancers, choirs, strolling musicians, jugglers, and puppeteers. This is the only time visitors are allowed to ascend to the top of the central tower to see the carillon; it's a tremendous climb, but you'll be rewarded with a spectacular view. For details, call 537-6200. A Saturday in late September or early October.

□ **Rock Creek Park Day.** A birthday party for Washington's largest park (1990 was its centennial). The celebration includes music, folk dancing, balloons, pony rides, international crafts and food booths, children's activities, and environmental exhibits. Call 426-6832 for details.

OCTOBER

- ☐ **Taste of D.C. Festival,** Pennsylvania Avenue between 9th and 14th Streets. Dozens of Washington's restaurants offer international food-tasting opportunities, along with live entertainment, dancing, storytellers, and games. Admission is free; purchase tickets for tastings. Call 724-4091 for details. Columbus Day weekend.
- ☐ **White House Fall Garden Tours.** For two days visitors have an opportunity to see the famed Rose Garden and South Lawn. Admission is free. A military band provides music. For details, call 456-2200. Mid-October.
- ☐ **Washington International Horse Show,** USAir Arena, 1 Harry S Truman Dr., Landover, Md. This is one of the nation's most important equestrian events, featuring a hunt night, Jack Russell terrier races, international team show jumping, and dressage. Admission is charged. Call 301/840-0281 for details, 432-SEAT for tickets. Eight days in late October.
- ☐ **Halloween.** Never officially organized, but with costumed revels on the increase every year. Giant block parties take place in the Dupont Circle area and Georgetown. Check the *Washington Post* for special parties and activities. October 31.

NOVEMBER

- ☐ **Marine Corps Marathon.** A 26-mile race beginning at the Iwo Jima Memorial in Arlington, the route passes some of Washington's major monuments. World-class runners compete. Call 703/690-3431 for details. First Sunday in November.
- ☐ **Veterans Day.** The nation's war dead are honored with a wreath-laying ceremony at 11am at the Tomb of the Unknowns in Arlington National Cemetery. The President of the United States or a very high-ranking government personage officiates. Military music is provided by the U.S. Army Band. Call 475-0843 for information. At the Vietnam Veterans Memorial (tel. 619-7222), observances include speakers, a wreath-laying, a color guard, and the playing of taps. November 11.

DECEMBER

- ☐ **Christmas Open House,** at the Washington National Cathedral. An evening for families that includes a visit from St. Nicholas, dancers, choral groups, crafts, caroling, bell ringing, and much more. Call 537-6200 for more information, or to inquire about other Christmas concerts, pageants, services, and children's activities. First week of December.
- ☐ **Christmas Pageant of Peace/National Tree Lighting,** at the northern end of the Ellipse. On a selected Thursday in early December between 5 and 6pm, the president lights the national Christmas tree to the accompaniment of orchestral and choral music. The lighting inaugurates the two-week Pageant of Peace, a tremendous holiday celebration

with seasonal music, caroling, a Nativity scene, 50 state trees, and a burning Yule log. Call 619-7222 for details. Early December.

☐ **White House Candlelight Tours.** On three evenings from 6 to 8pm, visitors can see the president's Christmas holiday decorations by candlelight. String music enhances the tours. Call 456-2200 for dates and details. Late December.

3. WHAT TO PACK

The most important aspect of a traveler's wardrobe is comfort. It can become very unpleasant trekking around even the most fascinating attractions when your shoes hurt or your clothing is too warm. In summer especially, the ideal ensemble is sneakers, shorts, and a T-shirt. You might, however, wish to carry a light jacket or shawl in hot weather, since interior spaces are often frigidly air-conditioned.

In winter, pack a coat, hat, and boots, but don't get carried away—this isn't Wisconsin. And since not every museum or attraction has a checkroom, light outerwear—like an easy-to-carry down jacket—is preferable. A fold-up umbrella is always a good idea, and if you don't use it, so much the better. People tend to dress up for dinner and evening entertainments (theater, concerts), so be sure to bring along one or two dressy outfits for nighttime wear. Jackets and ties for men are essential if you're going to an upscale restaurant, the theater, or a nightclub.

You don't need to pack a travel iron. Almost all hotels these days provide irons at the front desk, albeit sometimes with those tiny boards that make ironing even more hateful than usual. Find out if your hotel offers hairdryers before you pack one.

4. TIPS FOR THE DISABLED, SENIORS, SINGLES, STUDENTS & FAMILIES

FOR THE DISABLED

Some nationwide resources include the following: **Mobility International USA** (tel. 503/343-1284), offers accessibility information, has many interesting travel programs for the disabled, and publishes a quarterly newspaper called *Over the Rainbow* ($10 per year to subscribe). Help is also available from the **Travel Information Service** (tel. 215/456-9603).

Tour packager **Evergreen Travel Service,** 4114 198th Ave.

SW, Suite 13, Lynnwood, WA 98036 (tel. 206/776-1184, or toll free 800/435-2288), offers tours designed for the blind, the visually impaired, the hearing impaired, the elderly, and the physically or mentally disabled.

And a publisher called **Twin Peaks Press**, P.O. Box 129, Vancouver, WA 98666 (tel. 206/694-2462, or toll free 800/637-2256 for orders only), specializes in books for the disabled. Write for their *Disability Bookshop Catalog*, enclosing $3

Finally, a Washington phone number to keep on hand is 202/966-8081, the **Information, Protection and Advocacy Center for People with Disabilities.** This organization responds quickly to the needs of the visitor, whether it's locating emergency attendant care or replacing a missing part of a wheelchair. It also publishes a series of pamphlets called "Access Washington: A Guide to Metropolitan Washington for the Physically Disabled," which cover everything from hotels to restaurants to sightseeing attractions. There's a nominal fee for mailing, but it's well worth it. The center can help make your stay in Washington a worry-free, enjoyable experience

SIGHTSEEING ATTRACTIONS Washington, D.C., is one of the most accessible cities in the world for the disabled The **White House** has a special entrance on Pennsylvania Avenue for visitors arriving in wheelchairs, and the White House guides usually allow visually handicapped visitors to touch some of the items being described on tours For details, call 456-2322

All **Smithsonian museum buildings** (and the National Gallery) are accessible to wheelchair visitors, as are all museum floors The Smithsonian publishes large-print, braille, and cassette materials for several of its museums. On advance request, you may be able to arrange for a sign-language interpreter on museum tours. For details, and more specific information on programs of special interest to disabled visitors, call 786-2942 or 786-2414 (TTY). A comprehensive Smithsonian guide for the disabled is in preparation at this writing, call 357-2700 for details

The **Lincoln and Jefferson memorials** and the **Washington Monument** are also equipped to accommodate disabled visitors The last-named keeps a wheelchair on the premises and allows disabled visitors to go to the head of the waiting line

Call ahead to other sightseeing attractions for accessibility information and special services

SHOPPING For shoppers, places well equipped with wheelchair ramps and other facilities for the disabled include the Shops at National Place, the Pavilion at the Old Post Office, and Georgetown Park Mall

THEATER The **John F. Kennedy Center for the Performing Arts** rents headphones to hearing-impaired patrons, allowing them to adjust volume as needed All theaters in the complex are wheelchair accessible. Also inquire (in advance) about cassettes for the visually impaired, offering audio descriptions at select performances For details, call 416-8340, for other questions regarding patrons with disabilities call 416-8777

The **National Theatre** features special performances of its shows for visually- and hearing-impaired theatergoers. To obtain earphones for narration, simply ask an usher before the performance. The National also offers a limited number of half-price tickets to disabled patrons. For details, call 628-6161.

GETTING AROUND TOWN Each **Metro** station is equipped with an elevator (complete with braille number plates) to train platforms. Conductors make station and on-board announcements of train destinations and stops. The TTD number for Metro information is 638-3780.

Regular **Tourmobile** trams are accessible to physically impaired visitors. The company also operates special vans for immobile travelers, complete with wheelchair lifts. For information, call 544-5100. **Old Town Trolley** also has a vehicle for the disabled. For information, call 301/985-3021.

TRAVELING BY BUS, TRAIN & PLANE A companion can accompany a disabled person at no charge aboard a **Greyhound** bus. Call toll free 800/752-4841 at least 48 hours in advance to discuss special needs.

Amtrak (tel. toll free 800/USA-RAIL) provides redcap service, wheelchair assistance, and special seats with 72 hours' notice. The disabled are also entitled to a 25% discount on one-way regular coach fares. Documentation from a doctor or an ID card proving your disability is required. Amtrak also provides wheelchair-accessible sleeping accommodations on long-distance trains, and guide dogs are permissible and travel free of charge Write for a free booklet called *Amtrak's America* from Amtrak Distribution Center, P.O. Box 7717, Itasca, IL 60143, which has a chapter detailing services for passengers with disabilities.

Note: Washington offers redcap service, but check your own departure station.

When making your flight reservations, ask the airline or travel agent where your wheelchair will be stowed on the plane and if seeing or hearing guide dogs can accompany you

FOR SENIORS

Bring some form of photo ID that includes your birth date since many city attractions, theaters, transportation facilities, hotels, and restaurants grant special senior discounts.

If you haven't already done so, consider joining the **American Association of Retired Persons** (AARP), 601 E St. NW, Washington, DC 20049 (tel. 202/434-2277) Annual membership costs $8 per person or per couple. You must be at least 50 to join. Membership entitles you to many discounts. Write to Purchase Privilege Program, AARP Fulfillment, 601 E St. NW, Washington, DC 20049, to receive AARP's *Purchase Privilege* brochure—a free list of hotels, motels, and car-rental firms nationwide that offer discounts to AARP members. **AARP Travel Experience** from American Express (tel. toll free 800/927-0111 for tours, 800/745-4567 for cruises), arranges a wide array of discounted cruises and group tours for members

Another good source of reduced-price information is *The Discount Guide for Travelers Over 55* by Caroline and Walter Weinz (EP Dutton).

Elderhostel, a national organization that offers low-priced educational programs for people over 60 (your spouse or companion must be at least 50), sponsors frequent week-long residential programs in Washington. Some of these focus on government and American history, others on art, literature, and other subjects. Cost averages about $355 per person, including meals, room, and classes. For information, call 410/830-3437 or contact Elderhostel headquarters at 75 Federal St., Boston, MA 02110 (tel. 617/426-8056).

Saga International Holidays, 222 Berkeley St., Boston, MA 02116 (tel. toll free 800/343-0273), offers group tours designed for travelers over 60.

Amtrak (tel. toll free 800/USA-RAIL) offers a 15% discount off the lowest available coach fare (with certain travel restrictions) to people 62 or over.

Greyhound also offers discounted fares for senior citizens. Call your local Greyhound office for details.

FOR SINGLE TRAVELERS

Of major interest to single travelers is the opportunity to meet others. There is, of course, the bar scene (see Chapter 9). Another good way to meet people is to go on a hike, river-rafting trip, or other such excursion, many of which are listed in the *Washington Post* Friday "Weekend" section. You'll find other people-meeting activities listed there as well.

Another tip: Choose a bed-and-breakfast facility; it's easy to meet people over coffee and muffins in the communal dining room.

FOR STUDENTS

The key to securing discounts is a valid student ID. Be sure to carry one, and keep your eyes open for special student prices at attractions, theaters, transportation facilities, and other places

FOR FAMILIES

Careful planning can make all the difference between a successful, enjoyable vacation and one that ends with exhausted, irritable parents and cranky kids. Here are a few helpful hints:

Get the Kids Involved Let them, if they're old enough, write to the tourist offices for information and color brochures. Give them a map on which they can outline the route; let them help decide the itinerary.

Packing Although your home may be toddler-proof, accommodations are not. Bring portable gates for stairways and other off-limits areas, and also some blank plugs to cover electrical outlets.

En Route Carry a few simple games to relieve boredom while traveling. A few snacks will also help and will save money. Check Amtrak for special family discounts; the airlines, too, have reduced airfares for those under 17; both let those under 2 travel free

Accommodations   Children under a certain age usually stay free in their parents' room. Look for establishments that have pools and other recreational facilities. Reserve equipment such as cribs and playpens in advance.

Ground Rules   Set up ground rules before leaving home about issues such as bedtime and spending money on souvenirs.

Contact **Travel With Your Children, (TWYCH),** 45 W. 18th St., New York, NY 10011 (tel. 212/206-0688), to subscribe to the *Family Travel Times,* a newsletter about traveling with children. It's packed with useful information, and readers can call in for advice during certain periods each week.

5. GETTING THERE

BY AIR

Washington is served by three major airports—**Washington National Airport,** just across the Potomac in Virginia and a 15-minute drive from downtown; **Dulles International Airport,** about 45 minutes from downtown, also in Virginia; and **Baltimore-Washington International Airport,** between Baltimore and Washington, about 45 minutes from downtown. Most visitors come in via National, which is served by American, America West, Continental, Delta, Northwest, TWA, United, and USAir.

BEST-FOR-THE-BUDGET FARES   When evaluating airline fares, take into consideration bus and/or taxi fares to and from departure and arrival airports. The taxi and bus fares listed below will help you make these computations.

As we go to press, there's a major airline price restructuring going on throughout the country. With everything up in the air (so to speak), quoting specific fares here would be meaningless. Always remember, however, that it pays to book flights as far in advance as possible, since advance-purchase fares are often substantially lower. When you call, also inquire about money-saving packages that include essentials like hotel accommodations, car rentals, and tours with your airfare.

SHUTTLES TO & FROM NEW YORK   The **Delta Shuttle,** which flies out of LaGuardia's Marine Terminal in New York and Washington National Airport's Main Terminal (between Gates 15 and 16), has flights departing New York every hour on the half hour Monday to Friday, 6:30am to 8:30pm, with an extra departure at 9pm. Saturday flights are offered every hour on the half hour between 7:30am and 8:30pm. Sunday flights are scheduled every hour on the half hour between 8:30am and 8:30pm, with an extra departure at 9pm. The first weekday flight leaves Washington National at 6:45am, with flights every hour on the half hour after that until 9:30pm. Saturday flights depart every hour on the half hour between 7:30am and 8:30pm. Sunday flights are offered every

---

**ⓕ FROMMER'S SMART TRAVELER:
AIRFARES**

VALUE-CONSCIOUS TRAVELERS SHOULD TAKE
ADVANTAGE OF THE FOLLOWING:

1. Shop all the airlines that fly to Washington, D.C.
2. Always ask for the lowest fare, not just a discount fare.
3. Keep calling the airline to check fares. Availability of inexpensive seats changes daily, and as the departure date draws
   nearer, more seats are sold at lower prices.
4. Ask about discounts for seniors (usually 10%), children, and
   students.
5. Book in advance to obtain lower advance-purchase fares.

---

hour on the half hour between 8:30am and 9:30pm. At press time,
the price was $150 each way Monday to Friday and Sunday after
2:30pm, and $75 all day Saturday and through 1:30pm Sunday.
Since it's possible for prices and/or flight schedules to change,
double-check the above by calling Delta (tel. toll free 800/221-
1212).

The same prices are offered by the **USAir Shuttle,** which de-
parts from its own terminal at LaGuardia. Flights to Washington
National Airport leave New York Monday to Saturday every hour
on the hour from 7am to 9pm, and Sunday on the hour from 9am
to 9pm. Washington–New York flights leave at the same hours.
You can call USAir toll free at 800/428-4322.

At either airline, do inquire about special fares for seniors, children, and youth (up to age 24), as well as 7- and 14-day advance-
purchase fares.

BY TRAIN

Amtrak trains arrive at historic **Union Station,** 50 Massachusetts
Ave. NE, a turn-of-the-century beaux arts masterpiece that was
magnificently restored in the late 1980s at a cost of more than
$180 million. Offering a three-level marketplace of shops and res-
taurants, this stunning depot is conveniently located and connects
with Metro service. There are always lots of taxis available there.
For rail reservations, contact Amtrak (tel. toll free 800/USA-RAIL).
(For more on Union Station, see Chapters 6, 7, and 8.)

Like the airlines, Amtrak offers several discounted fares; although not all are based on advance purchase, you have more discount options by reserving early. At this writing, regular round-trip
coach fares and discount fares are as follows between Washington's
Union Station and five selected cities:

	Regular Fare	**Discount Fare**
N.Y.–D.C.	$136	$92
Chicago–D.C.	$211	$128
Atlanta–D.C.	$210	$126
L.A.–D.C.	$421	$259
Boston–D.C.	$179	$108

I also suggest that you inquire about money-saving packages that include hotel accommodations, car rentals, tours, etc., with your train fare. Call toll free 800/321-8684 for details.

Metroliner service—which costs a little more but provides faster transit and roomier, more comfortable seating—is available between New York and Washington, D.C., and points in between. The round-trip Metroliner fare between New York and D.C at this writing is $192. *Note:* Metroliner fares are substantially reduced on weekends

The most luxurious way to travel is **First Class Club Service,** available on all Metroliners and some other trains as well For an additional $50 each way, passengers enjoy roomier, more upscale seating in a private car; complimentary meals and beverage service; and Metropolitan Lounges (in New York, Chicago, Philadelphia, and Washington) where travelers can wait for trains in a comfortable, living room–like setting while enjoying free snacks and coffee.

BY BUS

Greyhound buses connect almost the entire United States with Washington, D.C. They pull in at a terminal at 1st and L Streets NE (tel. toll free 800/231-2222). The closest Metro station is Union Station, four blocks away. The bus terminal area is now what you'd call a showplace neighborhood, so if you arrive at night, it's best to take a taxi.

The fare structure on these buses is a little complex, and not necessarily based on distance traveled. The good news is that when you call Greyhound to make a reservation, the company will always offer you the lowest fare options. Call in advance and know your travel dates, since some discount fares require advance purchase.

BY CAR

Major highways approach Washington, D.C., from all parts of the country. The District is 240 miles from New York City, 40 miles from Baltimore, and 600 miles from Chicago and Atlanta.

CHAPTER 3

FOR FOREIGN VISITORS

1. **PREPARING FOR YOUR TRIP**
2. **GETTING TO & AROUND THE U.S.**
- **FAST FACTS: FOR THE FOREIGN TRAVELER**

Although American fads and fashions have spread across Europe and other parts of the world so that America may seem like familiar territory before your arrival, there are still many peculiarities and uniquely American situations that any foreign visitor will encounter.

1. PREPARING FOR YOUR TRIP

The **Services of Meridian International Center** (tel. 202/939-5566 or 939-5538) is a nonprofit, community volunteer organization that provides special services to D.C.'s many visitors from abroad. It has a language bank of volunteers on call who speak dozens of languages, and provides assistance (by phone) with accommodations, sightseeing, dining, and other traditional tourist needs.

Phones are answered seven days a week from about 6am to 10pm.

ENTRY REQUIREMENTS

DOCUMENT REGULATIONS Canadian citizens may enter the United States without visas; they need only proof of residence.

Citizens of the United Kingdom, New Zealand, Japan, and most Western European countries traveling on valid passports may not need a visa for fewer than 90 days of holiday or business travel to the United States, providing that they hold a round-trip or return ticket and enter the United States on an airline or cruise line participating in the visa waiver program.

(Note that citizens of these visa-exempt countries who first enter the United States may then visit Mexico, Canada, Bermuda, and/or the Caribbean islands and then reenter the United States, by any mode of transportation, without needing a visa. Further information is available from any U.S embassy or consulate.)

Citizens of countries other than those stipulated above, including citizens of Australia, must have two documents:

- a valid **passport,** with an expiration date at least six months later than the scheduled end of the visit to the United States; and

- a **tourist visa,** available without charge from the nearest U.S. consulate. To obtain a visa, the traveler must submit a completed application form (either in person or by mail) with a 1½-inch square photo and demonstrate binding ties to a residence abroad.

Usually you can obtain a visa at once or within 24 hours, but it may take longer during the summer rush from June to August. If you cannot go in person, contact the nearest U.S. embassy or consulate for directions on applying by mail. Your travel agent or airline office may also be able to provide you with visa applications and instructions. The U.S. consulate or embassy that issues your visa will determine whether you will be issued a multiple- or single-entry visa and any restrictions regarding the length of your stay.

MEDICAL REQUIREMENTS   No inoculations are needed to enter the United States unless you are coming from, or have stopped over in, areas known to be suffering from epidemics, particularly cholera or yellow fever

If you have a disease requiring treatment with medications containing narcotics or drugs requiring a syringe, carry a valid signed prescription from your physician to allay any suspicions that you are smuggling drugs.

CUSTOMS REQUIREMENTS   Every adult visitor may bring in free of duty: 1 liter of wine or hard liquor; 200 cigarettes or 100 cigars (but no cigars from Cuba) or 3 pounds of smoking tobacco; $100 worth of gifts. These exemptions are offered to travelers who spend at least 72 hours in the United States and who have not claimed them within the preceding six months. It is altogether forbidden to bring into the country foodstuffs (particularly cheese, fruit, cooked meats, and canned goods) and plants (vegetables, seeds, tropical plants, and so on). Foreign tourists may bring in or take out up to $10,000 in U.S. or foreign currency with no formalities; larger sums must be declared to Customs on entering or leaving.

INSURANCE

There is no national health system in the United States. Because the cost of medical care is extremely high, I strongly advise every traveler to secure health coverage before setting out.

You may want to take out a comprehensive travel policy that covers (for a relatively low premium) sickness or injury costs (medical, surgical, and hospital); loss or theft of your baggage; trip-cancellation costs; guarantee of bail in case you are arrested; costs of accident, repatriation, or death. Such packages (for example, "Europe Assistance" in Europe) are sold by automobile clubs at attractive rates, as well as by insurance companies and travel agencies.

MONEY

CURRENCY & EXCHANGE   The U.S. monetary system has a decimal base: one American **dollar** ($1) = 100 **cents** (100¢).

Dollar bills commonly come in $1 ("a buck"), $5, $10, $20, $50, and $100 denominations (the last two are not welcome when paying for small purchases and are not accepted in taxis or at subway ticket booths). There are also $2 bills (seldom encountered).

There are six denominations of coins: 1¢ (one cent or "penny"), 5¢ (five cents or "a nickel"), 10¢ (ten cents or "a dime"), 25¢ (twenty-five cents or "a quarter"), 50¢ (fifty cents or "a half dollar"), and the rare $1 piece.

TRAVELER'S CHECKS Traveler's checks denominated in U.S. dollars are readily accepted at most hotels, motels, restaurants, and large stores. But the best place to change traveler's checks is at a bank. Do not bring traveler's checks denominated in other currencies.

CREDIT CARDS The method of payment most widely used is the credit card: VISA (BarclayCard in Britain), MasterCard (EuroCard in Europe, Access in Britain, Chargex in Canada), American Express, Diners Club, Discover, and Carte Blanche. You can save yourself trouble by using "plastic money" rather than cash or traveler's checks in most hotels, motels, restaurants, and retail stores (a growing number of food and liquor stores now accept credit cards). You must have a credit card to rent a car. It can also be used as proof of identity (often carrying more weight than a passport), or as a "cash card," enabling you to draw money from banks that accept them.

Note: The "foreign-exchange bureaus" so common in Europe are rare even at airports in the United States, and nonexistent outside major cities. Try to avoid having to change foreign money, or traveler's checks denominated other than in U.S. dollars, at a small-town bank, or even a branch in a big city; in fact, leave any currency other than U.S. dollars at home—it may prove a greater nuisance to you than it's worth.

SAFETY

GENERAL While tourist areas are generally safe, crime is on the increase everywhere, and U.S. urban areas tend to be less safe than those in Europe or Japan. Visitors should always stay alert. This is particularly true of large U.S. cities. It is wise to ask the city's or area's tourist office if you're in doubt about which neighborhoods are safe. Avoid deserted areas, especially at night. Don't go into any city park at night unless there is an event that attracts crowds—for example, New York City's concerts in the parks. Generally speaking, you can feel safe in areas where there are many people, and many open establishments.

Avoid carrying valuables with you on the street, and don't display expensive cameras or electronic equipment. Hold on to your pocketbook, and place your billfold in an inside pocket. In theaters, restaurants, and other public places, keep your possessions in sight.

Remember also that hotels are open to the public, and in a large hotel, security may not be able to screen everyone entering. Always lock your room door—don't assume that once inside your hotel you are automatically safe and no longer need to be aware of your surroundings.

DRIVING   Safety while driving is particularly important. Question your rental agency about personal safety, or ask for a brochure of traveler safety tips when you pick up your car. Obtain written directions, or a map with the route marked in red, from the agency showing how to get to your destination. And, if possible, arrive and depart during daylight hours.

Recently more and more crime has involved cars and drivers. If you drive off a highway into a doubtful neighborhood, leave the area as quickly as possible. If you have an accident, even on the highway, stay in your car with the doors locked until you assess the situation or until the police arrive. If you are bumped from behind on the street or are involved in a minor accident with no injuries and the situation appears to be suspicious, motion to the other driver to follow you. *Never* get out of your car in such situations. You can also keep a premade sign in your car that reads: PLEASE FOLLOW THIS VEHICLE TO REPORT THE ACCIDENT. Show the sign to the other driver and go directly to the nearest police precinct, well-lighted service station, or all-night store.

If you see someone on the road who indicates a need for help, do *not* stop. Take note of the location, drive on to a well-lighted area, and telephone the police by dialing 911.

Park in well-lighted, well-traveled areas if possible. Always keep your car doors locked, whether attended or unattended. Look around you before you get out of your car, and never leave any packages or valuables in sight. If someone attempts to rob you or steal your car, do *not* try to resist the thief/carjacker—report the incident to the police department immediately.

You may wish to contact the local tourist information bureau in Washington, D.C., before you arrive. They may be able to provide you with a safety brochure.

2. GETTING TO & AROUND THE U.S.

Travelers from overseas can take advantage of the **APEX (Advance Purchase Excursion) fares** offered by all the major U.S. and European carriers. Aside from these, attractive values are offered by **Icelandair** on flights from Luxembourg to New York and by **Virgin Atlantic Airways** from London to New York/Newark.

Some large American airlines (for example, TWA, American Airlines, Northwest, United, and Delta) offer travelers on their transatlantic or transpacific flights special discount tickets under the name **Visit USA,** allowing travel between any U.S. destinations at minimum rates. They are not on sale in the United States, and must, therefore, be purchased before you leave your foreign point of departure. This system is the best, easiest, and fastest way to see the United States at low cost. You should obtain information well in advance from your travel agent or the office of the airline concerned, since the conditions attached to these discount tickets can be changed without advance notice.

The visitor arriving by air, no matter what the port of entry, should cultivate patience and resignation before setting foot on U.S. soil. Getting through Immigration control may take as long as two hours on some days, especially summer weekends. Add the time it takes to clear Customs and you'll see that you should make very generous allowance for delay in planning connections between international and domestic flights—an average of two to three hours at least.

In contrast, travelers arriving by car or by rail from Canada will find border-crossing formalities streamlined to the vanishing point. And air travelers from Canada, Bermuda, and some places in the Caribbean can sometimes go through Customs and Immigration at the point of departure, which is much quicker and less painful.

For information on transportation to Washington, D.C., from elsewhere in the United States, see "Getting There" in Chapter 2.

International visitors can also buy a **USA RAILPASS**, good for 15 or 30 days of unlimited travel on Amtrak. The pass is available through many foreign travel agents. Prices in 1994 for a 15-day pass are $208 off-peak, $308 peak; a 30-day pass costs $309 off-peak, $389 peak. (With a foreign passport, you can also buy passes at some Amtrak offices in the United States, including locations in San Francisco, Los Angeles, Chicago, New York, Miami, Boston, and Washington, D.C.) Reservations are generally required and should be made for each part of your trip as early as possible.

Visitors should also be aware of the limitations of long-distance rail travel in the United States. With a few notable exceptions (for instance, the Northeast Corridor line between Boston and Washington, D.C.), service is rarely up to European standards: delays are common, routes are limited and often infrequently served, and fares are rarely significantly lower than discount airfares. Thus, cross-country train travel should be approached with caution.

The cheapest way to travel around the United States is by **bus.** Greyhound, the nation's nationwide bus line, offers an **Ameripass** for unlimited travel for 7 days (for $250), 15 days (for $350), and 30 days (for $450). Bus travel in the United States can be both slow and uncomfortable, so this option is not for everyone.

FAST FACTS — FOR THE FOREIGN TRAVELER

Automobile Organizations   Auto clubs will supply maps, suggested routes, guidebooks, accident and bail-bond insurance, and emergency road service. The major auto club in the United States, with 955 offices nationwide, is the **American Automobile Association (AAA).** Members of some foreign auto clubs have reciprocal arrangements with the AAA and enjoy its services at no charge. If you belong to an auto club, inquire about AAA reciprocity before you leave. The AAA can provide you with an

International Driving Permit validating your foreign license. You may be able to join the AAA even if you are not a member of a reciprocal club. To inquire, call toll free 800/336-4357. In addition, some automobile rental agencies now provide these services, so you should inquire about their availability when you rent your car.

Automobile Rentals To rent a car you need a major credit card. A valid driver's license is required, and you usually need to be at least 25 years old. Some companies do rent to younger people but add a daily surcharge. Be sure to return your car with the same amount of gas you started out with; rental companies charge excessive prices for gasoline. For car-rental companies in Washington, D.C., see "Getting Around" in Chapter 4.

Business Hours Banks are open weekdays 9am to 3 or 4pm, although there's 24-hour access to the automatic tellers (ATMs) at most banks and other outlets. Generally, **offices** are open weekdays 9am to 5pm. **Stores** are open six days a week, with many open on Sunday, too; department stores usually stay open until 9pm at least one day a week.

Climate See "When to Go—Climate and Events" in Chapter 2.

Currency Exchange You will find currency exchange services in major airports with international service. Elsewhere, they may be quite difficult to come by. In New York, a reliable choice is **Thomas Cook Currency Services, Inc.,** which has been in business since 1841 and offers a wide range of services. They also sell commission-free foreign and U.S. traveler's checks, drafts, and wire transfers; they also do check collections (including Eurochecks). Their rates are competitive and service excellent. They maintain several offices in New York City (tel. 212/757-6915 for the Fifth Avenue office), at the JFK Airport International Arrivals Terminal (tel. 718/656-8444), and at LaGuardia Airport in the Delta terminal (tel. 718/533-0784).

Drinking Laws See "Liquor Laws" in "Fast Facts: Washington, D.C." in Chapter 4.

Electricity The United States uses 110–120 volts, 60 cycles, compared to 220–240 volts, 50 cycles, as in most of Europe. In addition to a 100-volt converter, small appliances of non-American manufacture, such as hairdryers or shavers, will require a plug adapter, with two flat, parallel pins.

Embassies/Consulates All embassies are located in Washington, D.C., as it's the nation's capital, and many consulates are located here as well. Among the embassies here are those for **Australia,** 1601 Massachusetts Ave. NW (tel. 202/797-3000); **Canada,** 501 Pennsylvania Ave. NW (tel. 202/682-1740); **France,** 4101 Reservoir Rd. NW (tel. 202/944-6000); **Germany,** 4645 Reservoir Rd. NW (tel. 202/298-4000); **Netherlands,** 4200 Linnean Ave. NW (tel. 202/244-5300); and the **United Kingdom,** 3100 Massachusetts Ave. NW (tel. 202/462-1340). You can obtain the telephone numbers of other embassies and consulates by calling "Information" in Washington, D.C. (dial 411 within D.C.'s 202 area code; elsewhere, dial 202/555-1212). Or consult the phone book in your hotel room.

Emergencies In all major cities you can call the police, an ambulance, or the fire brigade through the single emergency telephone number **911.** Another useful way of reporting an emergency is to call the telephone-company operator by dialing **0** (zero, *not* the letter "O").

If you encounter such travelers' problems as sickness, accident, or lost or stolen baggage, call the **Travelers Aid Society,** 512 C St. NE (tel. 546-3120), an organization that specializes in helping distressed travelers, whether American or foreign. See "Networks and Resources," in Chapter 4, for further details.

Gasoline [Petrol] One U.S. gallon equals 3.75 liters, while 1.2 U.S. gallons equals one Imperial gallon. You'll notice there are several grades (and price levels) of gasoline available at most gas stations. And you'll also notice that their names change from company to company. The unleaded ones with the highest octane are the most expensive (most rental cars take the least expensive "regular" unleaded) and leaded gas is the least expensive, but only older cars can take this now, so check if you're not sure.

Holidays On the following legal national holidays, banks, government offices, post offices, and many stores, restaurants, and museums are closed: January 1 (New Year's Day), third Monday in January (Martin Luther King, Jr., Day), third Monday in February (Presidents Day, Washington's Birthday), last Monday in May (Memorial Day), July 4 (Independence Day), first Monday in September (Labor Day), second Monday in October (Columbus Day), November 11 (Veterans Day/Armistice Day), fourth Thursday in November (Thanksgiving Day), December 25 (Christmas).

Finally, the Tuesday following the first Monday in November is Election Day, and is a legal holiday in presidential-election years.

Languages Major hotels often have multilingual employees. Unless your language is obscure, they can usually supply a translator on request.

Legal Aid The foreign tourist, unless positively identified as a member of the Mafia or of a drug ring, will probably never become involved with the American legal system. If you are pulled up for a minor infraction (for example, of the highway code, such as speeding), never attempt to pay the fine directly to a police officer; you may wind up arrested on the much more serious charge of attempted bribery. Pay fines by mail, or directly into the hands of the clerk of the court. If accused of a more serious offense, it's wise to say and do nothing before consulting a lawyer. Under U.S. law, an arrested person is allowed one telephone call to a party of his or her choice. Call your embassy or consulate.

Mail If you want your mail to follow you on your vacation and you aren't sure of your address, your mail can be sent to you, in your name, **c/o General Delivery** at the main post office of the city or region where you expect to be. The addressee must pick it up in person and produce proof of identity (for example, driver's license, credit card, or passport).

Generally to be found at intersections, mailboxes are blue with a red-and-white stripe and carry the inscription U.S. MAIL. If your mail is addressed to a U.S. destination, don't forget to add the five-figure postal code, or ZIP (Zone Improvement Plan) Code, after the two-letter abbreviation of the state to which the mail is addressed (CA for California, FL for Florida, NY for New York, and so on).

In Washington, the **main post office** is located opposite Union Station at Massachusetts Avenue and North Capitol Street (tel. 523-2628). It's open Monday to Friday 7am to midnight, Saturday and Sunday until 8pm.

Newspapers/Magazines   National newspapers include the *New York Times*, *USA Today*, and the *Wall Street Journal*. There are also a great many national newsweeklies including *Newsweek*, *Time*, and *U.S. News & World Report*. For information on local Washington, D.C., periodicals, see "Newspapers/Magazines" in "Fast Facts: Washington, D.C.," Chapter 4.

Radio/Television   Audiovisual media, with four coast-to-coast networks—ABC, CBS, NBC, and Fox—joined in recent years by the Public Broadcasting System (PBS) and the cable network CNN, play a major part in American life. In big cities, televiewers have a choice of about a dozen channels (including the UHF channels), most of them transmitting 24 hours a day, without counting the pay-TV channels showing recent movies or sports events. All options are usually indicated on your hotel TV set. You'll also find a wide choice of local radio stations, each broadcasting particular kinds of talk shows and/or music—classical, country, jazz, pop, gospel—punctuated by news broadcasts and frequent commercials.

Safety   See "Safety" in "Preparing for Your Trip," above.

Taxes   In the United States there is no VAT (value-added tax) or other indirect tax at a national level. Every state, and each city in it, has the right to levy its own local tax on all purchases, including hotel and restaurant checks, airline tickets, and so on.

In the District, in addition to your hotel rate, you pay 11% sales tax and $1.50 per room per night in occupancy tax. In Virginia, sales tax is 4.5%, while occupancy tax varies throughout the state. In Maryland, sales tax is 5%; occupancy tax, 9.5%.

Telephone/Telegraph/Telex   The telephone system in the United States is run by private corporations, so rates, especially for long-distance service, can vary widely—even on calls made from public telephones Local calls in the United States usually cost 25¢

Generally, hotel surcharges on long-distance and local calls are astronomical You are usually better off using a **public pay telephone,** which you will find clearly marked in most public buildings and private establishments as well as on the street. Outside metropolitan areas, public telephones are more difficult to find. Stores and gas stations are your best bet

Most **long-distance** and **international** calls can be dialed directly from any phone. For calls to Canada and other parts of the United States, dial 1 followed by the area code and the seven-digit number For international calls, dial 011 followed by the country code, city code, and the telephone number of the person you wish to call

For **reversed-charge or collect calls,** and for **person-to-person calls,** dial 0 (zero, *not* the letter "O") followed by the area code and number you want an operator will then come on the line, and you should specify that you are calling collect, or person-to-person, or both. If your operator-assisted call is international, ask for the overseas operator.

For local **directory assistance** ("information"), dial 411; for **long-distance information,** dial 1, then the appropriate area code and 555-1212.

Like the telephone system, **telegraph** and **telex** services are provided by private corporations like ITT, MCI, and above all, Western Union, the most important. You can bring your telegram in to the nearest Western Union office (there are hundreds across the country), or dictate it over the phone (a toll-free call, 800/325-6000). You can also telegraph money, or have it telegraphed to you, very quickly over the Western Union system.

Telephone Directory There are two kinds of telephone directories available to you. The general directory is the so-called **white pages,** in which private and business subscribers are listed in alphabetical order. The inside front cover lists the emergency number for police, fire, and ambulance, and other vital numbers (like the Coast Guard, poison-control center, crime-victims hotline, and so on). The first few pages are devoted to community-service numbers, including a guide to long-distance and international calling, complete with country codes and area codes.

The second directory, printed on yellow paper (hence its name, **yellow pages**), lists all local services, businesses, and industries by type of activity, with an index at the back. The listings cover not only such obvious items as automobile repairs by make of car, or drugstores (pharmacies), often by geographical location, but also restaurants by type of cuisine and geographical location, bookstores by special subject and/or language, places of worship by religious denomination, and other information that the tourist might otherwise not readily find. The yellow pages also include city plans or detailed area maps, often showing postal ZIP Codes and public transportation routes.

Time The United States is divided into four **time zones** (six, if Alaska and Hawaii are included). From east to west, these are: Eastern Standard Time (EST), Central Standard Time (CST), Mountain Standard Time (MST), Pacific Standard Time (PST), Alaska Standard Time (AST), and Hawaii Standard Time (HST) Always keep changing time zones in mind if you are traveling (or even telephoning) long distances in the United States. For example, noon in New York City (EST) is 11am in Chicago (CST), 10am in Denver (MST), 9am in Los Angeles (PST), 8am in Anchorage (AST), and 7am in Honolulu (HST)

Daylight Saving Time is in effect from the first Sunday in April through the last Saturday in October (actually, the change is made at 2am on Sunday) except in Arizona, Hawaii, part of Indiana, and Puerto Rico. Daylight Saving Time moves the clock one hour ahead of standard time

Tipping This is part of the American way of life, based on the principle that one should pay for any special service received Here are some rules of thumb: **bartenders:** 10% to 15%

bellhops: at least 50¢ per piece; $2 to $3 for a lot of baggage, **cab drivers:** 15% of the fare, **cafeterias, fast-food restaurants:** no tip, **chambermaids:** $1 a day, **checkroom attendants** (restaurants, theaters): $1 per garment, **cinemas, movies, theaters:** no tip, **doormen** (hotels or restaurants): not obligatory, **gas-station attendants:** no tip, **hairdressers:** 15% to 20%, **redcaps** (airport and railroad station): at least 50¢ per piece, $2 to $3 for a lot of baggage, **restaurants, nightclubs:** 15% to 20% of the check, **sleeping-car porters:** $2 to $3 per night to your attendant, **valet parking attendants:** $1.

Toilets Foreign visitors often complain that public toilets are hard to find in most U.S. cities. True, there are none on the streets, but the visitor can usually find one in a bar, restaurant, hotel, museum, department store, or service station—and it will probably be clean (although the last-mentioned sometimes leaves much to be desired). Note, however, a growing practice in some restaurants and bars of displaying a sign saying TOILETS ARE FOR THE USE OF PATRONS ONLY. You can ignore this sign, or better yet, avoid arguments by paying for a cup of coffee or soft drink, which will qualify you as a patron. The cleanliness of toilets at railroad stations and bus depots may be open to question. Some public places are equipped with pay toilets, which require you to insert one or more coins into a slot on the door before it will open.

AMERICAN SYSTEM OF MEASUREMENTS

LENGTH

1 inch (in.)	=	2.54cm			
1 foot (ft.)	=	12 in.	=	30.48cm	= .305m
1 yard	=	3 ft.	=	.915m	
1 mile (mi.)	=	5,280 ft.	=	1.609km	

To convert miles to kilometers, multiply the number of miles by 1.61 (for example, 50 mi. × 1.61 = 80.5km). Note that this conversion can be used to convert speeds from miles per hour (m.p.h.) to kilometers per hour (kmph).

To convert kilometers to miles, multiply the number of kilometers by .62 (for example, 25km × .62 = 15.5 mi.). Note that this same conversion can be used to convert speeds from kilometers per hour to miles per hour.

CAPACITY

1 fluid ounce (fl. oz.)	= .03 liter		
1 pint	= 16 fl. oz.	= .47 liter
1 quart	= 2 pints	= .94 liter
1 gallon (gal.)	= 4 quarts	= 3.79 liter
	= .83 Imperial gal.		

To convert U.S. gallons to liters, multiply the number of gallons by 3.79 (example, 12 gal. × 3.79 = 45.58 liters).

To convert U.S. gallons to Imperial gallons, multiply the number of U.S. gallons by .83 (example, 12 U.S. gal. × .83 = 9.95 Imperial gal.).

To convert liters to U.S. gallons, multiply the number of liters by .26 (example, 50 liters × .26 = 13 U.S. gal.).

To convert Imperial gallons to U.S. gallons, multiply the number of Imperial gallons by 1.2 (example, 8 Imperial gal. × 1.2 = 9.6 U.S. gal.).

WEIGHT

1 ounce (oz.)	= 28.35 grams		
1 pound (lb.)	= 16 oz.	= 453.6 grams	= .45 kilograms
1 ton	= 2,000 lb.	= 907 kilograms	= .91 metric ton

To convert pounds to kilograms, multiply the number of pounds by .45 (example, 90 lb. × .45 = 40.5kg).

To convert kilograms to pounds, multiply the number of kilos by 2.2 (example, 75kg × 2.2 = 165 lb.).

AREA

1 acre	= .41 hectare	
1 square mile (sq. mi.)	= 640 acres	= 2.59 hectares
	= 2.6 km	

To convert acres to hectares, multiply the number of acres by .41 (example, 40 acres × .41 = 16.4ha).

To convert square miles to square kilometers, multiply the number of square miles by 2.6 (example, 80 sq. mi. × 2.6 = 208km²).

To convert hectares to acres, multiply the number of hectares by 2.47 (example, 20ha × 2.47 = 49.4 acres).

To convert square kilometers to square miles, multiply the number of square kilometers by .39 (example, 150km² × 39 = 58.5 sq. mi)

TEMPERATURE

To convert degrees Fahrenheit to degrees Celsius, subtract 32 from °F, multiply by 5, then divide by 9 (example, 85°F – 32 × 5/9 = 29.4°C)

To convert degrees Celsius to degrees Fahrenheit, multiply °C by 9, divide by 5, and add 32 (example, 20°C × 9/5 + 32 = 68°F)

GETTING TO KNOW WASHINGTON, D.C.

Washington is one of America's most delightful cities—a fitting showplace for the nation's capital. It's a city designed for strolling, offering both natural beauty and stunning architecture. Learning your way around is quick and easy.

1. ORIENTATION

ARRIVING

BY PLANE Washington National Airport is right on the Blue and Yellow **Metro** lines from which you can reach just about any point in town. There is a courtesy van service between the airport terminal and the Metro station.

The Washington Flyer (tel. 703/685-1400) operates buses between the very centrally located Airport Terminal Building at 1517 K St. NW and both Dulles and National airports. Fares to/from Dulles are $16 one way, $26 round-trip; to/from National, $8 one way, $14 round-trip. Children 6 and under ride free. There are departures in each direction about every 30 minutes. At the K Street Terminal Building you can board a free loop shuttle that goes to eight Washington hotels—the Sheraton Washington, Omni Shoreham, Washington Hilton, Mayflower, Washington Renaissance, Grand Hyatt, J. W. Marriott, and Harrington. The Harrington alone requires advance reservation, since it's not on the loop unless someone requests it.

The Airport Connection II (tel. 301/261-1091 or 301/441-2345) runs buses between the Airport Terminal Building at 1517 K St. NW and Baltimore-Washington International Airport, with departures about every hour or two in each direction; call for exact times. The fare is $14 one way, $25 round-trip, free for children 5 and under.

Taxi fares come to about $9 between National Airport and the White House, $42 to $45 between the White House and Dulles or BWI. (From National, take a D.C. rather than a Virginia cab—it's cheaper.)

Note: There have been price-gouging incidents in which tourists going from the airports into town have been overcharged by taxi drivers. If you think you're being ripped off, make sure to write down the company name and number of the cab (they're on the door), get an accurate receipt for the fare, and, if possible, the license plate number of the cab and the driver's name. Call 331-1671 to report any problems.

BY TRAIN If you're traveling by train, Amtrak will leave at historic **Union Station,** Massachusetts Avenue and North Capitol Street. It's conveniently located and connects with Metro service. There are always plenty of taxis available at the station.

BY BUS Greyhound buses arrive at a terminal on 1st and L Streets NW (tel. toll free 800/231-2222); the closest Metro stop is Union Station. Since the bus terminal is not in a particularly safe neighborhood, if you arrive at night, consider taking a taxi to your hotel.

BY CAR If you're driving from New York or other points north, you'll probably take I-95 south to U.S. 50 west, which becomes New York Avenue in D.C. This avenue will be on your map, so you can easily figure out how to reach your hotel.

If you start elsewhere, your best bet, if you're a member of AAA, is to call for exact directions. Otherwise, the Convention and Visitors Association (tel. 202/789-7000) can help you find the way; have a map in front of you when you call.

TOURIST INFORMATION

On your arrival in D.C., be sure to visit the **Washington Visitor Information Center** in the Willard Collection of Shops (next to, but not in, the Willard Inter-Continental Hotel) between 14th and 15th Streets on Pennsylvania Avenue NW (tel. 789-7038). A block from the White House, the center provides information on every aspect of Washington and stocks a vast supply of free maps, brochures, and literature of interest to visitors. The center's friendly and knowledgeable staff can answer all your Washington-related questions. This service is open Monday to Saturday 9am to 5pm.

CITY LAYOUT

Pierre Charles L'Enfant designed Washington's great sweeping avenues crossed by numbered and lettered streets. At key intersections he placed spacious circles. Although the circles are enhanced with monuments, statuary, and fountains, L'Enfant designed them also to serve as strategic command posts to ward off invaders or marauding mobs. After what had happened in Paris during the French Revolution—and remember, that was current history at the time—his design views were quite practical.

MAIN ARTERIES & STREETS The primary artery of Washington is **Pennsylvania Avenue,** scene of parades, inaugurations, and other splashy events. Pennsylvania runs northwest in a direct line between the Capitol and the White House, continuing on a northwest angle to Georgetown from the White House.

Constitution Avenue, paralleled to the south most of the way by **Independence Avenue,** runs east-west flanking the Capitol and the Mall.

Washington's longest avenue, **Massachusetts Avenue,** runs north of and parallel to Pennsylvania. Along the way you'll find Union Station and Dupont Circle, central to the area known as Embassy Row. Farther out are the Naval Observatory (the vice-president's residence is on the premises), Washington National Cathedral, American University, and, finally, Maryland.

Connecticut Avenue, which runs more directly north, starts at Lafayette Square directly opposite the White House. It's the city's Fifth Avenue—the boulevard with elegant eateries, posh boutiques, and expensive hotels.

Wisconsin Avenue, from the point where it crosses M Street, is downtown Georgetown. Antiques shops, trendy boutiques, discos, restaurants, and pubs all vie for attention. Yet somehow Georgetown manages to keep its almost European charm.

FINDING AN ADDRESS Once you understand the city's layout, it's easy to find your way around. You'll find it helpful, when reading this, to have a map handy.

The city is divided into four basic quadrants—**northwest, northeast, southwest,** and **southeast.** If you look at your map, you'll see that some addresses—for instance, the corner of G and 7th Streets—appear in four different places. There's one in each quadrant. Hence you must observe the quadrant designation (NW, NE, SW, or SE) when looking for an address.

The **Capitol** dome is the center of the District of Columbia—the dividing point for the four quadrants: Each of the four corners of the District of Columbia is exactly the same distance from the dome. The White House and most government buildings and important monuments are west of the Capitol (in the northwest and southwest quadrants); so are important hotels and tourist facilities.

Numbered streets run north-south, beginning on either side of the Capitol with East 1st Street and West 1st Street. **Lettered streets** run east-west.

Avenues, named for U.S. states, run at angles across the grid pattern and often intersect at traffic circles. For example, New

---

IMPRESSIONS

If Washington should ever grow to be a great city, the outlook from the Capitol will be unsurpassed in the world. Now at sunset I seemed to look westward far into the heart of the continent from this commanding position.
—RALPH WALDO EMERSON

Like a city in dreams, the great white capital stretches along the placid river from Georgetown on the west to Anacostia on the east.
—ALLEN DRURY

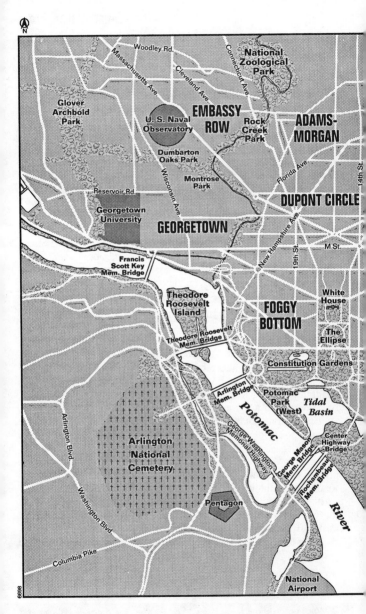

Hampshire, Connecticut, and Massachusetts Avenues intersect at Dupont Circle.

With this in mind, finding an address is a cinch. On **lettered streets,** the address tells you exactly where to go. For instance, 1776 K Street NW is between 17th and 18th Streets (the first two digits of 1776 tell you that) in the northwest quadrant (NW). *Note:* I Street is often written Eye Street to prevent confusion with 1st Street.

WASHINGTON, D.C.

To find an address on **numbered streets** you'll probably have to use your fingers. For instance, 623 8th Street SE is between F and G Streets (the sixth and seventh letters of the alphabet; the first digit of 623 tells you that) in the southeast quadrant (SE). One thing to remember though—there's no J Street (skipping the letter J was meant as a slap in the face to unpopular Chief Justice John Jay). So when counting, remember that K becomes the 10th letter, L the 11th, and so on.

As you go farther out—beyond Washington's original layout—the letter alphabetical system ends and a new one begins—two-syllable names in alphabetical order: Adams, Bryant, Channing, and so forth. When the two-syllable alphabet is used up, the system begins anew with three-syllable names—Albemarle, Brandywine, Chesapeake, and so on.

NEIGHBORHOODS IN BRIEF

The Mall This lovely tree-lined stretch of open space between Constitution and Independence Avenues, extending for 2½ miles from the Capitol to the Lincoln Memorial, is the hub of tourist attractions. It includes most of the Smithsonian Institution museums, and many other visitor attractions are close by. The 300-foot-wide Mall is used by natives as well as tourists—joggers, food vendors, kite-flyers, and picnickers among them.

Downtown Roughly the area between 7th and 22nd Streets NW going east to west, and P Street and Pennsylvania Avenue going north to south, downtown is a mix of Federal Triangle's government office buildings, K Street and Connecticut Avenue restaurants and shopping, F Street department stores, and much more. Too large an area to have a consistent character, it includes lovely Lafayette Park, Washington's tiny porno district, its slightly larger Chinatown, the convention center, and a half dozen or so sightseeing attractions.

Capitol Hill Everyone's heard of "the Hill," the area crowned by the Capitol. When people speak of Capitol Hill, they refer to a large section of town, extending from the western side of the Capitol to RFK Memorial Stadium going east, bounded by H Street NE and the Southwest Freeway north and south. It contains not only the chief symbol of the nation's capital, but the Supreme Court building, the Library of Congress, the Folger Shakespeare Library, Union Station, and the Botanic Garden. Much of it is a quiet residential neighborhood of tree-lined streets and Victorian homes. There are many restaurants in the vicinity.

Foggy Bottom The area west of the White House to the edge of Georgetown, Foggy Bottom was Washington's early industrial center. Its name comes from the foul fumes emitted in those days by a coal depot and gasworks, but its original name, Funkstown (for owner Jacob Funk), is perhaps even worse. There's nothing foul about the area today. The Kennedy Center and George Washington University are located here. Constitution and Pennsylvania Avenues are Foggy Bottom's southern and northern boundaries, respectively.

Dupont Circle Generally, when Washingtonians speak of Dupont Circle they don't mean just the park, they mean the area around it. The park itself, named for Rear Adm. Samuel Francis Dupont of the U.S. Navy, is centered around D.C.'s most famous fountain, at the intersection of Connecticut and Massachusetts Avenues, and is a popular rendezvous spot. Dupont Circle is one of the liveliest sections in town, rivaled only by Georgetown and Adams-Morgan for nightspots, movie theaters, and restaurants.

LEGEND

RED LINE:	Glenmont/Shady Grove
ORANGE LINE:	New Carrollton/Vienna
BLUE LINE:	Addison Road/Franconia-Springfield
GREEN LINE:	Branch Avenue/Greenbelt
YELLOW LINE:	Huntington/U Street-Cardozo

Georgetown This historic community dates back to colonial times. It was a thriving tobacco port long before the District of Columbia was formed, and one of its attractions, the Old Stone House, dates back to pre-Revolutionary days. Georgetown action centers on M Street and Wisconsin Avenue NW, where you'll find numerous boutiques (see Chapter 8 for details), chic restaurants, and popular pubs. But do get off the main drags and see the quiet tree-lined streets of restored colonial row houses, stroll through the beautiful gardens of Dumbarton Oaks, and check out the C&O Canal. One of the reasons so much activity flourishes in Georgetown is because of Georgetown University and its students.

Adams-Morgan This increasingly trendy multiethnic neighborhood is popular for its restaurants serving Jamaican, Ethiopian, Spanish, and other international cuisines. Try to plan at least one meal up here; it's a good opportunity to see an authentic, untouristy area of Washington. Adams-Morgan centers around Columbia Road and 18th Street NW.

2. GETTING AROUND

Washington is one of the easiest U.S. cities in which to get around. Only New York rivals its comprehensive transportation system, but Washington's clean, efficient subways put the Big Apple's underground nightmare to shame. There's also a complex bus system with routes covering all major D.C. arteries, and it's easy to hail a taxi anywhere at any time. Finally, Washington—especially the areas of interest to tourists—is pretty compact, and often the best way to get from here to there is on foot.

BY METRO

The Metrorail stations are immaculate, cool, and attractive, with terra-cotta floors and high, vaulted ceilings; the sleek subway cars are air-conditioned, carpeted, furnished with upholstered seats, and fitted with picture windows; the tracks are rubber-cushioned so the ride is quiet; the service is frequent enough so you usually get a seat; and the system is so simply designed that a 10-year-old can understand it.

Metrorail's 74 stations and 89 miles of track (83 stations and 103 miles of track are the eventual goal) include locations at or near almost every sightseeing attraction and extend to suburban Maryland and northern Virginia. If you're in Washington even for a few days you'll probably have occasion to use the system, but if not, I suggest you create one—perhaps dinner at a Dupont Circle restaurant. The Metro is a sightseeing attraction in its own right.

There are five lines in operation at this writing—**Red, Blue, Orange, Yellow,** and **Green**—with extensions planned for the future. The lines connect at several points, making transfers easy. All but the Yellow and Green Line trains stop at Metro Center; all but the Red Line trains stop at L'Enfant Plaza.

Metro stations are indicated by discreet brown columns bearing the station's name and topped by the letter M. Below the M is a colored stripe or stripes indicating the line or lines it serves. When entering a Metro station for the first time, go to the kiosk and ask the station manager for a free "Metro System Pocket Guide." It contains a map of the system, explains how it works, indicates parking lots at Metrorail stations, and lists the closest Metro stops to points of interest. The station manager can also answer questions about routing or purchase of farecards.

To enter or exit a Metro station you need a computerized **farecard,** available at vending machines near the entrance. The minimum fare to enter the system is $1, which pays for rides to and from any point within 7 miles of boarding during nonrush hours; during rush hours (Monday to Friday from 5:30 to 9:30am and 3 to 7pm) $1 only takes you for 3 miles. The maximum value allowed per card is $100. The machines take nickels, dimes, quarters, $1 bills, and $5 bills (some new machines also accept $10 and $20 bills), and they can return change (in coins only). If you plan to take several Metrorail trips during your stay, put more value on the farecard to avoid having to purchase a new card each time you ride. Otherwise you might waste time standing in long lines. There's a 5% fare discount on everything you purchase over $10, 10% on all farecards over $20. Up to two children under 5 can ride free with a paying passenger.

When you insert your card in the entrance gate, the time and location are recorded on its magnetic tape and your card is returned. Don't forget to snatch it up, and keep it handy—you have to reinsert it in the exit gate at your destination, where the fare will automatically be deducted. The card will be returned if there's any value left on it. If you arrive at a destination and your farecard doesn't have enough value, add what's necessary at the Exitfare machines near the exit gate.

If you're planning to continue your travel via Metrobus, pick up a **transfer** *at the station where you enter the system* (not your destination station) from the transfer machine on the mezzanine. It's good for full fare within D.C. plus a discount on bus fares in Maryland and Virginia. There are no bus-to-subway transfers.

Metrorail operates Monday to Friday from 5:30am to midnight and on weekends (and most holidays) from 8am to midnight. Call 637-7000 for information on Metro routes.

BY BUS

While a 10-year-old can understand the Metrorail system, the Metrobus system would probably perplex even Einstein. The 15,800 stops on the 1,489-square-mile route (it operates on all major D.C. arteries and in the Virginia and Maryland suburbs) are indicated by red, white, and blue signs. However, the signs tell you only what buses pull into a given stop (if that), not where they go. For **routing information,** call 637-7000; a transit information agent can tell you the most efficient route from where you are to where you want to go (using bus and/or subway) almost instantly. Calls are taken daily between 6am and 11:30pm, but the line is often busy, so don't wait until the last minute to call.

If you travel the same route frequently and would like a free map and time schedule, ask the bus driver or call 637-7000. Information about free parking in Metrobus fringe lots is also available from this number.

Base fare in the District is $1 and transfers are free. There are additional charges for travel into the Maryland and Virginia suburbs. Bus drivers are not equipped to make change, so be sure to *carry exact change or tokens.* The latter are available at 398 ticket outlets (call 637-7000 for locations and hours of operation). If you'll be in Washington for a while and plan to use the buses a lot, consider a two-week pass such as the **$21 D.C. Base Flash Pass,** good for unlimited Metrobus rides within the District and $4 worth of Metrorail rides. These are also available at ticket outlets. Other passes include zones in Virginia or Maryland.

Most buses operate daily almost around the clock. Service is quite frequent on weekdays, especially during rush hours. On weekends and late at night, your wait will be longer, but never more than 15 minutes.

There's a full bus information center at Metro Center Station (12th and F Streets), where tokens and special bus passes are available.

Up to two children under 5 ride free with a paying passenger on the Metrobus, and there are reduced fares for senior citizens (tel. 962-1179) and the handicapped (tel. 962-1245).

Should you leave something on a bus, on a train, or in a station, call Lost and Found (tel. 962-1195).

BY CAR

Within the District a car is a luxury, since public transportation is so comprehensive. Having a car can even be an inconvenience, especially during spring and summer, when traffic jams are frequent, parking spaces almost nonexistent, and parking lots ruinously expensive. But there's a great deal to see in the D.C. vicinity, and for most attractions in Virginia and Maryland you will want a car.

All the major car-rental companies are represented here. Some handy phone numbers: **Budget** (tel. toll free 800/527-0700), **Hertz** (tel. toll free 800/654-3131), **Thrifty** (tel. toll free 800/367-2277), **Avis** (tel. toll free 800/331-1212), and **Alamo** (tel toll free 800/327-9633)

BY TAXI

Surprise! You can take taxis in Washington without ruining your budget—at least in some cases. District cabs have a zone system. If you take a trip from one point to another in the same zone, you pay just $3.20 ($2.80 within a subzone of Zone 1), regardless of the distance traveled. So it would cost you $3.20 to travel a few blocks from the U S. Botanic Garden to the Museum of American History, but the same $3.20 would take you from the Botanic Garden all the way to Dupont Circle They re both in Zone 1 Also in Zone 1 are most other tourist attractions. the Capitol, the White House, most of the Smithsonian, the Washington Monument, the FBI, the National Archives, the Supreme Court, the Library of Congress, the Bureau of Engraving and Printing, the Old Post Office and Ford's Theatre If your trip takes you into a second zone the price is $4.40, $5.50 for a third zone, $6.60 for a fourth, and so on. You're unlikely to travel more than three zones unless you're staying in some remote section of town.

So far, the fares are pretty low. Here's how they can add up: There's a $1.25 charge for each additional passenger after the first, so a $3.20 Zone 1 fare can become $6.95 for a family of four (though one child under 6 can ride free). There's also a rush-hour surcharge of $1 per trip between 4 and 6:30pm weekdays. Surcharges are also added for large pieces of luggage and for arranging a pickup by telephone ($1.50).

The zone system is not used when your destination is an out-of-district address (such as an airport); the fare is then based on mileage covered—$2 for the first half mile or part thereof and 70¢ for each additional half mile or part. You can call 331-1671 to find out the rate between any point in D.C. and an address in Virginia or Maryland. Call 767-8380 to inquire about fares within the District.

It's generally easy to hail a taxi. There are about 7,500 cabs, and drivers are allowed to pick up as many passengers as they can comfortably fit. Expect to share. You can also call a taxi, though there's that $1.50 charge. Try **Diamond Cab Company** (tel. 387-6200), **Yellow Cab** (tel. 544-1212), or **Capitol Cab** (tel. 546-2400).

BY TOURMOBILE

You can save on shoe leather and see most Washington landmarks in comfort aboard Tourmobiles (tel. 544-5100)—open-air blue-and-white sightseeing trams that run along the Mall and as far out as Arlington National Cemetery and even (with coach service) Mount Vernon.

WASHINGTON/ARLINGTON CEMETERY TOUR You can take the Washington and Arlington Cemetery tour or tour Arlington Cemetery only. The former stops at 15 different sights on or near the Mall and three sights at Arlington Cemetery: the gravesites of the Kennedy brothers, the Tomb of the Unknowns, and Arlington House.

Here's how the system works. You can board a Tourmobile at 15 different locations: the White House, the Washington Monument/U.S. Holocaust Memorial Museum, the Arts and Industries Building/Hirshhorn Museum, the National Air and Space Museum, Union Station, the Capitol, the National Gallery of Art, the Museum of Natural History, the Museum of American History, the Bureau of Engraving and Printing, the Jefferson Memorial West Potomac Park, the Kennedy Center, the Lincoln Memorial/Vietnam Veterans Memorial, and Arlington National Cemetery

You pay the driver when you first board the bus Along the route, you may get off at any stop to visit monuments or buildings When you finish exploring each area, you step aboard the next Tourmobile that comes along without extra charge The buses travel in a loop, serving each stop every 20 to 30 minutes. One **fare** allows you to use the buses for a full day The charge for the Washington/Arlington Cemetery tour is $9 for adults, $4 for children 3–11 For Arlington Cemetery only, adults pay $3, children $1 50 Children under 3 ride free Buses follow "figure-8" circuits from the Capitol to Arlington Cemetery and back Between June 15 and Labor Day you can also buy a ticket after 4pm good for the rest of the afternoon and the following day ($11 for adults, $5 for children), the rest of the year the same offer is available after 2pm

Well-trained narrators give commentaries about sights along the route and answer questions.

Tourmobiles operate daily year-round on the following schedules. From June 15 to Labor Day, they ply the Mall between 9am and 6:30pm. After Labor Day, the hours are 9:30am to 4:30pm. From Arlington Cemetery, between October and March, they start at 8am and end at 5pm. April to September, the hours are 8am to 7pm.

OTHER TOURS Tourmobiles also run round-trip to **Mount Vernon** from April to October. Coaches depart from the Arlington National Cemetery Visitors Center and the White House at 10am, noon, and 2pm, and from the Washington Monument at 10:15am, 12:15pm, and 2:15pm. The price is $17 for adults, $8.25 for children, including admission to Mount Vernon. A combination tour of Washington, Arlington Cemetery, and Mount Vernon is $26.50 for adults, $13 for children—much cheaper than the Gray Line equivalent. Another offering (June 15 to Labor Day) is the **Frederick Douglass National Historic Site Tour,** including a guided tour of Douglass's home, Cedar Hill. Departures are from Arlington National Cemetery at 10am. Adults pay $5; children, $2.50. A two-day **Combination Frederick Douglass Tour and Washington-Arlington National Cemetery Tour** is also available at $16.50 for adults, $8 for children. For both the Mount Vernon and Frederick Douglass tours you must reserve at least an hour in advance.

BY OLD TOWN TROLLEY

A service similar to Tourmobile's is Old Town Trolley Tours of Washington (tel. 301/985-3020), in operation since 1986. For a fixed price, you can get on and off these green-and-orange vehicles as many times as you like within one loop at 16 locations in the District and at Arlington National Cemetery. Most stops are at or near major sightseeing attractions, including Georgetown. The trolleys operate seven days a week: Memorial Day to Labor Day hours are 9am to 5pm; the rest of the year, 9am to 4pm. The cost is $16 for adults, $8 for ages 5 to 12, free for children under 5. The full tour, which is narrated, takes two hours, and trolleys come by every 15 to 30 minutes. Stops are made at Union Station, the Hyatt Regency Hotel (near the National Gallery), the Pavilion at the Old Post Office, the Grand Hyatt (near Ford's Theatre), the J W Marriott (near the Renwick and Corcoran), the Hotel Washington (near the White House), the Capital Hilton (near the National Geographic Society), the Washington Hilton (near the Phillips Collection and Adams-Morgan restaurants), the Park Gourmet Washington (near the National Zoo), Washington National Cathedral, the Georgetown Park Mall, Arlington National Cemetery, the Lincoln Memorial, the Washington Monument/U.S Holocaust Memorial Museum, the Holiday Inn Capitol Hill (near Mall museums), and the Library of Congress

Tickets can be purchased at all stops except the Lincoln Memorial

FAST FACTS WASHINGTON, D.C.

Airports/Airport Transportation See "Arriving" under "Orientation," earlier in this chapter.

Ambulances See "Emergencies," below.

American Express There's an American Express Travel Service office at 1150 Connecticut Ave. NW (tel. 457-1300).

Area Code Within the District of Columbia, it's 202. In suburban Virginia, it's 703. In suburban Maryland, it's 410 or 301.

Babysitters Most hotels provide child-care services. If yours does not, contact Mother's Aides Inc. (tel. 703/250-0700). In business since 1979, this company uses only licensed and bonded sitters whose qualifications and personal history are carefully checked. Rates are $8 per hour for one child, $1 per hour for each additional sibling, $2 per hour for any other child. There's a four-hour minimum, a one-time $15 booking fee, and a $5 round-trip transportation charge. Call weekdays between 9am and 4:30pm.

Car Rentals See "Getting Around," earlier in this chapter.

Climate See "When to Go" in Chapter 2.

Crime See "Safety," below.

Congresspersons To locate a senator or congressional representative, call the Capitol switchboard (tel. 224-3121).

Convention Center The Washington, D.C., Convention Center, 900 9th St. NW, between H Street and New York Avenue (tel. 789-1600), is a vast multipurpose facility with 381,000 square feet of exhibition space and 40 meeting rooms.

Doctors/Dentists An organization called Prologue (tel. toll free 800/DOCTORS) can refer you to any type of doctor or dentist you need. Its roster of close to 800 practitioners includes just about every specialty. Phones are answered 24 hours a day. You can also call the Dental Referral Service (tel. 547-7615 Monday to Friday 8am to 4pm).

Drugstores Peoples, Washington's major drugstore chain (with about 40 stores), has two 24-hour locations: 14th Street and Thomas Circle NW, at Vermont Avenue (tel. 628-0720), and at Dupont Circle (tel. 785-1466), both with round-the-clock pharmacies. These drugstores also carry diversified merchandise ranging from frozen food and basic groceries to small appliances. Check your phone book for other convenient locations.

Embassies See "Fast Facts: The Foreign Traveler" in Chapter 3.

Emergencies Dial **911** to contact the police or fire department or to call an ambulance. See also "Hospital Emergency Wards," below.

Hairdressers/Barbers The Hair Cuttery, 1645 Connecticut Ave. near Dupont Circle (tel. 232-9685) is an inexpensive unisex hair salon offering trendy cuts, hair coloring, and styling on a walk-in, no-appointment-necessary basis. It's open Monday to Friday 8am to 8:30pm, Saturday 8:30am to 6:30pm, Sunday 11am to 4:30pm.

Holidays   See "When to Go" in Chapter 2.

Hospital Emergency Wards   Georgetown University Hospital, 3800 Reservoir Rd. NW (make a left off Wisconsin Avenue; tel. 784-2118), and George Washington University Hospital, 901 23rd St. NW (entrance on Washington Circle; tel. 994-3884), are both excellent.

Hotel Tax   In the District, in addition to your hotel rate, you pay 11% sales tax and $1.50 per room per night in occupancy tax. At Virginia hotels sales tax is 4.5%; hotel occupancy tax varies throughout the state. In Maryland, sales tax is 5%; hotel occupancy tax varies.

Libraries   The Martin Luther King, Jr., Memorial Library, 901 G St. NW (tel. 727-1186), is an extensive facility. It's open daily; hours vary seasonally, so call ahead.

Liquor Laws   Minimum drinking age is 21. Establishments can serve alcoholic beverages from 8am to 2am Monday to Thursday, until 2:30am Friday and Saturday, and 10am to 2am Sunday. Liquor stores are closed on Sunday.

Newspapers/Magazines   The major newspaper is, of course, the renowned *Washington Post*. The city's other daily is the *Washington Times*. Also informative are *Washingtonian* magazine and *The City Paper,* the latter a free newspaper available at restaurants, in bookstores, and other places around town.

Poison Control Center   625-3333 is a 24-hour emergency hotline.

Post Office   The city's main post office (tel. 523-2628) is located opposite Union Station at 2 Massachusetts Ave. NE (at G and North Capitol Streets). It's open Monday to Friday 7am to midnight, and on weekends until 8pm.

Religious Services   Every hotel keeps a list of places of worship for all faiths. Inquire at the front desk.

Safety   Whenever you're traveling in an unfamiliar city, stay alert. Be aware of your immediate surroundings. Wear a moneybelt or, better yet, check your valuables in a safety-deposit box at your hotel. Keep a close eye on your possessions, and be sure to keep them in sight when you're seated in a restaurant, theater, or other public place. Don't leave valuables in your car—even in the trunk. Every city has its criminals. It's your responsibility to be aware and alert even in the most heavily touristed areas.

Taxis   See "Getting Around," earlier in this chapter.

Tickets   A service called TICKETplace (tel. TICKETS [842-5387]) sells half-price tickets—on the day of performance only—to most major Washington-area theaters and concert halls. It also functions as a Ticketmaster outlet. See Chapter 9 for details

Time   Call 844-2525

Tourist Information   The Convention and Visitor Association's **Visitor Information Center,** Pennsylvania Avenue between 14th and 15th Streets NW (tel 789-7038), knows all, tells all. It's open Monday through Saturday from 9am to 5pm

Also be sure to visit the superb **Smithsonian Information Center,** 1000 Jefferson Dr SW (tel 357 2700) Open daily except

December 25 9am to 5:30pm, it's a must, especially for first-time visitors to the Smithsonian.

You can also call **Dial-a-Museum** (tel. 357-2020), the Smithsonian's number for recorded daily information on all its museum programs and activities, and **Dial-a-Park** (tel. 619-PARK) to find out about events in the National Capital Region parks.

Transit Information   See "Getting There" in Chapter 2; and "Orientation" and "Getting Around," earlier in this chapter.

Weather   Call 936-1212.

3. NETWORKS & RESOURCES

FOR ALL TRAVELERS

The **Travelers Aid Society** is a nationwide network of voluntary nonprofit social-service agencies providing help to travelers in difficulty. This might include anything from crisis counseling to straightening out ticket mix-ups, not to mention reuniting families accidentally separated while traveling, locating missing relatives (sometimes just at the wrong airport), and helping retrieve lost baggage (also sometimes at the wrong airport).

In Washington, Travelers Aid has a central office in the Capitol Hill area at 512 C St. NE (tel. 546-3120), where professional social workers are available to provide assistance. It's open only on weekdays 9am to 5pm.

There are also Travelers Aid desks at Washington National Airport (open Sunday to Friday 9am to 9pm and Saturday to 6pm; tel. 703/419-3972), on the lower concourse at the west end of Dulles International Airport (open Monday to Friday 10am to 9pm, Saturday and Sunday 10am to 6pm; tel. 703/661-8636), and at Union Station (open daily 9:30am to 5:30pm; tel. 546-3120); TTY or TDD (telecommunications device for the deaf) are provided at the above-mentioned locations.

FOR MILITARY PERSONNEL

If you're in a military service, you probably already know about **USO,** the congressionally chartered, nonprofit agency representing civilian concern for members of the armed forces and their families. You can stop by for assistance with accommodations, transportation, sightseeing, and other travel needs; find out about dozens of cultural events and recreational activities in the Washington area, many of them USO-sponsored for service families; pick up free tickets (when available) to theaters and sporting events; and learn about District discounts available on tours and travel, at hotels, restaurants, and elsewhere. Whatever your problems, USO will try to solve them. Call 703/696-2551 for information on theater/sporting events tickets.

You can also write to USO's Washington center at USO Metro, Post HQ, Bldg. 59, Rm. B-18, Fort Myer, VA 22211, or call 703/696-2628 weekdays 9am to 5pm. They can answer questions and provide information.

There's also a USO center complete with TV lounge and free coffee on the first floor of the North Terminal of Washington National Airport (tel. 703/920-6990). Also in the North Terminal at National is a USO information booth (tel. 703/920-2705). They're staffed by volunteers, so hours vary occasionally, but they try to keep one or the other of these airport facilities open daily 10am to 9pm.

FOR WOMEN

The **Women's Information Bank,** 3918 W St. NW, Washington, DC 20007 (tel. 202/338-8163), is a volunteer-staffed organization offering a number of services to women, such as help in finding safe, reasonably priced, long- and short-term accommodations. They often know of houses and apartments for rent, people who need roommates, and bed-and-breakfast places. Best of all, there's no fee, though donations are accepted. There's generally someone on hand daily 10am to 10pm, but call first. Sometimes they're slow to answer phone messages. Persevere. In addition, WIB hosts a walk-in open house nightly 7 to 9pm, sometimes with guest speakers.

FOR GAYS & LESBIANS

The complete source for the gay and lesbian community is *The Washington Blade,* a comprehensive weekly newspaper distributed free at about 400 locations in the District. Every issue provides an extensive events calendar and a list of about 300 resources, such as crisis centers, health facilities, switchboards, political groups, religious organizations, social clubs, and student activities; it puts you in touch with everything from groups of lesbian birdwatchers to the Asian Gay Men's Network. Gay restaurants and clubs are, of course, also listed and advertised. You can subscribe to the *Blade* for $30 a year or pick up a free copy at: Olsson's Books/Records, 1307 19th St. NW; Annie's Paramount Steak House, 1609 17th St. NW; and Kramerbooks, 1517 Connecticut Ave. NW, in the Dupont Circle area; the Biograph Theatre, 29th and M Streets NW, in Georgetown; Chesapeake Bagel Bakery, 215 Pennsylvania Ave. SE, on Capitol Hill. Call the *Blade* office at 797-7000 for other locations

CHAPTER 5

ACCOMMODATIONS IN WASHINGTON, D.C.

1. **VERY EXPENSIVE**
* **FROMMER'S SMART TRAVELER: HOTELS**
* **FROMMER'S COOL FOR KIDS: HOTELS**
2. **EXPENSIVE**
3. **MODERATE**
4. **INEXPENSIVE**
5. **BUDGET**
6. **BED & BREAKFAST**

Your first priority on a Washington visit is finding a place to stay. Luckily, with more than 63,000 hotel and motel rooms in the District and surrounding metropolitan area, there's no shortage of rooms. They exist in every category, from luxurious accommodations to budget guesthouses—with many more, alas, in the upper bracket than in the lower. Presented below are those establishments in all price categories that offer the best value for your money.

PRICE CATEGORIES Hotels listed as "Very Expensive" charge $200 or more for a double room, those charging $150 to $200 are listed as "Expensive," $100 to $149 as "Moderate," $65 to $99 as "Inexpensive," and under $65 as "Budget." B&Bs are listed in a separate section. Most of the recommendations in all price categories are located in the northwest sector, where you will also find a number of major sightseeing attractions and good restaurants. However, within each price category the hotels are listed by location.

TAXES Whatever your price range, remember that the sales tax here is 11% of your total bill, and the occupancy tax is $1.50 per night. If you have a car, inquire about the cost of parking when you reserve; some hotels charge as much as $22 a night!

GETTING THE MOST FOR YOUR DOLLAR

WEEKEND, OFF-SEASON & SPECIAL RATES In Washington, the majority of hotels, from budget to expensive, slash prices by almost half during weekends, and sometimes, weekdays in off-season (generally July through August and late December through January). When telephoning to make arrangements, be sure to verify that your reservation is at weekend rates before you hang up, and check on it again when you register. At many hotels, you must register in advance to obtain weekend rates. *Note:* Weekend rates listed for hotels in this chapter are, generally, subject to availability.

Contact the **D.C. Committee to Promote Washington**, P.O. Box 27489, Washington, DC 20038-7489 (tel. 202/724-4091, or toll free 800/422-8644), and request a copy of "Washington

Weekends." It lists weekend rates at more than 90 hotels in all price ranges.

Taj International Hotels, 1315 16th St. NW, Washington, DC 20036 (tel. 202/462-7104, or toll free 800/DC-VISIT), owns four centrally located Washington, D.C. hotels—the Hampshire Hotel, the Canterbury, the Quality Hotel, and Howard Johnson's Hotel & Suites—all of which are described in this chapter. Their weekend rates, also available sometimes on weekdays November to February and July and August, range from $59 to $99 per room per night. They also offer marvelous weekend packages with extras such as champagne and chocolates upon arrival. Write or call for details.

Also inquire about special packages. Many hotels offer special rates as a matter of course to senior citizens, families, active-duty military personnel, and government workers.

A RESERVATIONS SERVICE Make use of a free service offered by **Capitol Reservations,** 1730 Rhode Island Ave. NW, Suite 506, Washington, DC 20036 (tel. 202/452-1270, or toll free 800/VISIT-DC). They'll find you a hotel that meets your specific requirements and is within your price range, and they'll do the bargaining for you. "Because of the high volume of room nights we book," explains owner Thom Hall, "many properties offer discounts available only through this service." Capitol Reservations listings begin at about $55 a night for a double. Hotels are screened for cleanliness and other desirability factors, and they're all in safe neighborhoods.

GROUPS If you're planning a meeting, convention, or other group function requiring 10 rooms or more, you should know about a free service called **U.S.A. Groups** (tel. 202/861-1900, or toll free 800/872-4777). Representing hotel rooms at almost every hostelry in the Washington, D.C., and suburban Virginia/Maryland region—in categories from expensive to low cost—this organization works hard to find accommodations that fit your group's needs perfectly; this service will save you from having to make dozens of phone calls.

---

1. VERY EXPENSIVE

Whether they're old and grand or new and glamorous, all of these hostelries provide abundant luxuries and gracious service to guests. And they all feature beautiful gourmet restaurants, many of which merit a visit even if you stay at a less elegant address. Some proffer old-fashioned European-style services and traditions (shoeshine, bed turndown, concierge, etc.). Others offer wide-ranging facilities.

Another feature you'll frequently find in this category is the concierge floor. A special area of a hotel set aside for guests who pay a little bit more, it offers larger rooms with additional amenities, special concierge and housekeeping services, a private lounge where complimentary continental breakfasts and cocktail-hour hors d'oeuvres are served, and, in most cases, daily newspaper delivery and nightly turndown. Establishments in this section charge $200 and up per night for a double room.

DOWNTOWN

HENLY PARK, 926 Massachusetts Ave. NW (at 10th St.), Washington, DC 20001. Tel. 202/638-5200, or toll free 800/222-8474. Fax 202/638-6740. 90 rms; 6 suites. A/C MINIBAR TV TEL **Metro:** Metro Center or Gallery Place.

$ Rates: Weekdays $165–$215 single, $185–$235 double. Summer and weekends $89 single or double (including parking). Extra person $20; children under 14 stay free in parents' room. AE, CB, DC, DISC, ER, MC, V. **Parking:** $15.

⭐ Named for the quaint British town Henley-on-Thames, this intimate, English-style hotel is housed in a converted 1918 seven-story Tudor-style apartment house with 119 gargoyles on its facade. The lobby, with its exquisite Tudor ceiling, archways, and leaded windows, is particularly evocative of the period. Room decor is residential in the English country house mode. Furnishings are 18th-century styles—Hepplewhite, Chippendale, and Queen Anne—with lovely period beds (you might get a four-poster). Floral-print bedspreads and drapes are charming, walls are hung with framed botanical prints, and crown moldings harmonize with carpet hues. Baths offer phones, makeup mirrors, and luxury toiletries, and in-room amenities include remote-control cable TVs with pay-movie options and AM/FM alarm-clock radios.

Dining/Entertainment: The hotel's post French restaurant is **Coeur de Lion** (for Richard the Lion-Hearted, an English king of French descent). It's a lovely dining room, with walls of weathered brick and mirrors adorned with English oil paintings and a bacchanal-themed mural, glass windows, and a crystal chandelier suspended from a skylight. The menu features French cuisine, highlighting seafood, and the wine list is excellent. Adjoining the Coeur de Lion is **Marley's,** a delightful cocktail lounge, the setting for piano bar entertainment (and complimentary hors d'oeuvres) on weekdays 5 to 8pm and live jazz on weekend nights. Afternoon tea (with scones, finger sandwiches, and pastries) is served daily in the octagonal **Wilkes Room,** a charming and comfortably furnished parlor with a working fireplace.

Services: 24-hour concierge and room service, *Washington Post* delivery each weekday morning, complimentary shoeshine, nightly bed turndown with gourmet chocolate, complimentary weekday limo service to downtown and Capitol Hill locations.

Facilities: Access to health club a block away, which has treadmills, StairMasters, exercise bikes, and a Universal set.

J. W. MARRIOTT, 1331 Pennsylvania Ave. NW (at E St.), Washington, DC 20004. Tel. 202/393-2000, or toll free 800/228-9290. Fax 202/626-6991. 721 rms, 51 suites. A/C MINIBAR TV TEL **Metro:** Metro Center.

FROMMER'S SMART TRAVELER: HOTELS

1. Use reservations services such as Capitol Reservations; they obtain lower rates by booking rooms in volume.

2. Take advantage of reduced rates, often offered Friday to Sunday and sometimes off-season weekdays as well. They may be as much as 50% lower.

3. Bargain with the reservations clerk. An unoccupied room nets a hotel zero dollars, and any reasonable offer is better than that. This works best on the afternoon of your arrival, when the desk knows there will be empty rooms.

4. Ask about special discounts for students, government or corporate employees, senior citizens, or military personnel.

5. Using toll-free numbers, compare rates at a wide variety of hotels. Sometimes even expensive hostelries, which list rates as high as $200, will offer a rate as low as $75 on the phone.

6. At the hotel, if you don't like the first room you see, ask for another. Accommodations at the same property can vary considerably.

$ Rates: Weekdays $189–$209 single or double, $219–$229 concierge level single or double. Weekends $99–$129 single or double with full breakfast. Extra person free. AE, DC, DISC, ER, JCB, MC, V. **Parking:** $16.

This flagship property, opened in 1984 as part of the master plan to renovate historic Pennsylvania Avenue, is adjacent to the National and Warner theaters. It's stunning, combining futuristic architecture with warm color schemes and lush plantings to create an exciting but very livable environment.

Rooms are decorated in pleasing color schemes (sage and rose or celadon and apricot) and furnished with cherrywood pieces in traditional styles. They're equipped with remote-control TVs with cable and HBO, in-room voice mail, AM/FM alarm-clock radios, and plants. The concierge level, on the 14th and 15th floors, features a private lounge with a gorgeous view. Frills here include complimentary continental breakfast and cocktail-hour hors d'oeuvres, additional toiletries, nightly turndown with a Godiva chocolate, and an electric shoeshiner.

Dining/Entertainment: The hotel's most elegant facility is **Celadon,** in which Chinese Chippendale chairs (like the walls, upholstered in celadon green) and Oriental vases and screens create an Eastern ambience. Taped music varies from Vivaldi to show tunes. Lunch and dinner menus offer American/continental options ranging from filet mignon to pine-nut swordfish. The very pretty **National**

N

National
Zoological Park

Massachusetts Ave.

Rock Creek

24th St.
23rd St.

California St.

Florida Ave.

R St.

New Hampshire Ave.

16th St.

Q St.

**Dupont
Circle**

P St.

Wisconsin Ave.

34th St.
33rd St.
31st St.
30th St.
29th St.
28th St.

O St.

N St.

Connecticut Ave.

19th St.
18th St.

Rhode Island Ave.

M St.

N St.

M St.

**Washington
Circle**

New Hampshire Ave.

L St.

**Farragut
Square**

**McPhers
Squar**

K St.

Pennsylvania Ave.

I St.

**Lafayette
Square**

**Francis Scott Key
Mem. Bridge**

Georgetown Channel

H St.

**Theodore
Roosevelt
Island**

22nd St.
21st St.
20th St.

G St.

F St.

**The
White Hous**

**The
Ellipse**

Constitution Av

**Theodore Roosevelt
Mem. Bridge**

**Washington
Monument**

**Reflecting
Pool**

Virginia Ave.

Kutz Bridge

**Arlington
National
Cemetery**

Arlington Mem. Bridge

Potomac River

Tidal Basin

66

**Jefferson
Memorial**

6701

Adams Inn **20**	Embassy Inn **23**	Hotel Lombardy **9**
Barceló Washington Hotel **5**	Four Seasons **4**	Howard Johnson's Hotel & Suites **25**
Canterbury Hotel **21**	Georgetown Dutch Inn **2**	Howard Johnson's Lodge
Capital Hilton **29**	Hampshire Hotel **6**	J. W. Marriott **33**
Carlyle Suites **19**	Hay-Adams **30**	Jefferson **26**
Channel Inn **40**	Henley Park **36**	Kalorama Guest House **17**
Comfort Inn **39**	Holiday Inn Central **27**	Marriott's Residence Inn
Connecticut Avenue Days Inn **16**	Holiday Inn Franklin Square **31**	Mayflower **11**
Days Inn Downtown **34**	Hostelling International—Washington, D.C. **37**	Morrison Clark Inn **35**
	Hotel Anthony **10**	

WASHINGTON, D.C., ACCOMMODATIONS

Normandy Inn **14**
Omni Shoreham **15**
Washington Courtyard **13**
Quality Hotel Downtown **22**
The Reeds' Bed & Breakfast **26**
Ritz-Carlton **12**
Savoy Suites Georgetown **1**

State Plaza Hotel **8**
Washington, D.C., Renaissance Hotel **38**
Washington Hilton and Towers **18**
Willard Inter-Continental **32**
Windsor Inn **24**

Cafe utilizes a pink-and-peach Victorian/art nouveau motif and, in warm weather, has outdoor seating at umbrella-shaded tables. Lunch or dinner, the fare ranges from simple burgers and salads to heartier entrées. An "early-bird" dinner (soup, salad, entrée, and dessert) costs under $15. Alfresco dining is also a feature of **SRO** (for Standing Room Only), a friendly pub. And for piano entertainment and jazz bands nightly there's the skylit **Garden Terrace.**

Services: 24-hour room service.

Facilities: A connecting mall with 85 shops and restaurants, health club (with indoor swimming pool, Universal equipment, hydrotherapy pool, and sun deck), video-game arcade, full business center, gift shop.

WASHINGTON, D.C., RENAISSANCE HOTEL, 999 9th St. NW (at K St.), Washington, DC 20001. Tel. 202/898-9000, or toll free 800/228-9898. Fax 202/789-4213. 779 rooms, 21 suites. A/C MINIBAR TV TEL **Metro:** Gallery Place.

$ Rates: Weekdays $185–$205 single; $205–$225 double; club level $225 single, $245 double. Weekends $99 single or double. Extra person free. AE, CB, DC, DISC, MC, V. **Parking:** $14.

Opened in 1989 directly across the street from the D.C. Convention Center, this hotel is part of the $340-million World Technology Trade Center Complex. Though catering primarily to conventioneers and business travelers, it also delivers a lot of luxury and convenience to tourists.

For openers, the spiffy rooms are well equipped and attractive. Done up in teal/mauve or sage/sienna color schemes, with oak furnishings and Southwest-look bedspreads and drapes, they offer remote-control TVs (with cable stations, pay-movie options, and video message retrieval/checkout), alarm clocks, phones with voice mail and computer jacks, and AM/FM radios. An entire 15-story tower with 166 rooms constitutes the Renaissance Club, where guests are pampered with extra amenities such as three phones, hairdryers, and an extensive toiletries package. Club guests can also enjoy a private concierge-staffed lounge, a cozy domain where a lavish complimentary continental breakfast and afternoon hors d'oeuvres are served. Private registration/checkout is another plus.

Dining/Entertainment: The mahogany-paneled and crystal-chandeliered **Floreale** features American regional cuisine. Less formal is the **Café Florentine,** off the lobby, offering reasonably priced buffets and à la carte meals; it's cheerfully decorated with fruit- and vegetable-motif tiles. Surrounded by lush tropical plantings, the skylit **Marco Polo** piano bar resembles a Chinese pagoda. And the **Plaza Gourmet & Pastry Shop** offers take-out sandwiches, salads, and fresh-baked pastries.

Services: 24-hour room service, concierge.

Facilities: Gift shop, hairdresser, full business center, full health club (with lap pool, whirlpool, steam rooms, treadmills, StairMasters, free weights, bikes, and rowing machines).

WILLARD INTER-CONTINENTAL, 1401 Pennsylvania Ave. NW, Washington, DC 20004. Tel. 202/628-9100, or toll free 800/327-0200. Fax 202/637-7326. 304 rms, 37 suites. A/C MINIBAR TV TEL **Metro:** Metro Center.

$ **Rates:** Weekdays $255–$345 single, $285–$375 double. Weekends $199 single or double. Extra person $30; children under 12 stay free in parents' room. AE, DC, DISC, ER, JCB, MC, SAISON, V. **Parking:** $15.75.

Billed as the "crown jewel of Pennsylvania Avenue," the Willard Inter-Continental is actually the crown jewel of all Washington hotels. Reopened in 1986, it was built in 1901 as the grandest of grand hotels on the site of an earlier hostelry built by Henry Willard in 1850.

The original Willard's history is inextricably intertwined with the history of Washington. It flourished from pre–Civil War days (at one time there were separate entrances and floors for pro-Union and secessionist factions) until just after World War II. In the 1860s, Nathaniel Hawthorne said of the Willard, "You exchange nods with governors of sovereign States; you elbow illustrious men, and tread on the toes of generals. . . . You are mixed up with office seekers, wire pullers, inventors, artists, poets, prosers . . . until your identify is lost among them." Lincoln spent not only the eve of his inaugural here, but sometimes held staff meetings in front of the lobby fireplace. And it was at the Willard that Julia Ward Howe penned the words to the "Battle Hymn of the Republic."

In 1901 Henry Janeway Hardenbergh—architect of New York's Waldorf-Astoria and Plaza hotels—was hired to design the French Second Empire beaux arts palace that is still standing today. The hotel continued as a "residence of presidents." By the time the Willard closed its doors in 1968, however, it had deteriorated considerably.

Saved as a national landmark in 1974, restoration began in the 1980s, and a new building, designed to harmonize with the old, was constructed. In the original building, the exquisite plasterwork and scagliola marble were repaired or replicated, along with marble mosaic tile floors, carpeting, and chandeliers. The main lobby today is again an awesome entranceway, with massive marble columns ascending to a lofty ceiling decorated with 48 state seals and hung with huge globe chandeliers. Alaska and Hawaii seals are in Peacock Alley, a plush potted-palmed promenade.

Rooms are suitably sumptuous, decorated in Egyptian earth tones or sea and sky blues. Furnishings are Edwardian and Federal-period reproductions, and walls are hung with beautiful gilt-framed French prints. Phones have dual lines, and cable TVs (with remote control, pay-movie channels, video messaging, and video checkout) are concealed in armoires. And in the bath you'll find a hairdryer, scale, phone, TV speaker, and makeup mirror.

Dining/Entertainment: The **Willard Room** (the term "power lunch" originated here) is simply stunning. It's the setting for American regional cuisine meals, with piano music during dinner. (See Chapter 6 for details.) The circular **Round Robin Bar** is where Henry Clay mixed the first mint julep in Washington. The **Café Espresso** offers croissant sandwiches, pastas, pastries, and vintage wines by the glass, along with more substantial entrées. And the **Round Robin Lounge** offers afternoon tea daily from 3 to 5pm and jazz piano nightly.

Services: Twice-daily maid service, nightly bed turndown, complimentary shoeshine, 24-hour room service, concierge, currency exchange, airline/train ticketing.

Facilities: Full business center, fitness center (with multistation machine, treadmills, Lifecycles, StairMasters, and free weights).

NEAR THE WHITE HOUSE

THE CAPITAL HILTON, 16th St. NW (between K and L Sts.), Washington, DC 20036. Tel. 202/393-1000, or toll free 800/HILTONS. Fax 202/639-5784. 517 rms, 32 suites. A/C MINIBAR TV TEL **Metro:** Farragut West or McPherson Square.

$ Rates: Weekdays $240–$280 single, $265–$305 double; tower $310 single, $335 double. Weekends (including continental breakfast) $140 single or double. Extra person $25; children of any age stay free in parents' room. AE, CB, DC, DISC, ER, JCB, MC, V. **Parking:** $22.

This longtime Washington resident has hosted every American president since FDR, including Truman, who lived here while the White House (two blocks away) was being remodeled. The annual Gridiron Club Dinner and political roast is held in the ballroom each year.

During a five-year $55-million renovation in the late 1980s, the public areas were upgraded (note the gorgeous cherrywood paneling in the lobby). And in 1993 the rooms were redecorated in Federal-period motif with Queen Anne– and Chippendale-style furnishings. Each has three phones (desk, bath, bedside) equipped with call waiting, a digital alarm clock, an AM/FM radio, and a remote-control cable TV featuring pay-movie stations and account-review/message-retrieval options. In the bath you'll find a small TV and hairdryer. Floors 10 to 14 house the Towers accommodations, where guests enjoy nightly bed turndown with gourmet chocolates, private registration/checkout, a personal concierge, and complimentary continental breakfast in a plush private lounge

Dining/Entertainment: There's a **Trader Vic's** here with oak-paneled walls and plush red tufted-leather booths. Nautical art and ship models tastefully replace the usual Polynesian clutter associated with this chain. Its Asian/South Seas–influenced fare (mandarin orange beef, pupu platters, Tahitian bouillabaisse) is excellent; stop by for the $12.95 Polynesian buffet lunch. Another fine Hilton dining room is **Twigs,** a sunny gardenlike setting with lots of plants, white trelliswork, and seating amid potted palms; the more elegant **Twigs Grill** adjoins. Fare is American regional. Complimentary hors d'oeuvres are served in **The Bar,** a plushly furnished lobby lounge, weekdays from 5 to 7pm and a pianist entertains throughout the evening.

Services: 24-hour room service, 24-hour concierge, full business center tour and ticket desk

Facilities: Unisex hairdresser, gift shop, facial salon, shoeshine stand, jeweler, airline desks (American, Continental, Northwest), fitness center (with Nautilus equipment, treadmills, rowing machines, exercise bikes, StairMasters, steam, and sauna).

HAY-ADAMS, 1 Lafayette Sq. (at 16th and H Sts. NW), Washington, DC 20006. Tel. 202/638-6600, or toll free 800/424-5054. Fax 202/638-3803. 117 rms, 19 suites. A/C MINIBAR TV TEL **Metro:** Farragut West or McPherson Square.

$ Rates: Weekdays $210–$360 single or double. Weekends $135–$235 per room. Extra person $30; children under 12 stay free in parents' room. AE, CB, DC, JCB, MC, V. **Parking:** $19.

Few hotels have a more aristocratic air than this one, overlooking Lafayette Square. In 1927, famed Washington builder Harry Wardman created the Hay-Adams (on the site of the 19th-century homes of Theodore Roosevelt's secretary of state, John Hays, and noted historian Henry Adams) "to provide for the socially elite as well as men who loom large in the country's life." Its architecture evokes an Italian Renaissance palazzo with Doric, Ionic, and Corinthian orders and intricate ceiling motifs. Among the early guests were Amelia Earhart, Sinclair Lewis, Ethel Barrymore, and Charles Lindbergh. In the 1990s, the hotel is as elegant as ever—still a haunt of visiting royalty and powerful business leaders.

Rooms are individually furnished with antiques and appointments far superior to those usually found in today's hotels Though each is different, a typical accommodation might feature 18th-century-style furnishings, silk-covered walls hung with botanical prints and fine art, a gorgeous molded plaster ceiling, and French silk floral-print bedspreads, upholstery, and curtains. Many have ornamental fireplaces and/or French doors that open onto views of Lafayette Square and the White House. Amenities include fine toiletries, hairdryers, cosmetic mirrors, and phones in the bathrooms; terrycloth robes and slippers; AM/FM alarm-clock radios; and remote-control cable TVs with HBO.

Dining/Entertainment: The sunny **Lafayette Room,** overlooking the White House, is an elegant venue with comfortable mahogany chairs upholstered in Scalamandre silk and French Empire crystal candelabra chandeliers. Noted chef Patrick Clark's cuisine is contemporary American with international touches. The Tudor-style **John Hays Lounge**—its oak-paneled walls hung with reproductions of works by Hans Holbein the Younger and 17th-century French tapestries—is a stately setting for lunch, afternoon tea, cocktails, and nightly piano-bar entertainment

Services: Limousine service, 24-hour butler/room/concierge service, chocolates and petits fours with nightly bed turndown, complimentary shoeshine

Facilities: Guest access to several local health clubs, secretarial and business services

THE JEFFERSON, 1200 16th St. NW (at M St.), Washington, DC 20036. Tel. 202/347-2200, or toll free 800/368-5966. Fax 202/223-9039. 68 rms, 32 suites. A/C MINIBAR TV TEL

Metro: Farragut North.

$ Rates: Weekdays $220–$260 single, $235–$275 double. Weekends $160 single, $175 double. Extra person $25; children under 12 stay free in parents' room. AE, CB, DC, JCB, MC, OPT, V. **Parking:** $20.

Esquire magazine has called The Jefferson "one of the ten best hotels in the world." Opened in 1923 just four blocks from the White House, it has served as the Washington home of political personages, royalty, actors, writers, and other notables. Among those who've enjoyed The Jefferson's discreet small-hotel hospitality over the years are Edward R. Murrow, Helen Hayes, Robert Frost, Leonard Bernstein, and H. L. Mencken (his books are still in the room he occupied). With a very high staff-to-guest ratio, The Jefferson puts utmost emphasis on service: Staff members greet you by name, and, should you return, your preferences will be remembered. If you like, a butler will unpack your luggage and press clothes wrinkled in transit.

The Jefferson is impressive from the minute you set foot in the sedately elegant lobby. Beautiful Persian rugs adorn marble floors, Italian turn-of-the-century crystal chandeliers are suspended from a carved-plaster rosette-motif Adams ceiling, big bouquets of flowers adorn 18th-century tables, and moss-green velvet-covered Chippendale armchairs face a Georgian-reproduction fireplace. A Thomas Jefferson grandfather clock chimes the hour in dulcet tones. A very fine art collection graces public areas, rooms, and hallways. Each room is uniquely decorated. Yours might have a four-poster bed with plump eyelet-trimmed comforter and pillow shams (many are topped with canopies), a cherrywood bibliothèque from the Napoleonic period filled with rare books, a French Empire Louis XVI bureau, or a red lacquer chinoiserie case filled with objets d'art. In-room amenities include multiline phones with speakerphone option plus fax and computer jacks, remote-control cable TVs with VCRs, AM/FM alarm-clock radios, CD players, and, in the baths, terry robes, hairdryers, and phones.

Dining/Entertainment: Off the lobby is one of the city's premier dining venues (see Chapter 6). A marvelous high tea is served daily from 3 to 5pm in the reading room, its walls hung with framed original Thomas Jefferson letters and documents. Classical music enhances the ambience. There's also a cozy bar/lounge with a working fireplace, the setting for live jazz on Saturday night.

Services: 24-hour butler service, overnight shoeshine, nightly bed turndown with Godiva chocolate, morning newspaper delivery, 24-hour room and multilingual concierge service.

Facilities: Business/secretarial services; for a fee guests have access to full health club facilities at the University Club across the street (pool, Nautilus, sauna, whirlpool, and more)

DUPONT CIRCLE

MAYFLOWER, 1127 Connecticut Ave. NW (between L and M Sts.) Washington, DC 20036. Tel. 202/347-3000, or

toll free 800/HOTELS-1. Fax 202/466-9082. 559 rms, 80 suites.
A/C MINIBAR TV TEL **Metro:** Farragut North.

$ Rates: Weekdays $245–$305 single, $275–$335 double. Weekends $125–$170 single or double. Extra person $25; children under 18 stay free in parents' room. Inquire about "summer value rates." AE, CB, DC, DISC, ER, JCB, MC, V. **Parking:** $12.

Designed by the architectural firm whose masterpieces include Grand Central Terminal in New York, the Stouffer-owned May-flower (opened in 1925) is the grande dame of Washington hotels. Every president from Coolidge to Reagan held his inaugural ball in the gilded Grand Ballroom. FDR penned the words "The only thing we have to fear is fear itself" in Suite 776. JFK called the hotel home as a young congressman. And for 20 years before his death, FBI chief J. Edgar Hoover ate the same lunch (chicken soup, grapefruit, cottage cheese) in the Grille Room every day. One day he spotted Public Enemy No. 3 at an adjoining table and nabbed him. One could go on forever with Mayflower lore.

A major restoration in the 1980s uncovered large skylights and renewed the lobby's pink marble bas-relief frieze and the spectacular block-long promenade. Ceilings and columns were regilded and Italianate murals rediscovered.

In the graciously appointed guest rooms, hardwood crown moldings adorn high ceilings. Cream moiré wall coverings are complemented by accents of claret and teal, mahogany furnishings are period reproductions (Queen Anne, Sheraton, Chippendale, Hepplewhite), 25-inch remote-control TVs are discreetly concealed in handsome armoires, and amenities include three phones (bath, desk, bedside) and AM/FM alarm-clock radios. In the bath you'll find a terry robe, hairdryer, fine toiletries, and a small color TV.

Dining/Entertainment: The hotel's much-acclaimed premier restaurant, **Nicholas,** features superb American regional cuisine in a plush setting—crystal chandeliers and sconces illuminate walls hung with gilt-framed French oil paintings, tables are elegantly appointed, and windows are framed by swagged draperies.

Washington lawyers and lobbyists gather for power breakfasts in the posh **Café Promenade.** Under a beautiful domed skylight, the restaurant is adorned with Edward Laning's murals, crystal chandeliers, ficus trees, marble columns, and lovely flower arrangements. A full English tea is served here afternoons Monday to Saturday. The room originally was, in fact, used for thés dansants (tea dances). In the evening the café is a romantic venue for dinner.

The clubby, mahogany-paneled **Town & Country,** with its leather-upholstered chairs and sofas, is the setting for light buffet lunches, complimentary cocktail-hour hors d'oeuvres, and piano-bar entertainment nightly 5:30 to 8pm.

And the **Lobby Court,** an espresso bar just opposite the front desk, features coffee and fresh-baked pastries in the morning, champagne and caviar later in the day; it's open weekdays only.

Services: Coffee and newspaper with wake-up call, 24-hour room service twice-daily maid service, complimentary overnight shoeshine, complimentary limo within a 3-mile radius of the hotel, concierge.

Facilities: Business center, full on-premises fitness center (with sauna and Vectra exercise equipment, treadmills, Lifecycles, and StairMasters), florist, hair salon, gift shop, Cartier jeweler.

RITZ-CARLTON, 2100 Massachusetts Ave. NW, Washington, DC 20008. Tel. 202/293-2100, or toll free 800/241-3333. Fax 202/293-0641. 206 rms, 32 suites. A/C MINIBAR TV TEL **Metro:** Dupont Circle.

$ Rates: Weekdays $215–$285 single or double, $335 club single or double. Weekends $190 single or double. Extra person free. Inquire about packages. AE, CB, DC, ER, MC, V. **Parking:** $16 (valet only).

⭐ Built in 1924, the Ritz-Carlton is a gem, from its richly walnut-paneled lobby to its pristine Oriental-carpeted hallways and lovely residential rooms. The latter—decorated in muted tones (champagne or cream, with willow green, wheat, gray, and rose accents)—are handsomely furnished with traditional dark-wood pieces. Windows are framed by elegant tasseled draperies, walls hung with French architectural watercolor renderings. In-room amenities include remote-control cable TVs (with HBO movie stations) concealed in armoires, AM/FM alarm-clock radios, safes, three phones (desk, bath, and bedside), and terry robes. Gorgeous marble baths are equipped with hairdryers and upscale toiletries (some also have small black-and-white TVs). The seventh and eight floors comprise a club level where guests have use of a beautiful lounge overlooking neighboring embassies and a library housing travel books donated by ambassadors to Washington. Rates on these levels include, among other perks, the services of a private concierge, a video library (there's a VCR in your room), and elegant spreads for complimentary breakfasts, lunches, afternoon teas, cocktail-hour hors d'oeuvres and drinks, and late-night desserts and cordials.

Dining/Entertainment: The **Jockey Club** has long been one of Washington's most prominent restaurants (see details in Chapter 6). The **Fairfax Bar,** with a working fireplace and glossy knotty-pine walls hung with equestrian art, offers intimate seating for cocktails. The adjoining **Potomac Room,** with a dance floor in front of another working fireplace, features piano-bar entertainment Wednesday to Saturday nights. (*Note:* Michael Feinstein got his start playing piano at the Ritz-Carlton.) Room-service fare from the Jockey Club is available at both facilities. Check out the shadow boxes in the Potomac Room and see if you can find the tiny mouse in each of them.

Services: Complimentary morning newspaper delivery and shoeshine, nightly turndown with imported chocolates, complimentary limo transport weekdays within the District, 24-hour concierge and room service.

Facilities: Fitness room (with treadmills, stair machines, NordicTrack, free weights, Lifecycles, saunas), business center.

GEORGETOWN

THE FOUR SEASONS, 2800 Pennsylvania Ave. NW, Washington, DC 20007. Tel. 202/342-0444, or toll free 800/332-2442. Fax 202/944-2076. 166 rms, 30 suites. A/C MINIBAR TV TEL **Metro:** Foggy Bottom.

$ Rates: Weekdays $265–$295 single, $295–$320 double. Weekends $215–$235 single or double. Extra person $30; children under 18 stay free in parents' room. AE, CB, DC, ER, JCB, MC, V. **Parking:** $20.

Since it opened in 1979, this most glamorous of Washington's haute hotels has hosted everyone from Billy Joel (who took over the Garden Terrace piano and entertained delighted guests for an hour) to King Hussein of Jordan. During the course of their long and tempestuous courtship, Marla Maples once stalked out of the lobby after flinging a shoe—and a 7½-carat engagement ring—at Donald Trump. Another day, President Clinton stopped by for afternoon tea with Chelsea. But celebrity gossip aside, this is a magnificent property. Open the front door and you enter a plush setting where thousands of plants and palm trees grow, and large floral arrangements extend the gardenlike ambience. Fine china is displayed in a rare Chinese Chippendale mahogany breakfront, one of several notable antiques. And classical music is played throughout the public areas.

Exceptionally pretty accommodations, many of them overlooking Rock Creek Park or the C&O Canal, offer contrasting traditional dark-wood furnishings and charming print fabrics. Textured white walls are hung with gilt-framed antique prints, and the bedding is embellished with dust ruffles and scalloped spreads. Large desks and plump cushioned armchairs with hassocks contribute to the residential atmosphere. In-room amenities include remote-control cable TVs with free HBO and Spectravision pay-movie options, VCRs (movies and video games are available), CD players (the concierge stocks CDs), AM/FM alarm-clock radios, three phones (bedside, bath, and desk—one with two lines), bathrobes, and, in the baths, hairdryers, lighted cosmetic mirrors, and upscale toiletries.

Dining/Entertainment: The elegant and highly acclaimed **Seasons** serves contemporary cuisine that is international in scope (details in Chapter 6). Paneled in Australian ash, the delightful **Garden Terrace** is bordered by tropical plants, ficus trees, and flower beds. There's even a gurgling fountain. Comfy seating consists of upholstered wicker armchairs and sofas, and a wall of windows overlooks the canal. It's open for lunch, a lavish Sunday jazz brunch, and classic English-style afternoon teas. And guests are given temporary membership at the warmly intimate **Desirée,** a private on-premises nightclub.

Services: Twice-daily maid service, 24-hour room service and can-do-anything concierge, complimentary limousine service weekdays within the District, gratis newspaper of your choice, car windows washed when you park overnight, complimentary shoeshine.

Facilities: Beauty salon; gift shop; jogging trail; business facilities; children's programs; state-of-the-art fitness club with Lifecycles, StairMasters, treadmills, and rowing machines (all equipped with TVs, VCRs, and Walkmen; movie, music, and workout tapes are available), Nautilus equipment, free weights, lap pool, massage, whirlpool, sauna for women, steam for men, exercise classes, fitness evaluation, juice bar, workout clothes, and more.

WOODLEY PARK

OMNI SHOREHAM, 2500 Calvert St. NW (at Connecticut Ave.), Washington, DC 20008. Tel. 202/234-0700, or toll free 800/228-2121. Fax 202/265-5333. 745 rms, 55 suites. A/C TV TEL **Metro:** Woodley Park–Zoo.

$ Rates: Weekdays $205–$265 single, $225–$285 double. Off-season and weekends $79 single or double. Extra person $20; children under 18 stay free in parents' room. AE, CB, DC, DISC, ER, JCB, MC V. **Parking:** $12.

Set on 11 acres adjacent to verdant Rock Creek Park, the Shoreham is a resort hotel right in the heart of the city. And what a hotel it is! Built in 1930, this deluxe hostelry has been the scene of inaugural balls for every president since FDR. In the early years, prominent socialites such as Perle Mesta and Alice Roosevelt Longworth threw private parties here. Truman held poker games in Room D-106 while his limousine waited outside. JFK courted Jackie over drinks at the Shoreham and Richard Nixon introduced his cabinet-to-be over network television at a dinner here. The most ostentatious guest ever was King Saud who, traveling with a full complement of armed guards and 32 limos, dispensed solid-gold watches as tips.

Some years ago, the hotel's public areas were restored to their original grandeur. In the vast Renaissance lobby, Chinese carpets were laid on marble floors, exquisite stenciled artwork was restored on vaulted ceilings, clerestory windows were fitted with new glass, and opulent crystal chandeliers were cleaned. The spacious guest rooms—beautifully decorated in soft burgundies, subtle grays, and chalky blues—are equipped with remote-control cable TVs (with pay-movie options) and AM/FM alarm-clock radios.

Dining/Entertainment: The hotel's excellent restaurant, the **Monique Café et Brasserie,** is reminiscent of the famed La Coupole in Paris—a convivial enclave of polished brass, dark woodwork, simulated marble columns, potted palms, and Oriental mirrors. But, despite its French name and appearance, Monique specializes in continental/American fare with an emphasis on steak and seafood. The delightful **Garden Court,** under a 35-foot vaulted ceiling, is lushly planted with ficus trees and tropical foliage, all of it reflected in beveled-mirror walls. **Rock Creek Park** provides a fitting backdrop for this popular cocktail lounge. The hotel's nightlife centers on the art deco **Marquee Cabaret** (details in Chapter 9).

Services: Room service, concierge.

Facilities: Shops; travel/sightseeing desk; business center; extensive children's activity programs; 10 miles of jogging, hiking, and bicycle trails (winding off into Rock Creek Park), plus a 1½ mile Perrier parcourse with 18 exercise stations; three lighted Har-Tru tennis courts; Olympic-size swimming pool and kiddie pool; on-premises health club (with a full complement of Nautilus and Lifecycle equipment, StairMasters, treadmills, rowing machines, sauna, and more)

KALORAMA

WASHINGTON HILTON AND TOWERS, 1919 Connecticut Ave. NW (at T St.), Washington, DC 20009. Tel. 202/483-3000, or toll free 800/HILTONS. Fax 202/797-5755. 1,203 rms 82 suites. A/C MINIBAR TV TEL **Metro:** Dupont Circle.

$ Rates: Weekdays $200–$240 single, $220–$260 double; Towers rooms $225–$265 single, $245–$285 double. Weekends (and selected weekdays and holidays) $97 per room, $122 per Towers rooms. Extra person $20; children of any age stay free in parents' room. AE, CB, CH, DC, DISC, ER, JCB, MC, OPT, V. **Parking:** $12.

This is a kind of super-hotel/resort offering every imaginable amenity. A recent $42-million renovation spiffed up its accommodations, restaurants, and public areas, and it's looking great! The Hilton hosts numerous conventions and functions—inaugural balls, debutante cotillions, state banquets, and society shindigs.

ⓕ **FROMMER'S COOL FOR KIDS: HOTELS**

Channel Inn *(see p. 77)* This lovely hotel has a swimming pool, and adults will love the rooms with views of the boat-filled Washington Channel.

Howard Johnson's Hotel & Suites *(see p. 84)* Close to sightseeing attractions, it has a rooftop pool and video-game room. And most accommodations have kitchens, so you can prepare meals in your room—a big money-saver. Coin-op launderettes are here, too.

The OMNI Shoreham *(see p. 72)* Adjacent to Rock Creek Park, close to the zoo, and equipped with two outdoor pools—a large one for swimming laps and a kiddie pool—the Shoreham offers an extensive program of children's activities. Three lighted tennis courts are an additional attraction.

Washington Hilton and Towers *(see p. 73)* A large heated outdoor pool, a wading pool, video-game room, three tennis courts, shuffleboard, and bike rental. What more do you need?

The rooms are cheerful and attractively furnished in such colors as cinnamon, mauve, and sea-foam green. All have AM/FM alarm-clock radios and remote-control cable TVs with pay-movie stations, and many offer panoramic views of Washington. The 10th floor is called the Towers—a VIP hotel-within-a-hotel featuring a beautifully furnished private lounge (with a gorgeous view) and concierge service; it's the setting for complimentary continental breakfasts and afternoon hors d'oeuvres and cocktails. Special in-room amenities here include nightly bed turndown service and bathroom scales.

Dining/Entertainment: The handsome mahogany-paneled **1919 Grill,** embellished with the sporting gear and equestrian art, specializes in steaks, seafoods, and pasta dinners. The cheerful **Capital Café,** bordered by planters of flowers, has a wall of windows overlooking the pool. Open daily for all meals, it offers buffet meals and fancy coffee-shop fare—everything from croissant sandwiches to filet mignon. The **Gazebo,** an alfresco poolside eatery, serves light fare under a striped tent top in season. **McClellan's** (named for the Union general whose equestrian statue fronts the hotel) is a clubby lounge with a handsome brass-railed mahogany bar and commodious leather chairs—a comfortable place to imbibe. And **Capital Court,** an elegant lobby lounge, features a nightly piano bar.

Services: Room service during restaurant hours, transportation/sightseeing desk. Airport bus stops at the door.

Facilities: Extensive health club facilities (StairMasters, treadmills, rowing machines, Lifecycles, Cybex equipment, weight rooms, sun room, and massage), a large nightlit heated outdoor pool, children's pool, three nightlit Har-Tru tennis courts, numerous classes (including tennis and aerobics), pro/swim shop, shuffleboard, bike rental, and jogging path. Also, lobby shops, comprehensive business center, shoeshine stand, car-rental desk.

2. EXPENSIVE

The "expensive" category refers to establishments that charge $150 to $200 for a double room. As in all categories, weekend rates are considerably lower.

DUPONT CIRCLE

BARCELÓ WASHINGTON HOTEL, 2121 P St. NW, Washington, DC 20037. Tel. 202/293-3100, or toll free 800/257-5432. Fax 202/331-9719. 208 rms, 92 suites. A/C MINIBAR TV TEL **Metro:** Dupont Circle.

$ Rates: Weekdays $135–$160 single, $155–$180 double. Weekends $79–$109 single or double. Extra person $10; children under 12 stay free in parents' room. AE, CB, DC, DISC, MC, V. **Parking:** $13.

The Spanish-owned Barceló (previously the Omni Georgetown) opened with great fanfare in January 1994 when 11 Hispanic ambassadors joined Spain's ambassador Jaime de Ojeda and D.C. Mayor Sharon Pratt Kelly for a gala ribbon-cutting ceremony. The first American venture for this Mallorca-based firm, the Barceló offers friendly European-style service and an unbeatable location about midway between Dupont Circle and Georgetown. Recently renovated, its art deco marble-floored lobby is inviting, and its residential-look accommodations (formerly apartments) are enormous. Decorated in neutral tones with soft green accents (celadon and melon), they're furnished with traditional mahogany pieces. All offer workspaces with desks and living room areas containing sofas and armchairs. In-room amenities include remote-control cable TVs with free HBO and more than 200 pay-movie options, three phones with voice-mail and modem jacks, AM/FM alarm-clock radios, and marble baths with hairdryers.

Dining/Entertainment: Gabriel, one of the District's most exciting new restaurants, serves all meals (Spanish cuisine is featured) and tapas (details in Chapter 6). Its simpatico bar/lounge, popular with Washingtonians, is a big plus. Guests receive a coupon for a complimentary tapas appetizer or dessert upon registration.

Services: Concierge, room service, complimentary *Washington Post* mornings at front desk.

Facilities: Rooftop swimming pool and sun deck, sauna, small fitness room, coin-op washers/dryers, gift shop.

3. MODERATE

Establishments in this category charge about $100 to $149 for a double room. Some accommodations feature fully equipped kitchens.

DOWNTOWN

COMFORT INN, 500 H St. NW, Washington, DC 20001. Tel. 202/289-5959, or toll free 800/234-6423. Fax 202/682-9152. 197 rms. A/C TV TEL **Metro:** Gallery Place.

$ Rates: Weekdays $69–$119 single, $79–$139 double. Weekends from $59 single or double. Premier Plus Plan (includes upgraded room and amenities and full breakfast) $95 single, $105 double. Extra person $10; children under 18 stay free in parents' room. 30% senior citizen discount with a 30-day advance booking (call toll free, 800/221-2222 to obtain this rate). AE, CB, DC, DISC, ER, JCB, MC, V. **Parking:** $10.

A lower-priced offshoot of the Quality Inn chain, this hotel is within walking distance of many attractions—including Smithsonian museums. Recently renovated rooms are attractively decorated and offer cable TVs and AM/FM alarm-clock radios. The Comfort's **Cafe Express** offers buffet breakfasts and a reasonably priced salad bar and deli fare at lunch and dinner. On-premises facilities include a coin-op launderette and a sunny exercise room with

Universal equipment and a sauna. Reserve early. This popular hotel is close to Chinatown restaurants and just three blocks from the convention center.

STATE PLAZA HOTEL, 2117 E. St. NW, Washington, DC 20037. Tel. 202/861-8200, or toll free 800/424-2859. Fax 202/659-8601. 218 suites. A/C MINIBAR TV TEL **Metro:** Foggy Bottom.

$ Rates: Weekdays $125–$150 for an efficiency suite for one or two people, $175–$225 for a large one-bedroom suite (with dining room) for up to four people. Weekend (also, subject to availability, off-season weeknights) $89–$109. Extra person $20; children under 18 stay free in parents' room. AE, DC, ER, MC, V. **Parking:** $12.

⭐ I was charmed by the State Plaza from the moment I entered its antique-furnished lobby—a setting enhanced by beautiful floral arrangements and the soft strains of classical music. This all-suite hotel is deservedly popular with performers (including many ballet troupes) from the nearby Kennedy Center.

The spacious accommodations are just lovely, done up in pastel hues and pretty chintz fabrics, with Federal-style mahogany beds and Queen Anne chests. Framed botanical prints embellish the walls. Fully equipped kitchens have been fitted with shuttered windows and louver doors. Remote-control cable TVs offer Spectravision movie options. Amenities here include a coin-op launderette on the lower level, a fully equipped fitness center (treadmills, Lifecycles, StairMasters, free weights, exercise machines), a grocery-shopping service (a Safeway and gourmet shops are close by), complimentary shoeshine, and complimentary newspapers at the front desk.

The pristinely pretty **Garden** is a fine on-premises restaurant with an adjoining awning-covered patio for alfresco dining. Light and cheerful during the day, at night it's elegantly candlelit. The menu features continental and American regional cuisine, highlighting market-fresh fare.

NEAR THE WHITE HOUSE

HOLIDAY INN FRANKLIN SQUARE, 1155 14th St. NW (at Massachusetts Ave.), Washington, DC 20005. Tel. 202/737-1200, or toll free 800/HOLIDAY. Fax 202/783-5733. 208 rms. A/C TV TEL **Metro:** McPherson Square.

$ Rates: Weekdays $108–$113 single, $128–$133 double. Weekends $89 single, $109 double. Extra person $15; children under 18 stay free in parents' room. (For discount information, see below.) AE, CB, DC, DISC, JCB, MC, OPT, V. **Parking:** $8 (valet only).

Just five blocks from the White House, this centrally located, 14-story Holiday Inn is a good choice in the moderately priced category. Spacious rooms, decorated in mauve and earth tones, are equipped with remote-control satellite TVs offering free Showtime plus pay-movie stations, phones with call waiting and modem jacks, and AM/FM alarm-clock radios. There's a fairly large rooftop swimming pool and sun deck offering nice city views.

A restaurant on the premises serves buffet breakfasts. Other amenities include a coin-op launderette and a special parking lot for oversize vehicles.

At this writing, all Holiday Inns are featuring a "Great Rates" promotion, offering discounts of 20% to 50%, depending on the season and space availability. Be sure to inquire via the above toll-free number.

HOTEL ANTHONY, 1823 L St. NW, Washington, DC 20036. Tel. 202/223-4320, or toll free 800/424-2970. Fax 202/223-8546. 99 suites. A/C TV TEL **Metro:** Farragut North or Farragut West.

$ Rates: Weekdays $102–$129 suite for one, $112–$139 suite for two. Weekends $63–$73 suite for one or two. Extra person $10; children under 16 stay free in parents' suite. AE, CB, DC, DISC, JCB, MC, V. **Parking:** $10 (at nearby garage).

Fronted by an elegant gray awning, the Anthony offers suite accommodations in the heart of the downtown business/shopping/restaurant area and just five blocks from the White House. The large, comfortable suites are done in period styles—contemporary, art deco, or colonial. Most have full kitchens (the rest contain refrigerators and coffee-makers only), and all are equipped with cable TVs (offering free HBO), AM/FM alarm-clock radios, and Water Pik shower massages, among other amenities. Eleven suites offer wet bars.

There are dozens of restaurants in the surrounding streets, but adjoining the hotel itself is the cozy **Samantha's,** a cozy watering hole with a working fireplace. Reasonably priced deli sandwiches, burgers, quiches, salads, and omelets are featured, along with daily specials. Also on the premises is **Beatrice,** an Italian restaurant open for all meals.

Anthony extras include a copy of the *Washington Post* each weekday morning, room service, and gratis use of the nearby Bally's Holiday Spa, which has Nautilus and Universal exercise equipment, Lifecycles, treadmills, rowing machines, StairMasters, whirlpool, sauna, steam, and an indoor jogging track. A unisex hairstyling salon (also offering manicures, facials, and pedicures) is on the premises.

SOUTH OF THE MALL

CHANNEL INN, 650 Water St. SW (at 7th St. and Maine Ave.), Washington, DC 20024. Tel. 202/554-2400, or toll free 800/368-5668. Fax 202/863-1164. 100 rms. A/C TV TEL **Metro:** Waterfront.

$ Rates: Weekdays $100–$120 single, $110–$135 double. Weekends $80–$90 single or double. Extra person $10; children under 12 stay free in parents' room. AE, CB, DC, DISC, ER, JCB, MC, V. **Parking:** Free.

This is Washington's only waterfront hotel, built in 1973 as part of a redevelopment project that brought a marina and a row of seafood restaurants to the area Its rooms, most offering wonderful views of the boat-filled Washington Channel, are beautifully decorated in rich shades of teal and mauve, with floral chintz bedspreads and drapes, 18th-century-style mahogany furnishings, brass lamps, and plush velvet-upholstered armchairs. Some have high cathedral ceilings; all have balconies. Amenities include prettily wallpapered dressing rooms and AM/FM alarm-clock radios.

Dining/Entertainment: The inn has a moderately priced seafood/continental restaurant, the mahogany-paneled **Pier 7.** Under a peaked, beamed ceiling—from which are suspended immense wrought-iron and rope chandeliers with ship-lantern fixtures—it offers seating in comfortable red leather chairs and banquettes, many with marina and park views. Across the way is a sunny glass-walled coffee shop serving cafeteria-style breakfasts. The immense **Engine Room** lounge, featuring a cozy nautical decor and beautiful water views, offers a happy hour buffet of free hors d'oeuvres and a low-priced raw bar; stop by for live jazz and dancing Monday to Saturday until 1am.

Services: Concierge, room service (during restaurant hours).

Facilities: A pool and sun deck are out front; a golf course and indoor/outdoor tennis courts are within walking distance; the waterfront is an ideal place for jogging.

DUPONT CIRCLE

CANTERBURY HOTEL, 1733 N St. NW, Washington, DC 20036. Tel. 202/393-3000, or toll free 800/424-2950. Fax 202/785-9581. 99 junior suites. A/C MINIBAR TV TEL **Metro:** Dupont Circle.

$ Rates (including continental breakfast): Weekdays $125 suite for one, $135 suite for two. Weekends and off-season weekdays $89–$99 per room. Extra person $20; children under 12 stay free in parents' room. AE, CB, DC, DISC, ER, MC, V. **Parking:** $10.

The Canterbury Hotel is a small, European-style hostelry. Its prestigious address was once the home of both Theodore Roosevelt and Franklin D. Roosevelt. And though the hotel building is not the actual town house the Roosevelts occupied, it does attempt to recapture the elegance of an earlier era. It's entered via a graciously appointed lobby hung with hunting prints, a tranquil setting in which to plan your day's itinerary.

Each room is actually a junior suite, with a sofa/sitting area, dressing room, and kitchenette or full kitchen. Decorated in four color schemes (mauve/gray, mauve/burgundy, or tone-on-tone muted blues or sea greens), these spacious accommodations offer 18th-century mahogany English-reproduction furnishings (a few have four-poster beds). The look is pleasingly residential. Among the amenities: remote-control cable TVs with HBO movies, coffee-makers, multifeature phones, and AM/FM clock radios. Baths are supplied with cosmetic mirrors, hairdryers, phones, and baskets of fine toiletries.

Dining/Entertainment: Intimate and charming, **Chaucer's,** open for all meals, features British specialties such as cock-a-leekie soup, shepherd's pie, and prime rib with Lancashire pudding It's richly oak-paneled, with a beamed ceiling, gilt-framed mirrors, and crystal wall sconces. And the Tudor-beamed **Union Jack Pub,** complete with dart board and a menu featuring fish-and-chips, is the perfect place to relax after a busy day on the town. English beers on tap are served in pint mugs.

Services: Nightly turndown with fine chocolate, room service, morning delivery of the *Washington Post,* complimentary *Wall Street Journal* available in lobby and restaurant.

Facilities: Guests enjoy gratis use of the YMCA/National Capital Health Center nearby, offering Universal equipment, basketball/racquetball/handball/volleyball courts, a weight and exercise room, a 25-meter indoor heated pool, jogging track, StairMasters, treadmills, stationary bikes, steam room, whirlpool, and more.

HAMPSHIRE HOTEL, 1310 New Hampshire Ave. NW (at N St.), Washington, DC 20036. Tel. 202/296-7600, or toll free 800/368-5691. Fax 202/293-2476. 82 junior suites. A/C MINIBAR TV TEL **Metro:** Dupont Circle.

$ Rates: Weekdays $109 suite for one, $119 suite for two. Weekends and off-season weekdays $79–$89 per suite. Inquire, too, about low summer rates. Extra person $15; children under 12 stay free in parents' room. AE, CB, DC, DISC, ER, JCB, MC, V. **Parking:** $10.

Though it's on a quiet tree-lined street, the Hampshire is within easy walking distance of Georgetown and two blocks from Dupont Circle—convenient to numerous restaurants and nightspots.

Spacious junior-suite accommodations, furnished with 18th-century mahogany reproductions, are decorated, for the most part, in ecru/teal color schemes with cinnamon or plum accents. They're rather residential, with lots of closet space, big dressing rooms, couches and coffee tables, desks, and kitchenettes equipped with sinks, refrigerators, coffee-makers, and stoves or microwave ovens. There's a hairdryer in the bath. You'll find chocolates on arrival. AM/FM alarm-clock radios, multifeature phones (offering push-button access to everything from sports statistics to pizza delivery), and remote-control TVs with HBO movies are additional amenities.

Dining/Entertainment: The acclaimed **J. Sun Dynasty** serves Manchurian/Hunan specialties; it's open for all meals. A bar/lounge adjoins.

Services: Complimentary *Washington Post,* room service (during restaurant hours).

Facilities: Guests enjoy free use of the YMCA/National Capital Health Center nearby (see the Canterbury Hotel, above, for a rundown of facilities). Small business center.

HOLIDAY INN CENTRAL, 1501 Rhode Island Ave. NW, Washington, DC 20005. Tel. 202/483-2000, or toll free 800/248-0016 or 800/HOLIDAY. Fax 202/797-1078. 205 rms, 8 suites. A/C TV TEL **Metro:** McPherson Square or Dupont Circle.

$ Rates: Weekdays $97–$120 single, $120–$150 double. Weekends $79 single or double. Extra person $14; children 18 and under stay free in parents' room. Note also Holiday Inns' "Great Rates" program (see the Holiday Inn Franklin Square, above). AE, CB, DC, DISC, JCB, MC, V. **Parking:** $7.

This very well located hotel underwent a major renovation in 1991 and it sparkles. It's the typical "no surprises" hotel the Holiday Inn chain prides itself on offering. You'll find a souvenir shop and video-game room off the lobby and a pool and sun deck on the roof. A pleasant restaurant features competitively priced American fare, and guests also relax over cocktails in an adjoining lounge.

Rooms are decorated in shades of mauve and teal, with blond-wood furnishings and color-coordinated floral-motif drapes and bedspreads. All offer remote-control cable TVs with free movie stations and AM/FM alarm-clock radios. Other pluses here are a coin-op launderette, room service (from 6am to 11:30pm), and an exercise room with weights, treadmills, and Lifecycles.

WASHINGTON COURTYARD, 1900 Connecticut Ave. NW (at Leroy Place), Washington, DC 20009. Tel. 202/332-9300, or toll free 800/842-4211. Fax 202/328-7039. 147 rms. A/C TV TEL **Metro:** Dupont Circle.

$ Rates: Weekdays $85–$120 single, $120–$155 double. Weekends $69 single or double. Extra person $15; children under 18 stay free in parents' room. AE, CB, DC, DISC, MC, V. **Parking:** $10.

The Courtyard has the well-heeled look of a much more expensive hostelry with the amenities to match. It's right across the street from the deluxe Washington Hilton, where you can pick up sightseeing tour buses. You'll be pleased from the minute you step into the chandeliered lobby, where classical music is always playing. Guest rooms—off charming hallways—are decorated in either of two attractive color schemes: muted green with peach and rose accents or soft blues. Residential furnishings include in-room sofas, and among the in-room amenities are remote-control cable TVs (with pay-movie options) concealed in mahogany armoires, AM/FM alarm-clock radios, coffee-makers, and phones with modem jacks. Accommodations on higher floors offer panoramic views, and some rooms have stocked minibars.

In addition to a rooftop pool and sun deck, facilities include **Claret's,** a rather elegant restaurant with linen-covered tables and Waterford-crystal chandeliers overhead. It serves moderately priced American fare at all meals, including such upscale items as a croque-monsieur at lunch and grilled swordfish with artichokes and hearts of palm at dinner. **Bailey's,** a clubby bar with tapestried banquettes and equestrian art on the walls, adjoins. *USA Today* is available gratis at the front desk, and guests can enjoy nightly bed turndown on request. For a fee, guests can also use the well-equipped Washington Sports Club just across the street—treadmills, Lifecycles, StairMasters, rowing machines, Nautilus, Gravitron, and much more.

FOGGY BOTTOM/GEORGETOWN

HOTEL LOMBARDY, 2019 I St. NW, Washington, DC 20006. Tel. 202/828-2600, or toll free 800/424-5486. Fax

202/872-0503. 85 rms, 41 suites. A/C MINIBAR TV TEL **Metro:**
Farragut West or Foggy Bottom.

$ Rates: Weekdays $115 single, $130 double, $150 suite for one,
$165 suite for two. Weekends (and sometimes off-season week-
days) $59–$89 single or double; $109–$129 suite for one or two.
Extra person $20; children under 16 stay free in parents' room. AE,
CB, DC, ER, MC, V. **Parking:** $10 (subject to space availability).

From its rich wood-paneled lobby with carved Tudor ceilings to its
appealing restaurant and rooms, the Lombardy offers a lot of
luxury for the price—and the location, about five blocks west of
the White House. Rooms are charmingly residential, all but 20 with
fully equipped kitchens, large walk-in closets, and dining nooks. Entered via pedimented louver doors, they have fine cherrywood furnishings (including large desks), cotton chintz floral bedspreads and
drapes, dusty-rose carpeting, and Casablanca fans overhead. Cream-
colored walls are hung with gilt-framed mirrors and well-chosen
artworks. All offer AM/FM clock radios and remote-control cable
TVs with pay-movie options. The *Washington Post* is free at the
desk or in the café, shoes are shined gratis overnight, and a coin-op
launderette is located in the basement.

The **Café Lombardy,** a sunny glass-enclosed restaurant/bar/
lounge (with open-air seating, weather permitting), serves delicious
and authentic northern Italian fare. Try the pasta pancake. Yummy
desserts here, too.

THE GEORGETOWN DUTCH INN, 1075 Thomas Jefferson
St. NW (just below M St.), Washington, DC 20007. Tel.
202/337-0900, or toll free 800/388-2410. Fax 202/333-6526. 47
suites. A/C TV TEL **Metro:** Foggy Bottom. **Bus:** M Street buses
go to all major Washington tourist attractions.

$ Rates (including continental breakfast): Weekdays $110–$130 one-
bedroom suite for one, $125–$150 for two; $200–$300 two-bedroom
duplex penthouse quad (sleeps six). Weekends $99 one-bedroom
suite for one or two, $180–$220 penthouse suite. Extra person $20;
children under 14 stay free in parents' room. AE, CB, DC, DISC, ER,
MC, V. **Parking:** Free.

The Dutch Inn is superbly located in the heart of
Georgetown, just half a block from the C&O Canal (many
rooms offer water views), on a charming brick-paved street
lined with maple trees. Thomas Jefferson once lived on this street.
Accommodations are rather spacious one- and two-bedroom suites,
nine of them ultra-luxurious duplex penthouses with two baths.
Staying here is like having your own Georgetown apartment. You'll
have a full living room with a comfy queen-size convertible sofa,
dining area, and desk, plus a complete kitchen (the maid does your
dishes, and the hotel offers food-shopping service). Decor is classic
residential—handsome mahogany furnishings, brass lamps, beige
carpeting, textured beige walls hung with gilt-framed botanicals and
historic prints of Washington, a forest green sofa, a burgundy wing
chair, and attractive striped bedspreads and drapes in the same
Ralph Lauren–like color scheme. Amenities include remote-control

cable TVs with free HBO, AM/FM alarm-clock radios, and three phones (bedside, living room, and bath). You'll also find upscale toiletries in the bath. The Dutch Inn's reputation as a comfortable home away from home draws the occasional celebrity client. Nell Carter stayed here during *Ain't Misbehavin*'s revival at the National, as did many of the *Les Misérables* cast members.

There's no on-premises restaurant; however, an extensive room-service menu offers a nice selection of sandwiches, salads, pizzas, and hot entrées. Of course, since you're in the heart of Georgetown, there are dozens of eating places within a block or two. Complimentary continental breakfast is served in the charming lobby each morning, and free newspaper delivery is available on request. Guests also enjoy free use of the many facilities at the West End Fitness Center at 24th and M Streets—StairMasters, treadmills, exercise bikes, NordicTrack, rowing machines, racquetball/squash/ basketball courts, a full complement of Cybex equipment, lap pools, steam, sauna, tanning, massage, classes, and much more.

MARRIOTT'S RESIDENCE INN, 1000 29th St. NW (between K and M Sts.), Washington, DC 20007. Tel. 202/ 298-1600, or toll free 800/331-3131. Fax 202/333-2019. 78 suites. A/C TV TEL **Metro:** Foggy Bottom.

$ Rates (including extended continental breakfast): $145 studio suite (for one or two), $170 one-bedroom suite (for up to four). Weekends $99 studio suite, $109 one-bedroom suite. Rollaways or sleep sofa $10 extra. Discounts for stays of seven days or more. AE, CB, DC, DISC, JCB, MC, V. **Parking:** $13.

This home-away-from-home concept was designed to meet the needs of business travelers making extended visits, but it's marvelous even if you're spending only one night. Residence Inn accommodations are luxurious apartments, with fully-equipped kitchens, living rooms, and dining areas. This particular inn, in the heart of Georgetown, is entered via a brick courtyard with flowering plants in terra-cotta pots and Victorian white wooden benches. Inside, off the lobby, is a comfortable lounge equipped with a cable TV, games, books, magazines, and daily newspapers. Here, tea and coffee are available throughout the day, and a substantial continental breakfast (danish, muffins, bagels, hot and cold cereals, fresh fruit, juice, tea and coffee) is served daily. Monday to Thursday afternoons, complimentary beer, wine, and soft drinks are offered to guests between 5:30 and 7pm, along with snacks such as nachos or sloppy joes. Wednesday afternoon that snack is a full dinner— perhaps spaghetti and salad or barbecue.

Attractive resortlike accommodations are decorated in taupe/teal or ecru/mauve color schemes and equipped with large desks, remote-control cable TVs with HBO, AM/FM alarm-clock radios, hairdryers, and irons and ironing boards. On-premises facilities include an outdoor barbecue grill for guest use, occasional organized parties and activities, coin-op washers and dryers, and a small workout room with a Nautilus multistation machine, StairMaster, treadmill, and Lifecycle. Hotel services include complimentary grocery shopping and food delivery from nearby restaurants. M Street buses (a block away) will take you to most major D.C. attractions.

4. INEXPENSIVE

The following are all reputable hotels with double rooms priced from $65 to $99.

DOWNTOWN

DAYS INN DOWNTOWN, 1201 K St. NW, Washington, DC 20005. Tel. 202/842-1020, or toll free 800/562-3350 or 800/325-2525. Fax 202/289-0336. 220 rms. A/C TV TEL **Metro:** Metro Center.

$ Rates: Weekdays $77–$87 single, $87–$97 double. Weekends $75 single or double. Extra person $10; children under 18 stay free in parents' room. Lower "Super Saver" rates (about $49) are sometimes available if you reserve in advance (the earlier the better) via the toll-free number, 800/325-2525—it's worth a try. AE, CB, DC, DISC, ER, MC, V. **Parking:** $8.

This hotel is conveniently located near the Convention Center. Rooms with woven wall coverings and attractive blond-wood furnishings are cheerfully decorated in blue/mauve or mauve/aqua color schemes and equipped with remote-control satellite TVs (with free and pay-movie channels). Half the rooms are equipped with small refrigerators, and a few have kitchenettes.

Buckley's Grill, a pleasant on-premises restaurant, specializes in reasonably priced steak, seafood (there are lobster tanks), and pasta dishes. The adjoining **Buckley's Lounge**—offering dart boards, TV monitors for airing sporting events, and snack fare—halves food prices weekdays from 5 to 7pm. And **Buckley's Deli** serves breakfast and lunch (sandwiches, chili, salads) weekdays. A small rooftop pool with a sun deck and a video-game room makes this a good choice for families with young children. Additional amenities: room service, a fitness center (with workout equipment including a treadmill and exercise bikes) and a car-rental agency just across the street. Inquire about special packages when you reserve.

DUPONT CIRCLE

CARLYLE SUITES, 1731 New Hampshire Ave. NW (between R and S Sts.), Washington, DC 20009. Tel. 202/234-3200, or toll free 800/964-5377. Fax 202/387-0085. 176 suites. A/C TV TEL **Metro:** Dupont Circle.

$ Rates: Weekdays $69–$119 studio suite for one, $79–$129 for two; $150 one-bedroom suite. Weekends $69 suite for one or two. Extra person $10; children under 18 stay free in parents' suite. AE, CB, DC, MC, V. **Parking:** Free but limited.

On a quiet residential street near Dupont Circle—the kind of street with a neat little garden and a shade tree in front of each house—Carlyle Suites occupies a converted landmark building. Its exterior art deco elements are complemented by similarly styled interior silver moldings, light fixtures, and cove ceilings.

Only the suites eschew the art deco motif. Cheerfully decorated in pastel shades (mauve, grape, and ice gray), they have oak beds, white stucco walls, gray drapes, charcoal carpeting, and cheerful print bedspreads with matching pillow cushions on the sofa. All accommodations are equipped with huge closets, remote-control TVs with pay-movie choices, AM/FM radios, small but complete kitchens (a huge Safeway is two blocks away), cozy seating areas with sofas, and dining nooks.

Dining/Entertainment: The **Neon Cafe**—decorated in shades of gray with purple neon tubing, glass-brick walls, and a black-and-white checkerboard floor—is one of the hotel's great assets. Its period ambience is enhanced by background music from the 1930s/1940s. Moderately priced American/continental fare is served; entrées run the gamut from tortellini pesto to deli sandwiches and salads. There's live music here (a singer and combo) weekend nights.

Services: Carry-out food available from the café.

Facilities: Coin-op launderette; gratis access to a nearby health club with Nautilus and Universal exercise equipment, Lifecycles, exercise bikes, treadmills, rowing machines, StairMasters, whirlpool, sauna, steam room, and more.

HOWARD JOHNSON'S HOTEL & SUITES, 1430 Rhode Island Ave. NW, Washington, DC 20005. Tel. 202/462-7777, or toll free 800/368-5690. Fax 202/332-3519. 168 minisuites, 18 one-bedroom suites. A/C MINIBAR TV TEL **Metro:** Dupont Circle.

$ Rates: Weekdays $79–$99 minisuite for one or two, $99–$129 one-bedroom suite. Weekends (and off-season weekdays) $59 suite for one or two. Extra person $10; children under 18 stay free in parents' room. AE, CB, DC, DISC, ER, MC, V. **Parking:** $7.

Set on a tranquil tree-lined street close to Mall attractions, Dupont Circle, and the White House, this hotel is popular with government employees, businesspeople, and families. It has a handsome marble-floored lobby and attractive residential-style rooms with ecru walls and floral-print or paisley bedspreads. There are dining areas and full kitchens in all but 20 of the units. In-room amenities include cable TVs (with HBO and Spectravision movies), safes, and AM/FM radios. Eighteen one-bedroom suites additionally offer a full living room with a sofabed plus a bedroom with a king-size bed, with phones and TVs in each. Among the on-premises facilities are a coin-op launderette, a small video-game room, and a rooftop pool and sun deck. Guests enjoy complimentary use of the YMCA/National Capital Health Center nearby (see the Canterbury Hotel, in "Moderate," above, for a rundown of facilities).

Off the lobby is the cozy **Kitchen Cabinet,** with balloon-curtained windows and fresh flowers on every table. Open for all meals, it features moderately priced American fare and a special menu for children. Cocktails are served in the **Civil Servant Lounge,** an inviting low-ceilinged pub with shelves of books and a pool table.

NORMANDY INN, 2118 Wyoming Ave. NW (at Connecticut Ave.) Washington, DC 20008. Tel. 202/483-1350, or toll free 800/424-3729. Fax 202/387-8241. 75 rms. A/C TV TEL **Metro:** Dupont Circle.

$ Rates: Weekdays $94 single, $104 double. Weekends $69 single or double. Extra person $10; children under 18 stay free in parents' room. AE, CB, DC, MC, V. **Parking:** $10.

⭐ This gracious small hotel blends in perfectly with neighboring embassies. Pristinely charming rooms have tapestry upholstered mahogany furnishings in 18th-century styles. Huntergreen and white flora-printed bedspreads harmonize nicely with lemon-colored walls hung with gilt-framed botanical prints. Amenities include refrigerators, AM/FM alarm-clock radios, coffee-makers, and remote-control cable TVs with pay-movie options.

Continental breakfast (juices, tea or coffee, croissants, English muffins, toast, and cold cereals) is available in your room or in the comfortable **Tea Room** off the lobby for $5. Coffee and tea are served throughout the day from an antique oak sideboard in the Tea Room, and cookies are put out at 3pm. In nice weather you can take these snacks outside to umbrella tables on a garden patio. Tuesday nights, complimentary wine and cheese are served to guests. Numerous restaurants are located nearby, and guests enjoy access to a large swimming pool a block away.

A weekend package includes continental breakfast; guests must stay both Friday and Saturday or Saturday and Sunday nights.

QUALITY HOTEL DOWNTOWN, 1315 16th St. NW (between Rhode Island Ave. and O St.), Washington, DC 20036. Tel. 202/232-8000, or toll free 800/368-5689. Fax 202/667-9827. 125 rms, 10 suites. A/C TV TEL **Metro:** Dupont Circle.

$ Rates: Weekdays $79–$109 single or double, $99–$129 onebedroom suite. Weekends $59 single or double. Extra person $15; children under 18 stay free in parents' room. AE, CB, DC, DISC, ER, JCB, MC, V. **Parking:** $8.50.

A few years back the Quality underwent a total renovation from a homey, family-style hotel to a rather luxurious property. The good news is that despite its plush new look, it's still charging very moderate rates. And, in fact, it's still a good bet for families.

For openers, each of the rooms here is actually a large suite, with a fully equipped kitchen. Done up, for the most part, in shades of muted teal and pale rose/mauve, the rooms feature French country pine or dark-wood furnishings in traditional style. Most accommodations feature dining areas and sofas, and all have cable TVs with free HBO (plus pay movies) and dressing rooms. Baths, with shiny brass fixtures, offer hairdryers and baskets of fine toiletries. Some rooms have handsome desks, and a few feature Murphy beds—an innovation appreciated by people who conduct business in their hotel rooms. Even the public areas of the hotel have been attractively upgraded.

The Quality's restaurant, **Wondi's Cafe,** is pleasant and pretty, with green-and-white-checkered tablecloths and numerous plants flourishing in the sunlight. At night **Scott's** is cozily candlelit. Open for all meals, it serves (in addition to American fare), Asian and Ethiopian specialties. **Bleeker's Lounge,** a cozy pub off the lobby, has a billiards table.

Guests have gratis use of the nearby YMCA/National Capital Health Center (see the Canterbury Hotel in "Moderate," above, for a rundown of facilities). Room service, a coin-op basement launderette, free use of the swimming pool at a nearby hotel, and a very central location are additional pluses. Gray Line tours depart from the lobby.

Note: Bill Clinton attends Sunday services at the Baptist church across the street and often greets guests outside the hotel.

FOGGY BOTTOM/GEORGETOWN

HOWARD JOHNSON'S LODGE, 2601 Virginia Ave. NW (at New Hampshire Ave.), Washington, DC 20037. Tel. 202/965-2700, or toll free 800/654-2000. Fax 202/965-2700, ext. 7910. 192 rms. A/C TV TEL **Metro:** Foggy Bottom.

$ Rates: Weekdays $50–$91 single, $58–$99 double. Weekends $57 single or double. Extra person $5; children under 18 stay free in parents' room. AE, DC, DISC, ER, JCB, MC, V. **Parking:** Free (maximum height 6'2").

Just two blocks from the Kennedy Center is a HoJo with a nicely landscaped entrance where rose bushes bloom in season. Attractively furnished modern rooms have AM/FM radios, desks, small refrigerators, and VCRs (movies can be rented). Some rooms feature sofas, and over half provide balconies. A **Bob's Big Boy** on the premises offers typical American fare, including inexpensive all-you-can-eat buffets at breakfast and lunch. A coin-op launderette, sightseeing bus tours, a large L-shaped rooftop pool with sun deck and Ping-Pong room, a gift/sundry shop, and video games are additional amenities.

NORTH WASHINGTON

CONNECTICUT AVENUE DAYS INN, 4400 Connecticut Ave. NW (between Yuma and Albermarlie Sts.), Washington, DC 20008. Tel. 202/244-5600, or toll free 800/325-2525 or 800/952-3060. Fax 202/244-6794. 150 rms, 5 suites. A/C TV TEL **Metro:** Van Ness.

$ Rates (including continental breakfast): Weekdays $59–$119 single, $59–$129 double, $99–$139 suites. Weekends $59–$79 single or double. Extra person $10; children under 18 stay free in parents' room. Inquire about senior-citizen rates. Lower "Super Saver" rates are sometimes available if you reserve at least 29 days in advance via the corporate toll-free number, 800/325-2525. AE, CB, DC, DISC, MC, V. **Parking:** $5.

If you don't mind a 10- to 15-minute Metro or bus ride into the heart of town, you can do very nicely here This Days Inn is located in a very pleasant neighborhood, and its recently refurbished rooms are in tip-top condition Furnished in teak Danish modern pieces, with brass-framed art prints on grass-cloth-covered walls, they offer remote-control cable TVs with HBO and pay-movie options and AM/FM radios, and refrigerators. Families can book a parlor suite that includes an extra room (and an extra TV). Complimentary continental breakfast is served in the lower lobby each morning—coffee, juice, herbal teas, cold cereals, danishes, muffins, and doughnuts. Room service is available from a number of nearby restaurants. There's a gift shop in the rather charming Queen Anne–style lobby. A coin-op launderette is close by.

SAVOY SUITES GEORGETOWN, 2505 Wisconsin Ave. NW (above Calvert St.) Washington, DC 20007. Tel. 202/ 337-9700, or toll free 800/944-5377. Fax 202/337-3644. 150 rms. A/C TV TEL **Bus:** Even-numbered buses stop in front of the hotel and connect to Georgetown, Dupont Circle, and the Mall.

$ Rates: Weekdays $69–$119 single, $79–$129 double. Weekends $69 single or double. Extra person $10; children under 18 stay free in parents' room. AE, CB, DC, MC, V. **Parking:** Free.

This moderately priced luxury hotel is in a sedate embassy district, just five minutes from the heart of Georgetown by bus or car. Many restaurants are within walking distance, and Washington National Cathedral is just four blocks away.

The accommodations, half of them suites with fully stocked kitchens and dining areas, are decorated with French provincial pieces, marble-topped bureaus, and faux malachite desks with cabriole legs. Grasspaper-covered walls are hung with gilt-framed 18th-century color lithographs. All rooms offer remote-control cable TVs with pay-movie stations and AM/FM radios. Many have large walk-in closets and/or in-room steam baths, and about half offer panoramic city views over the treetops. Eighth-floor guests enjoy large in-room Jacuzzis.

The owner hired a set designer to liven up the hotel's public areas. A stunning art nouveau lobby is set against a garden-motif restaurant called **On Wisconsin,** with seating amid ficus trees, potted plants, and floral arrangements. The walls serve as gallery space for exhibits by local artists. Popular with neighborhood residents, On Wisconsin features reasonably priced American/continental fare—great chilis, focaccia pizzas, and entrées ranging from roast duck to couscous paella. In warm weather the Savoy also has a tree-shaded outdoor café serving light fare.

Other on-premises amenities include a room of food-vending machines, a small sun deck, and a laundry room with a TV and coin-op washers and dryers. The front desk proffers conciergelike hospitality, and there's a complimentary shuttle bus to and from the Woodley Park Metro stop. Guests also enjoy free use of a nearby health club featuring treadmills, StairMasters, Nautilus and Universal equipment, rowing machines, and an Olympic-size swimming pool.

By the way, note the ornate fence fronting the Savoy Suites. Made in 1890, it's from the original lion's cage of the National Zoo.

5. BUDGET

This budget section lists only one accommodation. For fancier, good-value accommodations, see the bed-and-breakfast listings in the next section.

DOWNTOWN

HOSTELLING INTERNATIONAL—WASHINGTON, D.C., 1009 11th St. NW (at K St.), Washington, DC 20001. **Tel. 202/737-2333.** 250 beds. A/C **Metro:** Metro Center. **$ Rates:** $17 for AYH members. $20 for nonmembers. MC, V.

The best bet among budget hotels is this spiffy youth hostel, which opened in late 1987. Situated in a fully renovated eight-story brick building, it offers freshly painted dorm rooms (with 4 to 14 beds) and clean baths down the hall. Though the accommodations are basic, the facility itself provides a lot of features you won't find at a hotel. These include a huge self-service kitchen where you can cook your own meals (a supermarket is two blocks away), a dining room, a comfortable lounge, coin-op launderette, storage lockers, and indoor parking for bicycles. There's street parking.

Upon registering, you'll be given an information sheet detailing local services. HIW offers special activities for guests—volleyball games, cookouts, lectures, movies, travel seminars, and more. And near the entrance, knowledgeable volunteers staff a comprehensive information desk to help guests with sightseeing and other travel questions.

The hostel's location is excellent—just three blocks from the Metro, six blocks from the Mall. And the clientele is monitored, so it's a perfectly safe place to send your college-age kids or, for that matter, your mother

Those in all age groups are welcome, but since the dorms are for men or women only, couples are separated. (Subject to availability, there are a limited number of rooms for families and couples October to March; reserve them early) Maximum stay is six nights, but that limit may be extended with permission, subject to available space. You must supply your own linens, towels, and soap (blankets and pillows are provided); sleeping bags are not allowed. You can rent the requisite sleep sheet here for $2 a night or buy one. Call as far in advance as possible to reserve (there are only 250 beds and they go fast), and assure your reservation with a 50% deposit

6. BED & BREAKFAST

One of the most enjoyable ways to travel on a budget is to stay at B&B accommodations Prices are reasonable rooms are often charming, and you have an opportunity to meet local people and other travelers.

In addition to specific B&B accommodations, I've listed two services that represent numerous homes that rent out rooms on this basis. Call as far in advance as possible so that you will have the largest choice of locations and the lowest rates, and be sure to specify your needs and preferences: For instance, discuss children, pets, smoking policy, preferred locations (do you require convenient public transportation?), parking, availability of TV and/or phone, preferred breakfast, and choice of payment.

The **Bed and Breakfast League/Sweet Dreams and Toast,** P.O. Box 9490, Washington, DC 20016 (tel. 202/363-7767), is a reservation service representing more than 70 B&Bs in the District. Through them, you might find a room in a mid-1800s Federal-style Capitol Hill mansion, a Georgetown home with a lovely garden, or a turn-of-the-century Dupont Circle town house filled with Victorian furnishings. Those are just a few of the many possibilities. The accommodations are all screened, and guest reports are given serious consideration. Hosts are encouraged, though not required, to offer such niceties as fresh-baked muffins at breakfast. All listings are convenient to public transportation. Rates for most range from $40 to $115 for a single, $50 to $130 for a double, and $10 to $25 per additional person. There's a two-night minimum-stay requirement and a booking fee of $10 (per reservation, not per night). AE, DC, MC, V.

A similar service, **Bed & Breakfast Accommodations Ltd.,** P.O. Box 12011, Washington, DC 20005 (tel. 202/328-3510; fax 202/332-3885), has about 80 homes, inns, guesthouses, and unhosted furnished apartments in its files. Some are in historic District homes. Its current roster offers, among many others, a Georgian-style colonial brick home on a tree-lined avenue in Tenley Circle; an 1899 Victorian home on Capitol Hill owned by a network news producer (a well-stocked library is a plus); and a Dupont Circle Victorian town house with a two-level deck. Rates are $50 to $100 single, $55 to $110 double, $15 for an extra person, and from $65 for a full apartment. At guesthouses and inns, rates run the gamut from $75 to $180 for a single, $85 to $225 for a double AE, DC, MC, V

DUPONT CIRCLE

EMBASSY INN, 1627 16th St. NW (between Q and R Sts.), Washington, DC 20009. Tel. 202/234-7800, or toll free 800/423-9111. Fax 202/234-3309. 38 rms (all with bath). A/C TV TEL **Metro:** Dupont Circle.

$ Rates (including continental breakfast): $69–$89 single, $79–$99 double. Weekends $55 single or double. Extra person $10; children 14 and under stay free in parents' room. AE, CB, DC, MC, V.

This four-story brick building, built in 1922 and an inn for two decades (1940–62), was rescued from demolition some years back, spruced up, and transformed once more into a quaintly charming small hotel Its Federal-style architecture harmonizes with other town houses on the block, some of which were actually designed by Thomas Jefferson. The comfortably furnished pale-lemon lobby, with its plushly upholstered sofas and armchairs, doubles as a parlor. Breakfast (fresh-baked blueberry muffins, croissants, cold cereals, juice, and coffee) is served here daily, and fresh coffee brews all day; it's complimentary, along with tea, cocoa, and evening sherry. You can buy Tourmobile tickets here, too, pick up maps and brochures, read a complimentary *Washington Post*, or request sundries you may have forgotten (toothbrush, razor, and the like). Soft classical music is piped into the lobby, and brass planters grace every hallway. There's also a basement lounge with a color TV, ice machines, a small refrigerator, and a supply of books.

The rooms are furnished with 18th-century-style mahogany pieces. Bedspreads and curtains in attractive floral prints, pale-lemon walls hung with turn-of-the-century lithographs and historic prints of Washington, and new carpeting combine to create a homey atmosphere. Everything is freshly painted, pristine, and neat. All accommodations have AM/FM clock radios. Baths have showers only (no tubs). *Note:* There is no elevator, and there's street parking only.

THE REEDS' BED & BREAKFAST, P.O. Box 12011, Washington, DC 20005. Tel. 202/328-3510. 5 rms (with shared bath), 1 apt (with bath). A/C TV TEL **Metro:** McPherson Square or Dupont Circle (about six blocks from either).

$ Rates (including breakfast): $60–$80 single, $70–$80 double. Apt (no breakfast) $65–$80 for one, $75–$85 for two. Extra person $15; children 18 and under $10; crib $5 extra. AE, DC, MC, V. **Parking:** $5.

Even by the most exacting standards, the Reeds' restored Victorian mansion is a masterpiece of good taste. Built in 1887 by notable Washington builder John Shipman, it had a long succession of subsequent owners. When Charles and Jackie Reed bought it in 1975, it was in such disrepair that they spent nine years on a renovation they say "took on the appearance of a Pentagon cost overrun." They combed antiques shops and auction houses for period/reproduction furnishings and art, landscaped the garden, and added fountains. Today, the house is a gorgeous Victorian/art nouveau showplace with carved fireplace mantels, shuttered bay windows, leaded glass, and rich oak and mahogany paneling The living room is furnished with a velvet Chesterfield, a Jacobean oak armchair, Oriental carpet, and a turn-of-the-century player piano. Breakfast is served at a Victorian banquet table in a formal dining room complete with 19th-century stained-glass windows and a working fireplace.

The rooms, reached by a grand carved-oak staircase with intricate fretwork and a leaded-glass skylight above, are charmingly decorated in period styles. Yours might have a floral-print chaise, Eastlake Victorian bed, ornamental fireplace, white wicker daybed and rocker, Empire bureau, or Regency lady's writing desk. All are supplied with AM/FM clock radios and books and magazines. Completely separate from the main building is a one-bedroom apartment with a private bath and a fully equipped kitchen; it easily accommodates five people. There's no maid service, however, and you'll have to get your own breakfast.

Guests are encouraged to use the gorgeous Victorian-style lattice porch, fountained patio, and barbecue facilities. Breakfast is continental (featuring fresh-baked breads and muffins, cereals, fruit, and juice) on weekdays, a full bacon-and-eggs meal on weekends. A computer and a treadmill are available on request, and there's a washer and dryer for guest use. No charge for local calls here.

The Reeds' doesn't take walk-ins, hence you'll note the P.O. Box address above. You must call to reserve.

WINDSOR INN, 1842 16th St. NW (at T St.), Washington, DC 20009. Tel. 202/667-0300, or toll free 800/423-9111. Fax 202/667-4503. 37 rms (all with bath), 10 suites. A/C TV TEL **Metro:** Dupont Circle.

$ Rates (including continental breakfast): Weekdays $69–$89 single, $79–$99 double; $125–$150 suite accommodating up to five people. Weekends $55 single or double. Extra person $10; children under 14 stay free in parents' room. AE, CB, DC, MC, V.

The Windsor Inn, a neat brick building on a tree-lined residential street, was built in the 1920s as a boarding house, then renovated and run as an inn through 1963. A wealthy owner subsequently let the property stand empty until the Windsor folks discovered and purchased it in 1985, along with an adjacent building fronted by a neoclassic portico. Accommodations are located in both. Some of the public areas are done up in art deco motif, and hallways are especially nice, lit by sconces and crystal chandeliers and hung with lovely gilt-framed lithographs. Rooms, neat as a pin and handsomely furnished with mahogany antique reproductions, utilize mauve or sea-green color schemes. Some have floral wall friezes, many are adorned with botanical prints or silk flower arrangements, and you may get a sofa and/or decorative fireplace. Suites are worthy of a first-class hotel—but much cheaper. Lower-level rooms face a skylit terrace with lawn furnishings and flower boxes, but I prefer the sunnier upstairs accommodations. All accommodations offer AM/FM alarm-clock radios. A continental breakfast—fresh-baked muffins, cold cereals, fruit juices, and tea or coffee—is served in the comfy lobby. During the day, complimentary coffee, tea, and hot chocolate are available, and sherry is offered evenings from 5 to 7pm. There are ice machines and a refrigerator for guest use. A very friendly multilingual staff is a big plus. Guests also enjoy free use of a beautiful small conference room that seats 10. *Note:* There is no elevator, and parking is on the street.

ADAMS-MORGAN/WOODLEY PARK

ADAMS INN, 1742–1748 Lanier Place NW (between Calvert St. and Ontario Rd.), Washington, DC 20009. Tel. 202/745-3600. 25 rms (12 with bath). A/C **Metro:** Woodley Park–Zoo (seven blocks away).

$ Rates (including continental breakfast and tax): $45 single without bath, $60–$95 single with bath; $55 double without bath, $70–$95 double with bath. Extra person $10. Weekly rates available. AE, CB, DC, DISC, MC, V. **Parking:** $7.

While many B&B accommodations are decorator homey with rooms in *Architectural Digest* good taste, the Adams is down-to-earth, for-real homey—like your Aunt Edna's house. It occupies three turn-of-the-century brick town houses on a residential tree-lined street fronted by small gardens and porches. All have cozily furnished Victorian parlors or lounges with decorative fireplaces and lace-curtained windows; they're stocked with books, games, and magazines for guests. The most attractive public areas and rooms are at no. 1742; request it when you book.

Accommodations, furnished with flea market and auction finds, have a kitschy charm. They're all very clean and freshly painted or papered, and some have bay windows or handsome oak paneling. No phones or TVs here, but you do get a clock radio. Rooms that share baths have in-room sinks. A substantial continental breakfast (including fresh-baked breads and muffins) is served each morning in the dining room; in warm weather you can take your breakfast out to the front porch or a small garden patio. Tea, coffee, and doughnuts are available throughout the day.

A coin-op washer/dryer is available in the basement, there are pay phones in the lobby, and the desk takes incoming messages. Other pluses: a refrigerator, microwave oven, iron/ironing board, and TV lounge. The location is close to Adams-Morgan eateries and a Safeway supermarket. Anne Owens is your genial host.

Note: No smoking is permitted on the premises. No pets, but children are welcome.

KALORAMA GUEST HOUSE, 1854 Mintwood Place NW (between 19th St. and Columbia Rd.), Washington, DC 20009. Tel. 202/667-6369. 31 rms (12 with bath). A/C **Metro:** Woodley Park–Zoo.

$ Rates (including continental breakfast): $45–$70 single with shared bath, $65–$90 single with bath; $45–$75 double with shared bath, $65–$95 double with bath; $95 two-room suite ($5 each additional occupant). AE, CB, DC, DISC, MC, V. **Parking:** $5 (limited).

This San Francisco–style B&B guesthouse was so successful it expanded in a short time from a six-bedroom Victorian town house (at 1854 Mintwood) to include four houses on Mintwood Place and two on Cathedral Avenue NW. A great effort was made to create charming rooms and public areas. Owner Roberta Pieczenik regularly haunts antique stores, flea markets, and auctions to find beautiful furnishings.

Many rooms are furnished with brass beds and perhaps lovely floral-print bedspreads and matching ruffled curtains. Other possibilities: Oriental throw rugs, a cane-backed rocking chair, an oak mirror shelf with a display of antique bottles, and walls hung with turn-of-the-century artwork or vintage photographs. Whatever you find, it will be a delight. Live plants and/or fresh flowers grace the rooms, and you're likely to get a dish of candy, too. All rooms have AM/FM alarm-clock radios.

Over at 1854 is the cheerful breakfast room with plant-filled windows and park benches at marble tables. Breakfast consists of bagels, croissants, English muffins, orange juice, and tea or coffee. Adjoining amenities include a seldom-used TV, a phone (local calls are free), a phone for long-distance credit- or charge-card calls, a vending machine for soft drinks, a washing machine and dryer, and a refrigerator. Upstairs in the parlor, which has a working fireplace, there's a decanter of sherry on the buffet for complimentary evening apéritifs; magazines, games, and current newspapers are provided. There's a garden behind the house with umbrella tables. At 1859 Mintwood (also a Victorian town house) is another cozy parlor with two working fireplaces. A lower level here has additional laundry and ironing facilities and a refrigerator. Though the rooms have no phones, incoming calls are answered around the clock, so people can leave messages for you. Maid service is provided daily.

The Mintwood Place location is very good—near Metro stations, dozens of restaurants, nightspots, and Connecticut Avenue shops. And the Cathedral Avenue houses (tel. 202/328-0860), even closer to the Metro, provide similarly wonderful amenities and facilities.

DOWNTOWN

MORRISON CLARK INN, Massachusetts Ave. NW (at 11th St.), Washington, DC 20001. Tel. 202/898-1200, or toll free 800/332-7898. Fax 202/289-8576. 40 rms (all with bath), 14 suites. A/C TV TEL **Metro:** Metro Center.

$ Rates (including continental breakfast): Weekdays $115–$175 single, $125–$195 double. Weekends $85 single or double. Extra person $20; children under 12 stay free in parents' room. AE, CB, DC, DISC, MC, V. **Parking:** $10.

This magnificent inn, occupying twin 1865 Victorian brick town houses—with a newer wing in converted stables across an interior courtyard—is on the National Register of Historic Places. Its arresting Victorian/Chinois facade features Shanghai porches with Chinese Chippendale railings and a pagodalike mansard roof. Guests enter via a turn-of-the-century parlor, with velvet-upholstered Victorian furnishings, swag-curtained bay windows, and a large floral centerpiece on a piecrust table under a converted gaslight chandelier. Continental breakfast—oven-fresh cakes, muffins, danish, and croissants—is served in the adjoining Club Room with lace-curtained 13-foot windows flanking gold-leafed mahogany-framed pier mirrors on either side of the room. Ornate white marble fireplaces, large potted palms in Chinese cachepots, and a 19th-century carved rosewood screen with Chinese paintings on silk in glass panels are further adornments.

Exquisite, high-ceilinged guest rooms are individually decorated. Yours might be neoclassical in feel, with coffered ceilings and wall columns. Some are furnished in antique wicker pieces with floral chintz balloon shades on the windows and matching bed ruffles. Others have floral swag friezes and/or decorative fireplaces. Color schemes utilize delicate hues like rose, muted gray/blue, and cream. Artwork runs the gamut from Rajasthani paintings on silk to illuminated manuscripts of poems by Lord Byron, bibelots from Dresden figurines to antique Chinese vases. Four rooms have private porches, a few are octagonal with bay windows, and many have plant-filled balconies (with umbrella tables) overlooking a fountained courtyard garden with flower beds amid crepe myrtle and dogwood trees. In-room amenities include remote-control cable TVs housed in handsome armoires, VCRs (tapes are available at the front desk), and two phones (bed and bath) equipped with computer jacks. Baths are supplied with an array of Caswell-Massey toiletries.

Room service is available from the inn's highly acclaimed American regional restaurant (see Chapter 6). Other amenities here include twice-daily maid service with Belgian chocolates at bed turndown, complimentary daily newspapers, overnight shoeshine, concierge, many business services, and fresh flowers in every room. An on-premises fitness center is equipped with treadmills, StairMasters, exercise bikes, and a Universal set.

DINING IN WASHINGTON, D.C.

1. **VERY EXPENSIVE**
2. **EXPENSIVE**
3. **MODERATE**
- **FROMMER'S SMART TRAVELER: RESTAURANTS**
- **FROMMER'S COOL FOR KIDS: RESTAURANTS**
4. **INEXPENSIVE**
5. **RESTAURANTS AT SIGHTSEEING ATTRACTIONS**
6. **SPECIALTY DINING**

In the 1980s, Washington residents, like many other Americans, discovered food. Once a culinary boondocks, Washington today is on a par with major American cities and European capitals. The District supports dozens of first-rate restaurants, whose chefs are not only up-to-date on the latest culinary trends but in the vanguard. And in a city filled with foreign embassies, numerous eateries cater to the international contingent, offering everything from Spanish tapas to Ethiopian zilzil wat. Here, too, you can join the rich and powerful at select spots where historic decisions are made over gravlax and champagne or perhaps rub elbows with a justice at the Supreme Court cafeteria or with your senator in a Capitol restaurant. Fresh seafood comes in from Chesapeake Bay, hence crabcakes are a staple of Washington menus. And this is also a southern town, where biscuits are on many breakfast menus, and it's not too hard to find greens and grits. It all adds up to an excitingly diverse dining scene.

I have listed my restaurant choices first by price and then by geographical area, using four **price categories:** "Very Expensive" (dinner typically costs more than $50 per person for a full meal, including a glass of wine, tip, and tax), "Expensive" (main courses at dinner average $13 to $19), "Moderate" (a full dinner can be had for about $20 to $25 per person), and "Inexpensive" (main courses at dinner are under $10).

Keep in mind that the above categories refer to dinner prices, and some very expensive restaurants offer affordable lunches and/or early-bird dinners. Also, I'm assuming that you're not going to stint when you order. Some restaurants, for instance, have entrées ranging from $12 to $20. In most cases you can dine for less if you order carefully.

Note: A Metro station is indicated when it's within walking distance of a restaurant. If you need bus-routing information, call 637-7000.

My favorite restaurants are marked with a star. However, I must say that every restaurant listed here is actually a favorite of mine, and I wish I could star them all. I guarantee a marvelous dining experience at all of these establishments. Bon appétit!

1. VERY EXPENSIVE

These upper-bracket restaurants are distinguished by truly excellent food and beautiful settings.

DOWNTOWN

MORRISON CLARK INN, Massachusetts Ave. NW, at 11th St. Tel. 898-1200.
  Cuisine: AMERICAN REGIONAL. **Reservations:** Recommended.
  Metro: Metro Center.
$ Prices: Appetizers $5.25–$6.50 at lunch, $5.50–$9.50 at dinner; main courses $11.75–$14.25 at lunch, $15.75–$20 at dinner; three-course Sun brunch (including unlimited champagne) $19.50. AE, CB, DC, MC, V.
  Open: Lunch Mon–Fri 11:30am–2:30pm; dinner nightly 6–9pm; brunch Sun 11:30am–2pm.

The dining room at the Morrison Clark, an exquisite upscale accommodation (see Chapter 5), is one of the District's most fashionable restaurants (Barbara Bush celebrated a birthday here). Its setting is a National Register Victorian town house, and the interior decor beautifully evokes that period. The dining room is symmetrical, with floor-to-ceiling mahogany- and gilt-valanced lace-curtained windows flanking pier mirrors at either end. Also paired are ornately carved white marble fireplaces. The room centers on a circular settee upholstered in a gorgeous floral print and crowned by a stunning flower arrangement. At night, soft lighting emanates from Victorian brass candelabras, crystal candelabra chandeliers suspended from intricate ceiling medallions, and the glow of candlelight. During the day, sunlight streams in through those massive windows. A smaller dining area adjoins, its trellised walls hung with plants, and you can also dine alfresco at courtyard umbrella tables.

Chef Susan Lindeborg's seasonally changing menus are elegant and inspired. At dinner you might begin with an appetizer of Maryland crab, glazed with cognac and crème fraîche and served in two lemon crêpe cornets with a green herbed-butter sauce. Entrées on my last visit included juicy grilled salmon on a bed of green lentils mixed with applewood-smoked bacon, the fish topped with creamed horseradish sauce; sautéed Catalan-style duck breast in a garlicky saffron-flavored tomato sauce, served with Spanish green olives, basmati rice, haricots verts, and a crunchy garnish of pickled red onions; and apple-stuffed pork loin served with spätzle and cardamom-glazed carrots. Everything is beautifully presented and accompanied by divine side dishes. Similar fare is available at lunch. A reasonably priced wine list offers a variety of premium wines by the glass, plus a good choice of champagnes and sparkling wines. Desserts—such as maple crème brûlée served in a pecan tulip with Grand Marnier–marinated strawberries—are fittingly fancy.

RED SAGE, 605 14th St. NW, at F St. Tel. 638-4444.
Cuisine: SOUTHWESTERN. **Reservations:** Required. **Metro:** Metro Center.

$ Prices: Appetizers $7.50–$9.50 at lunch, $7.50–$11 at dinner; main courses $8.75–$14.25 at lunch, $16–$27.50 at dinner. AE, CB, DC, MC, V.

Open: Restaurant, lunch Mon–Fri 11:30am–2:15pm; dinner Mon–Sat 5:30–10:30pm. Sun 5–10pm. Upstairs Chili Bar, Mon–Sat 11:15am–11:30pm, Sun 4:30–11:30pm. Bar, Sun–Thurs to 2am, Fri–Sat to 3am.

One of the brightest stars in Washington's culinary galaxy, Red Sage is the stunning creation of owner/distinguished chef Mark Miller, who brings brilliant inspiration to traditional southwestern cookery. His dynamic setting—in a stunning beaux arts building—is an elegantly whimsical Wild West fantasy. The main dining area comprises a warren of cozy, candlelit dining nooks under a curved ponderosa log–beamed ceiling. Native American (Zapotec) rugs are strewn on flagstone floors, and etched-glass panels by Sante Fe artist Kit Carson depict western motifs. Special dining areas include an exhibition kitchen, a wine bar, a hogan (Native American hut), and a library where Persian rugs enhance century-old pine floors and "bookshelves" in arched niches are used to display wines.

Upstairs, the less expensive, more casual high-ceilinged Chili Bar—with its large white cloud (emitting bolts of blue lightning) overhead, western-landscape mural, and buffalo-hide upholstery and table lamps is a romantic venue for drinks and light fare. At this writing, the Red Sage is adding a new dining area adjacent to the Chili Bar where a 24-monitor video wall will air old westerns.

The menu changes seasonally. During my recent visit, memorable appetizers included a buttermilk-corn pancake topped with large grilled shrimp in chipotle-butter sauce. Among the entrées, I loved the fan of grilled tender duck breast. Another notable choice was a pecan-crusted chile lamb chop, served with spicy smoked lamb sausage, goat cheese mashed potatoes atop a bed of spinach and mustard greens, and a garnish of yam chips to which molido chilies added piquancy Red Sage desserts are sublime Two standouts: a rich, moist, warm, chocolate-truffle cake surrounded by small mounds of malted vanilla ice cream and drenched in white-chocolate fudge sauce and a silky smooth caramelized goat's-milk flan topped with crunchy crushed pralines and served with a scoop of chocolate ancho ice cream and chocolate sauce. The well-researched wine list is very extensive

WILLARD ROOM, in the Willard Inter-Continental Hotel, 1401 Pennsylvania Ave. NW. Tel. 637-7440.
Cuisine: CLASSICAL AMERICAN. **Reservations:** Required.
Metro: Metro Center.

$ Prices: Appetizers $8.50–$11.50 at lunch, $9–$12.50 at dinner, main courses $18–$26 at lunch, $26.50–$32 at dinner; three-course fixed-price brunch $27.50–$38.50. AE, DC, DISC, ER, JCB, MC SAISON, V

Aditi ◆3
America ◆48
Au Pied de Cochon ◆7
Bamiyan Afghan ◆2
Bombay Palace ◆28
Cafe at The Corcoran ◆32
Café Petitto ◆21
Café Promenade ◆33
Center Cafe ◆49
Chesapeake Bagel Bakery ◆51
Cities ◆18
City Lights of China ◆24
Clyde's ◆5

Concourse Buffet ◆49
Dean & Deluca ◆3
Dirksen Senate Office Building
 South Buffet Room ◆47
Duke Zeibert's ◆31
Encore Cafe ◆15
Flight Line ◆46
Gabriel ◆23
Garden Terrace ◆13
Georgetown Bagelry ◆3
Greek Port Restaurant ◆5
House of Representatives
 Restaurant ◆47

Houston's ◆9
Iron Gate ◆34
Jaleo ◆43
Jean-Louis ◆14
Jefferson ◆37
Jockey Club ◆23
Kramerbooks &
 Afterwords, A Café ◆
La Ruche ◆6
Le Lion d'Or ◆29
Library of Congress
 Cafeteria ◆50
Mick's ◆28

WASHINGTON, D.C., DINING

Open: Breakfast Mon–Fri 7:30–10am; lunch Mon–Fri 11:30am–2pm; dinner nightly 6–10pm; brunch Sun 11am–2pm.

⭐ Since the reopening of the magnificent Willard Inter-Continental Hotel in 1986, its restaurant has become one of Washington's most prestigious see-and-be-seen dining rooms. This is nothing new. An 1880 guidebook to the city described the Willard Room as "a most agreeable and pleasing spectacle where refined people enjoy an unequaled table." Today that "refined" clientele includes upper-crust Washingtonians, visiting presidents and premiers, movie and sports stars, and often a king or two. To ensure an ongoing "unequaled table," the restaurant shops the markets of the world to stock its larders, from the pâtés of Strasbourg to West Virginia's finest mountain brook trout. And the room itself has been re-created to reflect its original turn-of-the-century splendor in every detail—the gorgeous carved oak paneling, towering scagliola columns, brass and bronze torchères and chandeliers, and faux-bois beamed ceiling have all been restored or faithfully reproduced. "The Willard Room is so elegant," said *Dossier* magazine, "that one could eat a hot dog here and still think it was the dining experience of a lifetime."

Chef Guy Reinbolt, who, like many great *cuisiniers,* hails from Alsace, trained at the noted Michelin-starred restaurants of France and Germany, picking up Créole and regional southern approaches during stints in New Orleans and Memphis. His menus change seasonally. At a recent dinner, a companion and I shared appetizers of Norwegian smoked salmon (with goat cheese, marinated tomatoes, and Kalamata olive tapenade) and a leek/wild mushroom terrine crowned with sautéed foie gras on duck jus flavored with raspberry vinegar. An entrée of sautéed black sea bass wrapped in phyllo dough was served on a bed of acorn squash sabayon. Fillets of Dover sole and grilled salmon in scallion beurre blanc came with fried green tomatoes and roast leeks julienne. And roasted Pennsylvania wood pigeon with a cumin-cabbage marmalade relish was enfolded in creamy Anna potatoes. Desserts ran the gamut from a classic crème brûlée or soufflé au chocolat to a tropical fruit strudel served with ginger-orange sorbet on vanilla sauce. A list of more than 250 fine wines mentions Thomas Jefferson's notes from his voyages in the vineyards of France.

Note. If you want to enjoy the splendor of the Willard Room but not the prices, drop by for continental breakfast—a mere $11.50 for coffee, juice, and a basket of fresh-baked breads and croissants.

NEAR THE WHITE HOUSE

DUKE ZEIBERT'S, in the Washington Square Building, 1050 Connecticut Ave. NW. Tel. 466-3730.

Cuisine: AMERICAN. **Reservations:** Recommended. **Metro:** Farragut North.

$ Prices: Appetizers $2.95–$9.95 at lunch, $5.95–$9.95 at dinner, main courses $11.50–$17.50 at lunch, $17.50–$25.95 at dinner. AE, CB, DC, MC, V.

Open: Mon–Sat 11:30am–11:30pm. Sun 5–10pm. **Closed:** Sun July–Aug.

Duke Zeibert's is a reincarnated venerable on the D.C. dining scene. Opened in 1950, it closed in 1980 when the building it occupied was torn down, then reopened in 1983 in the new building that went up on the same spot. Washington legend and lore abound at Duke's. In the old days it was a Runyonesque hangout into which few women ventured. ("Ladies go to Georgetown," said the *Washington Star*. "Macho Washington dines at Duke Zeibert's.") Both Jimmy Hoffa and J. Edgar Hoover frequented the old Duke's.

Though the new Duke's is less macho (he's selling 10 times more white wine), the old gang is still here in force. It's not unusual to note George McGovern, David Brinkley, Art Buchwald, Redskins owner Jack Kent Cooke, or talk-show host Larry King among the lunchtime crowd. It was at Duke's that Jimmy the Greek wrecked his TV career with an infamous remark about the breeding of black athletes. And it certainly caused a stir when President Clinton dined here with his chief congressional adversary, Sen. Bob Dole. The main dining room is under an eight-story atrium skylight. The ambience is light and airy opulence; you may feel as though you're dining in a crystal. Adornments include art deco lighting fixtures and numerous photos of sports figures and famous guests lining mahogany-paneled walls. Food is also served in the bar, and cocktails and light fare are offered on a tree-lined terrace. Duke and his son, Randy, are always on hand to greet customers.

On every table is a basket of assorted rolls and a silver bowl of New York pickles—a Zeibert trademark. The latter go well with overstuffed sandwiches made with freshly cooked meats and served at lunch—for example, a combo of breast of turkey, smoked tongue, Swiss cheese, onion, homemade coleslaw, and Russian dressing. In fact, though it's much more upscale, you'll note many New York deli characteristics at Duke's, not the least of them the red-jacketed waiters who would fit in at any Gotham pastrami house. Furthermore, appetizers include matzoh-ball soup, chopped liver, and creamed herring. However, you could also—and wisely—begin your meal with a bluepoint oyster cocktail, followed by feathery light crabcakes served with mashed potatoes and coleslaw For dessert, strawberry cheesecake—the rich Lindy's variety—is recommended. A good wine list is a plus.

THE JEFFERSON, 1200 16th St. NW, at M St. Tel. 347-2200.

Cuisine: AMERICAN REGIONAL. **Reservations:** Recommended. **Metro:** Farragut North.

$ Prices: Appetizers $5.75–$6.50 at lunch, $5.75–$9.75 at dinner; main courses $13.50–$18.50 at lunch, $22.75–$25 at dinner; Sun jazz brunch $21.50–$23.50 for appetizer, main course, dessert, and coffee. AE, CB, DC, JCB, MC, OPT. V.

Open: Mon–Sat 11:30am–2:30pm; dinner nightly 6–10:30pm; brunch Sun11:30am–2:30pm.

Built in 1923 as a residence for Washington s social elite, The Jefferson remains the city's most exclusive hotel discreetly catering to royalty and other distinguished visitors. Its dining room is, of course, fittingly elegant, offering the kind of exquisite fare and impeccable service you'd expect in such a prestigious establishment. Cozy, rather than intimidatingly plush, it has bare oak floors and flower-bedecked tables covered with brown-and-cream tattersall-plaid cloths. Walls and ceiling are handsomely painted in faux tortoiseshell, the former adorned with intricately carved moldings and hung with 1830s hand-colored lithographs by Charles Bird King, James Otto Lewis, and other notable American artists. Seating is in deep-brown tufted-leather banquettes.

Award-winning chef Will Greenwood offers a seasonally changing menu of American regional dishes. Virginia cuisine is highlighted, but his wide-ranging food sources are international—from a farm in Maryland that supplies organically raised free-range game birds to fresh salmon flown in from Scandinavia. A delectable appetizer from a recent menu was roast quail stuffed with braised red cabbage and pecans served with foie gras and orange butter sauce. Another excellent starter was a plantation corncake topped with smoked salmon and chive cream. Typical entrées from the same day's menu included sautéed lamb loin with goat-cheese croutons and a layered eggplant casserole; smoked duck breast in honey date/cumin sauce with turnip potato cake; and roasted pheasant with wild mushroom/pistachio sausage and country ham spoon bread. For dessert: whiskey almond pound cake with Southern Comfort sauce. An extensive wine list, predominantly French and Californian and including many by-the-glass selections, complements the menu.

LE LION D'OR, 1150 Connecticut Ave. NW., at M St. Tel. 296-7972.
  Cuisine: FRENCH. **Reservations:** Required. **Metro:** Farragut North.
$ Prices: Appetizers $6–$12 at lunch. $11–$22 at dinner; main courses $12–$22 at lunch, $20–$32 at dinner. AE, CB, DC, MC, V.
  Open: Lunch Mon–Fri noon–2pm; dinner Mon–Sat 6–10pm.

Under the creative and skillful direction of owner/chef Jean Pierre Goyenvalle, Le Lion d'Or is one of Washington's most highly esteemed bastions of haute cuisine It opened in 1976 to immediate acclaim, Goyenvalle having previously garnered a loyal following in a decade of classic cookery at other noted area restaurants. This talented chef continues to excel; in the late 1980s he received the prestigious Toque d'Argent award from the Maître Cuisiniers de France—a rare honor for a chef in this country. Le Lion d'Or is patronized by visiting kings, presidents, and power brokers. You might overhear major policy decisions in the making over lunch.

Though the restaurant is down a flight of steps from the street, you'll quickly forget you're underground in a delightful French country setting with seating in dark-brown tufted-leather banquettes under tented silk canopies. Ecru silk walls are adorned with provincial French Faience platters, copper cooking implements, and gilt-framed oil paintings of pastoral scenes Soft lighting emanates from brass chandeliers and shaded sconces. A single rose in a vase graces every pink-linen-covered table.

The food is classic French cuisine at its best, beautifully presented and graciously served. A not-to-be-missed hors d'oeuvre is the petit soufflé de homard, a feather-light hot lobster mousse, delicately pink and lightly browned on top in lobster-cream sauce flavored with a soupçon of tarragon and parsley. Another excellent beginning: ravioli de foie gras—a large poached pasta pocket stuffed with fresh duck foie gras marinated in white port wine and served in a canard glaze with small diced vegetables. A red snapper entrée "aux senteurs de Provence" (with the aroma of Provence) comes lightly roasted in extra-virgin olive oil and served on a bed of fennel—a marvelously flavorful foil to the fish—with a side dish of new potatoes and a colorful garnish of julienned tomatoes and spinach. And tender, juicy roast rack of lamb is coated just before completion with a Dijon-mustard meringue, crushed green peppercorns, and herbed breadcrumbs; it's served with an array of fresh seasonal vegetables. Dessert options include hot soufflés (orange, raspberry, chocolate, and passionfruit), scrumptious pastry cart selections, or possibly a gratin of broiled seasonal fruits marinated in Cointreau and served in sabayon sauce. A dish of cookies or miniature pastries is complimentary. Le Lion d'Or offers an extensive wine list, primarily French and Californian, and house wines are bottled with the restaurant's own label.

PRIME RIB, 2020 K St. NW. Tel. 466-8811.

Cuisine: STEAK/CHOPS/SEAFOOD. **Reservations:** Recommended. **Metro:** Farragut West. **Parking:** Free (valet) after 6pm.

$ Prices: Appetizers $6–$12; main courses $10–$16.50 at lunch, $18–$26 at dinner. AE, CB, DC, MC, V.

Open: Lunch Mon–Fri 11:30am–3pm; dinner Mon–Thurs 5–11pm, Fri–Sat 5–11:30pm.

Washington Post restaurant critic Phyllis Richman calls the Prime Rib "Washington's most glamorous setting for plain old steak and roast beef." Modeled after Central Park South hotel restaurants, it is indeed glamorous—in a substantial, well-heeled fashion—with gold-trimmed black walls, comfortable black leather chairs and banquettes, white-linened tables softly lit by shaded brass lamps, swagged white curtains, and large floral displays. Waiters are in black tie, a pianist at the baby grand plays show tunes, and the art on the walls includes dozens of gilt-framed Louis Icart art deco lithographs.

As for that "plain old" steak and roast beef, they are thick, tender, juicy, and prepared from meat of the best grain-fed steers that has been aged for four to five weeks. And it's served exactly the way you ordered it. For less carnivorous diners there are about a dozen seafood entrées. A bountiful basket of fried potato skins with a big bowl of sour cream is a must. Lunch or dinner might begin with an appetizer of smoked fresh trout with Dijon-mustard sauce or creamy lobster bisque and end with a gorgeous hot-fudge sundae over amaretto pound cake Bar drinks here, by the way, are made with fresh-squeezed juices and Evian water

DUPONT CIRCLE

THE JOCKEY CLUB, in the Ritz-Carlton Hotel, 2100 Massachusetts Ave. NW. Tel. 659-8000.
   Cuisine: FRENCH. **Reservations:** Required. **Metro:** Dupont Circle.
$ Prices: Appetizers $8.50–$10.50 at lunch, $9.50–$15.50 at dinner; main courses $12–$23 at lunch, $24–$31 at dinner. AE, CB, DC, ER, MC, V.
   Open: Daily lunch 11:30am–3pm, dinner 6–11pm.

The Jockey Club has perhaps been Washington's most "in" restaurant since it opened in 1961, the night before JFK's inauguration. Jackie came in the next week, and it immediately became a Kennedy-clan favorite. JFK once quipped that when he wanted to reach a staff member, he first called their office, then their home, then the Jockey Club. During the Reagan years Nancy was a regular, as was Barbara during the Bush years. Humorist Art Buchwald has a designated table, as do notables ranging from Boutros Boutros-Ghali to Princess Michael of Kent.

The big surprise when you first visit this society page tableau-vivant is its total lack of pomp and crystal-chandeliered pretension. Instead it is cheerful and pubby, with red-leather banquettes and bentwood chairs, a random-plank oak floor, lantern suspended from a low beamed ceiling (the subdued amber lighting is as cozy as the glow of a fireplace), and walls of stucco or aged oak paneling hung with English equestrian prints. The tables are covered in red-and-white tattersall check and bedecked with single red roses.

Chef Hidemasa Yamamoto brings Eastern nuance to classic French cookery. For instance, an appetizer of sautéed quail with California artichokes and green lentils is garnished with oba (Japanese basil). And an entrée of truffle-studded sautéed Dover sole, in a white wine–infused pale-pink lobster cream sauce, comes with bok choy as well as artichokes, julienne roast peppers, and puréed truffled potatoes. An excellent beginning here, by the way, is purée of fennel soup afloat with delicate sturgeon quenelles and a garnish of Sevruga caviar. For your main course, the big fluffy crabcakes meunière is the restaurant's signature dish. And there's also a marvelous pan-fried lobster entrée with a trinity of *boules*—avocado, mango, and red beets—in a sauterne beurre blanc sauce with fresh ginger and cilantro. I'm listing a lot of seafood. Other choices include a black peppercorn–crusted roasted loin of lamb with basil sauce and fried shiitake mushrooms (it's served with ratatouille, mixed beans, and a mille-feuille of potato, broccoli, and parmesan). And New York strip steak comes with roasted garlic purée and pommes soufflés. Salads—such as fresh seafood with three sauces—are popular at lunch. Crusty sun-dried tomato, cheese, and basil breads are served warm. For dessert there are silky smooth soufflés dusted with powdered sugar, or you can opt for cart selections such as a lemon meringue tart with fresh orange and raspberry sauce. After dinner, enjoy piano-bar music and a cognac by the fireplace in the adjoining Fairfax Bar.

Note: Want to see it? Can't afford it? Come by for breakfast served daily from 6:30 to 10:30am.

NORA, 2132 Florida Ave. NW, at R St. Tel. 462-5143.
Cuisine: MULTIETHNIC/ORGANIC. **Reservations:** Recommended. **Metro:** Dupont Circle.
$ Prices: Appetizers $6.95–$8.95; main courses $17.95–$23.95. MC, V.
Open: Dinner Mon–Thurs 6–10pm, Fri–Sat 6–10:30pm.

This charming Washington restaurant, where owner-chef Nora Pouillon brings haute panache to healthful organic cookery, is a favorite of the Clintons and the Gores (who celebrated Tipper's 45th birthday here). Other Clinton-administration devotees include Janet Reno, George Stephanopoulos, and White House press secretary Dee Dee Myers. The ever fit Jane Fonda comes in when she's in town, and fit wannabee Ted Kennedy is a regular. Actor Harrison Ford, who dined here recently, quipped of the free-range chicken, "it's free, but it's dead." Housed in a turn-of-the-century building, the restaurant is entered via a cozy bar. The skylit main dining room is a converted stable, with a weathered-looking beamed pine ceiling, damask-covered tables lit by shaded paraffin lamps, and a display of Amish and Mennonite patchwork crib quilts on pale-gray brick walls. Handmade Windsor chairs enhance the Early American feel. Especially lovely is the intimate brick-walled patio with its vast window box of dried flowers and a large shade tree creating leafy shadows over the skylight. And when it's busy Nora opens a rather elegant dining room upstairs—otherwise the scene of private parties.

The chemical-free, organically grown, free-range fare is extremely healthful, but not of the brown-rice-and-bean-sprout variety. However, the water you're served is filtered and purified, and fresh-baked breads come with extra-virgin olive oil for dipping instead of butter. Menus vary nightly. Salads here make good beginnings—perhaps mixed Asian greens with spring onions and crispy noodles in piquant chili-lemongrass vinaigrette. Or you might opt for something like grilled natural shrimp served with jalapeño-studded black bean salad, red and green salsas, and mizuna (a mustard green). Entrées on my recent visit included lamb curry in a fragrant orange-tomato sauce, served with apricot and raisin chutney, poori bread, mint raita, basmati rice, and greens; skewers of beef satay marinated with lemongrass and chili, served with peanut sauce, turmeric couscous, carrot salad tossed in coconut milk–lime dressing, and crunchy broccoli; and free-range chicken breast with jalapeño cornbread-orange stuffing, pumpkinseed mole sauce, black beans, and sugar snap peas. Most desserts are light and utilize fruits and nuts, for instance, a Macintosh apple and dried cherry cobbler served with French vanilla ice cream. An extensive wine list includes—but is not limited to—selections made with organically grown grapes. I promise you won't miss any of the bad-for-you ingredients at Nora, and you will experience the vivid and earthy flavors of natural foods.

VIDALIA, 1990 M St. NW. Tel. 659-1990.

   Cuisine: PROVINCIAL AMERICAN. **Reservations:** Recommended. **Metro:** Dupont Circle. **Parking:** Complimentary valet parking at dinner.

$ Prices: Appetizers $4.75–$6.50 at lunch, $5.50–$6.75 at dinner; main courses $9.25–$11.50 at lunch, $14.50–$19 at dinner. AE, DC, MC, V.

   Open: Lunch Mon–Fri 11:30am–2:30pm; dinner Mon–Sat 5:30–10:30pm. Onion Bar, Mon–Sat to midnight.

⭐ Down a flight of steps from the street is one of Washington's finest new restaurants, the charmingly country-cozy Vidalia, named for a variety of sweet Georgia onion. It's entered via a watermelon-green foyer where an oak table is used to display baskets overflowing with fresh flowers, breads, and onions. The oak-floored bi-level dining room centers on a similar display table. Its cream stucco walls are hung with gorgeous dried-flower wreaths and works by local artists, soft lighting emanates from graceful Georgian-style brass chandeliers and sconces, family china is displayed in antique cabinets, and seating is in sturdy oak chairs or forest-green tapestried banquettes. It's a lovely setting, enhanced by exquisite flower arrangements, big terra-cotta pots of chrysanthemums, and bowls of fruit.

   Talented chef Jeff Buben's "provincial American" menus (focusing on southern-accented regional specialties) change frequently, but his highly recommended crisp East Coast lump crabcakes (the lightest, fluffiest ever, with a piquant dash of capers and cayenne) are a constant among appetizer choices; they're served with a mound of celery seed–studded pepper slaw and coriander mayonnaise. Another signature appetizer is his magnificent wild-mushroom ragoût—a mix of exotic seasonal mushrooms and finely diced Smithfield Virginia ham served over a rosemary biscuit soaked with cream gravy. On my recent visit, entrée selections—aesthetically arranged on colorful fioriware platters—included a scrumptious fan of pan-roasted moularde duck sauced with saffron, honey, and lemon and served with seared cabbage and creamy soufflé of cheese grits. At lunch, in addition to similar entrées there are hearty sandwiches such as grilled olive bread, garnished with sun-dried tomatoes. Meals here include an assortment of fresh-baked breads such as wheatberry, onion focaccia, and moist cornbread studded with chewy creamed-corn niblets. Either meal, save room for a dessert of buttery-crusted lemon chess pie with strawberry sauce—or pig out over a dessert sampler plate. Tapas—such as warm lentil salad with duck sausage and smoked chicken quesadillas—are served in the very simpatico adjoining Onion Bar. A carefully chosen wine list highlights American vintages.

GEORGETOWN

MORTON'S OF CHICAGO, 3251 Prospect St. NW. Tel. 342-6258.

   Cuisine: STEAKS/CHOPS/SEAFOOD. **Reservations:** Recommended. **Parking:** Free valet parking.

$ Prices: Appetizers $7.50–$8.95, main courses $15.95–$29.95. AE, CB, DC, JCB, MC, V.

Open: Dinner only. Mon–Sat 5:30–11pm. Sun 5–10pm.

⭐ Part of a national restaurant empire created by Arnie Morton, a flamboyant former Playboy Enterprises executive, this is far and away the best steak house in town. It attracts a celebrity-studded clientele: You might spot James Carville and Mary Matalin, Janet Reno, CNN's Larry King, or Sen. Ted Kennedy among the beef eaters. It's also a favorite of athletes; the Washington Redskins served as waiters for a Special Olympics fundraiser here. And National Symphony Orchestra conductor Mstislav Rostropovich dined here one night with a famous classical pianist, both wearing headphones! But, basically, one comes to eat, not gawk at the glitterati.

Huge portions of succulent USDA prime midwestern beef and scrumptious side dishes are the real attraction. Start off with an appetizer such as smoked Pacific salmon or a lump-crabmeat cocktail served with rémoulade sauce. Steaks (rib eye, double filet mignon, porterhouse, or New York sirloin) are perfectly prepared to your specifications. Other entrée choices include prime rib, lamb chops, fresh swordfish steak, lemon-oregano chicken, and baked Maine lobster. Side orders of flavorfully fresh al dente asparagus served with hollandaise or hash browns are highly recommended. A loaf of onion bread on every table is complimentary. Consider taking home a doggy bag if you want to leave room for dessert—perhaps a soufflé Grand Marnier or rich and creamy cheesecake.

Morton's plush interior is cozy and convivial. Large framed LeRoy Nieman sports prints adorn wainscoted stucco walls. Seating is in comfortable cream-colored leather booths at white-linen-covered tables adorned with flowers and lit by pewter oil lamps in the shape of donkeys or elephants. The display kitchen is hung with gleaming copper pots.

RIVER CLUB, 3223 K St. NW. Tel. 333-8118.

Cuisine: PAN-EUROPEAN. **Reservations:** Recommended. **Parking:** Complimentary valet parking.

$ Prices: Appetizers $8.50–$9.50, main courses $22.50–$25, four-course fixed-price tasting menu $45 ($60 with wines for each course). AE, CB, DC, DISC, MC, V.

Open: Dinner Tues–Thurs 6–11pm, Fri–Sat 6pm–midnight; late supper Tues–Thurs to midnight, Fri–Sat to 1am. Dancing till 2am Tues–Thurs. 3am Fri–Sat.

⭐ It's not often that a restaurant can best be described as glamorous—especially in an essentially bureaucratic town like Washington. This is a setting evocative of old movies, a posh supper club where elegantly attired men and women sip champagne, dine, and dance to romantic music. The last word in art deco elegance, its $1.3-million interior features graceful etched-glass murals (one of them a marble-framed panel under a cascading waterfall), gleaming silver and black-lacquer columns, a cove ceiling subtly aglow in pink neon, and a 50-foot serpentine marble bar. Seating is in comfy-cozy alcoves at tables ringing a sunken circular dance floor.

Chef Frank Ruta—who has been sous-chef in the White House and in two-star restaurants of northern Italy—likes diners to graze on a variety of small dishes. His menu changes frequently. Last time I looked in, he featured an appetizer of baked Portuguese sardines in a flaky pastry tart, drizzled with fennel oil and served with a tangy salad of olives, greens, and lemon wedges. Another—buffalo mozzarella wrapped in applewood-and cherrywood-smoked salmon—was served atop a confit of juniper/balsamic-flavored red cabbage in extra-virgin olive oil. Entrées included in Indian-spiced steamed fresh sea bass served on a cauliflower vinaigrette infused with lemongrass and lemon segments; it was served with sautéed Yukon gold potatoes and haricots verts. And a roast rack of lamb came with salsify/wheatberry ragoût and herbed potato purée. A unique dessert was citrus soup—a purée of blood and navel oranges, clementines, and grapefruit garnished with citrus fruit sections and topped with a dollop of white chocolate mousse.

A pianist plays show tunes Friday and Saturday nights from 7 to 10pm. Do take advantage of the River Club's knowledgeable and friendly sommelier, Tony Foreman—the champagnes, wines, and dessert wines he recommends for each course will immensely enhance your meal. The River Club is the kind of place where you can manage to spend hundreds on caviar and champagne—or dine modestly at about $60 for two. Don your best duds and make a night of it (see Chapter 9 for further details).

SEASONS, in the Four Seasons Hotel, 2800 Pennsylvania Ave. NW. Tel. 944-2000.

Cuisine: CONTINENTAL WITH REGIONAL AMERICAN SOURCES. **Reservations:** Recommended. **Parking:** Free valet parking.

$ Prices: Appetizers $6.75–$8 at lunch, $6–$13.50 at dinner; main courses $12.75–$18 at lunch, $16–$29 at dinner. AE, CB, DC, ER, JCB, MC, V.

Open: Lunch Mon–Fri noon–2:30pm; dinner nightly 6–10:30pm.

In the fall of 1993, the upscale but casual-in-concept Seasons replaced the more formal Aux Beaux Champs as the hotel's signature restaurant. This does not mean that the restaurant is funky, but the atmosphere is more relaxed, there's no dress code, and waitstaff and wine captains are friendly and unintimidating. It remains a beautiful room. Elegantly appointed tables—adorned with orchids, white freesia, or flowering plants in small clay pots—are draped in white linen over black-and-white table skirts depicting scenes of ancient Rome. Diners are comfortably ensconced in plush booths, neoclassic-design club chairs, or boardroom chairs, upholstered in a mix of hunter green, burgundy, or black velvet. Slate floors are strewn with black-wool carpets abloom with red and white roses on a green trellis. And glossy hunter-green lacquer walls display Italian engravings of birds from an 18th-century text. Seasons is candlelit at night; during the day, light streams in from a wall of windows overlooking the C&O Canal.

Talented Scottish chef William Douglas McNeill's cuisine focuses on fresh market fare. In search of the highest quality ingredients, he plucks baby lettuces from the garden just hours before serving, raises free-range venison on a 600-acre Texas ranch, and has fresh fish flown in from Maine and Florida within hours of the catch. And his passion for wine is behind Seasons' extensive and *recherché* list encompassing major wine-growing regions of France and California as well as vintage ports. The menu changes seasonally. A recent dinner offered appetizers of seared raw tuna médaillons in a spicy pocket of saffroned raw and smoked salmon on a julienne of snow peas and Japanese seaweed; thick corn blini with Scottish smoked salmon, flying fish caviar, and a dollop of sour cream; and ravioli stuffed with julienned wild mushrooms and a nugget of goose foie gras on a truffle-infused tomato-butter sauce. An entrée of crisp-fried sea bass was served on a bed of julienned and gingered Oriental vegetables. And roast rack of lamb encrusted with Indian spices came with saffroned rice studded with raisins, pine nuts, morsels of dried apricot, pistachios, and slivered almonds. McNeill's menus always include lighter "alternative cuisine" items such as a large bowl of spinach linguine tossed in a coarse tomato-vermouth sauce with a zesty nuance of basil pesto and a crunchy contrast of julienned zucchini and yellow squash. Meals are accompanied by a basket of scrumptious fresh-baked breads—rosemary flat bread, sun-dried tomato bread drizzled with parmesan, seven-grain sourdough, and others. And desserts might range from ambrosial mango crème brûlée garnished with mint and crème fraîche to a warm apple tart on caramel sauce marbleized with crème anglaise and topped with homemade honey ice cream.

1789, 1226 36th St. NW, at Prospect St. Tel. 965-1789.
   Cuisine: AMERICAN REGIONAL. **Reservations:** Recommended.
   Parking: Complimentary valet parking.
$ **Prices:** Appetizers $6–$10, main courses $21–$28, fixed-price pretheater menu $23. AE, DC, DISC, MC, V.
   Open: Dinner only, Sun–Thurs 6–10pm, Fri–Sat 6–11pm.

One of Washington's most elegantly charming restaurants, 1789 (its name commemorating not the French Revolution but the year the village of Georgetown was incorporated) is as cozy as a country inn. Housed in a Federal town house, its intimate dining areas include the John Carroll Room, where the walls are hung with Currier and Ives prints and old city maps, a log fire blazes in the hearth, and a gorgeous flower arrangement is displayed atop a hunting-themed oak sideboard. In the smaller Manassas Room, rough-hewn pine walls (siding from an 1860s Maryland barn) are covered with prints of the Civil War period. And the pubby bar area, with seating in oak-backed tufted-leather banquettes, has a stunning gas chandelier overhead and walls embellished with shelves of pewterware, hunting prints, and 18th-century hand-colored English caricatures. Throughout, silk-shaded brass oil lamps provide romantic lighting at crisp, white-linen-covered tables set with Limoges china. One could go on and on with interior detail here; 1789 is a virtual decorative arts museum of period furnishings and museum-quality paintings, prints, and objets d'art. It's also one of the city's prime see-and-be-seen dining venues, where you might spot anyone from Bill and Hillary Clinton to Stacy Keach at the next table.

Talented chef Michael Patton's menus change seasonally. A recent one offered appetizers of basil-potato stuffed dumplings (garnished with julienned Petrossian smoked salmon in a light and lemony cream sauce) and grilled Gulf Coast shrimp coated with bourbon-pecan barbecue sauce and served on a bed of fresh sweet corn purée. Consider a salad course here, such as sautéed artichoke bottoms served warm with roasted red- and yellow-pepper strips and crisp radicchio in herbed vinaigrette. An entrée of roast rack of lamb with garlicky Napa goat-cheese crust was served au jus on an array of sautéed mixed southern greens (mustard, turnip, spinach, and collard) with potatoes au gratin. Also notable were Patron's lumpmeat crabcakes (with zesty infusions of garlic, cayenne, and Dijon mustard) served with fire-roasted tomato sauce, grilled ratatouille, and Cheddar-cheese grits. Homemade breads such as basil parmesan and whole-wheat walnut accompany entrées, desserts might range from tira misu to pecan-crusted lemon soufflé pie with raspberry sauce, and the wine list is long and distinguished. A great bargain here: the pretheater menu offered between 6 and 6:45pm, including appetizer, entrée, dessert, and coffee for just $23!

KENNEDY CENTER

JEAN-LOUIS, in the Watergate Hotel, 2650 Virginia Ave. NW. Tel. 298-4488.
  Cuisine: "INSTINCTIVE" FRENCH. **Reservations:** Required.
  Metro: Foggy Bottom. **Parking:** Free valet parking.
$ Prices: Pretheater four-course dinner $43, five-course dinner $85, six-course dinner $95, not including wine, tax, or gratuity. AE, CB, DC, DISC, MC, V.
  Open: Dinner Tues–Sat 5:30–10pm; pretheater seating from 5:30–6:30pm, second seating 8–8:30pm.

Washington's most prestigious restaurant—under the auspices of one of America's most brilliant chefs, Jean-Louis Palladin—occupies an unlikely precinct—the basement of the Watergate Hotel. This intimate dining room (it seats only 42) is entered via a glass-walled corridor where the restaurant's extensive wine offerings (750 labels, most of them French) are displayed. Its interior decor features an arrangement of back-lit gold and copper silk banners, flower-bedecked white-linen-covered tables lit by hurricane lamp candles, a mirrored tile ceiling, and soft green carpeting. Its most notable feature, however, is a panel of mirror that girds the room at eye level, allowing diners to 'scope the crowd without being conspicuous

Jean-Louis began his culinary apprenticeship at the age of 12 in his native Gascony, and, by the time he was 28, he had his own Michelin two-star establishment there. Enticed by an American ambassador, he came to Washington in 1979 to open his eponymous Watergate restaurant. His food sources include an organic farm in Virginia hunt country, where superior-quality beef, veal, lamb, eggs, and poultry are raised to his specifications Other farms grow organic produce for him, and he is a partner in a local fish market He imports only a few items that cannot be found in America, for instance, French and Italian truffles, Brazilian hearts of palm, and, interestingly, salt from France ("I don't like American salt," says Jean-Louis). He defines his "instinctive" cuisine as grounded in rich classical gastronomy but seasoned with the magic of inspiration and spontaneity.

His fixed-price menus change nightly. What comprises a typical $95 six-course dinner? Let me tantalize you with one I recently enjoyed. After we had been seated, a complimentary nugget of smoked salmon arrived at our table, followed by a quail egg nestled in toasted brioche with ossetra caviar garnish. The first actual course was chestnut soup (a rich chicken-broth-based purée of chestnuts, ham, shallots, and foie gras) afloat with chicken wings stuffed with wild mushrooms and delicate quenelles filled with chestnut meat and black truffles. Next came a plate of lightly smoked halibut gravlax atop a mélange of seaweeds in ginger dressing. Duck foie gras came on a sweetish quince–duck jus purée with poached quince garnish. This was followed by broiled fresh rouget (red mullet) seasoned with thyme and rosemary and served with a julienne of pumpkin sautéed with cardamom and cumin and spiced pumpkin coulis. Roasted noisettes of Texas venison in a red wine–venison reduction sauce were accompanied by a gratin de pommes. And dessert was a napoleonlike almond feuilleté layered with dried, sweetened pineapple and served on blueberry coulis with a dollop of pineapple sherbet. Like the wines recommended for each course by friendly sommelier Vincent Feraud, the breads also change with each course (anchovy-buttered brioches, country French breads, and others).

Note: If you would like to experience Jean-Louis's culinary expertise at slightly lower prices, dine at his new Watergate restaurant, **Palladin** (tel. 298-4455), where lunch entrées range from $6.50 to $12.50, and dinner entrées from $13.50 to $19.95.

2. EXPENSIVE

Most of the restaurants in this category also offer selections—such as pizzas, pastas, and sandwiches—in the moderate price range.

DOWNTOWN

OLD EBBITT GRILL, 675 15th St. NW, between F and G Sts. Tel. 347-4801.
    Cuisine: AMERICAN. **Reservations:** Recommended. **Metro:** McPherson Square or Metro Center.
$ Prices: Appetizers $4.50–$6.50; main courses $7.95–$10.95 at lunch, $9.95–$15.95 at dinner; burgers and sandwiches $6.50–$7.95; breakfast/brunch $4.95–$6.95, AE, DC, DISC. MC, V.
    Open: Breakfast Mon–Fri 7:30–11am, Sat 8–11:30am; lunch Mon–Fri 11am–5pm, Sat 11:30am–4pm; dinner Mon–Fri 5pm–midnight. Sat–Sun 4pm–midnight; brunch Sun 9:30am–4pm. Bar Sun–Thurs to ⅃am Fri–Sat to 3am

Located two blocks from the White House is the city's oldest saloon, founded in 1856. Presidents Grant, A. Johnson, McKinley, Cleveland, Theodore Roosevelt, and Harding were patrons, and among its artifacts are Alexander Hamilton's wooden bears—one with a secret compartment in which it's said he hid whiskey bottles from his wife. However, don't expect to find a fusty old tavern. The existing facility is a plush reconstruction loosely based upon the original. Fronted by a grandiose beaux arts facade, it has Persian rugs on beautiful oak and marble floors, beveled mirrors, gas lighting, etched-glass panels, and other elements evocative of turn-of-the-century Washington saloons. Old Ebbitt heirlooms are scattered throughout—the Hamilton bears and animal trophies bagged by Teddy Roosevelt among them. The street level comprises a dining area and three bars, plus a glassed-in atrium dining room with umbrella tables amid much greenery. The main dining room, hung with period oil paintings, has lace-curtained windows and forest-green velvet banquettes and booths. Other areas include the Old Bar (where the Ebbitt's famed collection of antique beer steins is displayed), the Oyster Bar, and Grant's Bar, complete with a classic gilt-framed bar nude. The Ebbitt is a stunning setting for meals, cocktails, or a romantic rendezvous.

Menus change daily, but lunch entrées might include anything from a fried oyster sandwich to fettuccine tossed with spinach and walnuts in cream sauce. Typical dinner entrées: a half chicken (roasted with lemon, herbs, and honey, and served with rice and fresh vegetables) and straw and hay pasta tossed with prosciutto, peas, onions, mushrooms, olive oil, and fresh-grated parmesan. At either meal you can order a sandwich (perhaps a Reuben or turkey club), a hamburger, or a half a dozen raw oysters, thus enjoying the luxe ambience at low cost. Desserts range from a hot-fudge sundae made with homemade vanilla ice cream to toll house pie studded with chocolate morsels and walnuts, spiked with bourbon, and served warm with vanilla ice cream.

THE PEASANT RESTAURANT & BAR, 801 Pennsylvania Ave. NW. Tel. 638-2140.

Cuisine: AMERICAN/CONTINENTAL. **Reservations:** Recommended at dinner. **Metro:** Archives–Navy Memorial.

$ Prices: Appetizers $6.95–$9.95; main courses $7.95–$10.95 at lunch, $11.95–$22.95 at dinner. AE, CB, DC, DISC, MC, V.

Open: Lunch Mon–Fri 11am–3pm; dinner Mon 5:30–10pm, Tues–Sat 5:30–11pm, Sun 5–9pm.

Part of a first-rate Atlanta-based restaurant group, the Peasant belies its name with a plushly clubby interior. High ceilings are adorned by carved moldings, mahogany-wainscoted cream walls are hung with turn-of-the-century French silhouette portraits, crisply white-linened tables are lit by brass candle lamps, and additional muted lighting emanates from elegant brass chandeliers and sconces. It's a romantic setting, with seating amid potted palms and soothing light jazz or classical background music. During the day, weather permitting, you can dine alfresco at café tables on the Navy Memorial Plaza

Service is smooth and gracious, and the fare both original and delicious. A marvelous appetizer is herb-marinated warm goat cheese served with grilled French bread, roasted tomatoes, and big savory cloves of roasted elephant garlic. If you plan to kiss someone later, skip this garlicky treat and order the plump and fluffy scallion-studded crabcakes, zestily spiced with a little cumin and hot peppers; they're served with fresh tomato salsa. Entrées come with incredible fresh-baked parmesan bread, a salad, vegetables, and rice or potatoes du jour. Some examples: Tuscan-style grilled rack of lamb (four large chops) served with mixed bean relish, Asian pasta (lo mein noodles tossed with sautéed jumbo shrimp, julienned vegetables and shiitake mushrooms, and snow peas in orange-ginger sauce), and grilled North Atlantic salmon with juniperberry-butter sauce. This is the kind of food that excites the senses, and dazzling desserts provide a fitting climax. Chocolate-toffee pie is a symphony of tastes and textures—a rich mocha mousse whipped into a chocolate wafer crust and smothered in whipped cream, hot caramel, and chocolate-covered toffee. And there's blackberry-peach cobbler with crunchy brown-sugary streusel topping served with cinnamon ice cream. The wine list is reasonably priced, with many premium wines available by the glass.

DUPONT CIRCLE

GABRIEL, in the Barceló Washington Hotel, 2121 P St. NW. Tel. 293-3100.

Cuisine: PAN-HISPANIC. **Reservations:** Recommended. **Metro:** Dupont Circle.

$ Prices: Appetizers/tapas $2.50–$6.25 at lunch, $2.50–$8.50 at dinner; main courses $7.25–$13.50 at lunch, $13.25–$18.50 at dinner. AE, CB, DC, DISC, MC, V.

Open: Lunch Mon–Sat 11:30am–2:30pm; dinner Sun–Thurs 6–10:30pm, Fri–Sat 6–11:30pm; brunch Sun noon–3pm; tapas and bar daily 11:30am–midnight.

Gabriel, opened in 1994, brought an exciting new cuisine and a sophisticated setting to the Washington dining scene. Its warmly inviting interior, in sienna and turquoise, offers seating in roomy upholstered mahogany armchairs, booths, and banquettes. Café-au-lait stucco walls are hung with colorful prints, café curtains adorn high windows, and soft lighting flatters diners. A large rectangular mahogany bar is the centerpiece of a convivial lounge area. Noted Washington chef Greggory Hill, who years ago honed his craft as sous-chef at the French embassy, spent months studying with major chefs in various regions of Spain and Mexico before creating Gabriel's dazzlingly innovative—and ever-changing—menu.

You can graze on tapas at the bar or begin a meal with them. Salvadorean pupusas (chili-flavored corn/potato pancakes) are served with large grilled scallops and chunks of hot and spicy chorizo sausage in a smoked garlic/cilantro cream sauce with a side of cayenne slaw Pimento, filled with raisins, pine nuts, sautéed spinach, grilled portobello mushrooms, and creamy chèvre, is served over crunchy shredded cabbage braised in Reisling and sherry—a marvelous mélange of textures and flavors, And radicchio leaves, rubbed with Spanish olive oil and stuffed with black olive goat cheese, oven-dried tomatoes, and roasted peppers, are grilled over oak, applewood, and hickory. Many dishes can be ordered in appetizer or entrée portions—among them flour tortillas filled with rotisseried shredded duck and sweet corn mushrooms, served with tomatillo/smoked-jalapeño salsa and feta cheese garnish. Less exotic but equally satisfying is rotisserie free-range chicken with lemony-herb gravy, grilled eggplant slices, and garlic mashed potatoes. Resist the temptation to fill up on crusty-chewy fresh-baked sourdough bread dipped in rosemary/garlic-infused olive oil. There's a good wine list, with several by-the-glass selections including dry and sweet sherries—the ideal complement to tapas. Incredible desserts here, too. An amaretto-crusted chocolate-hazelnut fudge cake is served on crème anglaise flavored with Spanish brandy. And a phyllo purse stuffed with custard, papaya, pineapple, berries, and pistachio nuts is poised atop cinnamon custard marbleized with apricot raspberry coulis.

IRON GATE RESTAURANT & GARDEN, 1734 N St. NW. Tel. **737-1370.**
   Cuisine: MEDITERRANEAN. **Reservations:** Recommended.
   Metro: Dupont Circle.
$ Prices: Appetizers $4.50–$6 at lunch, $5–$6.50 at dinner; main courses $9.50–$12.50 at lunch, $15.50–$19 at dinner. AE, MC, V.
   Open: Lunch Mon–Fri 11:30am–5pm; dinner Mon–Sat 5–10pm, Sun 5–9pm. **Closed:** Sun July–Aug.

Housed in a converted 19th-century stable, the Iron Gate is probably Washington's most romantic dining venue. In winter, it's the coziest place in town: A big fire blazes in an immense brick fireplace hung with gleaming copper pots, and the smell of burning wood is as alluring as the aromas emerging from the kitchen. Exposed brick walls are hung with exquisite dried flower arrangements and wreaths. There's additional seating upstairs in a room with another working fireplace. And spring through fall, you can dine alfresco under a grape-and-wisteria arbor in an enchanting brick-walled garden with a splashing fountain and lovingly tended flower beds.

With its superb ambience, the Iron Gate has always been a local favorite, all the more so since 1991 when Nabeel and Karen David took over and created a menu worthy of the setting. Everything is fresh (even herbs are grown out back) and prepared with finesse using the finest possible ingredients. An excellent beginning is a baked goat-cheese torte with charred-pepper coulis. There are fantastic soups such as potato-leek topped with lebne (rich, creamy drained yogurt) and parsley. And the mesclun salad is a refreshing mix of greens (radicchio, baby lettuces, endive, baby bok choy, frisé) with chopped tomato and crumbled goat cheese in a tasty balsamic vinaigrette. Entrées are served with fresh-baked focaccia breads (herb, parmesan, walnut, sun-dried tomato) and coins of herbed butter. A totally satisfying pasta dish is fettuccine tossed with grilled shrimp, pancetta, and sugar peas. Crisp-skinned roast free-range chicken (you'll taste the difference) is served in a lemony jus de poulet with fresh veggies and wild-rice pilaf in golden raisin/pine nut vinaigrette. And there's also a savory vegetable tajine with couscous. Divine desserts include mint-garnished almond flan in caramel sauce and a chocolate-truffle pie with dark cookie crust on a raspberry coulis topped with fresh whipped cream. There's a full bar, a good choice of wines, even fresh-squeezed lemonade. Keep the Iron Gate in mind not only for meals, but as the perfect place for leisurely afternoon tea/espresso/cappuccino or cocktails.

GEORGETOWN

PAOLO'S, 1301 Wisconsin Ave. NW, at N St. Tel. 333-7353.

> **Cuisine:** CALIFORNIA-STYLE ITALIAN. **Reservations:** Accepted at lunch only.
>
> **$ Prices:** Appetizers $4.95–$7.95, pastas $7.95–$16.95, pizzas $7.95–$8.95, main courses $13.95–$17.95 lunch specials $7.50–$11.95. AE, CB, DC, DISC, MC, MOST, V
>
> **Open:** Mon–Thurs 11:30am–midnight, Fri–Sat 11:30am–12:30am, Sun 11am–midnight. Bar, Sun–Thurs to 1:30am, Fri–Sat to 2:30am.

Under the same auspices as the River Club (see "Very Expensive," above), Paolo's is one of Georgetown's hottest restaurants. Restaurateur Paul Cohn is a virtuoso when it comes to creating a scene that crackles with excitement. "It's the closest thing to show business," he says. "You're on every night." I never tire of the show at Paolo's. For one thing, the setting is *molto simpático*. Tables spill out onto the street from an open-air patio, and the front room, with a stunning peach-hued Italian marble floor and black marble bar, centers on the warm glow of a pizza-oven fire. Red peppers, dried herbs, and strings of garlic are suspended above the wood-burning brick oven, which is fronted by a colorful display of pizza toppings—creamy white bowls filled with pine nuts, peppers, sausage, sun-dried tomatoes, and more. Here diners can watch the chef preparing his luscious golden-crusted pies. The pack room, richly paneled in cherrywood and agleam with copper mirrors, also centers on an open exhibition kitchen. Paolo's is a major D.C. see-and-be-seen celebrity haunt. Ted Kennedy, Tipper Gore, and Jack Kent Cooke come in often; Muhammed Ali signed autographs one night; and when they were in town, Alec Baldwin and Kim Basinger ate lunch and dinner here for two days in a row!

Steve Roberts applies subtle nouvelle principles to traditional Italian fare, but don't worry—he doesn't skimp on portion size. A delightful surprise arrives as soon as you're seated—a bowl of tapenade (a Mediterranean spread of puréed olives, chick-peas, and roasted red peppers) along with oven-fresh sesame-studded chewy breadsticks made from pizza dough. The same menu is offered all day. You can dine lightly on a pizza with toppings running the gamut from oak-grilled chicken to goat cheese. Pastas include such temptations as grilled garlic-fennel sausage served with peppers and onions over saffron fettuccine in marinara sauce. Among the nonpasta entrées is a mixed grill of jumbo shrimp wrapped around a sea scallop, médaillon of beef tenderloin, and marinated chicken breast, served with saffron risotto cake, tomato-fennel relish, and fresh vegetables. Wines, many available by the glass, are *de rigueur* with this food. Desserts include a white-chocolate banana-cream pie. Paolo's takes no reservations at dinner, so plan a before-dinner drink in the bar.

THE SEA CATCH, 1054 31st St. NW, just below M St. Tel. 337-8855.

Cuisine: SEAFOOD. **Reservations:** Recommended.

$ Prices: Appetizers $5.95–$8.95 at lunch, $6.75–$11.95 at dinner; main courses $7.75–$13.95 at lunch, mostly $15.75–$19.95 at dinner. AE, CB, DC, MC, V.

Open: Lunch Mon–Sat noon–3pm; dinner Mon–Sat 5:30–10:30pm.

I love the C&O Canal, so I was especially thrilled when this stunning restaurant opened in 1988 offering canalside seating. Outside on the long awning-covered wooden deck, mulberry and ailanthus trees form a verdant archway over the canal. The marble-topped tables are romantically candlelit in the evening; by day, watch ducks, punters, and mule-drawn barges glide by while you dine. But don't pass up Sea Catch on days that are less than ideal for alfresco meals; the restaurant, housed in a historic Georgetown stone-and-brick building, is as beautiful within as without. There's a white Carrara-marble raw bar adorned with exquisite floral and food displays and backed by a rustic stone wall. A deluxe brasserie under a low inn-style beamed ceiling adjoins; large windows overlook the canal, and there's a working fireplace. And the main dining room—with its rift-sawn white oak ceiling, random-plank oak floor, and rough-hewn walls made of fieldstone dug from Georgetown quarries is also warmed by a working fireplace. Classic jazz tapes provide a fine acoustical background.

A dinner here might begin with an appetizer of white calamari rings marinated in lime juice and herbs served with roasted eggplant/sweet garlic custard. Of course, plump farm-raised oysters, fresh Florida jumbo stone crabs with mustard sauce, and other raw-bar offerings also merit consideration. The entrée focus is on daily-changing fresh fish and seafood specials, such as grilled hickory-smoked tuna on diced eggplant with fresh sage butter served with potato casserole and a mélange of fresh corn and black-eyed peas. The kitchen willingly prepares fresh fish and seafood dishes to your specifications, including live lobster from the tanks. Don't miss the soft-shell crab when it's in season here. At lunch seafood salads are a recommendable option. An extensive wine list highlights French, Italian, and American selections and features five premium wines by the glass each day.

ADAMS-MORGAN

CITIES, 2424 18th St. NW. Tel. 328-7194.

Cuisine: INTERNATIONAL. **Reservations:** Recommended.

$ Prices: Appetizers $3.95–$7.95, main courses $10–$21. AE, DC, MC, V.

Open: Dinner only, Mon–Thurs 6–11pm, Fri–Sat 6–11:30pm. Bar, Sun–Thurs 5pm–2am, Fri–Sat 5pm–3am.

Housed in a century-old former five-and-dime store, Cities is a restaurant-cum-travelogue. Every six or seven months, following a comprehensive research expedition by the owner and chef, the restaurant is revamped to reflect the cuisine, character, and culture of a different city. Even the music reflects the city under consideration, and the waiters are in native dress or some facsimile thereof. When the city was Bangkok, for instance, vases were filled with large bird-of-paradise and bamboo arrangements, corrugated steel sheets overhead suggested Thai roofing, beautiful photographs of rickshaws and rice paddies lined the walls, and Thai sculpture, paper umbrellas, fans, tapestries, and other artifacts provided further evocation. On one of my visits, the highlighted city was Paris, and the decor replicated a Montparnasse-style brasserie, with French street lamps, flower boxes, murals of Parisian park and café scenes, and French bistro menus on the walls. My Parisian meal began with an appetizer of escargots served with shiitake mushrooms and sautéed spinach in a garlicky Pernod-flavored butter sauce with a gratinée of fresh Gruyère and parmesan. That was followed by an entrée of poulet grillé served in a fan of slices on a bed of leeks in butter-cream-chèvre reduction sauce with classic pommes frites. And dessert was chef Mary Richter's divine interpretation of a marquise au chocolat—layers of crunchy hazelnut meringue filled with hazelnut-butter cream on a crème anglaise marbleized with raspberry and garnished with fresh raspberries, mint, and crème chantilly. *Formidable!* Of course, by the time you read this, the cuisine and setting will be entirely different—that's part of the fun. Not to worry—Cities' fare is always excellent. There's a small but expertly conceived wine and champagne list enhanced by alcoholic beverages representing the city cuisine, and premium wines are offered by the glass.

The adjoining bar, open-air in summer and one of the most simpatico spots for imbibing in the Adams-Morgan district, is also redecorated with every city change. It offers a light-fare menu with items in the $4.50 to $7.50 range. For Paris, these included a croque-monsieur, plat de fromages, and pâté served with cornichons, radishes, and bread.

PETITTO'S, 2653 Connecticut Ave. NW, between Calvert St. and Woodley Rd. Tel. 667-5350.

Cuisine: ITALIAN. **Reservations:** Recommended. **Metro:** Woodley Park–Zoo.

$ Prices: Appetizers $3.75–$6.75 at lunch, $4.25–$8 at dinner; main courses $6.75–$11.75 at lunch, $11.25–$18.25 at dinner. AE, CB, CHOICE, DC, MC, V.

Open: Lunch Mon–Fri 11:30am–2:30pm; dinner Mon–Sat 6–10:30pm. Sun 6–9:30pm. Dolce Finale, Mon–Thurs 5pm–12:30am, Fri–Sat 5pm–1:30am.

The superb Petitto's features the cuisine of Rome and Abruzzi—plus a few southern specialties—in a very charming setting. There are three dining rooms in this converted turn-of-the-century town house, each with its own working fireplace. Seating, in bentwood chairs at white-linen-clothed tables, sets a traditionally elegant tone, and soft, suffused lighting is provided by hanging lamps wrapped in creamy silk scarves. Operatic arias make very appropriate background music. In good weather you can dine alfresco at umbrella tables on the street.

A shared pasta entrée makes a marvelous appetizer course—perhaps falasche alla Petitto (homemade spinach and egg noodles tossed with mushrooms, prosciutto, and peas in a cream sauce) or penne all' amatriciana (a zitilike pasta with chunks of thickly sliced bacon and hot peppers in a lusty red sauce flavored with freshly grated romano cheese). Two exquisite pasta dishes available as entrées only are pappardelle (wide fettuccine) mixed with chunks of sautéed chicken breast, exotic mushrooms, and prosciutto in a sage-marjoram-rosemary–flavored butter-wine sauce and fettuccine primavera tutto giardino—with seasoned vegetables and a lemon-cream sauce; the recipe for the latter has appeared in *Bon Appétit*. A salad course here is a must. Light and refreshing is a harmonious arrangement of tomatoes (always bright red and delicious here; off-season they're imported from Holland or Mexico) and homemade mozzarella in an olive oil/basil dressing. Also noteworthy: an exquisite affair of marinated squid and seafood with red peppers, onions, and black olives vinaigrette.

Nonpasta entrées change weekly, but always include excellent fresh seafood dishes such as plump jumbo shrimp grilled in garlic, oil, and fresh oregano. And cacciucco—an array of shellfish (lobster, scallops, mussels, clams, and squid)—is served with linguine in a sauce of olive oil, garlic, and fresh tomatoes. Entrées are accompanied by flavorful al dente fresh vegetables and new potatoes prepared in various ways. Breads—pan-fried in olive oil, flavored with garlic and parmesan, or toasted with tomato, parmesan, and basil—are famed house specialties, but you might forgo them in a good cause: leaving room for dessert. Recommended choices include a great tira misu, zuppa inglese (a sponge cake layered with custard, real whipped cream, and fresh raspberries, saturated with Chambord liqueur), and the creamiest ever orange cheesecake topped with fresh fruit. A moderately priced and well-chosen list of Italian wines is augmented by costlier vintages (including French and California selections); a few premium wines are available by the glass each night.

Dolce Finale, in Petitto's cozily candlelit, brick-walled wine cellar, features a variety of cappuccinos, wines, grappas, liqueurs, fruits and cheeses, and an array of sumptuous desserts. It can be visited separately from the restaurant.

3. MODERATE

The following moderate selections are restaurants most of us prefer for everyday dining. They all offer excellent meals at reasonable prices, in many cases with a fair amount of ambience thrown in for good measure. Many ethnic eateries are included in this category.

DOWNTOWN

JALEO, 480 7th St. NW, at E St. Tel. 628-7949.

   Cuisine: SPANISH REGIONAL/TAPAS. **Reservations:** Accepted before noon for lunch and before 6:30pm for dinner only. **Metro:** Archives or Gallery Place.

$ Prices: Tapas $2.95–$7.50 (most under $5), lunch specials $6.75–$8.25, dinner specials $9.75–$14.25. AE, DC, DISC, MC, V.

   Open: Lunch Mon–Sat 11:30am–2:30pm (with a limited tapas menu served 2:30–5:30pm); dinner Sun–Mon 5:30–10pm, Tues–Thurs 5:30–11pm, Fri–Sat 5:30pm–midnight.

The exuberantly colorful Jaleo, specializing in tapas (little dishes) "reflective of the diversity of classical and contemporary Spanish cuisine," is the creation of two successful local restaurateurs. Housed in the Civil War–era Lansburgh building, it has a corner location that allows light to stream in through café-curtained windows on two sides. The casual-chic interior focuses on a large mural of a flamenco dancer based on John Singer Sargent's painting *Jaleo,* also the inspiration for the restaurant's name. There's a large bar area with Saltillo-tile floors and a copper-topped bar faced with turquoise ceramic tile. Background music ranges from the Gypsy Kings to classical Spanish guitar.

You'll want to return again and again to sample all of Jaleo's zesty tapas. Peruse the menu over a gratis dish of Spanish olives and roasted almonds. There's a mild but savory warm goat cheese served with toast points. Angel-hair pasta, deep-fried before cooking for extra crunch, is then thrown into a garlicky casserole with fish broth and mushroom stock, tossed with sautéed wild mushrooms and vegetables, and topped with a dollop of aïoli (garlicky Basque mayonnaise). The humble potato reaches an apogee in patatas bravas—crisp fried chunks of red potato topped with a piquant tomato-chili sauce and aïoli. Steamed mussels in a marinade of garlic, paprika, sherry wine vinegar, and extra-virgin olive oil are served cold on a bed of haricots verts And a delicious eggplant flan comes with roasted red pepper sauce. Spanish wines, sangrías, and sherries selected to complement these items are available by the glass, and fresh-baked chewy bread comes in handy for soaking up tangy sauces. For dessert try the musician's tart—a compote-filled pastry of dates, prunes, apricots, hazelnuts, and almonds atop sherry cream. Other choices include a light chocolate-hazelnut cake on coffee crème anglaise or, taking another tack, a plate of Spanish cheeses

NEAR THE WHITE HOUSE

BOMBAY PALACE, 2020 K St. NW. Tel. 331-4200.

   Cuisine: NORTH INDIAN. **Reservations:** Recommended. **Metro:** Farragut North or Farragut West

$ Prices: Appetizers $3.95–$5.50, main courses $6.50–$16.95 (most are under $12), fixed-price three-course lunch (Mon–Fri) $10.95–$13.95, lunch buffet (Sat–Sun) $9.95. AE, MC, V.

Open: Lunch daily 11:30am–2:30pm; dinner Sun–Thurs 5:30–10pm, Fri–Sat 5:30–10:30pm; brunch Sat–Sun noon–2:30pm.

Created by international restaurant "moghul" Sant Chatwal, Bombay Palace features the Mughlai cooking of northern India, famous for its subtle mélanges of full-flavored spices and creamy yogurt-based marinades. Many senators (for example, Al D'Amato, Pat Moynihan, Bob Dole) and ambassadors are regulars here. Beautifully decorated in burgundy-accented soft tones of mauve and beige, with gleaming etched-mirror walls and columns, the ambience is both restful and pleasingly plush. Recessed lighting casts a rosy glow over crisp, linen-covered tables; a large aquarium of tropical fish occupies the back wall; and comfortable upholstered banquettes and armchairs comprise most of the seating. Soft Indian music and bas-relief sculptures of Indian deities provide the requisite exotic note.

Start off with a selection of appetizers such as aloo papri chat (a medley of chick-peas and potato and flour crisps topped with chutney-yogurt dressing) and samosas (flaky pastries stuffed with lightly spiced potatoes and peas). Tandoori (clay oven–baked) specialties range from large juicy prawns to an Afghani version of lamb chops marinated with ginger and herbs (ask for curry sauce with it). One of my favorite dishes here is Makhani chicken, which is also tandoor-baked and served in a fragrant tomato cream sauce spiced with coriander, ginger, garlic, and chili. If you're sharing dishes with a companion, order it along with an entrée of Hyderabadi biryani (tender lamb cubes marinated in yogurt and fried spices tossed with steam-baked long-grain basmati rice). Make sure to order one of the tandoor-baked breads with your meal—either a simple chewy and delicious naan or a more complex affair such as naan stuffed with cashews and dried fruits. For dessert try gulab jamun (milk dumplings flavored with rose water and green cardamom). There's a full bar, and the wine list recommends selections for specific dishes

SICHUAN PAVILION, 1820 K St. NW. Tel. 466-7790.

Cuisine: SZECHUAN. **Reservations:** Recommended. **Metro:** Farragut North or Farragut West.

$ Prices: Appetizers $2–$4.50 at lunch, $2.50–$5 at dinner; main courses $6.95–$14.95 at lunch, $7.95–$15.95 at dinner; fixed-price brunch (Sat–Sun) $10.95. AE, DC, DISC, MC, V.

Open: Lunch Mon–Fri 11:30am–3pm; dinner nightly 5–10:30pm; brunch Sat–Sun noon–4pm.

The Sichuan Pavilion is unique in several ways Though it s American-owned, its chefs are recruited from the highest ranks of the People's Republic of China's Chengdu Service Bureau, which operates luxurious hotels and restaurants for visiting dignitaries and prepares sumptuous state banquets These chefs, supplied from home with special seasonings and spices not otherwise available in the United States, are masters of Szechuan cuisine The Chinese embassy sent its cook here for training, and when Premier Zhao Ziyang visited Washington, the Sichuan Pavilion prepared special meals for him. The setting is unpretentious but elegant, with white-linen-covered tables, crystal chandeliers, and walls hung with paintings and calligraphy from the Chungking Institute of Fine Arts. And the food is beautifully presented (since these chefs are also trained in food sculpture, they adorn platters with exquisite carrot and leek flowers). It's also light—never greasy—low in salt, and prepared without MSG.

Do begin with an appetizer of tangy dumplings in spicy red hot sauce or crispy but feather-light spring rolls. And keep in mind that though some of the dishes sound familiar—moo shu pork, Kung Pao chicken, twice-cooked shredded duck—their subtle flavors distinguish them from Szechuan fare you've had elsewhere. The chef's specialties include tinkling bells with 10 ingredients (sliced shrimp, crab, beef, and chicken sautéed with vegetables and topped with Sichuan dumplings) and crispy fried sea bass in Sichuan sauce. Each dish is a revelation; dining here is like discovering new colors in the culinary spectrum. As a concession to Western palates, there are dessert choices such as cheesecake—though you can also opt for almond tofu custard.

DUPONT CIRCLE

CAFE PETITTO, 1724 Connecticut Ave. NW. between R and S Sts. Tel. 462-8771.

Cuisine: ITALIAN. **Reservations:** Not accepted. **Metro:** Dupont Circle.

$ Prices: Appetizers $4.25–$6; main courses $7.95–$12.95 at lunch, $8.95–$12.95 at dinner, $5.95–$9.25 at brunch; salad bar $5.95 a plate; pizzas from $5.25; sandwiches and hoagies $5–$6.50; Sat–Sun brunch buffet $8.95. AE, DC, MC, V.

Open: Mon–Thurs 11:30am–midnight, Fri–Sat 11:30pm–1am, Sun 11:30am–11pm.

Roger and Byron Petitto, original owners of the upscale Petitto's (see "Expensive," above), launched this exciting, moderately priced venture in 1985. They lure diners inside with an exquisite antipasto display in the front window—about 50 items including stringbean and fava-bean salads, marinated eggplant, snow peas with oil-cured olives, creamy egg salad, stuffed grape leaves, cold fried eggplant, pasta salads, escarole and pancetta (Italian bacon), homemade potato salad, rice/peas/pepper salad, and much more. It's always changing, always fabulous, and you can sample as much as you can stack on a plate. Then there are the scrumptious Calabrian pizzas, on flavorful bready dough that's lightly fried in olive oil before toppings are added and the entirety grilled. For $7 95 you'll get a pizza ample for two with Italian plum tomatoes, mozzarella, and fresh basil. Optional additions, priced from 75¢ to $2 75, include more than 30 choices, among them hot sausage, pancetta, artichoke hearts, sun-dried tomatoes, grilled eggplant, roasted peppers, baby clams and smoked mozzarella A third menu category is sandwiches (for example, grilled eggplant, fresh mozzarella, pepper, and tomato on toasted peasant bread) served with roasted potatoes. Daily specials always include great pasta dishes. Italian wines are reasonably priced and available by the glass. And fresh-baked desserts—such as ricotta cheesecake and pecan spice cake with caramel sauce—change daily. Additional breakfast items such as eggs Benedict are offered at brunch, but you can't beat the lavish all-you-can-eat brunch buffet for value and quality.

The original dining room here has pine-wainscoted walls hung with a veritable Petitto family album—mom, dad, and brother Tony at 9 months, among others. A gorgeous adjoining bar (open till 3am nightly and a good choice for happy hour) and a sunken dining room were added in 1993. Arrive off-hours to avoid waiting in line.

CITY LIGHTS OF CHINA, 1731 Connecticut Ave. NW, between R and S Sts. Tel. 265-6688.

> **Cuisine:** CHINESE. **Reservations:** Recommended. **Metro:** Dupont Circle.
>
> **$ Prices:** Appetizers $2–$4.50 at lunch, $2–$4.95 at dinner; main courses mostly $5.95–$9.95 at lunch, $6.95–$11.95 at dinner (a few are pricier). AE, CB, DC, DISC, MC, V.
>
> **Open:** Mon–Thurs 11:30am–10:30pm, Fri 11:30am–11pm, Sat noon–11pm, Sun noon–10:30pm (dinner from 3pm daily).

George McGovern, Jesse Jackson, former Attorney General Dick Thornburgh, Lloyd Bentsen, Bruce Babbitt, and political commentator Martin Agronsky are just a few of the many Washington insiders who make City Lights a regular stop on their dining itinerary. Like myself, they're hooked on the irresistible Mandarin/Cantonese/Szechuan dishes prepared by talented Taiwanese chef (and part owner) Kuo-Tai Soug. The setting is pretty but unpretentious—a three-tiered dining room with much of the seating in comfortable pale-green leather booths and banquettes. Neat white-linen-covered tables set with peach napkins, cloth flower arrangements in lighted niches, and green neon track lighting complete the picture.

There are wonderful appetizers like crisp-fried Cornish hen prepared in a cinnamon-soy marinade and served with a tasty dipping sauce, garlicky Chinese eggplant with a hot red-pepper tang, sesame noodles tossed with shreds of cucumber and scrambled eggs, and plump, delicious dumplings (steamed or pan-fried) stuffed with artfully seasoned pork, chives, scallions, and green peppers. As for entrées, the pièce de résistance (listed under "chef's specialties") is the crisp fried shredded beef—a delicate mix of finely julienned beef, carrot, scallion, and celery in a crunchy peppercorn hot-caramel sweet glaze. Also exemplary here: stir-fried spinach richly flavored with sesame and garlic and pan-fried noodles—a crunchy Chinese kugel topped with shrimps, scallops, and vegetables. There's a full bar.

KRAMERBOOKS & AFTERWORDS, A CAFE, 1517 Connecticut Ave. NW, between Q St. and Dupont Circle. Tel. 387-1462.

FROMMER'S SMART TRAVELER: RESTAURANTS

1. Eat your main meal at lunch when prices are lower; you can enjoy gourmet entrées for a fraction of what they cost at dinner.
2. Washington abounds with parks and beautifully landscaped squares. You'll not only save money by occasionally buying food and lunching alfresco, but you'll also probably find it more relaxing than a crowded museum cafeteria.
3. Note restaurants in the listings below offering fixed-price dinners; they usually represent good values.
4. Some accommodations listed in Chapter 5 include breakfast in the rates or have rooms with fully equipped kitchens; for families, these can represent substantial savings.
5. Many bars in D.C. offer fairly extensive happy-hour buffets. If you're a light eater, or you've had a big lunch, this could suffice for a meal.

Cuisine: AMERICAN. **Reservations:** Not accepted. **Metro:** Dupont Circle.

$ Prices: Appetizers $4.25–$5.75; main courses $7.75–$12.95. AE, DISC, MC, V.

Open: Mon–Thurs 7:30am–1am, around the clock Fri 7:30am–Sun 1am.

This schmoozy bookstore-cum-café is the kind of congenial place you go for cappuccino after the movies, for an intense discussion of your love life over a platter of fettuccine, or to linger over a good book and a cognac (both of which can be purchased here) on a sunny afternoon. There's cozy seating indoors under a low beamed ceiling, at the bar, upstairs on a balcony in a two-story glassed-in solarium, and at outdoor café tables.

The café opens early serving items like cream cheese and Nova on a bagel. At Sunday brunch—served from 9:30am to 3pm—a glass of champagne or a Bloody Mary is just $1.25. Entrées at lunch or dinner include salads (perhaps whole-wheat noodles tossed with sweet peppers, broccoli, snow peas, and grated carrots in French sesame dressing); hot entrées such as cheese-filled tortellini tossed with pancetta and field mushrooms in creamy basil parmesan sauce; and sandwiches such as sliced chicken breast with hickory bacon, grilled sweet peppers, and onion on focaccia bread. Meats are roasted on the premises, fish are fresh, and there are many vegetarian dishes. Other options include margaritas ($17.50 for a large pitcherful) served with nachos, banana splits and ice-cream sundaes, luscious desserts like chocolate/coconut/sour cream blackout cake, and rum-spiked ice-cream drinks, as well as a selection of premium wines offered by the glass. Friday and Saturday nights there's live entertainment—piano, folk, jazz, or blues.

MICK'S, 1220 19th St. NW, between M and N Sts. Tel. 785-2866.

> **Cuisine:** CASUAL AMERICAN. **Reservations:** Not accepted.
> **Metro:** Dupont Circle (south exit).

$ Prices: Appetizers $3.95–$6.95, salads/burgers/sandwiches $4.95–$7.95, main courses $6.95–$12.95 (most are under $10). AE, CB, DC, DISC, MC, V.

> **Open:** Mon–Thurs 11am–11pm, Fri 11am–midnight, Sat noon–midnight. **Closed:** Sun.

I was thrilled to note the coming of Mick's, a branch of an Atlanta-based eatery that offers vast portions of great food at moderate prices. Down a flight of stairs from the street, this Mick's has a handsome Ralph Lauren look. Softly lit by lamps and shaded sconces, its main dining room has black walls with light-pine moldings, tweed carpeting, and banquettes upholstered in classic plaids. Mirror panels enlarge the perceived space. A second room, entered via French doors, displays gilt-framed equestrian prints on knotty-pine walls. Riding boots and other horsey paraphernalia are displayed here and there. The background music is mellow rock.

Mick's is great for anything from a snack to a full meal. Many people patronize the large, comfortable bar up front, especially weekdays from 5 to 7:30pm when drink prices are reduced a dollar and a generous spread of complimentary hors d'oeuvres is set out. Nachos here are as good as nachos get—piled high with melted Monterey jack cheese, sliced jalapeños, and (optionally) grilled chicken breast or chili. This is also a good opportunity to sample crisp, cornmeal-battered-fried green tomatoes topped with roasted red pepper sauce and melted Montrachet cheese. A hickory-grilled burger au poivre (the meat studded with crushed black peppercorns) comes with mustard-cognac sauce on a whole-grain bun and a side of fries or homemade pasta salad. Also hickory-grilled are thick center-cut pork chops topped with fresh sage butter and served with a baked potato and grilled broccoli. There's even old-fashioned meatloaf with mashed potatoes and mushroom gravy. Whatever you order, leave room for dessert—incredible Oreo cheesecake, strawberry shortcake (made with fresh berries, topped with vanilla ice cream, and smothered in real whipped cream), or silky smooth chocolate cream pie. Beverages include many wines by the glass, international and draft beers, specialty concoctions, malts, and milkshakes.

There's another **Mick's** at 2401 Pennsylvania Ave. NW (tel. 331-9613). It's open the same hours as the above, plus Sunday from 11am to 10pm, with a special brunch menu served until 3pm. The closest Metro is Farragut West.

GEORGETOWN

ADITI, 3299 M St. NW. Tel. 625-6825.

> **Cuisine:** INDIAN. **Reservations:** Recommended.

$ Prices: Appetizers $1.25–$4.95; main courses $5.95–$7.50 at lunch, $6.95–$13.95 at dinner. AE, DC, DISC, MC, V.

Open: Lunch Mon–Sat 11:30am–2:30pm, Sun noon–2:30pm; dinner Sun–Thurs 5:30–10pm, Fri–Sat 5:30–10:30pm.

This pristinely charming restaurant provides a serene setting in which to enjoy first-rate Indian cookery—the kind where everything is made from scratch and each dish is uniquely spiced and sauced. You enter a small, red-carpeted, cream-walled front room, where tables are set with white linen, fresh flowers, and candles. Above the bar is a display of Kathakali figurines, representing the classic dance forms of India. A staircase spirals its way past niches filled with plants to the larger second-level dining space. Soft Indian music sets the tone for your meal.

A "must" here is the platter of assorted appetizers—bhajia (a deep-fried vegetable fritter), deep-fried cheese and shrimp pakoras lightly flavored with chili powder and dry-roasted herbs, and vegetable samosa (a crispy turnover stuffed with spiced potatoes and peas). It comes with a tangy green cilantro chutney. Favorite entrées include lamb biryani, an aromatic saffron- and rosewater-flavored basmati rice pilaf tossed with savory pieces of lamb, cilantro, raisins, and almonds. I also love the chicken pasanda (in a mild yogurt-cream sauce seasoned with onion, cumin, fresh cilantro, and almond paste) and the skewered jumbo tandoori prawns, chicken, lamb, or beef—all fresh and fork tender—barbecued in the tandoor (clay oven). Sauces are on the mild side, so if you like your food fiery, inform your waiter. A kachumber salad—diced cucumber, tomato, bell pepper, lettuce, and onion, topped with yogurt and spices—is a refreshing accompaniment to entrées. Excellent vegetable dishes like malai kofta (deep-fried croquettes in a creamy sauce) and fresh-from-the-tandoor-baked breads (like hot, chewy naan) also merit consideration. For dessert, try kheer, a cooling rice pudding garnished with chopped nuts. There's a full bar, including a good choice of wines. Do note that a $4.95 lunch is offered weekdays.

BAMIYAN AFGHAN, 3320 M St. NW. Tel. 338-1896.

Cuisine: AFGHAN. **Reservations:** Recommended.

$ Prices: Appetizers $2.75–$3.25; main courses $5.25–$5.95 at lunch, $7.25–$13.95 at dinner; fixed-price meal for two $35. AE, MC, V.

Open: Lunch Mon–Fri 11:30am–3pm; dinner nightly 5:30–11pm.

When an ambassador from Afghanistan returned home, his chef stayed behind to open this restaurant. Its cuisine is both interesting—because it consists largely of dishes new to most Americans—and delicious. Bamiyan Afghan is also quite an attractive place, with its dining room upstairs and a cozy bar/lounge on the street level. White walls are hung with Afghan rugs and a large oil painting depicting *booz keshi*, the wild national game played on horseback and using a dead goat for the ball! Tablecloths of cheerful Afghani geometric prints, hanging plants, curtained windows, and candles in glass holders combine to create a cozy atmosphere, which is enhanced by taped Afghani music.

The food is spicy but not hot unless you request it that way. A multicourse fixed-price dinner for two includes a demi-carafe of wine; noodle and vegetable soup with yogurt and ground beef;

deep-fried pastries stuffed with ground beef, chick-peas, and parsley; chicken pieces marinated in herbs and spices on a skewer; scallion-filled dumplings topped with yogurt and meat sauce; rice; salad; Afghani bread; desserts of baklava, firni (custard), or fried pastry dusted with sugar, cardamom, and pistachio nuts; and coffee or Afghani tea. You can, of course, also order à la carte. The lunch menu highlights beef, chicken, and lamb kebabs served with brown rice, salad, homemade bread, and hot sauce.

CLYDE'S, 3236 M St. NW. Tel. 333-9180.

Cuisine: AMERICAN. **Reservations:** Recommended.

$ Prices: Appetizers $5–$6; burgers, ribs, omelets, salads, sandwiches $5.50–$10.95; dinner specials $8.95–$13.95. AE, DC, DISC, MC, V.

Open: Mon–Thurs 11:30am–2am, Fri 11:30am–3am, Sat 9am–3am, Sun 9am–2am; brunch Sat–Sun 9am–4pm.

Clyde's has been a favorite watering hole for an eclectic mix of Washingtonians since 1963. You'll see university students, Capitol Hill types, affluent professionals, Washington Redskins, romantic duos, and well-heeled "ladies who lunch" bogged down with shopping bags from Georgetown's posh boutiques.

Clyde's is your classic New York–style saloon—a warren of pubby bars and cozy dining areas furnished with bentwood chairs at checkered-cloth-covered tables. The Back Room has wide-plank oak floors, dark oak walls, and amber globe lamps overhead. Ornate brass filigree antique elevator doors divide this room from the Main Bar, which is always mobbed at night. The smaller Atrium Bar has a train theme, with railroad lamps flanking an 1880s mother-of-pearl-inlaid painting of the *Rocky Mountain Limited*. The sunnier Omelette Room, up front, lit by authentic gaslight sconces, features an exhibition kitchen under a copper hood and dark oak walls hung with gilt-framed turn-of-the-century French posters. And last, there's my favorite Clyde's precinct—the light and airy brick-walled Patio Room, a jungle setting with dozens of plants, trees, vines, and ferns flourishing under a skylight ceiling. Big papier-mâché toucans and parrots amid the lush foliage add to the tropical ambience.

At weekend brunch you can get terrific omelets prepared to order or eggs Benedict with thinly sliced smoked salmon. Throughout the day the menu lists burgers, homemade soups, delicious Maryland lump crabmeat sandwiches, award-winning chili, hickory-smoked barbecued ribs, and salads—plus daily lunch specials such as fresh-made fettuccine tossed with Cajun andouille sausage, tomatoes, and herbs. At dinner, similar specials might include thin-sliced London broil served with roasted potatoes and a vegetable or broiled salmon in hot basil vinaigrette served with rice pilaf and wax-bean salad. A special snack menu offered from 4 to 7pm features "Afternoon Delights" ($2.50 to $4) such as beer-batter shrimp with orange-mustard sauce and hard smoked salmon with black bread and horseradish sauce. Beverage choices range from premium wines by the glass, to Clyde's famous lager, to a milkshake made with Ben & Jerry's ice cream. Desserts—such as a classic creamy cheesecake or a rich mousse made from Belgian Callebaut chocolate—also merit attention.

GREEK PORT RESTAURANT, 1736 Wisconsin Ave. NW, between R and S Sts. Tel. 333-0111.

Cuisine: GREEK. **Reservations:** Recommended.

$ Prices: Appetizers mostly $3.95–$4.50, main courses $7.85–$12.50. MC, V.

Open: Lunch Mon–Fri 11:30am–2:30pm; dinner Mon–Sat 5:30–11pm.

Macedonian immigrants Moskos and Despina Nomikos opened this homey mom-and-pop restaurant in 1984. It's an unpretentious setting. Light-blue walls are hung with photographs of Greece, and diners sit at tables covered with plastic cloths. Eating here is like visiting a kindly aunt and uncle who delight in providing you with a good, filling meal. Regular customers (of which there are many) kiss Despina good-bye and shake hands with Moskos when they leave. Despina does all the cooking and marketing, somehow managing to procure the best tomatoes of the season for her delicious tomato salad layered with feta cheese and thin-sliced onions and garnished with black olives. Share an order of it along with her homemade taramasalata, soaking up the juices with chunks of French bread. Also worth sharing are entrées of vine leaves stuffed with rice and ground beef and, the pièce de résistance, roast lamb marinated in lemon and garlic, and served with roasted potatoes. Order up a bottle of Boutari (a Greek white wine), and save room for Despina's homemade baklava and a cup of rich Greek coffee. It's a totally satisfying meal. There's a full bar.

HOUSTON'S, 1065 Wisconsin Ave. NW, just below M St. Tel. 338-7760.

Cuisine: AMERICAN. **Reservations:** Not accepted.

$ Prices: Appetizers $1.25–$6.45; main courses $6.25–$15.95 AE, MC, V.

Open: Sun–Thurs 11:15am–11pm. Fri–Sat 11:15am–1am.

Arrive before or after peak lunch and dinner hours to avoid long lines at the very popular Houston's, where the barbecued ribs are tender and juicy enough to eat with a knife and fork, the large and delicious burgers are made from fresh-ground chuck, and the soups, salads, and desserts are prepared from scratch. A very simpatico ambience further enhances this restaurant's appeal. Exposed brick walls are hung with framed mirrors and an old American flag, and there are rough-hewn wood rafters overhead. Most seating is in roomy red leather booths at oak tables, lighting—from dark-green enamel lamps with amber bulbs and flickering gaslight sconces—is subdued, and the background music is mellow rock and country. An area in the back has many large plants growing under a skylight ceiling.

The same menu is offered throughout the day. A hickory-grilled cheeseburger is served with a choice of iron skillet beans, couscous, fresh-cut thick fries, or coleslaw. You can choose two of these side dishes with an order of barbecued chicken breast or ribs. If you're in the mood for something heartier, there's prime rib with a baked potato, creamed spinach, and house salad; something lighter might be a grilled chicken salad tossed with honey-lime vinaigrette and garnished with a light peanut sauce. The bar serves drinks made with premium liquor brands only and fresh-squeezed juices. And for dessert, an immense chewy brownie topped with vanilla ice cream and Kahlúa is hard to surpass.

LA RUCHE, 1039 31st St. NW, a block below M St. Tel. 965-2684.

Cuisine: COUNTRY FRENCH. **Reservations:** Recommended.

$ Prices: Appetizers $3–$5; main courses $6.50–$8.50 at lunch, $9–$14.50 at dinner; fixed-price brunch $9.95. AE, MC, V.

Open: Mon–Fri 11:30am–midnight, Sat 10am–1am, Sun 10am–11pm; brunch Sat–Sun 10am–3pm.

This is a pretty little plant-filled restaurant with cushioned wicker-seated chairs, flower-bedecked tables (candlelit at night), and white walls adorned with framed art posters, French street signs, and baskets. The French countryside ambience is furthered by an outdoor courtyard café with umbrella tables amid lots of plants.

Inside, your eye is likely to be caught by the pastry case filled with exquisite fresh-baked desserts—banana tart with custard and bittersweet chocolate, gâteau amande chocolat layered with meringue and whipped cream, a classic tarte aux pommes, and more. Many people take an afternoon break from Georgetown rambles just for dessert and coffee here. Throughout the day menu offerings

---

ⓕ FROMMER'S COOL FOR KIDS: RESTAURANTS

The Dirksen Senate Office Buffet *(see p. 138)* Getting here involves a subway ride through the belly of the Capitol; there's a reduced price for children, and, for dessert, a make-your-own-sundae bar.

Flight Line *(see p. 142)* At this airy, very pleasant cafeteria the kids can dig into burgers and pizza, while adults enjoy many other options, even wine. Before you get here, pick up astronaut freeze-dried ice cream for the kids at any museum shop, an intriguing dessert.

Union Station Food Court *(see p. 145)* Something for everyone, and the setting is very pleasant.

Houston's *(see p. 127)* Burgers, barbecue, and an ice-cream-topped brownie for dessert.

Sholl's Cafeteria *(see p. 132)* Pleasant surroundings, a wide choice of freshly made high-quality fare, and low, low prices. You can't beat it with a stick.

include a hearty potage parisien with fresh chopped leeks, potatoes, and cream; salade niçoise; a wedge of Brie with apple and French bread; croque-monsieur (toasted French bread with ham and cheese); and escargots aux champignons—all the traditional specialties of a Paris brasserie. In addition, there are daily "spécialités du chef Jean-Claude," which might include mussels niçoises, bouillabaisse, Algerian couscous (a hearty dish replete with chunks of chicken, eggplant, zucchini, peppers, and chick-peas), and a duck à l'orange served with tomato provençal, haricots verts, and sautéed potatoes. There's a full bar, and wines are offered by the bottle, glass, and carafe. The fixed-price brunch includes a mimosa, entrée, and pastry.

NEKEYSA, 1564 Wisconsin Ave., just below Q St. Tel. 337-6500.

Cuisine: PERSIAN. **Reservations:** Recommended.

$ Prices: Appetizers $3.95–$4.50, main courses $6.95–$11.95, complete dinner for two $32. DISC, MC, V.

Open: Mon–Thurs noon–10pm, Fri–Sat noon–11pm. Sun noon–9pm.

This charming restaurant offers a tranquil setting enhanced by traditional Persian music. Exposed brick walls are hung with Iranian calligraphic art, there are brass urns and live plants, and a posy of fresh flowers adorns each table. More important than its ambience, however, is Nekeysa's moderately priced and totally authentic fare, which will add new and exciting colors to your culinary palette.

Begin with an assortment of appetizers such as kashke bademjan (sautéed mashed eggplant in yogurt sauce with a crunchy contrast of mint-flavored crisp-fried onions), mirza ghasemi (eggplant charcoal-roasted to create a charred tang, sautéed with egg, tomatoes, and garlic, and puréed), and fresh grape leaves stuffed with a slightly honey-sweetened mixture of ground beef, rice, split peas, and herbs (mint, coriander, and tarragon). Excellent entrée choices include a kebab of lime-marinated charcoal-grilled boneless chicken breast, subtly spiced and served with basmati rice and grilled tomato; fesenjan (a piquant sweet-and-sour stew with chunks of tender chicken simmered in a spicy sauce of pomegranate, ground walnuts, and sun-dried tomatoes, also served with basmati rice); and shirin polo and murgh (a baked-chicken dish embellished with shredded almonds, candied orange peel, pistachios, and saffron over a bed of sweetened rice). A side dish of homemade yogurt with chopped cucumbers and crushed dried mint makes a perfect foil for these sweetish entrées, as do salad selections. A basket of homemade lavash bread accompanies all entrées. For dessert, I like the light and delicate rollet—a golden cake filled with homemade whipped cream. Nekeysa has no liquor license, so you might want to pick up a bottle of wine at the store across the street

ADAMS–MORGAN

PEYOTE CAFE, 2319 18th St. NW, between Belmont and Kalorama Rds. Tel. 462-8330.

Cuisine: SOUTHWEST/TEX-MEX. **Reservations:** Recommended. **Metro:** Woodley Park–Zoo.

$ Prices: Appetizers $3.25–$7.95; sandwiches, salads, burgers $3.50–$9.95; main courses $5.95–$14.95 at dinner, mostly $3.95–$5.95 at brunch. AE, CB, DC, MC, MOT, V.

Open: Mon–Fri 5pm–1am, Sat–Sun noon–1am. Bar, Sun–Thurs to 2am, Fri–Sat to 3am.

Sharing an Adams-Morgan town house with Roxanne (see below), the Peyote Cafe, occupying the downstairs level, evokes a southwestern roadside eatery with Texas-themed ornament lights (shaped like cowboy boots, lizards, cacti) over the bar, neon beer signs, Sante Fe peach walls decorated with coyotes and armadillos, and a jukebox stocked with country-western tunes. You can dine at the bar or seated on high chairs at round tables.

It's a casual place, but there's nothing casual about the kitchen. This is inspired cookin'. The café's chili is Lone Star State quality—thick and stewlike with tender chunks of sirloin, tomatoes, and pinto beans, its spicy sauce spiked with Dos Equis beer. Similarly spiked is the chile con queso, a melted-cheese-and-jalapeño dip you eat with tortilla chips. Another noteworthy appetizer: vegetable quesadillas—pan-crisped flour tortillas wrapped around finely minced vegetables spiced with chili peppers; they're served with fresh-made guacamole. Everything here is good, but two entrées are especially irresistible. One is the Tex-Mex mixed grill (pork chop, chicken breast, and chorizo sausage) served with skin-on mashed potatoes (the best ever, topped with ancho-chili gravy), corn on the cob, and chunky homemade applesauce. The other is tacos al carbón—flour tortillas stuffed with grilled pork, melted asadero cheese, shredded lettuce, homemade pico de gallo (made with the freshest market tomatoes), guacamole, and sour cream. At brunch, served weekends, the regular menu is supplemented by entrées like New Orleans pain perdu—rum-soaked French toast topped with pecans, fresh berries, whipped cream, and powdered sugar. There's a full bar, and specialty drinks run the gamut from frozen margaritas and daiquiris (made from scratch) to liqueur-coffee concoctions topped with fresh whipped cream. For dessert, cheesecake studded with chunks of dark and white chocolate and topped with dark cocoa, cherry sauce, chocolate fudge, and fresh strawberries makes an opulent finale

ROXANNE/ON THE ROX, 2319 18th St. NW, between Belmont and Kalorama Rds. Tel. 462-8330.

Cuisine: SOUTHWEST. **Reservations:** Recommended. **Metro:** Woodley Park–Zoo.

$ Prices: Appetizers $3.25–$7.95; sandwiches, salads, burgers $3.95–$8.95; main courses $7.95–$14.95 at dinner, mostly $3.95–$5.95 at brunch. AE, CB, DC, MC, MOST, V.

Open: Mon–Fri 5pm–1am, Sat–Sun noon–1am. Bar, Sun–Thurs to 2am, Fri–Sat to 3am.

Up a flight of stairs from the Peyote Cafe (see above), Roxanne offers similar fare (some menu items are identical) Decorated in soft southwest-evocative pastels (adobe, peach, turquoise, and ocher), its banquette upholstery utilizes Native American motifs, cacti grow on the sills of a bay window up front, and a colorful iguana relief sculpture adorns an exposed brick wall. Though Roxanne is cozy, weather permitting, head to the candlelit rooftop deck area (called On the Rox). Warmed by big heaters, the Rox is open most of the year. It's a delightful setting for alfresco brunches and dinners.

The food is worthy of its romantic, starlit venue. There are two specially scrumptious appetizers: Spicy chicken wings are served with a celestial cilantro- and lime-flavored chunky peanut sauce. And plump poached shrimp and scallops, marinated in a mix of avocado, Serrano Chilies, lime, and cilantro, are served with grenadine-rimmed tequila-soaked orange slices. Enfolded in warm flour tortillas, the mix of flavors is ambrosial. Entrées include the Tex-Mex grill described at Peyote Cafe, always a great choice. Crisp-skinned grilled Muscovy duck, moist and tender, is served over garlicky wilted spinach studded with roasted pumpkin seeds in a green mole (sauce); it comes with blue-corn crêpes. I also like Roxanne's thin-crust pizzas and a pasta dish called fettuccine Toluca, which is tossed with shrimp, chorizo sausage, plum tomatoes, poblano chilies, roasted red peppers, mushrooms, and fresh basil. Like the Peyote, Roxanne adds brunch items (such as blue-cornmeal pancakes served with honey-maple butter) on weekends. Drinks and desserts are also the same (see above). I usually don't want dessert after such filling fare. One exception is a refreshing gratin of lightly grilled fresh berries in sabayon sauce topped with powdered sugar. There's live music some weekend nights—general, R&B, jazz, or blues.

4. INEXPENSIVE

Washington is filled with low-priced restaurants. Actually, I often patronize those listed below for reasons other than monetary—the food is great or they're comfortable places to hang out Many of the "Restaurants at Sightseeing Attractions," below, are also inexpensive eateries

CAPITOL HILL/UNION STATION

CHESAPEAKE BAGEL BAKERY, 215 Pennsylvania Ave. SE. Tel. 546-0994.

Cuisine: SANDWICHES/SALADS. **Metro:** Capitol South.

$ Prices: Salads $1.50–$4.50, bagel and croissant/sandwiches $1.40–$5. No credit cards.

Open: Mon–Fri 6:30am–8pm, Sat 7am–6pm, Sun 7am–5pm.

For a good quick meal near the Capitol, its hard to beat this pleasant minicafeteria with impressionist art posters adorning gallery-white walls The bagels are baked from scratch on the premises, and the aroma is divine. There are 12 varieties running the gamut from cinnamon raisin to pumpernickel, and sandwich fillings include cream cheese, walnuts, raisins, and carrots; cream cheese and Nova, chicken salad; chopped liver; and hummus and sprouts, among others. There are also sandwiches on fresh-baked croissants—for example, roast beef with lettuce and mayo or a ham, turkey, Swiss combo with sliced tomato and sprouts. A cup of coffee is 80¢, and for dessert there are brownies, blondies, carrot cake, and such.

There's a Dupont Circle location at 1636 Connecticut Ave. NW, between Q and R Streets (tel. 328-7985), and another at 818 18th St. NW (tel. 775-4690). The menus are pretty much the same.

NEAR THE WHITE HOUSE

SHOLL'S CAFETERIA, Esplanade Mall, 1990 K St. NW. Tel. 296-3065.
   Cuisine: AMERICAN. **Reservations:** Not accepted. **Metro:** Farragut West.
$ Prices: Appetizers 80¢–90¢; main courses $1.65–$5.25. No credit cards.
   Open: Mon–Sat, breakfast 7–10:30am; lunch 11am–2:30pm; dinner 4–8pm.

In March 1928, Pennsylvania Dutchman Evan A. Sholl opened this Washington cafeteria, offering fresh, wholesome, inexpensive fare, prayers, and patriotism. Though Mr. Sholl died in 1984, the current owner, his nephew, upholds his uncle's traditions. On every table is a sheet announcing the weekly special (for example, baked ham with peach half), along with a biblical quote or prayer, the slogan "We pray together. . . . We stay together," Sholl's motto ("Live well for less money with quality food at more reasonable prices"), and perhaps an inspirational poem as well. Sholl's is a homey environment, with soft lighting and carpeted floors. Photographs of the president and Pope John Paul II are prominently displayed on the cream-colored walls.

Everything served here is prepared on the premises. All vegetables are fresh, pies and cakes are homemade, and chopped meat is ground daily. And the prices are not to be believed. At breakfast, load up your tray with scrambled eggs, bacon, biscuits, coffee, orange juice, and home fries for under $3.50. Lunch or dinner entrées might include braised beef and rice, roast turkey and dressing, roast beef, or beef stew with potatoes, carrots, celery, and onions. Add corn or broccoli and a scoop of mashed potatoes for another $1.30, a piece of homemade peach or pumpkin pie for $1.15. Eating here is cheaper than preparing your own meals at home. Or, to quote a Sholl's flyer, "If you have problems with breakfast or dinner, just a meal at Sholl's and you'll be a winner."

There's a second location not far from the White House at 1750 Pennsylvania Ave. (tel. 737-5259). In addition to the above-mentioned fare, it features an extensive salad bar with items priced at 20¢ an ounce. It's open Monday to Friday 6:30am to 4pm and Sunday 8:30am to 4pm.

DOWNTOWN

REEVE'S RESTAURANT AND BAKERY, 1306 G St. NW. Tel. 628-6350.

Cuisine: AMERICAN. **Reservations:** Not accepted. **Metro:** Metro Center.

$ Prices: Main courses $4.75–$6.50, sandwiches $2.95–$5.75, buffet breakfast $4.95 Mon–Fri, $5.95 Sat and holidays. MC, V.

Open: Mon–Sat 7am–6pm.

There's no place like Reeve's, a Washington institution since 1886. J. Edgar Hoover used to send a G-man to pick up chicken sandwiches, Lady Bird Johnson and daughter Lynda Bird worked out the latter's wedding plans over lunch here, and the late Helen Hayes always stopped by when she was in town. Closed for a few years when its former building was demolished, Reeve's has reincarnated at a new address offering the identical famous fare and retaining something of its vintage ambience. It's still fronted by a long bakery counter filled with scrumptious pies and cakes. One exultant reviewer compared the strawberry pie—Bess Truman's favorite, by the way—to desserts at Maxim's in Paris. It's delicious, with enormous juicy berries atop a cakey crust. And the familiar brass-railed counter seating on both floors utilizes the original 19th-century wooden stools. The ambience is cheerful. Oak-wainscoted cream walls are hung with pictures of Washington, and soft lighting emanates from wall sconces. Much of the seating is in cozy booths and banquettes.

Reeve's has managed to reassemble most of the old staff, many of whom have been employees for three or four decades. Everything is homemade with top-quality ingredients—the turkeys, chickens, salads, breads, desserts, even the mayonnaise. At breakfast, you can't beat the all-you-can-eat buffet—for scrambled eggs, home fries, French toast, pancakes, cinnamon and sticky buns, corned-beef hash, grits, bacon, sausage, stewed and fresh fruit, and biscuits with sausage gravy. At lunch, try a roast turkey sandwich on fresh-baked bread, perhaps with an order of homemade coleslaw or potato salad. Hot entrées run the gamut from golden-brown Maryland crabcakes with fries and coleslaw to Italian sausage subs, to country-fried chicken (three pieces) with mashed potatoes and gravy. And leave room for one of those fabulous pies—strawberry, peach, chocolate cream, key lime, coconut custard . . . you name it. Or, if you like, a butterscotch sundae. No alcoholic beverages are served.

DUPONT CIRCLE

TRIO, 1537 17th St. NW, at Q St. Tel. 232-6305.

Cuisine: AMERICAN. **Reservations:** Not accepted. **Metro:** Dupont Circle (Q Street exit).

$ Prices: Appetizers $1–$3; main courses $1.95–$5.35 at breakfast. $4.25–$8.50 at lunch and dinner; burgers and sandwiches $1.75–$5. AE, MC. V.

Open: Daily 7:30am–midnight.

The Trio is a real find. Its comfortable and roomy burgundy leather booths (the kind with coathooks) are filled each morning with local folk checking out the *Washington Post* over big platters of bacon and eggs. Multipaned windows are hung with plants, there are fresh flowers on every table, and in warm weather, the awning-covered outdoor café is always packed. The Trio has been around for four decades—originally Pete and Helen Mallios' mom-and-pop business, now run by son George—and it's on its way to becoming a Washington legend.

The food is fresh and you can't beat the prices. The same menu is offered throughout the day, but there are very low-priced lunch specials such as crabmeat cakes with tartar sauce, grilled pork chops with applesauce, turkey with cornbread dressing and cranberry sauce, and fried oysters—all served with two side dishes (perhaps baked macaroni au gratin and buttered fresh carrots) and a beverage. The same kind of specials are featured at dinner, when they also include soup or juice and a dessert such as homemade rice pudding. In addition, an extensive menu features such typical coffee-shop fare as a chef's salad, chili con carne, and a turkey-salad sandwich. There's a full bar, so a glass of wine with your meal is an option. In fact, there's a surprisingly extensive wine list. A soda fountain turns out hot-fudge sundaes and milkshakes. And that's not all—specialty drinks (Irish coffee topped with whipped cream, a Fuzzy Navel, and others) are also available at this eclectic eatery.

GEORGETOWN

DEAN & DELUCA, 3276 M St. NW. Tel. 342-2500.

Cuisine: INTERNATIONAL. **Reservations:** Not accepted.

$ Prices: Croissants, muffins, and breakfast pastries $1.95–$3; sandwiches, salads, and hot dishes $4–$5.95. AE, MC, MOST, V.

Open: Café, Sun–Thurs 9am–8pm, Fri–Sat 9am–10pm, with extended hours in summer. Store, Sun–Thurs 10am–8pm, Fri–Sat 10am–9pm.

Occupying an 1865 markethouse, this renowned fine food emporium (I think of its culinary offerings as "museum quality") adjoins an awning-covered brick-walled and brick-floored café with forest-green and cream wicker-weave bamboo bistro chairs at marble-topped tables. It's rather European in feel; you can even buy *Le Figaro* at the counter. Come by in the morning for scrumptious buttery almond and chocolate croissants, scones, and fresh-baked muffins with espresso or cappuccino. Later in the day there are sandwiches (such as tomato, homemade mozzarella, and basil drizzled with extra-virgin olive oil on fresh-baked focaccia bread), soups, an array of tempting salads, and a daily hot dish such as polenta with wild mushroom sauce or bowtie pasta quattro formaggi. But you needn't limit yourself to counter offerings; you can buy anything at the store and eat it in the café. This includes a vast selection of cheeses and pâtés, oven-roasted vegetables, exquisite salads, olives, fresh produce, dried fruits, charcuterie meats, fresh-baked breads and cakes, and gourmet ice creams—and that's not the half of it. You don't just eat at Dean & Deluca—you engage in a romance with food. Fine wines are available by the glass.

GEORGETOWN BAGELRY, 3245 M St. NW. Tel. 965-1011.

Cuisine: SANDWICHES.

$ Prices: Sandwiches $3–$5.50. No credit cards.

Open: Mon–Sat 6am–9pm, Sun 6am–6pm.

Here, ex–New Yorker and bagel maven Erik Koefoed turns out about 5,000 bagels a day—plain, sesame, poppyseed, onion, garlic, salt, garlic-salt, caraway, rye, onion rye, pumpernickel, oatmeal-raisin, cinnamon-raisin, whole-wheat, and bran. And that's not to mention bialys. You can get them spread with cream cheese and lox or an array of other fillings such as homemade chicken salad, hummus and sprouts, even hot pastrami. Homemade brownies, carrot cakes, fruit salad, and other desserts are also inexpensive. Come by early in the morning to enjoy an oven-fresh bagel with fresh-squeezed orange juice and coffee over the morning paper (it's sold here, too). It's nice to sit by the big windows and watch Georgetown coming to life.

PATISSERIE CAFE DIDIER, 3206 Grace St. NW, off Wisconsin Ave. just below M St. Tel. 342-9083.
   Cuisine: CONTINENTAL/PATISSERIE. **Reservations:** Not accepted.
$ Prices: Main courses $7.95–$8.50; breakfast pastries, muffins, croissants, and desserts $1.10–$4.95. DC, DISC, MC, V.
   Open: Tues–Sat 8am–7pm, Sun 8am–5pm.

This is the most delightful place in town for continental breakfasts, light lunches, and afternoon teas. Dieter Schorner, former pastry chef at New York's haute-cuisine bastions Le Cirque and La Côte Basque, came to D.C. in 1988 as pâtissier of restaurateur Warner LeRoy's Potomac. Potomac went under, but Schorner stayed behind and opened this Georgetown café specializing in classic European pastries. His marvelous creations have already graced many of Washington's most fashionable parties. For National Symphony Orchestra Director Mstislav Rostropovich's 60th birthday, he fashioned a cello-shaped birthday cake complete with bow and strings of pulled sugar—plus 800 miniature replicas for guests!

His café is charming—light and sunny, with 18th-century lithographs on pale-peach walls, fresh flowers adorning peach linen-covered tables, plants in terra-cotta pots, and a flower box in the window. The tempting pastries are displayed in a glass case—oven-fresh croissants worthy of Paris, classic tarte Tatins, lemon tarts, strudels, mini-fruit tartlets and éclairs, and sumptuous creations such as a rich Swiss chocolate cake lavishly iced and filled with chocolate ganache. And while you're decadently eating cake for breakfast, why not enjoy it with real hot chocolate made from scratch with chunks of Belgian chocolate? Great coffee, cappuccino, espresso, freshly brewed tea, and café au lait are also options. At lunchtime, you can enjoy homemade soups (for example, saffron-flavored cream of mussel) served with a basket of fresh-baked breads, quiches, soufflés (shrimp, spinach, cheese, mushroom), a daily changing menu of sandwiches (perhaps tarragon chicken salad on baguette or croissant), salads, small European-style pizzas, cold platters (seafood, saucisson, chicken, cheese plates), and hot items such as crabcakes, lamb couscous, or grilled trout served with fresh vegetables and new potatoes.

THE TOMBS, 1226 36th St. NW, at Prospect St. Tel. 337-6668.

Cuisine: AMERICAN. **Reservations:** Not accepted.

$ Prices: Appetizers/light fare $4.25–$5.75; burgers, sandwiches, salads $3.95–$7.75; main courses mostly $6.50–$8.95. AE, DISC, MC, V.

Open: Mon–Thurs 11:30am–2am, Fri–Sat 11am–3am, Sun 9:30am–2am; brunch Sun 10am–3pm.

For good food, moderate prices, and simpatico ambience, you can't beat this classic college watering hole, which occupies a converted 19th-century Federal-style home. Its name derives from a London pub in T. S. Eliot's *Old Possum's Book of Practical Cats.* Innlike and cozy, with low ceilings, brick floors, and a working fireplace, it's a favorite hangout of both local residents and Georgetown University students (Bill Clinton was a frequent patron during his college years) and faculty. They congregate at the central bar and surrounding tables, where walls are hung with old sporting prints and lithographs from the original *Harper's,* Spanish-American War recruiting posters, and brass lanterns. I prefer to sit in the less rambunctious room called "the Sweeps." Down a few steps, its exposed brick walls are hung with vintage rowing-motif prints, along with oars from Yale, Columbia, and other college teams. Seating is in comfortable red leather banquettes.

The menu offers a wide selection of burgers and sandwiches served with steak fries (the latter range from a Philadelphia cheese steak sub to avocado, sprouts, roasted red peppers, and Muenster cheese with eggplant caviar spread on fresh-baked multigrain bread), chili, and salads, along with a few more serious entrées such as sliced London broil with a baked potato and vegetable. From 5pm on there are low-priced nightly specials—perhaps broiled salmon fillet stuffed with spinach, topped with herbed cream sauce, and served with rice and vegetables. There are similar specials at lunch. Everything on the menu is fresh and delicious. Beer prices are low to accommodate the student crowd, and a few premium wines are offered by the glass each night. Lager, brewed to German standards with no additives or preservatives, is a specialty. And the fresh-baked desserts are stupendous. Try the toll-house pie or densely moist chocolate brownie topped with ice cream and a dollop of real whipped cream. A special brunch menu offering items such as eggs Maryland (spinach, crabmeat, and poached eggs on an English muffin topped with hollandaise) is featured on Sunday. Arrive at off-peak hours to avoid a wait for tables.

ZED'S, 3318 M St. NW. Tel. 333-4710.

Cuisine: ETHIOPIAN. **Reservations:** Accepted for large parties only.

$ Prices: Appetizers and salads $4.25–$4.75; main courses $5.95–$8.95 at lunch, mostly $6.95–$11.75 at dinner. AE, MC, V.

Open: Sun–Thurs 11am–11pm, Fri–Sat 11am–1am.

Though this spicy cuisine has long been popular in Washington, it's not always easy to find restaurants offering truly authentic, high-quality Ethiopian fare. Such a one is Zed's, a charming little place with Ethiopian paintings, posters, and artifacts adorning pine-paneled walls and peach- or burgundy-colored table-cloths on tables set with fresh flowers. Ethiopian music enhances the ambience. Zed's three dining floors are particularly cozy at night by candlelight.

Everything here is made from scratch using spices imported from Ethiopia. This is a healthy cuisine, with a minimum of fat used in cooking. It's eaten *sans* utensils—a sourdough crêpelike bread called injera (made fresh daily from an African grain called teff) is used to scoop up food. Items listed as *watt* are hot and spicy; *alitchas* are milder and more delicately flavored. I love both the chicken dishes here. Doro watt is chicken stewed in a tangy red-chili-pepper sauce; it comes with a hard-boiled egg that has simmered in the sauce. I love that egg, but equally scrumptious is infillay—strips of tender chicken breast flavored with seasoned butter and honey wine and served with a delicious chopped spinach and rice side dish. Also highly recommended are the flavorful lamb dishes, a deep-fried whole fish, and steamed shrimp with sautéed onions, garlic, and red chili peppers. And vegetables have never been tastier. You get a choice of one with each entrée, but consider ordering extras such as garlicky chopped collard greens, red lentil purée in spicy red-pepper sauce, or a purée of roasted yellow split peas mixed with onions, peppers, and garlic (it's served cold, a refreshing taste contrast). Half-portions are available. Other marvelous side dishes are cooked bulgur wheat blended with herbed butter and marvelous lemony fresh-made tomato or potato salads spiked with hot green chili peppers. There's a full bar. Drink options include Ethiopian wines and beers as well as after-dinner coffees with liqueurs. And should have the inclination, there are Italian pastries for dessert.

ADAMS-MORGAN

MIXTEC, 1792 Columbia Rd. Tel. 332-1011.
  Cuisine: MEXICAN. **Reservations:** Not accepted. **Metro:** Woodley Park–Zoo.
$ Prices: Appetizers $2.50–$5.25, main courses $4.75–$9.95. MC, V.
  Open: Sun–Thurs 11am–10:30pm, Fri–Sat 11am–midnight.

This Adams-Morgan eatery serves up authentic regional cuisine in a cheerful setting, with an open kitchen and white walls hung with color photographs of menu items. Colorful paper lanterns are suspended overhead, and Mexican music provides south-of-the-border ambience. Dozens of brightly painted cut-tin creations (birds, fish, butterflies) adorn an adjoining dining room.

Delicious made-from-scratch corn tortillas enhance whatever they're stuffed with. Start out with an appetizer of queso fundido—a bubbling hot dish of broiled Chihuahua cheese topped with shredded spicy chorizo sausage and flavored with jalapeños and cilantro. The freshly prepared guacamole is also excellent. An interesting side dish is cebollitas al carbón—spring onions lightly grilled in olive oil and flavored with fresh lime juice. Tacos al carbón, pieces of spicy grilled beef, come wrapped in small corn tortillas with three sauces—a purée of green tomatillos flavored with onion and garlic, a hot red-chili sauce, and a salsa cruda of chopped tomatoes, onions, jalapeños, and cilantro. A similar dish, tacos al pastor, comprises small corn tortillas stuffed with pork that has been marinated overnight in mild guajillo peppers, fresh garlic, cumin, black pepper, and chicken broth. All these dishes are in the $2.50 to $4.50 range, and if you order a few of them you'll enjoy a hearty meal and diverse culinary thrills. Full entrées served with rice and beans include the house specialty, mole mexicano—broiled chicken in a rich sauce of five peppers (mulato, gaujillo, pasillo, ancho, and arbol), sunflower and sesame seeds, onions, garlic, almonds, cinnamon, and chocolate. There's a nice choice of Mexican beers. For dessert, try homemade flan flavored with brandy and orange and lemon peel.

5. RESTAURANTS AT SIGHTSEEING ATTRACTIONS

Given the hectic round of Washington sightseeing, you'll sometimes want to save time by eating at or near various attractions. Here's a rundown of restaurants right in the Smithsonian, the Capitol, and other major sights. Check out other sections of this chapter to locate additional restaurants close to sights you'll be visiting.

Note: In addition to the below-listed, spring through fall there's usually a rather nice outdoor café at the Hirshhorn.

THE CAPITOL

You can rub elbows with senators and congresspeople if you dine in the Capitol—a good choice when you're touring the building.

DIRKSEN SENATE OFFICE BUILDING SOUTH BUFFET ROOM, 1st and C Sts. NE. Tel. 224-4249.
   Cuisine: AMERICAN. **Reservations:** Not accepted. **Metro:** Capitol South or Union Station.
$ Prices: Fixed-price buffet $7.75 adults, $5.25 children under 12, plus 15% gratuity. MC, V.
   Open: Lunch only, Mon–Fri 11:30am–2:30pm.

This is a marvelous lunchtime choice, featuring lavish all-you-can-eat meals. To get here, you can take a free subway that runs through the underbelly of the Capitol, a fun trip—ask Capitol police for directions. You can also go directly to the Dirksen Building, of course, in which case your closest Metro is Union Station. The marble-colonnaded art deco setting for these buffets is most attractive, with seating in comfortable leather chairs at white-linen-covered, flower-bedecked tables. You can help yourself to unlimited viands from the carvery station (perhaps roast beef or leg of lamb), about eight additional hot entrées, vegetables, potatoes, rice, pasta, a full salad and fruit bar, a make-your-own-sundae bar, soft drinks, and tea, coffee, or milk.

HOUSE OF REPRESENTATIVES RESTAURANT, Room H118, at the south end of the Capitol. Tel. 225-6300.

Cuisine: AMERICAN REGIONAL. **Reservations:** Not accepted. **Metro:** Capitol South.

$ Prices: Appetizers $1.20–$6.95, main courses mostly $5.25–$8.75. AE, DC, DISC, MC, V.

Open: Breakfast Mon–Fri 8–11am; lunch Mon–Fri 1:30–2:30pm when Congress is in session, Mon–Fri 8am–2:30pm when Congress is not in session.

Most impressive of all Capitol eateries open to the public, the House Restaurant consists of two plush dining rooms. Both are beautifully appointed. In one, walls are hung with gilt-framed Federal mirrors, historic prints, and a Bierstadt landscape, and lighting emanates from crystal sconces and graceful Georgian chandeliers. The other has high ceilings with beautiful moldings, floor-to-ceiling windows framed by swagged satin draperies, and a large gilt-framed Brumidi fresco of George Washington receiving Cornwallis's letter of surrender at Yorktown. White-linen-covered tables are adorned with fresh flowers.

Bean soup has been a feature menu choice here since 1904, when Speaker of the House Joseph G. Cannon ordered it only to find that it had been omitted from the menu because the day was too hot for hearty soups. "Thunderation," roared Cannon, "I had my mouth set for bean soup. . . . From now on, hot or cold, rain, snow, or shine, I want it on the menu every day!" And so it has been ever since. Prices are very reasonable for such a lofty setting. A breakfast of two eggs, homemade biscuits, sausage patty, fresh-squeezed orange juice, and coffee is about $5. At lunch, the famous bean soup is $1.50. Other choices might include grilled Pacific salmon, Maryland crabcakes, or New York strip steak. There are also deli sandwiches, salads, and burgers, and daily specials always include one low-cholesterol/low-salt entrée. Seven wines (representing various regions of the country) are offered by the glass daily. For dessert, a butterscotch sundae is a treat, though apple pie seems more appropriate Who knows, you might even get to see your congressperson.

REFECTORY, first floor, Senate side of the Capitol. Tel. 224-4870.

Cuisine: AMERICAN. **Reservations:** Not accepted. **Metro:** Capitol South.

$ Prices: Main courses $3.50–$9.95. MC, V.

Open: Mon–Fri 8am–4pm (later if the Senate is in session).

Another good choice for Capitol meals, this charming dining room with vaulted ceilings and wainscoted walls offers light fare. Continental breakfast fare includes fresh-baked muffins. Lunch runs the gamut from a roast-beef sandwich with mashed potatoes and gravy to a cold chunky chicken salad plate with seasonal fruits. There are also sandwiches (including the three-decker senator's club), burgers, and salads. Try hot pecan pie or a hot-fudge sundae for dessert

THE CORCORAN

CAFE AT THE CORCORAN, 17th St. NW, between E St. and New York Ave. Tel. 638-3211.

Cuisine: AMERICAN/CONTINENTAL. **Reservations:** Not accepted. **Metro:** Farragut West or Farragut North.

$ Prices: Main courses $5.95–$9.95; afternoon tea sampler $5.95 for one, $9.95 for two; buffet jazz brunch $15.95 adults, $8.50 children under 12. No credit cards.

Open: Wed–Mon 10am–5pm, Thurs till 9pm; brunch Sun 11am–2pm.

⭐ This museum café couldn't be more lovely. Under a lofty skylight ceiling, it's ensconced by fluted Doric columns and neoclassic marble statuary. Flower-bedecked tables are set amid tall palms in terra-cotta pots. The menu is quite "haute" for a museum eatery, featuring entrées like boneless breast of chicken with banana-curry sauce and wild-mushroom salad, a Caesar salad topped with grilled chicken, and paper-thin slices of smoked salmon served with herbed Neufchâtel cheese, garden-fresh tomatoes, and focaccia bread. Fresh-baked desserts include key lime pie. For afternoon tea, there's a selection of cheeses with tea biscuits, fresh fruit, a pot of tea, and freshly baked currant scones with Devonshire cream and strawberry preserves.

Do stop by on Sunday for a buffet brunch, with live jazz and gospel music. The fare highlights Créole and southern dishes—catfish étouffé, oyster-and-corn pudding, blackened redfish, andouille sausage, sticky chicken, grits, dirty rice, and more—along with a honey-baked ham or steamship of beef, potato dishes, salads, fresh fruits and vegetables, breads, desserts, coffee or tea, and a mimosa or orange juice.

KENNEDY CENTER

ENCORE CAFE, New Hampshire Ave. NW, at Rock Creek Pkwy. Tel. 416-8560.

Cuisine: AMERICAN. **Metro:** Foggy Bottom

$ Prices: Most items $4.50–$6. No credit cards.

Open: Daily 11am–8pm.

An inexpensive choice is this attractive cafeteria with windows all around providing gorgeous city views Typical entrées here: baked trout with mashed potatoes and a medley of fresh vegetables, Spanish paella, and chilled salmon fillet with pecan-studded wild rice Sandwiches, homemade soups, pizza, salads, wine, and beer are available, and there are fresh-baked pastries such as apple-cinnamon cobbler for dessert. From 5 to 8pm you can order a fresh-carved prime-rib dinner here, with baked potato and vegetable, for $10 95

ROOF TERRACE RESTAURANT, New Hampshire Ave. NW, at Rock Creek Pkwy. Tel. 416-8555.

Cuisine: AMERICAN REGIONAL. **Reservations:** Recommended. **Metro:** Foggy Bottom.

$ Prices: Roof Terrace, appetizers $4–$6 at lunch, $6–$9 at dinner; main courses $10–$14 at lunch $22–$24 at dinner, fixed-price buffet brunch $19.95, fixed-price three-course dinner $33. Hors d'Oeuvrerie, light-fare items $8–$12. AE, CB, DC, MC, V.

Open: Roof Terrace, lunch daily 11:30am–3pm; dinner nightly 5:30–9pm; brunch Sun 11:30am–3pm. Hors d'Oeuvrerie, daily 5pm–half an hour after the last show. *Note:* The Roof Terrace is occasionally closed when the show schedule is scant; call before you go.

A meal in this fine dining room adds a glamorous note to an evening at the theater. It's extremely plush, with ornate crystal candelabra chandeliers suspended from a lofty ceiling, immense windows providing panoramic views of the Potomac, and Louis XV–style chairs at white-linen-covered tables. Potted palms and big floral arrangements further adorn the luxe ambience.

Menus change seasonally. During my recent visit, dinner appetizers included crabcakes served with herbed aïoli, smoked duck with asparagus strudel, and a grilled vegetable and goat-cheese terrine. Among the entrées were walnut- and herb-roasted rack of lamb and grilled salmon steak with potato-leek crust. The signature dessert here is chocolate Concorde cake—chocolate meringue topped with chocolate ganache and chocolate mousse. At lunch, lighter fare—such as a Mediterranean vegetable frittata with roasted tomato salsa—is an option. And Sunday brunch features a vast buffet (see details below under "Brunch" listings). Many premium wines are offered by the glass.

After-theater munchies and cocktails are served in the adjoining and equally plush **Hors d'Oeuvrerie.** I love to stop here after a show for a glass of wine and late supper—perhaps a smoked duck on mustard cress drizzled with red lentil oil or cold lobster and papaya salad. It's gourmet snack fare. Desserts and coffee are also available.

LIBRARY OF CONGRESS

CAFETERIA, James Madison Memorial Building of the Library of Congress, 101 Independence Ave. SE. Tel. 707-8300.

Cuisine: AMERICAN. **Metro:** Capitol South.

$ Prices: Main courses $2.50–$4, sandwiches $2–$3.80. No credit cards.

Open: Breakfast Mon–Fri 9–10:30am; lunch, Mon–Fri 12:30–2pm; light fare Mon–Fri 2–3:30pm.

This building has a classy sixth-floor cafeteria that is open to the public The decor is tasteful (wall-to-wall carpeting, Breuer chairs at oak-framed white tables, a wall of windows for panoramic city views), the food fresh and homemade. Hot entrées change daily; they might include old-fashioned beef stew, Swedish meatballs over noodles, homemade pizza, or crabcakes with tartar sauce A stir-fry station and special-event station (serving daily-changing fare—Mexican, pasta, Chinese, etc.) are options. Selections from the salad bar begin at 29¢ an ounce for such things as greens, tomatoes, pasta salads, Greek salad, Caesar salad, egg salad, mushrooms, chick-peas, beans, cheeses, and sprouts. Vegetables might include broccoli, noodles with mushrooms, mashed and au gratin potatoes, sautéed dilled tomatoes, and spinach soufflé. There are also sandwiches, fresh-baked pies and cakes, and a full array of breakfast foods.

MONTPELIER ROOM, James Madison Memorial Building of the Library of Congress, 101 Independence Ave. SE. Tel. 707-8300.
   Cuisine: AMERICAN. **Reservations:** Recommended for parties of four or more. **Metro:** Capital South.
$ Prices: Fixed-price lunch $8.50. MC, V.
   Open: Lunch Mon–Fri 11:30am–2pm. **Closed:** Aug to mid-Sept.

   Adjoining the James Madison cafeteria (details above), the Montpelier Dining Room offers a marvelous midday buffet. It's a lovely carpeted room, with panoramic views (including the Capitol dome) from white-draped windows on two sides, tables adorned with fresh flowers, oak-paneled walls, and an elegant dessert display table with a floral centerpiece. The fixed-price lunch served here is one of the best deals in town. Menus change daily. During my recent visit it included cream of broccoli soup, prime rib, lyonnaise potatoes, honeyed carrots, bread and butter, beverage, and salad bar; desserts were $1.75 extra. Wine and beer are available by the glass. Friday is the Montpelier's prime-rib day.

NATIONAL AIR & SPACE MUSEUM

FLIGHT LINE, Independence Ave. at 4th St. SW. Tel. 371-8778.
   Cuisine: AMERICAN. **Metro:** L'Enfant Plaza.
$ Prices: Main courses, sandwiches, salads $2.65–$6.95. MC, V.
   Open: Daily 10am–5pm.

This major Mall museum features a 39,400-square-foot restaurant complex consisting of Flight Line, an 800-seat cafeteria on the main level, and the Wright Place (see below), an elegant full-service dining room on the mezzanine. The two eateries occupy a conservatorylike glass building, with floor-to-ceiling windows on both levels offering panoramic views of the Mall and Capitol. Surrounding terraces are lushly planted and landscaped with seasonal flowers.

   Flight Line, under a Tinker-Toy assemblage of white-steel tubing, is carpeted in forest green and handsomely furnished with marble-topped pine tables. Needless to say, with all those windows it's bright and sunny inside. The self-service fare is reasonably priced, fresh, and tasty. It's displayed on an immense octagonal food counter with buffet stations for salads, hot entrées (such as baked lasagne, meatloaf, and fried chicken), hot soups and chili, burgers, vegetables, fresh-baked breads and pastries, pastas and pizzas, fresh fruit, sandwiches, wine and beer, even bottled waters.

THE WRIGHT PLACE, Independence Ave. at 4th St. SW. Tel. 371-8777.
   Cuisine: AMERICAN. **Reservations:** Recommended (you must call between 9 and 11am). **Metro:** L'Enfant Plaza.
$ Prices: Main courses $7.50–$11.50, sandwiches and salads $6.75–$9.50. AE, DISC, MC, V.
   Open: Daily 11 30am–3pm

Upstairs from Flight Line (see above), this is a plush, full-service restaurant enclosed by a chrome railing and planters of greenery. Tables are adorned with fresh flowers, and pale-gray walls are hung with vintage aviation photographs from the museum's collection. The city views here, being higher up, are especially great. The menu changes seasonally. Choices might include appetizers of smoked salmon salad or white pizza (topped with smoked provolone, parmesan, and goat cheeses with a julienne of fresh basil). And entrées run the gamut from sandwiches (such as pulled pork with barbecue sauce on a kaiser roll, served with battered crispy fries) to a hearty Brunswick stew served with salad and fresh-baked corn muffins. Wine and microbrewery beers are available, and there's a low-priced children's menu with foods such as a grilled-cheese sandwich, fries, and milk. Yummy fresh-baked desserts—like key lime pie and warm apple cobbler with a scoop of vanilla ice cream—change daily.

NATIONAL GALLERY OF ART

CONCOURSE BUFFET, on the Mall, between 3rd and 7th Sts. NW. Tel. 347-9401.
   Cuisine: AMERICAN. **Metro:** Archives or Judiciary Square.
$ Prices: Main courses $4–$5.50. AE, MC, V.
   Open: Mon–Sat 10am–3pm, Sun 11am–4pm.

Set in the concourse connecting the two buildings of the National Gallery is this cheerful cafeteria with seating amid planters and potted palms. Good acoustics keep the noise level bearable, and efficient operations keeps the lines moving quickly. Selections include homemade soups and tasty salads, and a choice of four fresh vegetables each day. In addition, there are croissant sandwiches, pizza, frozen yogurts with varied toppings, burgers and hot dogs, a carvery for deli sandwiches, even a few hot entrées each day—perhaps roast beef with mashed potatoes, Idaho rainbow trout, or Italian vegetable quiche. Fresh-baked desserts and wine and beer are available.

NATIONAL GALLERY RESTAURANTS, on the Mall, between 3rd and 7th Sts. NW. Tel. 347-9401.
   Cuisine: INTERNATIONAL. **Reservations:** Not accepted. **Metro:** Archives or Judiciary Square.
$ Prices: Cascade Espresso Bar, menu items $3.75–$5.95. Terrace and Garden cafés, main courses $5.95–$10. AE, MC, V.
   Open: Cascade Espresso Bar, Mon–Sat noon–4:30pm, Sun noon–5:30pm. Terrace Café, Mon–Sat 11:30am–3pm, Sun noon–4:00pm. Garden Café, Mon–Sat 11:30am–3pm, Sun noon–6:30pm (extended hours in summer).

There are two charming full-service restaurants within the National Gallery itself, both of which provide restful settings and good food. And an attractive lunch spot with waiter service is nothing to scorn when you've been trudging around museums all day. The **Terrace Café,** in the East Building, overlooks the Mall, and the fern- and flower-bordered **Garden Café,** in the West Building, is under a skylight with tables around a marble fountain with a late Renaissance bronze *Venus and Cupid.*

The Terrace and Garden cafés have similar menus listing about five items each day. They change from time to time (often reflecting current exhibits), but might typically include a plate of chilled poached salmon served on a bed of spinach pasta with a basket of bread; a salmagundi salad (greens with Cheddar cheese, eggs, black olives, anchovies, and Virginia ham); a cheese-and-fruit plate served with pâté and a glass of wine; a Caesar salad topped with grilled chicken; and English spring lamb stew. Fresh-baked pastries and fresh fruit are among your dessert options at both eateries, as are wine, beer, and cappuccino/espresso.

The **Cascade**, an espresso/cappuccino/wine bar, features mini-croissant and tea sandwiches (for example, marinated salmon or sliced beef) served with fresh fruit, fruit and cheese plates, and exquisite desserts. It overlooks an indoor waterfall, and patrons sit at marble tables amid potted palms.

NEAR THE NATIONAL ZOO

UPTOWN BAKERS, 3313 Connecticut Ave. NW, just north of Macomb St. Tel. 362-6262.
   Cuisine: SANDWICHES/PASTRIES. **Metro:** Cleveland Park.
$ Prices: Sandwiches $3.75–$5.50, pastries $1.50–$2.75. No credit cards.
   Open: Daily 7am–8pm.

Although there are eateries in the zoo, their fast-food menus are less than inspiring. A better bet is an alfresco lunch at one of the zoo's nice picnic areas. Get the fixings at Uptown Bakers—sandwiches on scrumptious fresh-baked breads (baguette, raisin-nut, sourdough, olive, herb, challah, and many more) with yummy fillings like country pâté and Brie and grainy mustard, lean roast beef with creamed horseradish, and fresh mozzarella with roasted red peppers, olive tapenade, and watercress. Focaccia pizzas, too. Uptown's coffee is a blend of Amazon and French roast beans. And oven-fresh desserts run the gamut from the world's best sticky buns to an apple tart topped with light calvados cream and caramel crunch.

SUPREME COURT

SUPREME COURT CAFETERIA, 1st St. NE, between E. Capitol St. and Maryland Ave. Tel. 479-3246.
   Cuisine: AMERICAN. **Metro:** Capitol South.
$ Prices: Main courses and sandwiches $2.40–$3.95. No credit cards.
   Open: Breakfast Mon–Fri 7:30–10:30am; lunch Mon–Fri 11:30am–2pm (closed to public noon–12:15pm and 1–1:10pm).

Like the Capitol restaurants, the Supreme Court cafeteria is run in the belief that members of each branch of government have to eat but can't always get out to do so. It's likely you'll see a justice or two in the attractive ground-floor cafeteria here. The food is good and low priced, with daily soup-and-entrée specials such as New

England clam chowder with fish-and-chips or navy bean soup followed by baked stuffed green pepper with whipped potatoes and broccoli. Sandwiches on fresh-baked croissants, stuffed with chicken salad or roast beef, are served with potato chips and pickles. Full breakfasts are available here as well (with fresh-baked muffins). There's a salad bar, and homemade pies and cakes are just 95¢ to $1.50.

UNION STATION

Since its renovation in the late 1980s, Union Station has become an extremely popular dining choice for both locals and tourists. It offers dozens of restaurants and food vendors in different price ranges, and when you're through dining you can browse the diverse shops (see Chapter 8) or take in a movie at the nine-screen cinema complex on the lower level. Other events here might include strolling singers, orchestral performers, choral groups, and art exhibits. There's validated parking for 1,600 cars (entrance on H Street or Massachusetts Avenue), and of course, the Union Station Metro takes you right to the door.

At this writing, a new restaurant is about to open in the station's most exalted setting—the Presidential Suite, where in the heyday of rail travel presidents officially greeted visiting monarchs and dignitaries. Called **B. Smith's,** it will specialize in southern cuisine.

On the lower level is a vast **Food Court,** offering an incredible array of low- to medium-priced options. It's all cafeteria-style, with food vendors selling blintzes, falafel, stuffed baked potatoes, burgers, fresh seafood, enchiladas, sushi, fresh-squeezed juices, salad-bar items, fresh baked goods, homemade ice cream, chili, pastrami sandwiches, pizzas, fried-oyster po'boys, biryani, barbecue, and much more. Ordinarily I do not like food courts because they're big, noisy, and sterile-looking. This one, however, in line with the lofty quality of the station's renovation, is a totally different story. It's a really attractive facility, enhanced by extensive use of oak and pine, colorful canvas umbrellas over some tables, subtle lighting, live plants, and an exquisite marble floor. In addition, the vast space is divided into a number of seating areas, creating a more intimate ambience.

Also noteworthy here:

AMERICA, Union Station, 50 Massachusetts Ave. NE. Tel. 682-9555.

    Cuisine: AMERICAN. **Reservations:** Recommended. **Metro:** Union Station.

$ Prices: Appetizers $4.75–$6.25; main courses $5.95–$15.95 (most items are $10 or less). AE, DC, MC, V.

    Open: Sun–Thurs 11:30am–midnight, Fri–Sat 11:30am–1am. Bar stays open a few hours later.

    I always enjoy eating at this New York transplant, with seating on three levels and café tables spread out into the Main Hall. Its essentially art deco interior includes WPA-style murals, a large painting of the American West, and a whimsical frieze depicting surfers, athletes, astronauts, and superheroes in outer space. I especially like sitting by the balcony rail so I can see the action below. A vast American-classic menu consisting of hundreds of items is offered throughout the day. Some choices: delicious baked macaroni and cheese, Pecos red chili con carne, sandwiches (Philadelphia cheese steak, New Orleans po'boy, and a New York Reuben, among others), burgers, salads, egg dishes and omelets, and entrées running the gamut from crabcakes to New England roast turkey with stuffing, giblet gravy, and cranberry compote. A list of about 20 desserts includes white-chocolate macadamia-nut brownies, peanut butter pie with vanilla ice cream, and ultra-rich "death-by-chocolate" cake. All bar drinks are available, including a wide selection of domestic beers; nonalcoholic beverages range from milkshakes to lemonade.

CENTER CAFE, Union Station, 50 Massachusetts Ave. NE. Tel. 682-0143.

    Cuisine: AMERICAN/MEXICAN/ASIAN. **Reservations:** Accepted for large parties only. **Metro:** Union Station.

$ Prices: Appetizers $4.75–$7.95; main courses $8.95–$14.95. AE, CB, DC, MC, V.

    Open: Sun–Thurs 11:30am–10:30pm (bar, to 11:30pm), Fri–Sat 11:30am–midnight (bar, to 12:30am).

This handsome two-level oval mahogany restaurant, the hub of the Main Hall, offers a diverse menu of salads, sandwiches, quesadillas, and fancy pizzas. Entrées include crabmeat-filled lobster ravioli in herbed tomato-cream sauce, blue-corn enchiladas stuffed with chicken and chilies, and hacked roast Oriental chicken with peanut sauce and sesame noodles. The café is also an oyster bar. Good desserts here, too, such as key lime mousse and a "death by chocolate" flourless torte.

SFUZZI, Union Station, 50 Massachusetts Ave. NE. Tel. 842-4141.

    Cuisine: ITALIAN. **Reservations:** Recommended. **Metro:** Union Station.

$ Prices: Appetizers $3.25–$5 at lunch, $4.50–$7.25 at dinner; main courses $8.75–$11 at lunch, $11–$21.50 at dinner; brunch Sun $14. AE, CB, DC, MC, V.

    Open: Lunch Mon–Sat 11:30am–5pm; dinner nightly 6–9pm (bar open nightly to 2am); brunch Sun 10:30am–3pm.

An elegant multilevel restaurant in an alcove off the Main Hall, Sfuzzi serves California-influenced Italian fare. Entrées range from pizzas with gourmet toppings (smoked chicken, wild oregano, goat cheese) to grilled salmon in basil-citrus sauce with green beans and new potatoes. There are also many pasta dishes such as spinach lasagne layered with grilled vegetables, portobello mushrooms, and asiago cheese. There's a full bar, and an extensive wine list includes many by-the-glass selections. A fixed-price Sunday brunch includes an extensive antipasto bar, an entrée, and dessert.

6. SPECIALTY DINING

FOR BRUNCH

I love Sunday brunches—the kind that go on for hours fueled by free-flowing champagne. The following, all worthy choices for this leisurely repast, are described fully in earlier sections in this chapter (see the Restaurant Index at the back of this book for the page numbers). Reservations are recommended at all of these establishments.

The **Old Ebbitt Grill,** 675 15th St. NW (tel. 347-4801), a stunning reconstructed 19th-century saloon, serves Sunday brunch (à la carte) from 9:30am to 4pm. Entrées are $5 to $7. Very elegant.

Bombay Palace, 2020 K St. NW (tel. 331-4200), offers a marvelous brunch buffet for just $9.95—an opportunity to sample a variety of gourmet northern Indian dishes—tandoori chicken, curries, salads, rice pilafs, breads, and more. Brunch is served on Saturday and Sunday from noon to 2:30pm.

Or perhaps you'd like a Chinese brunch. Another elegant dining room, **Sichuan Pavilion,** 1820 K St. NW (tel. 466-7790), offers a $10.95 fixed-price brunch on Saturday and Sunday from noon to 4pm. It includes an appetizer, soup, entrée, a glass of wine or a mimosa, and tea.

Combine a Kennedy Center tour or Sunday matinee with a lavish brunch at its on-premises **Roof Terrace Restaurant** (tel. 416-8555). This ornate establishment invites guests into the kitchen where a stunning array of food is displayed—soups, dozens of salads, pâtés and terrines, cheeses, made-to-order omelets/waffles/French toast, pastas in succulent sauces, a carvery for prime rib au jus and salmon, chicken quesadillas, smoked meats and fish, and an array of oven-fresh breads and desserts. Your meal includes a glass of champagne or a mimosa, and musicians (flute and guitar) entertain while you dine. The price is $19.95; Sunday hours are 11:30am to 3pm. An à la carte menu is also an option.

Café Petitto, 1724 Connecticut Ave. NW (tel. 462-8711), has one of the best deals in town—an all-you-can-eat buffet brunch for just $8.95, served Saturday and Sunday from 11:30am to 3pm. It includes sausages with peppers, bruschetta, stuffed grape leaves, dozens of salads, cheeses, cold cuts, pizzettes, frittatas, poached and deviled eggs, calzones, fried cauliflower, breads, pastries, and more.

Gabriel, the exciting Spanish restaurant at the Barceló Hotel, 2121 P St. NW (tel. 956-6690), offers tapas, roast potatoes with aïoli, olive and fig breads, and a quesadilla bar, along with the usual carving/omelet and waffle stations, salads, cheeses, cold cuts, and desserts that make up a traditional brunch buffet. Served Sundays from noon to 3pm, it includes a glass of champagne, mimosa, or Bloody Mary. The price is $16.75 for adults, $11.75 for children under 12.

The **Café Promenade,** at the Mayflower Hotel, 1127 Connecticut Ave. NW (tel. 347-2233), an exquisite gardenlike setting under a domed skylight, offers a fixed-price $28 brunch (half price for children under 12) Sundays from 11am to 2:30pm. It includes champagne, mimosas, and kir royales; fresh-squeezed juices; arrays of fresh fruit, cheeses, salads, and seafood; smoked fish and deli meats; clam chowder; pâtés and terrines; a Caesar salad station; a choice of entrées (perhaps broiled lamb chops with roasted garlic and rosemary au jus or poached eggs Benedict on crabmeat), and fresh-baked pastries, tortes, and mousses.

AFTERNOON TEA

Afternoon tea is total self-indulgence—a decadent lingering over things sweet and caloric in the middle of the day. Two luxurious settings for this very civilized repast are:

The **Café Promenade,** at the Mayflower Hotel, 1127 Connecticut Ave. NW (tel. 347-2233; described above under "Brunch" listings), features à la carte afternoon teas Monday to Saturday from 3 to 5pm. Prices range from $8 to $12.50, the latter for a selection of tea sandwiches, English pound cake, raisin scones, toasted crumpets, Devonshire cream and preserves, a fruit tartlet, and a pot of fresh-brewed tea.

Equally divine, and also gardenlike with lush plantings and picture windows overlooking the C&O Canal, the **Garden Terrace** at the Four Seasons Hotel, 2800 Pennsylvania Ave. NW (tel. 342-0444), offers soothing piano music during afternoon tea. A choice of three teas is offered Monday through Saturday from 3 to 5pm and Sunday from 3:30 to 5pm. For $12.25 you can enjoy a choice of pinwheel and finger sandwiches, fresh-fruit tartlets, assorted English tea breads and biscuits, a Scottish sultana scone with double Devonshire cream and homemade preserves, and a pot of fresh-brewed tea. Or for $11.25, there's a tea featuring sugar-dusted fresh strawberries with strawberry fruit coulis, lemon curd, and Devonshire cream. Vintage ports, sherries, and champagne are also available.

LATE-NIGHT/24-HOUR DINING

Washington's not a late-night town unless you count the action at 5 or 6am when the workaholic population gets into gear for the workday ahead. In Georgetown, **Au Pied de Cochon,** 1335 Wisconsin Ave. NW (tel. 333-5440), is one place that never closes. A Parisian-style café/brasserie, it offers traditional bistro fare—fresh-baked croissants, quiche Lorraine, duck à l'orange, salade niçoise, and so forth. Prices are low to moderate. **Kramerbooks & Afterwords, A Café,** 1517 Connecticut Ave. NW, at Dupont Circle (tel. 387-1462), keeps late weekend hours, staying open continuously from Friday at 7:30am through Sunday at 1am.

WHAT TO SEE & DO IN WASHINGTON, D.C.

People often come to Washington for a weekend expecting to see all the sights. Talk about life in the fast lane! The Smithsonian Institution alone consists of more than a dozen museums plus the National Zoo. Then there are the monuments and memorials, the White House, the Capitol, the Supreme Court, the Library of Congress, the FBI, the Kennedy Center, the Holocaust Museum, the National Archives, and Washington National Cathedral—major sights one and all. About a dozen other very interesting attractions vie for your sightseeing time, and it's nice to get over to Georgetown, take a stroll on the canal, or visit nearby Mount Vernon, Arlington, and Alexandria.

There's so much to see that you should consider spending at least a week. Even then, remember that you can't see everything, and it's more rewarding to see a few attractions thoroughly than to race through dozens. To make the most of your time, read the following listings and plan a reasonably relaxed sightseeing itinerary focusing on the sights that interest you most. As you plan, keep in mind geographic proximity (don't waste energy zigzagging back and forth across town); days and hours attractions are open; and applicable warnings about arriving early to avoid long lines or secure necessary tickets. "Special Passes for VIP Tours" in "Before You Go" (Chapter 2) tells you how to obtain tickets ahead of time for VIP tours to some attractions.

Since friends whom I've personally counseled to take it easy while sightseeing in Washington have wound up exhausting themselves, I suspect that my advice to program relaxation into your touring day will go unheeded. For the record, I suggest an occasional long leisurely lunch and visits to relaxing outdoor attractions. Tour the beautiful gardens at Dumbarton Oaks, take a river cruise, or plan a picnic at the Arboretum—anything that gets you off your museum-weary feet for a while. Speaking of those feet, you'll be on them a lot in Washington. Comfortable shoes are essential to bearing up under the rigors of sightseeing; during sweltering summer days running shoes, shorts, and a T-shirt (or whatever minimum attire you feel comfortable with) is the ideal outfit.

Most museums offer highlight tours (call in advance for exact hours)—a good way to get a useful overview in a short time.

The good news: Almost everything is free.

SUGGESTED ITINERARIES

IF YOU HAVE 1 DAY Make the Mall your destination, visiting whichever museums best suit your interests. Rest up, have a leisurely dinner (this advice goes for every day's itinerary), and visit the Lincoln Memorial at night.

IF YOU HAVE 2 DAYS Spend your first day as suggested above. Start your second day with a tour of the Capitol, followed by a tour of the Supreme Court. After a relaxing lunch, spend the afternoon visiting the Washington Monument, walking around the Tidal Basin, and seeing the Jefferson Memorial. If the weather makes this plan unfeasible, continue visiting Mall museums (you won't even have scratched the surface in one day). Have dinner in Georgetown and browse the shops.

IF YOU HAVE 3 DAYS Spend your first two days as outlined above.

In the morning of your third day, tour the White House and the National Archives. In the afternoon, visit the Vietnam Veterans Memorial, and, if you haven't already done so, the Lincoln Memorial. Or in bad weather, tour the Washington National Cathedral or some of the non-Mall art museums (for example, the Phillips Collection, National Portrait Gallery, Museum of American Art, or the Corcoran). See Chapter 9 for evening suggestions.

IF YOU HAVE 5 DAYS OR MORE Spend your first three days as suggested above.

On the fourth day, get an early start taking the FBI tour, and spend the rest of the morning at Ford's Theatre. Spend the afternoon in outdoor activities—the zoo, a hike along the C&O Canal, the museum and gardens at Dumbarton Oaks, or the Arboretum Or in bad weather, visit the indoor U.S. Botanic Garden and Union Station. See Chapter 9 for evening suggestions.

On the fifth day, plan an entire day visiting Alexandria, Virginia. Or spend the morning touring Mount Vernon and the afternoon seeing the sights you've missed. See Chapter 9 for evening suggestions

1. THE TOP ATTRACTIONS

Although these are the sights most tourists choose to visit in Washington, they may or may not strike you as major, and nowhere is it written that you must see them all. You might want to consider other sights and outdoor activities (listed later in this chapter) when planning your itinerary

THE THREE MAJOR HOUSES OF GOVERNMENT

Three of the most visited sights in Washington are the buildings housing the executive, legislative, and judicial branches of the U.S. government. All stunning edifices, they offer considerable insight into the workings of our system.

THE WHITE HOUSE, 1600 Pennsylvania Ave. NW (visitor entrance gate on E. Executive Ave.). Tel. 456-7041 or 755-7798.

Note: In the spring of 1995, a new White House Visitor Center will open on Pennsylvania Avenue between 14th and 15th Streets in the Department of Commerce Building. It will become the new ticket center and offer exhibits and interactive videos about the White House.

"I never forget," said Franklin Delano Roosevelt in one of his fireside chats, "that I live in a house owned by all the American people." Not only do Americans own the White House, they're welcome to visit, making it almost unique among world residences of heads of state. The White House has been the scene of many great moments in American history. It is the central theater of government, where decisions on national and international policies are made. And, of course, it's also the private home of the president and his family, their personal doings and dramas as much a focus of national interest as any happenings in the political arena. Its interior is a repository of art and furnishings, reflecting the tastes of our chief executives and first ladies from the early years of the American Republic. Highlights of the tour include the following rooms:

The gold-and-white **East Room,** scene of great and gala receptions, weddings of presidents' daughters (Lynda Bird Johnson, for

---

FROMMER'S FAVORITE WASHINGTON EXPERIENCES

A Picnic Along the C&O Canal Hike the scenic canal towpath from Georgetown (about 3 miles) to Fletcher's Boat House where there are picnic tables and grills Spend the day—bring kites, watercolors, whatever

Afternoon Tea Fresh-baked scones with homemade preserves and Devonshire cream, finger sandwiches, and pots of your favorite tea. See listings on p. 148.

A Day in Alexandria Just a short Metro ride from the District is George Washington's Virginia hometown Roam the quaint cobblestone streets, browse charming boutiques and antiques stores, visit the boyhood home of Robert E. Lee and other historic attractions, and dine in one of Alexandria's fine restaurants

N

National Zoological Park

24th St.
California St.
23rd St.
Florida Ave.
New Hampshire Ave.

R St.
Massachusetts Ave.
Dupont Circle

Wisconsin Ave.
Q St.
29th St.
30th St.
31st St.
28th St.
33rd St.
34th St.
P St.
O St.
Connecticut Ave.
Rhode Island Ave.
M St.

N St.
M St.
Washington Circle
29
New Hampshire Ave.
19th St.
18th St.
L St.
K St.
Farragut Square
McPher Squar

Francis Scott Key Mem. Bridge
Georgetown Channel
Pennsylvania Ave.
I St.
H St.
Lafayett Square
The White Hou

Theodore Roosevelt Island
Virginia Ave.
22nd St.
21st St.
20th St.
G St.
F St.
E St.
Constitution Hall
The Ellipse

Theodore Roosevelt Mem. Bridge
Constitution A
Washingto Monumer

Arlington Mem. Bridge
Reflecting Pool
Kutz Bridge
Tidal Basin

Arlington National Cemetery
66
Potomac River
Jefferson Memorial

Rock Creek

Arts and Industries Building ⑱	Freer Gallery of Art ⑮
Arthur M. Sackler Gallery ⑯	Hirshhorn Museum
Bureau of Engraving	& Sculpture Garden ⑲
and Printing ⑭	Jefferson Memorial ⑫
Capitol ㉜	John F. Kennedy Center
Constitution Hall ⑧	for the Performing Arts ⑤
Corcoran Gallery ⑨	Library of Congress ㉞
Dumbarton Oaks ②	Lincoln Memorial ⑥
Federal Bureau of Investigation ㉕	National Air and Space
Folger Shakespeare Library ㉟	Museum ⑳
Ford's Theatre	National Archives ㉖
& Lincoln Museum ㉔	

WASHINGTON, D.C., ATTRACTIONS

one), and other dazzling events. Here, heads of state have been entertained, seven presidents who died in office lay in state, and Nixon delivered his resignation speech. The room is decorated in the early 20th-century style of the Theodore Roosevelt renovation, with parquet Fontainebleau oak floors and white-painted wood walls with fluted pilasters and relief inserts illustrating Aesop's fables. Note the famous Gilbert Stuart portrait of George Washington that Dolley Madison saved from the British torch during the War of 1812.

The **Green Room** (named in the 19th century for its green upholstery), today used as a sitting room, was Thomas Jefferson's dining room. He designed a revolving door with trays on one side, so servants could leave dishes on the kitchen side. Then he would twirl the door, take the food from the shelves, and serve his own guests. Thus he retained his privacy. Walls here are covered in green watered-silk fabric, and some of the early 19th-century furnishings are attributed to the famous cabinetmaker Duncan Phyfe. There are notable paintings by Gilbert Stuart and John Singer Sargent.

The oval **Blue Room,** where presidents and first ladies have officially received guests since the Jefferson administration, is today decorated in the French Empire style chosen by James Monroe in 1817. It was, however, Van Buren's decor that began the "blue room" tradition. The walls, on which hang portraits of five presidents (including Rembrandt Peale's portrait of Thomas Jefferson and G. P. A. Healy's of Tyler), are covered in a reproduction of French Directoire paper from 1800, and a settee and seven of the original gilded armchairs Monroe ordered from French cabinetmaker Pierre-Antoine Bellangé remain. Grover Cleveland, the only president ever to wed in the White House, was married in the Blue Room; the Reagans, Nancy wearing symbolic yellow, here greeted the 53 Americans returned after being held hostage in Iran for 444 days; and every year it's the setting for the White House Christmas tree.

Several portraits of past presidents—plus Albert Bierstadt's *View of the Rocky Mountains* and a Gilbert Stuart portrait of Dolley Madison—hang in the **Red Room.** It's used as a reception room, usually for small dinners. The satin-covered walls and most of the Empire furnishings are red, with white wainscoting and moldings.

The white-walled, gold-accented **State Dining Room** is a superb setting for state dinners and luncheons. Its architecture is modeled after late 18th-century neoclassical English houses. Theodore Roosevelt, a big-game hunter, had a large moose head over the fireplace and other trophies on the walls. Below G. P. A. Healy's portrait of Lincoln is an inscription written by John Adams on his second night in the White House (FDR had it carved into the mantel): "I Pray Heaven to Bestow The Best of Blessings on THIS HOUSE and on All that shall hereafter Inhabit it. May none but Honest and Wise Men ever rule under This Roof."

History   Since its cornerstone was laid in 1792, the White House has gone through numerous changes. It was designed by Irishman James Hoban, so it isn't surprising that it resembles the house of the duke of Leinster of Dublin. The South Portico was added in 1824, the North Portico in 1829. Electricity was first installed during Benjamin Harrison's presidency in 1891.

In 1902, repairs and refurnishings of the White House cost almost $500,000. No other great change took place until Harry Truman added his controversial "balcony" inside the columns of the South Portico. Also in 1948, after the leg of Margaret Truman's piano cut through the dining room ceiling, nearly $6 million was allotted for reconstruction of the building. The Trumans lived at Blair House across the street for four years while the White House interior was taken apart and put back together again, piece by piece. Steel girders and concrete shored up the place. It's as solid as Gibraltar now.

In 1961 Mrs. John F. Kennedy formed a Fine Arts Committee to help restore the famous rooms to their original grandeur. Her artistic touch will be in evidence for generations to come.

Seeing the White House   More than 1.2 million people line up annually to see the Executive Mansion. Your best bet is to obtain tickets in advance from your congressperson or senator for the VIP tours at 8:15, 8:30, and 8:45am (see Chapter 2 for details). This will ensure your entrance, even during the tourist season when more than 6,000 people try to squeeze in during the two hours each day the White House is open. It will also entitle you to a more extensive—and guided tour; during the regular visiting hours, there are guides on hand to answer questions, but no actual tour is given. A good idea, before you take any tour, is to pick up a book called *The White House: An Historic Guide,* available in District bookstores and at many of the top sights. Then you'll know what to look for in each room, and your experience will be greatly enhanced. You can order it in advance (as well as another book, *The Living White House,* which gives more biographical information about the presidents and their families) from the **White House Historical Association,** 740 Jackson Place NW, Washington, DC 20503 (tel. 202/737-8292). Send $5.75 for a paperback or $7.50 for a hardcover edition of either book.

Most of the year, if you don't have VIP tour tickets, you just join the line at the East Gate before 10am (visitors enter in groups between 10am and noon). Arrive early to be sure to get in. *Note: Between Memorial Day and Labor Day tickets are required.* They are available (only one per person) at one of the kiosks on the Ellipse (at 15th Street and Constitution Avenue NW) beginning at 8am on the day of your visit only; lines begin forming even earlier. There's no charge. Once you've obtained your ticket (the tour time is stamped on it), you can go to a nearby hotel for breakfast, such as the Washington at 15th Street and Pennsylvania Avenue, or the classier, and pricier, Hay-Adams at 1200 16th St. Or you can sit and wait in the bleachers while glee clubs and bands entertain.

Admission: Free.

Open: Tues–Sat 10am–noon. **Closed:** Some days for official functions; check before leaving your hotel by calling the above 24-hour number. **Metro:** McPherson Square

THE CAPITOL, at the east end of the Mall, entrance on E. Capitol St. and 1st St. NW. Tel. 225-6827.

⭐ As our most tangible national symbol since its first wing was completed in 1800, and the place where all our laws are debated, the Capitol is perhaps the most important edifice in the United States. It's also one of the most beautiful. Historian Allan Nevins called it "the spirit of America in stone." For 134 years it sheltered not only both houses of Congress but the Supreme Court, and for 97 years the Library of Congress as well.

On the massive bronze doors leading to the **Rotunda** are portrayals of events in the life of Columbus. The Rotunda—a huge circular hall some 97 feet across and under a 180-foot dome—is the hub of the Capitol. Nine presidents have lain in state here; when Kennedy's casket was displayed, the line of mourners stretched 40 blocks. On the circular walls are eight immense oil paintings of events in American history, such as the reading of the Declaration of Independence and the surrender of Cornwallis at Yorktown. In the dome is an allegorical fresco masterpiece by Constantino Brumidi, *Apotheosis of Washington,* a symbolic portrayal of George Washington surrounded by Greek gods and goddesses watching over the progress of the nation. A trompe l'oeil frieze overhead depicts events in American history from Columbus through the Wright brothers' flight at Kitty Hawk. There's also a life-size marble statue of Lincoln.

National Statuary Hall was originally the chamber of the House of Representatives. In 1864 it became Statuary Hall, and the states were invited to send two statues each of native sons and daughters to the hall. As the room filled up, statues spilled over into the Hall of Columns, corridors, and anywhere that might accommodate the bronze and marble artifacts. Many of the statues honor individuals who have had important roles in American history, such as Henry Clay, Ethan Allen, and Daniel Webster.

The south and north wings are occupied by the House and Senate chambers, respectively. The House of Representatives chamber is the largest legislative chamber in the world. The president delivers his annual State of the Union address there.

Seeing the Capitol As at the White House, VIP tour tickets from a congressperson or senator for the morning tours (between 8 and 9am) are a definite advantage (see Chapter 2 for details). Also

---

IMPRESSIONS

The Capitol is the first temple dedicated to the sovereignty of the people, embellishing with Athenian taste the course of a nation looking far beyond the range of Athenian destinies.
—Thomas Jefferson

It is our national center. It belongs to us, and whether it is mean or majestic, whether arrayed in glory or covered with shame, we cannot but share its character and its destiny.
—Frederick Douglass

request visitors' passes for each member of your party to view a session of the House and/or Senate. If you don't get advance tickets, free 30-minute guided tours leave from the Rotunda every 15 minutes (more often in spring and summer) between 9am and 3:45pm. And if you don't receive visitors' passes in the mail (not every senator or representative sends them), they're obtainable at your senators' office on the Constitution Avenue side of the building or your representative's office on the Independence Avenue side (noncitizens can just present a passport at the first-floor appointment desk on the Senate side or at the third-floor House gallery and ask for a pass). You'll know when the House or Senate is in session when you see flags flying over their respective wings of the Capitol. Or you can check the weekday "Today in Congress" column in the *Washington Post* for details on times of House and Senate committee meetings. This column also tells you which sessions are open to the public, allowing you to pick one that interests you.

Admission: Free.

Open: Daily 9am–4:30pm (tours 9am–3:45pm). The Rotunda is open till 8pm Memorial Day–Labor Day most years (this is decided each year). **Closed:** Jan 1, Thanksgiving Day, and Dec 25. **Metro:** Capitol South. **Parking:** Union Station.

SUPREME COURT, east of the Capitol on 1st St. NE, between E. Capitol St. and Maryland Ave. Tel. 479-3000.

⭐ In these oft-turbulent times, I find it reassuring to visit the massive Corinthian marble palace that houses the Supreme Court, its serene classical dignity reinforced by the pledge etched in a frieze over the colonnaded entrance: "Equal Justice Under Law." The Court's subtle excitement is well described by Justice Oliver Wendell Holmes, Jr., who wrote, "We are very quiet . . . but it is the quiet of a storm center." The highest tribunal in the nation, the Supreme Court is charged with deciding whether actions of Congress, the president, the states, and lower courts are in accord with the Constitution and with interpreting that document's enduring principles and applying them to new situations and changing conditions. It has the power of "judicial review"—authority to invalidate legislation or executive action that conflicts with the Constitution. Out of the 6,500 cases submitted to it each year, the Supreme Court hears only about 120 cases, many of which deal with issues vital to the nation. The Court's rulings are final, reversible only by another Supreme Court decision, or in some cases, an Act of Congress or a Constitutional amendment.

Until 1935 the Supreme Court met in the Capitol. Architect Cass Gilbert designed the stately Corinthian marble palace that houses the Court today. The building was considered rather grandiose by early residents: One justice remarked that he and his colleagues ought to enter such pompous precincts on elephants.

If you're in town when the Court is in session, try to see a case being argued. The Court meets Monday through Wednesday from 10am to 3pm (with a lunch-hour recess from noon to 1pm) from the first Monday in October through late April, alternating, in approximately two-week intervals, between "sittings" to hear cases and deliver opinions and "recesses" for consideration of business before the Court. Mid-May to early July, you can attend brief sessions (about 15 minutes) at 10am on Monday, when the justices release orders and opinions. You can find out what cases are on the docket by checking the *Washington Post*'s "Supreme Court Calendar." Arrive at least an hour early—even earlier for a highly publicized case—to line up for seats, about 150 of which are allotted to the general public.

At 10am the entrance of the justices is announced by the marshal, and all present rise and remain standing while the justices are seated following the chant: "The Honorable, the Chief Justice and Associate Justices of the Supreme Court of the United States. Oyez! Oyez! Oyez! [French for "Hear ye!"] All persons having business before the Honorable, the Supreme Court of the United States, are admonished to draw near and give their attention, for the Court is now sitting. God save the United States and this Honorable Court!" There are many rituals here. Unseen by the gallery is the "conference handshake"; following a 19th-century tradition symbolizing a "harmony of aims if not views," each Justice shakes hand with each of the other eight when they assemble to go to the bench. The Court has a record before it of prior proceedings and relevant briefs, so each side is allowed only a 30-minute argument.

If the Court is not in session during your visit, you can attend a free **lecture** in the courtroom about Court procedure and the building's architecture. Lectures are given from 9:30am to 3:30pm every hour on the half hour.

After the talk, explore the Great Hall and go down a flight of steps to see the 20-minute film on the workings of the Court. The ground floor is a good vantage point to view one of two grand spiral staircases here similar to those at the Vatican and the Paris Opéra. There are also interesting exhibits and a gift shop on this level, and good meals are served at the adjoining cafeteria (see "Restaurants at Sightseeing Attractions," in Chapter 6, for details).

Admission: Free.

Open: Mon–Fri 9am–4:30pm. Closed: Weekends and all federal holidays. Metro: Capitol South or Union Station.

TRIUMVIRATE OF PRESIDENTIAL MEMORIALS

Only three American presidents have been singled out for recognition with great monuments in Washington, D.C.: George Washington, Abraham Lincoln, and Thomas Jefferson.

The first monument to be built (to Washington) was begun in 1848, the last (to Jefferson) was dedicated in 1943 during cherry-blossom time. There are wreath-laying ceremonies on (or close to) Lincoln's and Jefferson's birthdays at their respective monuments.

WASHINGTON MONUMENT, directly south of the White House at 15th St. and Constitution Ave. NW. Tel. 426-6839.

The 555-foot stark marble obelisk that shimmers in the sun and glows under floodlights at night is the city's most visible landmark. It is, like the Eiffel Tower in Paris or London's Big Ben, a symbol of the city.

The idea of a tribute to George Washington first arose 16 years before his death at the Continental Congress of 1783. An equestrian statue was planned, and Washington himself approved the site for it—on the Mall, west of the future Capitol and south of the "President's Palace." However, more than a century elapsed before a very different monument was completed. The new nation had more pressing problems, and funds were not readily available. It wasn't until the early 1830s, with the 100th anniversary of Washington's birth approaching, that any action was taken. Then there were several fiascos. A mausoleum was provided for Washington's remains under the Capitol Rotunda, but a grand-nephew, citing Washington's will, refused to allow the body to be moved from Mount Vernon. In 1830 Horatio Greenough was commissioned to create a memorial statue for the Rotunda. He came up with a bare-chested, seated Washington, draped in classical Greek garb; a shocked public claimed he looked as if he were "entering or leaving a bath," and so the statue was relegated to the Smithsonian. Finally, in 1833 prominent citizens organized the Washington National Monument Society. Treasury Building architect Robert Mills's design (originally with a circular colonnaded Greek temple base, but later discarded for lack of funds) was accepted. The cornerstone was laid on July 4, 1848; for the next 37 years, watching the monument grow—or not grow—was a local pastime. The Civil War and lagging funds brought construction to a halt at an awkward 150 feet. The unsightly stump remained until 1876 when President Grant approved federal monies to complete the project. Rejecting plans for ornate embellishment that ranged from English Gothic to Hindu pagoda designs, authorities put the U.S. Army Corps of Engineers to work on the obelisk. Dedicated in 1885, it was opened to the public in 1888.

The 360° views are spectacular. To the east are the Capitol and Smithsonian buildings; to the north, the White House; to the west, the Lincoln and Vietnam memorials, and Arlington National Cemetery beyond; and to the south, the gleaming-white shrine to Thomas Jefferson and the Potomac River. It's a marvelous orientation to the city.

During the tourist season, arrive before 8am to avoid long lines. Climbing the 897 steps is verboten, but a large elevator whisks

---

IMPRESSIONS

May the spirit of which animated the great founder of this city descend to future generations.
—JOHN ADAMS

Every dedicated American could be proud that a dynamic experience of democracy in his nation's capital had been made visible to the world.
—MARTIN LUTHER KING, JR., after the 1963 March on Washington

visitors to the top in just 70 seconds. If, however, you're avid to see more of the interior, **"Down the Steps" tours** are given, subject to staff availability, weekends at 10am and 2pm (more often in summer). For details, call before you go or ask a ranger on duty. On this tour you'll learn more about the building of the monument and get to see the 193 carved stones inserted into the interior walls. They range from a piece of stone from the Parthenon to plaques presented by city fire departments.

Light snacks are sold at a snack bar on the grounds, where you'll also find a few picnic tables. There's free two-hour parking at the 16th Street Oval.

Admission: Free.

Open: First Sun in Apr–Labor Day, daily 8am–midnight; the rest of the year, daily 9am–5pm. Last elevators depart 15 minutes before closing. **Closed:** July 4 (usually) and Dec 25. **Metro:** Smithsonian; then a 10-minute walk.

LINCOLN MEMORIAL, directly west of the Mall in Potomac Park, at 23rd St. NW, between Constitution and Independence Ave. Tel. 426-6895.

The Lincoln Memorial attracts some 6 million visitors annually. It's a beautiful and moving testament to a great American, its marble walls seeming to embody not only the spirit and integrity of Lincoln, but all that has ever been good about America. Visitors are silently awed in its presence.

The monument was a long time in the making. Although it was planned as early as 1867, two years after Lincoln's death, it was not until 1912 that Henry Bacon's design was completed, and the memorial itself was dedicated in 1922.

A beautiful neoclassical templelike structure, similar in architectural design to the Parthenon in Greece, the memorial has 36 fluted Doric columns representing the states of the Union at the time of Lincoln's death, plus two at the entrance. On the attic parapet are 48 festoons symbolic of the number of states in 1922 when the monument was erected. Hawaii and Alaska are noted in an inscription on the terrace. To the west, the Arlington Memorial Bridge crossing the Potomac recalls the reunion of North and South. To the east is the beautiful Reflecting Pool, lined with American elms and stretching 2,000 feet toward the Washington Monument and the Capitol beyond.

The memorial chamber, under 60-foot ceilings, has limestone walls inscribed with the Gettysburg Address and Lincoln's Second Inaugural Address. Two 60-foot murals by Jules Guerin on the north and south walls depict, allegorically, Lincoln's principles and achievements. On the south wall, an Angel of Truth freeing a slave is flanked by groups of figures representing Justice and Immortality. The north-wall mural depicts the unity of North and South and is flanked by groups of figures symbolizing Fraternity and Charity. Most powerful, however, is Daniel Chester French's 19-foot-high seated statue of Lincoln in deep contemplation in the central chamber. Its effect is best evoked by these words of Walt Whitman: "He was a mountain in grandeur of soul, he was a sea in deep

? DID YOU KNOW . . . ?

- Architect Pierre L'Enfant's bill for designing Washington came to $95,000; years later he finally accepted Congress's offer of $2,500.
- In 1835 Pres. Andrew Jackson paid off the national debt; it was the first—and last—time in U.S. history that the federal books have been balanced.
- Ambassadors to Washington in the early days were given "hardship pay" for enduring the inconveniences of living there.
- The classic novel *Little Lord Fauntleroy* was written by Frances Hodgson Burnett on I Street in 1886.
- A famous beverage was concocted for a Missouri lobbyist, Col. J. K. Rickey; originally rye whiskey was used, but later some "barbarous New Yorkers" substituted gin—hence, "Gin Rickey."

undervoice of mystic loneliness, he was a star in steadfast purity of purpose and service and he abides." It is appropriate to the heritage of Lincoln that on several occasions those who have been oppressed have expressed their plight to America and the world at the steps of his shrine. Most notable was a peaceful demonstration of 200,000 people on August 28, 1963, at which another freedom-loving American, Dr. Martin Luther King, Jr., proclaimed "I have a dream."

An information booth and bookstore are on the premises. Ranger talks are given on request.

Admission: Free.

Open: Daily 24 hours; park staff on duty 8am–midnight. **Metro:** Foggy Bottom; then about a 15-minute walk.

JEFFERSON MEMORIAL, south of the Washington Monument on Ohio Dr., at the south shore of the Tidal Basin. Tel. 426-6822.

Pres. John F. Kennedy, at a 1962 dinner honoring 29 Nobel Prize winners, told his guests they were "the most extraordinary collection of talent, of human knowledge, that has ever been gathered together at the White House, with the possible exception of when Thomas Jefferson dined alone." Jefferson penned the Declaration of Independence, spoke out against slavery, and was George Washington's secretary of state, John Adams's vice president, and our third president. And he still found time to establish the University of Virginia and to pursue wide-ranging interests including architecture, astronomy, anthropology, music, and farming.

The site for the Jefferson Memorial, in relation to the Washington and Lincoln memorials, was of extraordinary importance. The Capitol, the White House, and the Mall were already located in accordance with L'Enfant's plan, and there was no spot for such a project if the symmetry that guided L'Enfant was to be maintained. So the memorial was built on land reclaimed from the Potomac River, now known as the Tidal Basin. Franklin Delano Roosevelt had all the trees between the Jefferson Memorial and the White House cut down, so that he could see it every morning and draw inspiration from it.

It's a beautiful memorial, a columned rotunda in the style of the Pantheon in Rome, which Jefferson so admired. On the Tidal Basin side, the sculptural group above the entrance depicts Jefferson with

Benjamin Franklin, John Adams, Roger Sherman, and Robert Livingston, who worked on drafting the Declaration of Independence. The domed interior of the memorial contains the 19-foot bronze statue of Jefferson standing on a 6-foot pedestal of black Minnesota granite. The sculpture is the work of Rudulph Evans, who was chosen from more than 100 artists in a nationwide competition. Jefferson is depicted wearing a fur-collared coat given to him by his close friend, the Polish general, Tadeusz Kosciuszko. Inscriptions from Jefferson's writing engraved on the interior walls expand on Jefferson's philosophy, which is best expressed in the circular frieze quotation: "I have sworn upon the altar of God eternal hostility against every form of tyranny over the mind of man."

Park rangers give short talks to visitors on request. Spring through fall, a refreshment kiosk at the Tourmobile stop offers snack fare. A bookshop is on the premises. There's free one-hour parking.

Admission: Free.

Open: Daily 24 hours; park staff on duty 8am–midnight.
Transportation: Tourmobile.

SMITHSONIAN INSTITUTION

No longer referred to as "the nation's attic," which seemed somewhat musty, the Smithsonian Institution has been redubbed, "the nation's showcase." That doesn't totally explain the Smithsonian either, for its collection of more than 140 million objects pertains to the entire world and its history, as well as its peoples and animals (past and present) and our attempts to probe into the future. The sprawling institution employs about 6,000 people, who are assisted by almost as many volunteers. Nine immense Smithsonian buildings are located between the Washington Monument and the Capitol on the Mall. Other buildings devoted to specialized exhibits are within walking distance of the Mall. And farther out, the National Zoological Park (the zoo) and the Anacostia Museum are also Smithsonian responsibilities. Thousands of scientific expeditions sponsored by the Smithsonian have pushed into remote frontiers in the deserts, mountains, polar regions, and jungles. Traveling exhibits are sent to other museums, schools, and libraries. And all this is a mere hint of the Smithsonian's scope and involvement.

The Smithsonian Institution began with a $500,000 bequest from James Smithson, an English scientist who had never visited this country. When he died in 1829, he willed his entire fortune to the United States "to found at Washington an establishment for the increase and diffusion of knowledge. . . ." In 1846 Congress created a corporate entity to carry out Smithson's will, and the federal government agreed to pay 6% interest on the bequeathed funds in perpetuity.

Since then, other munificent private donations have swelled Smithson's original legacy many times over. Major gallery and museum construction through the years stands as testament to thoughtful donors. In 1987 the **Sackler Gallery** (Asian and Near Eastern art) and the **National Museum of African Art** were added to the Smithsonian's Mall attractions. The **National Postal Museum** opened in 1993. And future plans call for moving the **National Museum of the American Indian** (currently in New York) here by the end of the decade.

If you're at the Smithsonian at lunchtime or just want to rest your feet and refuel, check "Restaurants at Sightseeing Attractions" (Chapter 6) for descriptions of the restaurants in the various museums here.

More Information, Please If you want to know what's happening at any of the Smithsonian museums, just get on the phone; **Dial-a-Museum** (tel. 357-2020) will bring you news of special events.

SMITHSONIAN INFORMATION CENTER, 1000 Jefferson Dr. SW. Tel. 357-2700.

For years, visitors were left to explore the intimidatingly vast Smithsonian complex with only a scanty orientation. But that all changed with the 1989 opening of the high-tech Smithsonian Information Center, located in the "Castle" on the Mall. It is appropriately housed in the original Victorian red sandstone Smithsonian building, named for its resemblance to a Norman castle. Today the Castle is fronted by a lovely flower garden and entered via the ornate Oriental-motif Children's Room. Designed at the turn of the century for exhibits displayed at a child's eye level, this charming room has a gold-trimmed ceiling decorated to represent a grape arbor with brightly plumed birds and blue sky peeking through the trellis. Furnishings are peacock-themed, and large Chinese paintings adorn the walls.

The main information area, however, is the Great Hall, where a 20-minute video overview of the institution runs throughout the day in two theaters. There are two large schematic models of the Mall (as well as a third in braille) detailing sights, Metro and Tourmobile stops, as well as major architectural structures. Interactive videos, some of them at children's heights, offer comprehensive information about the Smithsonian and other capital attractions and transportation (the menus seem infinite).

The entire facility is handicapped-accessible, and all information is available in a number of foreign languages. In addition, there's a large light-up map of Washington sights that allows visitors to locate 70 popular attractions electronically; daily Smithsonian events are displayed on monitors; and the information desk's multilingual staff can answer all your questions and help you plan a Smithsonian sightseeing itinerary. James Smithson's crypt is also on the premises.

You can pick up brochures and parking maps here. A stop at the center is highly recommended, especially for first-time visitors to the Smithsonian. Most of the museums are within easy walking distance of the facility.

Open: Daily 9am–5:30pm. **Closed:** Dec 25. **Metro:** Smithsonian.

NATIONAL MUSEUM OF AMERICAN HISTORY, on the north side of the Mall between 12th and 14th Sts. NW,

with entrances on Constitution Ave. and Madison Dr. Tel. 357-2700.

⭐ The National Museum of American History deals with "everyday life in the American past" and the external forces that have helped to shape our national character. Exhibits run the gamut from a Revolutionary War general's tent to Archie Bunker's chair.

Exhibits on the **first floor** (enter on Constitution Avenue) explore the development of farm machines, power machinery, transportation, timekeeping, phonographs, and typewriters. The Palm Court on this level, a turn-of-the-century re-creation, includes the interior of Georgetown's Stohlman's Confectionery Shop as it appeared around 1900 and part of an actual 1902 Horn & Hardart Automat. You can have your mail stamped Smithsonian Station at a post office that had been located in Headsville, West Virginia, from 1861 to 1971, when it was brought lock, stock, and barrel to the museum. An important first-floor exhibit, "A Material World," deals with the changing composition of artifacts—from predominantly natural materials such as wood and stone, to manufactured materials such as steel, to the vast range of synthetics we have today. Also on this level is "Engines of Change: The American Industrial Revolution 1790–1860," which tells the story of America's transformation from an agricultural to an industrial society. "Information Age: People, Information, & Technology," looks at the ways information technology has changed society during the past 150 years. And a vast exhibit called "Science in American Life" analyzes the impact of science on society from the 1870s to the present. Exhibits range from an Indiana fallout shelter to a display on gene-based medical research.

If you enter from the Mall, you'll find yourself on the **second floor** facing the original Star-Spangled Banner, 30 by 42 feet, that inspired Francis Scott Key to write the U.S. national anthem in 1814. "After the Revolution," a major exhibition, focuses on the everyday activities of ordinary 18th-century Americans—their work, family life, and communities. "Field to Factory: Afro-American Migration, 1915–40," is an in-depth study of America's social and demographic history from an African-American perspective. And "American Encounter" on this level commemorates the Columbus quincentennial. Perhaps the most fascinating exhibit is the Foucault Pendulum, a copy of the original model that was exhibited in Paris in 1851 with the accompanying teaser, "You are invited to witness the earth revolve." The heavy pendulum, suspended from the roof, swings monotonously from one side to the other, never varying in its arc, yet knocking over, one by one, a series of red pointers that firm a circle around it. How? The pendulum has an unvarying arc, but the earth revolves beneath it. Also on the second floor you will find the first ladies' gowns displayed in an exhibit called "First Ladies: Political Role and Public Image."

A vast collection of ship models, uniforms, weapons, and other military things is located on the **third floor,** where major exhibits focus on the experiences of GIs in World War II (and the postwar world) as well as the wartime internment of Japanese-Americans. Other areas include Money and Medals, Textiles, Printing and Graphic Arts, and Ceramics. Here, too, is the first American Flag to be called Old Glory (1824).

Inquire at the information desks about highlight tours, Demonstration Center hands-on activities for children and adults, films, lectures, and concerts. Many events are scheduled during holiday periods. There are several museum shops (most noteworthy is the Smithsonian bookstore, offering books and objects on all aspects of Americana), and there is a cheerful cafeteria on the premises.

Admission: Free.

Open: Daily 10am–5:30pm. **Closed:** Dec 25. **Metro:** Smithsonian or Federal Triangle.

NATIONAL MUSEUM OF NATURAL HISTORY, on the north side of the Mall between 9th and 12th Sts. NW, with entrances on Madison Dr. and Constitution Ave. Tel. 357-2700.

The National Museum of Natural History contains more than 120 million artifacts and specimens—everything from one of the largest African elephants ever bagged by a hunter in our time (it dominates the Rotunda on the Mall—entrance level) to the legendary Hope Diamond.

Free highlight **tours** are given daily at 10:30am and 1:30pm, but if you have the time, the self-guided audio tour, narrated by Meryl Streep, provides the most comprehensive commentary on exhibits. It's available at the Rotunda information desk for a nominal fee. A **Discovery Room,** filled with creative hands-on exhibits for children, is on the first floor; it's open Monday to Friday noon to 2:30pm, Saturday and Sunday 10:30am to 3:30pm. Children under 12 must be accompanied by an adult. Tickets are available from 15 minutes prior to opening at the Discovery Room. If you have kids, this is a "must."

On the **Mall Level,** off the Rotunda, evolution is traced back billions of years in Fossils, comprising such exhibits as a 3.5-billion-year-old stromatolite (blue-green algae clump) fossil—one of the earliest signs of life on earth—and a 70-million-year-old dinosaur egg. "Life in the Ancient Seas" features a 100-foot-long mural depicting primitive whales, a life-size walk-around diorama of a 230-million-year-old coral reef, and more than 2,000 fossils that chronicle the evolution of marine life. Dinosaurs, of course, loom large—giant skeletons of creatures that dominated the earth for 140 million years before their extinction about 65 million years ago. On balconies over Dinosaur Hall are exhibits on ancient birds, including a life-size model of the pterosaur, which had a 40-foot wingspan. Also residing above this hall is an ancient shark—or at least the jaw of one, the carcharodon megalodon, that lived in our oceans 5 million years ago. A monstrous 40-foot-long predator, its teeth were 5 to 6 inches long, and it could have consumed a Volkswagen "bug" in one gulp! Here, too: the World of Mammals and Life in the Sea, the latter including a spectacular living coral reef in a

? DID YOU KNOW . . .?

- When the *Washington Post* sponsored a public music competition, John Philip Sousa was asked to compose a march for the awards ceremony; the result was *The Washington Post March,* for which Sousa earned the grand sum of $35.
- The only presidential inauguration ceremony to be held in the White House was that of Franklin D. Roosevelt, in 1941.
- Herbert Hoover was the first president to have a telephone on his desk.
- The desk in the Oval Office, carved from the British ship *Resolute,* was a gift to Rutherford B. Hayes from Queen Victoria.
- The first first lady to fly to a foreign country was Eleanor Roosevelt, in 1934.

3,000-gallon tank. A second 3,000-gallon tank houses a subarctic sea environment typical of the Maine coast. And an exhibit called "In Search of Giant Squid" focuses on the world's largest invertebrates.

On the **second floor,** along with the Hope Diamond, are such dazzling gems as the 182-carat Star of Bombay sapphire that belonged to Mary Pickford, a rare red diamond (one of only five in the world), and Marie Antoinette's diamond earrings. Nearby are geological specimens ranging from meteorites to moon rocks. Kids will enjoy the Orkin Insect Zoo's Plexiglas cages housing tarantulas, centipedes, and the like—not to mention a crawl-through model of an African termite mound (many other fascinating entomological displays here range from cave insects to swamp bugs). Numerous skeletons—from the gigantic extinct Stellar sea cow to the tiny pocket mouse—are displayed in "Bones." Additional exhibits include "South America: Continent and Culture," with objects from the Inca civilization, among others, and "Origin of Western Culture"—from about 10,000 years ago to A.D. 500.

The **ground level** houses changing exhibits.

There's a plant-filled cafeteria off the Rotunda. Museum shops feature books on natural history and anthropology for adults and children, jewelry, crafts, fossil reproduction kits, shells, and more. On the second floor are the Dinostore (all dinosaur merchandise) and a gem and mineral store.

Note: Due to renovations, the Gem and Mineral Hall and the restaurant may be closed during your visit.

Admission: Free.

Open: Daily 10am–5:30pm, with extended hours in summer some years. **Closed:** Dec 25. **Metro:** Smithsonian or Federal Triangle.

NATIONAL AIR AND SPACE MUSEUM, on the south side of the Mall between 4th and 7th Sts. SW, with entrances on Jefferson Dr. or Independence Ave. Tel. 357-2700, 357-1686 for IMAX ticket information.

The National Air and Space Museum chronicles the story of man's mastery of flight—from Kitty Hawk to outer space—in 23 galleries filled with exciting exhibits. Plan to devote at least three or four hours exploring these exhibits and, especially during the tourist season and on holidays, arrive before 10am to make a rush for the film-ticket line when the doors open. The not-to-be-missed **IMAX films** shown in the Samuel P. Langley Theater here, on a screen five stories high and seven stories wide, are immensely popular; tickets tend to sell out quickly. There are five or more films playing each day, most with nature or space-exploration themes. See as many as you have time for. Tickets cost $3.25 for adults, $2 for children 2 to 16, students, and seniors over 55, and are free to children under 2. You can also see IMAX films most evenings after closing (call for details and ticket prices).

You'll also want to catch a show (same prices) at the **Albert Einstein Planetarium,** so after you've purchased IMAX tickets, go to the planetarium ticket booth on the second floor.

In between shows, you can view the exhibits; free 1¹/₂-hour highlight **tours** are given daily at 10:15am and 1pm. Recorded tours, narrated by astronauts, are also available for rental. Interactive computers and slide and video shows enhance the exhibits throughout.

Highlights of the **first floor** include famous airplanes (such as *The Spirit of St. Louis*) and spacecraft (the *Apollo 11* command module); the world's only touchable moon rock; numerous exhibits on the history of aviation and air transportation; galleries in which you learn how a helicopter works, design your own jet plane, and study astronomy; and rockets, lunar-exploration vehicles, manned spacecraft, and guided missiles. A major exhibit on the *Enola Gay,* the plane that dropped the atomic bomb on Hiroshima, will open here in 1995. All the aircraft, by the way, are originals.

Kids love the "walk-through" Skylab orbital workshop on the **second floor.** Other galleries here highlight the solar system, U.S. manned space flights, sea-air operations, aviation during both world wars, and artists' perceptions of flight. An important exhibit is "Beyond the Limits: Flight Enters the Computer Age." Occupying seven exhibit areas, it illustrates the primary applications of computer technology to aerospace.

A very attractive cafeteria and a rather elegant restaurant, **Flight Line** and the **Wright Place,** respectively, are on the premises (see "Restaurants at Sightseeing Attractions" in Chapter 6 for details). And the museum shop sells everything from model kits to freeze-dried astronaut ice cream.

Admission: Free.

Open: Daily 10am–5:30pm (some years the museum has extended hours during East week and in summer). **Closed:** Dec 25. **Metro:** L'Enfant Plaza (Smithsonian Museums exit).

NATIONAL MUSEUM OF AMERICAN ART, 8th and G Sts. NW. Tel. 357-2700.

The NMAA owns more than 35,000 works representing two centuries of our national art history. A rotating sampling of about 1,000 of these works is on display at any given time, along with special exhibitions highlighting various aspects of American art. The collection, along with the National Portrait Gallery (described below), is housed in the palatial quarters of the 19th-century Greek Revival Old Patent Office Building, partially designed by Washington Monument architect Robert Mills and Capitol dome architect

Thomas U. Walter. Philip Johnson called it "the greatest building in the world." Fronted by a columned portico evocative of the Parthenon, it was originally a multipurpose facility housing an eclectic mix of items ranging from the original Declaration of Independence to a collection of shrunken heads.

Twentieth-century art occupies the most exalted setting, the third-floor Lincoln Gallery, with vaulted ceilings and marble columns. In this room, 4,000 revelers celebrated Lincoln's second inaugural in 1865. On view are works of post–World War II artists (de Kooning, Kline, Noguchi, and others). Other 20th-century works on this floor include paintings commissioned during the New Deal era.

Mid- to late-19th-century artists—such as Winslow Homer, Mary Cassatt, Albert Pinkham Ryder, and John Singer Sargent—are on the second floor, as is the Hiram Powers Gallery housing the contents of the 19th-century neoclassic sculptor's Florence studio. Here, too: works by such early American masters as Charles Willson Peale, Benjamin West, and Samuel F. B. Morse.

A unique work of folk art on the first floor is James Hampton's visionary religious piece (completely covered in aluminum and gold foil), *Throne of the Third Heaven of the Nation's Millennium General Assembly.* Other first floor displays include the $1.4-million Herbert Waide Hemphill, Jr., Fold Art Collection (19th and 20th centuries) and an Art of the West Gallery featuring paintings by John Mix Stanley and Charles Bird King, along with George Catlin's Native American portraits from the collection he showed in Paris in the 1840s (the museum owns 445 of them).

When you enter, pick up a map and calendar of events and ask about current temporary exhibits at the information desk. Free walk-in tours are given at noon weekdays and at 2pm Saturday and Sunday. There is a lovely courtyard cafeteria on the premises.

Admission: Free.

Open: Daily 10am–5:30pm. **Closed:** Dec 25. **Metro:** Gallery Place.

THE NATIONAL PORTRAIT GALLERY, 8th and F Sts. NW. Tel. 357-2700.

The "heroes and villains, thinkers and doers, conservatives and radicals" who have made "significant contributions to the history, development, and culture of the United States" are represented here in paintings, sculpture, photography, and other forms of portraiture. Although the museum didn't open until 1968, the concept of a national portrait gallery first arose in the mid-19th century when Congress commissioned G. P. A. Healy to paint a series of presidential portraits for the White House. And American portraiture dates back even further, as evidenced by the Gilbert Stuart and Rembrandt Peale portraits of George and Martha Washington on display here, not to mention those predating the Revolution (of Pocahontas, among others). It's great fun to wander the corridors here, sometimes putting faces to famous names for the first time.

In addition to the Hall of Presidents (on the second floor), notable exhibits include Gilbert Stuart's famed "Lansdowne" portrait of George Washington, a portrait of Mary Cassatt by Degas,

19th-century silhouettes by French-born artist August Edouart, Jo Davidson's sculpture portraits (including a Buddha-like Gertrude Stein), and a self-portrait by John Singleton Copley. On the mezzanine, the Civil War is documented in portraiture, including one of the last photographs ever taken of Abraham Lincoln. Take a look at the magnificent Great Hall on the third floor. Originally designed as a showcase for patent models, it later became a Civil War hospital, where Walt Whitman came frequently to "soothe and relieve wounded troops."

Pick up a calendar of events at the information desk to find out about the museum's comprehensive schedule of temporary exhibits, lunchtime lectures, concerts, films, and dramatic presentations. Walk-in tours are given at varying hours—usually between 10am and 3pm (call 357-2920 for details).

Admission: Free.

Open: Daily 10am–5:30pm. **Closed:** Dec 25. **Metro:** Gallery Place.

RENWICK GALLERY OF THE NATIONAL MUSEUM OF AMERICAN ART, Pennsylvania Ave. and 17th St. NW. Tel. 357-2700.

A department of the National Museum of American Art, the Renwick is housed in a historic mid-1800s landmark building of the French Second Empire style. The original home of the Corcoran Gallery, it was saved from demolition by President Kennedy in 1963, when he recommended that it be renovated as part of the Lafayette Square restoration. In 1965 it became part of the Smithsonian and was renamed for its architect, James W. Renwick, who also designed the Smithsonian "Castle." Although the setting—especially the lavish Octagon Room and the magnificent Victorian Grand Salon with its wainscoted plum walls and 38-foot skylight ceiling—evokes another era, the museum's contents are mostly contemporary. The Renwick is a national showcase for American creativity in crafts. The rich and diverse display of objects here includes both changing exhibitions of contemporary works and pieces dating from 1900 to the present that belong to the museum's permanent collection. Typical exhibits run the gamut from "American Wicker: 1870–1930" to a Louis Comfort Tiffany show. The two abovementioned Victorian galleries on the second floor are furnished in opulent 19th-century style, their walls hung with gilt-framed paintings by 18th- and 19th-century artists.

The Renwick has a comprehensive schedule of events, lectures, concerts, and films. Inquire at the information desk. And check out the museum shop near the entrance for books on crafts, design, and decorative arts, as well as craft items, many of them for children.

Admission: Free.

Open: Daily 10am–5:30pm. **Closed:** Dec 25. **Metro:** Farragut West or Farragut North.

HIRSHHORN MUSEUM AND SCULPTURE GARDEN, on the south side of the Mall at Independence Ave. and 7th St. SW. Tel. 357-2700.

⭐ Latvian-born immigrant Joseph H. Hirshhorn, the 12th of 13 children, came to America in 1905 at the age of 6 with his widowed mother. He dropped out of school at 13, and two years later got his first Wall Street job, earning $12 a week. In 1916 he invested his savings of $255, became a stockbroker, and went on to amass a fortune in the market and in uranium mining. At age 18 he acquired his first works of art—two Dürer etchings—thus beginning a lifelong passion for collecting. Over the years, he amassed the world's most extensive private collection of 20th-century art. In 1966 he donated the entire collection—more than 4,000 drawings and paintings and some 2,000 pieces of sculpture—to the United States "as a small repayment for what this nation has done for me and others like me who arrived here as immigrants." At his death in 1981, Hirshhorn bequeathed an additional 5,500 artworks to the museum; numerous other donors have since greatly expanded Hirshhorn's legacy.

Constructed 14 feet above the ground on sculptured supports, the museum's contemporary cylindrical concrete-and-granite building shelters a verdant plaza courtyard where sculpture is displayed. The light and airy interior follows a simple circular route that makes it easy to see every exhibit without getting lost in a honeycomb of galleries. Natural light from floor-to-ceiling windows makes the inner galleries the perfect venue for viewing sculpture, second only, perhaps, to the magnificently beautiful tree-shaded sunken sculpture garden across the street (don't miss it). Paintings and drawings are installed in the outer galleries, artificially lit to prevent light damage.

A rotating show of about 600 pieces is on view at all times. The collection features just about every well-known 20th-century artist and provides a comprehensive over-view of major trends in Western art from the turn of the century to the present. Among the best-known pieces are Rodin's *The Burghers of Calais*, four bas-reliefs by Matisse known as *The Backs*, and an important collection of the works of Henry Moore.

Pick up a free calendar when you come in to find out about free films, lectures, concerts, and temporary exhibits. Free docent **tours** are given mornings and early afternoons (call for schedule). Art books, posters, and prints are sold at the museum shop.

Admission: Free.

Open: Daily 10am–5:30pm. **Closed:** Dec. 25. **Metro:** L'Enfant Plaza (Smithsonian Museums exit).

ARTHUR M. SACKLER GALLERY, 1050 Independence Ave. SW. Tel. 357-2700.

⭐ Opened in 1987, the Sackler, a museum of Asian art, presents traveling exhibitions from major cultural institutions in Asia, Europe, and the United States. In the recent past, these have focused on such wide-ranging areas as 15th-century Persian art and culture, ancient Buddhist and Hindu sculpture from Sri Lanka, Chinese porcelain, 19th-century Japanese woodblock prints, and the opulent court arts of Indonesia. Supplementing these exhibits are items from the permanent collection, which includes Chinese bronzes from the Shang (1700–1028 B.C.) through the Han (206

B.C.–A.D. 220) dynasties; Chinese jade figures spanning the millennia from 3000 B.C. to the 20th century; Chinese paintings and lacquerware (from the 10th through the 20th century); 20th-century Japanese ceramics and works on paper; ancient Near Eastern works in silver, gold, bronze, and clay; and stone and bronze sculptures from South and Southeast Asia. Since the museum's opening, Sackler's original gift has been enhanced by significant collections such as the Vever assemblage of 11th- to 19th-century Persian and Indian paintings, manuscripts, calligraphies, miniatures, and book-bindings.

Architecturally, but in no other way, the Sackler is linked to the adjoining National Museum of African Art in a complex housing both facilities. Although 96% of the buildings' exhibition space is subterranean, there are two above-ground pavilions, both designed to harmonize with neighboring landmark buildings. The pyramidal silhouette of the Sackler is related to the Victorian Arts and Industries Building, and its exterior is faced with dark-beige Rockville granite. Subterranean areas are enlivened by dramatic descents, vast north-facing skylights, a spacious concourse, and lush plantings. Roofing material is copper, treated to oxidize green as it ages. The Sackler shares its staff and research facilities with the adjacent Freer Gallery and is connected to it via an underground exhibition space.

While you are visiting, be sure to browse the vast gallery shop, which offers a wide array of books on Asian art, posters, and art reproductions, along with marvelous gifts—Indian mirrorwork fabrics, Balinese masks, jade jewelry, Japanese kimonos, bonsai kits, and much more. For information about museum programs (including many wonderful experiences for children and families), highlight tours (highly recommended), films, events, and temporary exhibits, inquire at the information desk.

Admission: Free.

Open: Daily 10am–5:30pm. **Closed:** Dec 25. **Metro:** Smithsonian.

NATIONAL MUSEUM OF AFRICAN ART, 950 Independence Ave. SW. Tel. 357-2700 or 357-4600.

This is the only national art museum in the United States devoted to research in, and the collection and exhibition of, African art. Founded in 1964, and part of the Smithsonian since 1979, it moved to the Mall in 1987 to share a building (though not an entrance) with the Sackler Gallery (see above). Its domed pavilions reflect the arch motif of the neighboring Freer.

Although the museum collects and exhibits ancient and contemporary art from the entire African continent, its permanent collection more than 7,000 objects (shown in rotating exhibits) highlights the traditional arts of the vast sub-Saharan region. Most of the collection dates from the 19th and 20th centuries, with works from the western part of Sudan and the Guinea Coast particularly well represented. Also among the museum's holdings are the Eliot Elisofon Photographic Archives, comprising 300,000 photographic prints and transparencies and 120,000 feet of film on African arts and culture. Permanent exhibits include a display of Royal Benin art from Nigeria, "The Art of the Personal Object" (everyday items such as chairs, headrests, snuff boxes, bowls, and baskets), and "Purpose and Perfection: Pottery as a Woman's Art in Central Africa." Specific objects or themes are explored in depth in a small exhibition space called the Point of View Gallery.

Inquire at the desk about special exhibits, workshops (including excellent children's programs), storytelling, lectures, docent-led tours, films, and demonstrations. A comprehensive events schedule here (together with exhibitions) provides a unique opportunity to learn about the diverse cultures and visual traditions of Africa.

Admission: Free.

Open: Daily 10am–5:30pm. **Closed:** Dec. 25. **Metro:** Smithsonian.

ENID A. HAUPT GARDEN, 10th St. and Independence Ave. SW. Tel. 357-2700.

With its central parterre and 1870s cast-iron furnishings, elaborate flower beds and borders, plant-filled turn-of-the-century urns, and lush baskets hung from 19th-century-style lampposts, this tranquil, beautiful oasis on the Mall is named for its donor, a noted supporter of horticultural projects. Although on ground level, it's really a rooftop garden above the subterranean Sackler and African art museums. The magnolia-lined parterre has multicolored swags and ribbon beds adapted from the 1876 Philadelphia Centennial Exposition's horticultural hall. The swags are composed of 30,000 green and yellow Alternanthera, supplemented by seasonal displays of spring pansies, begonias, or cabbage and kale. A winter Oriental garden near the Sackler Gallery, entered via a 9-foot moongate, has benches backed by English boxwoods under the shade of weeping cherry trees; half-round pieces of granite in its still pool are meant to suggest ripples. A summer Islamic garden outside the African art museum provides granite seating walls shaded by hawthorn trees, with tiny water channels fed by fountains and a waterfall or "chadar" inspired by the gardens of Shalimar. Three small terraces, shaded by black sour gum trees, are located near the Arts and Industries Building. And five majestic linden trees shade a seating area around the Downing Urn, a memorial to American landscapist Andrew Jackson Downing. Additional features include wisteria-covered dome-shaped trellises, clusters of trees (Zumi crabapples, ginkgoes, and American hollies), a weeping European beech, and rose gardens. Elaborate cast-iron carriage gates made according to a 19th-century design by James Renwick, flanked by four pillars made from the same red Seneca sandstone used to construct the "castle," have been installed at the Independence Avenue entrance to the garden.

Admission: Free.

Open: Memorial Day–Labor Day, daily 7am–8pm; the rest of the year, daily 7am–5:45pm. **Closed:** Dec 25. **Metro:** Smithsonian.

NATIONAL POSTAL MUSEUM, 2 Massachusetts Ave. NE, at 1st St. Tel. 357-2700.

This newest addition to the Smithsonian complex (opened in 1993) appropriately occupies the palatial beaux arts quarters of the

City Post Office Building designed by brilliant architect Daniel Burnham. Created to house and display the Smithsonian's national philatelic and postal history collection of more than 16 million objects, it is, somewhat surprisingly, a great deal of fun to visit. Dozens of intriguing interactive exhibits range from Nickelodeon "films" about train wrecks and robberies to a video game that challenges visitors to get 20 bags of mail from Philadelphia to New Orleans in the 1850s via train, boat, or stagecoach. The game is programmed so that 17,000 problems can arise en route! The museum documents America's postal history from 1673 (about 170 years before the advent of stamps, envelopes, and mailboxes) to the present.

In the central gallery, titled "Moving the Mail," three planes that carried mail in the early decades of the 20th century (including a converted World War I bomber) are suspended from a 90-foot atrium ceiling. Here, too: a railway mail car, an 1851 mail/passenger coach, a Ford Model A mail truck, and a replica of an airmail beacon tower atop an oil derrick. In "Binding the Nation," historic correspondence (letters from slaves and Native Americans, from a Revolutionary War soldier to his wife, from immigrants keeping in touch with their relatives back home, and from pioneers during America's westward expansion) illustrate how mail served to bind families together in the developing nation. Several exhibits deal with the famed Pony Express, a service that lasted less than two years but was romanticized to legendary proportions by Buffalo Bill and others. In the Civil War section you'll learn about Henry "Box" Brown, a slave who had himself "mailed" from Richmond to a Pennsylvania abolitionist in 1856. "Customers and Communities" explores how a growing America dealt with the vast increase in mail volume generated by an expanding population—via pneumatic tubes that carried mail underground, mail metering, ZIP Codes, and technological advance. Here you can try to decipher addresses on dead letters, and find out how marketers view the demographics of your ZIP Code. Entertaining exhibits include whimsical folk art mailboxes on rural routes and an array of mail frauds such as an advertisement for a "solar clothes dryer" that turned out to be a clothespin! "The Art of Cards and Letters" gallery displays personal correspondence from World War I through Operation Desert Storm, as well as greeting cards, travel postcards, and disaster postcards documenting earthquakes, fires, and floods; these were popular in the days before newspapers carried photographs. An 800-square-foot gallery focuses on federal duck stamps (first issued in 1934 to license waterfowl hunters), with displays on the hobby of duck hunting and the ecology of American water birds. There are, of course, stamps on display here too, ranging from the rare and valuable to fakes and forgeries. In addition, the museum houses a vast research library for philatelic researchers and scholars, a stamp store, and a museum shop.

Admission: Free.

Open: Daily 10am–5:30pm. **Closed:** Dec 25. **Metro:** Union Station.

FREER GALLERY OF ART, on the south side of the Mall at Jefferson Dr. and 12th St. SW. Tel. 357-2700.

A gift to the nation of 9,000 works from Charles Lang Freer, a collector of Asian art and American works from the 19th and early 20th centuries, the Freer Gallery opened in 1923. Freer's original interest was, in fact, American art, but his good friend James McNeill Whistler encouraged him to collect Asian works as well. Eventually the latter became predominant. Freer's gift included funds to construct a museum and an endowment to add objects of the highest quality to the Asian collection only, which has been greatly augmented over the years. It includes Chinese and Japanese sculpture, printing, lacquer, metalwork, and ceramics; early Christian illuminated manuscripts; Japanese screens and woodblock prints; Chinese jades and bronzes; Korean ceramics; Near Eastern manuscripts, metalwork, and miniatures; ancient Near East metalware; and Indian sculpture, manuscripts, and paintings.

Among the American works, not surprisingly, are more than 1,200 pieces by Whistler, including the famous Peacock Room permanently installed here. Originally a dining room designed by an architect named Thomas Jeckyll for the London mansion of F. R. Leyland, the Peacock Room contained a Whistler painting called *The Princess from the Land of Porcelain.* But after his painting was installed, Whistler was dissatisfied with the room as a setting for his work. When Leyland was away from home, Whistler painted over the very expensive gilded leather interior, embellishing it with paintings of golden peacocks. A permanent rift ensued between Whistler and Leyland. After Leyland's death, Freer purchased the painting and shipped the entire room here from London. Other American painters represented in the collections are Childe Hassam, Thomas Wilmer Dewing, Dwight William Tryon, Abbott Henderson Thayer, and John Singer Sargent. (*Note:* About 90% of the American works are in their original frames, many of them designed by Stanford White or Whistler.)

Housed in an Italian Renaissance–style granite-and-marble building, the Freer is a pleasant museum, with plants and trees adorning its skylit galleries. In 1993, a 4½-year, $26-million expansion and renovation project was completed. The main exhibit floor centers on a garden court open to the sky. There's a museum shop featuring books relating to the collection and reproductions from it; there are wonderful gifts here, too. An underground exhibit space connects the Freer to the neighboring Sackler Gallery. The museum's Meyer Auditorium is the setting for free chamber music concerts, dance performances, Asian feature films, and other programs. Inquire about these, as well as children's programs, at the information desk

Admission: Free.

Open: Daily 10am–5:30pm. **Closed:** Dec 25 **Metro:** Smithsonian (Mall or Independence Avenue exit)

ARTS AND INDUSTRIES BUILDING, on the south side of the Mall at 900 Jefferson Dr. SW. Tel. 357-2700.

Completed in 1881 as the first national museum, this red-brick-and-sandstone structure was the scene of President Garfield's Inaugural Ball. Since 1976 it has housed exhibits from the 1876 United States International Exposition in Philadelphia—a celebration of America's 100th birthday that featured the latest advances in technology. The Exposition was re-created here in 1976 for the Bicentennial. The entrance floor is like a turn-of-the-century mall with display cases of Victorian furnishings, fashions, clocks, musical instruments, tools, photographic equipment, and medicines. In areas off the magnificent central Rotunda there's machinery that probably evoked oohs and aahs in the 19th century—steam and gas engines, printing presses, corn mills, refrigerator compresses, and tool builders, as well as a considerable display of weaponry and vehicles. Some machines are rather large, such as a steam locomotive. There are also state exhibits highlighting California wines, Kansas corn and wheat, Tennessee lumber, and so forth, as well as international displays.

Singers, dancers, puppeteers, and mimes perform in the Discovery Theater (October to July, Tuesday to Saturday—call 357-1500 for show times and ticket information; admission is charged). Don't miss the charming Victorian-motif shop on the first floor that sells books, jam and jellies, china, needlepoint patterns and samplers, antique reproduction dolls, and more. Most of the year, there's a 19th-century carousel in operation across the street.

Admission: Free.

Open: Daily 10am–5:30pm. **Closed:** Dec 25. **Metro:** Smithsonian.

NATIONAL ZOOLOGICAL PARK, adjacent to Rock Creek Park, main entrance in the 3000 block of Connecticut Ave. NW. Tel. 673-4800 or 673-4717.

Established in 1889, the National Zoo is home to more than 5,000 animals of some 500 species, many of them rare and/or endangered. A leader in the care, breeding, and exhibition of animals, it occupies 163 beautifully landscaped acres and is one of the country's most delightful zoos. Star resident is Hsing-Hsing, the giant panda donated by the People's Republic of China. The best time to catch him is at feeding time, 11am and 3pm.

It's best to enter the zoo at the Connecticut Avenue entrance, which puts you right by the Education Building. Here you can pick up a map and, on occasion, see films about animals and activities at the zoo's Conservation and Research Center. Friday through Sunday, you can also get tickets for **ZOOlab** (available on a first-come, first-served basis), a learning lab where visitors can handle and examine such objects as hummingbird eggs, read zoology texts, and peer at specimens through a microscope. Similar in concept is the **Reptile Discovery Center** (for the study of reptiles and amphibians; no tickets required). There's also a learning center at the

---

IMPRESSIONS

Take an umbrella, an overcoat, and a fan, and go forth.
—MARK TWAIN

It has a damp, wheezy, Dickensian sort of winter hardly equalled by London, and a steaming tropical summer not surpassed by the basin of the Nile.
—ALISTAIR COOKE

birdhouse. ZOOlab is open Friday to Sunday 10am to 2pm. The Reptile Discovery Center is open daily 10am to 4:30pm. And the Bird Resource Center is open Saturday and Sunday 10am to 2pm.

Of course, the main reason to come to the zoo is to see the animals. They live in large open enclosures simulating their natural habitats on two easy-to-follow numbered paths, Olmsted Walk and the Valley Trail. You can't get lost, and you won't unintentionally miss anything. In total, there are 3½ miles of trails. Signs indicate the presence of baby animals born on the premises.

Lions, tigers, leopards, monkeys, apes, reptiles, and small animals live in proximity to one another on the Rock Creek side of the zoo. Nearby, in an immense glass-domed building, is **Amazonia,** an exhibit of fish, plants, and animals from the Amazon River region. Also grouped are the four largest land mammals—hippos, rhinos, giraffes, and elephants. Hsing-Hsing is bracketed with kangaroos, camels, and antelopes at the center of the park. Deer and Malayan tapirs coexist with abundant birdlife. Additional residents include North American mammals, otters, seals, and sea lions.

The invertebrate exhibit is the only one of its kind in the country. On display are starfish, sponges, giant crabs, anemones, insects, and other spineless creatures.

Zoo facilities include stroller-rental stations, a number of gift shops, a bookstore, and several paid-parking lots. The lots fill up quickly, especially on weekends, so arrive early or take the Metro.

Snack bars and ice-cream kiosks are scattered throughout the park. Most notable is the **Panda Cafe,** with umbrella tables overlooking the outdoor habitat of Hsing-Hsing; fast food is featured. The largest facility is the **Mane Restaurant,** near the Beach Drive entrance. A pleasant alternative is an alfresco lunch at one of the zoo's very nice picnic areas. Buy picnic fare at **Uptown Bakers** (details in Chapter 6) or at the zoo eateries.

Admission: Free.

Open: Apr 15–Oct 15, daily (weather permitting): grounds, 8am–8pm; animal buildings, 9am–4:30pm. Oct 16–Apr 14, daily: grounds, 8am–6pm; animal buildings, 9am–4:30pm. **Closed:** Dec 25. **Metro:** Cleveland Park or Woodley Park–Zoo.

ANACOSTIA MUSEUM, 1901 Fort Place SE, off Martin Luther King Ave. Tel. 287-3382 or 357-2700.

This unique Smithsonian establishment was created in 1967 as a neighborhood museum, whose major focus is the history and cultural interests of the predominantly black Anacostia community. Expanding its horizons over the years to include every aspect of black history, art, and culture, both American and worldwide, the permanent collection now includes about 5,000 items, ranging from videotapes of African-American church services to art, sheet music, and historic documents. In addition, the Anacostia produces a varying number of shows each year and offers a comprehensive schedule of free educational programs and activities in conjunction with exhibit themes. For instance, to complement an exhibition called "The African American Presence in American Quilts," the museum featured a video about artist/quiltmaker Faith Ringgold, quilting workshops for adults and children, talks by local quilting societies, and storytelling involving quilts.

Call for an events calendar (which always includes children's activities) or pick one up when you visit.

Admission: Free.

Open: Daily 10am–5pm. **Closed:** Dec 25. **Metro:** Anacostia; then take a W1 or W2 bus directly to the museum.

OTHER TOP ATTRACTIONS

LIBRARY OF CONGRESS, 1st St. SE, between Independence Ave. and E. Capitol St. Tel. 707-5458.

Note: Due to ongoing renovations, the tour procedure will be in flux for some time. Call 707-8000 before you go for up-to-the-minute tour information.

This is the nation's library, established in 1800 "for the purchase of such books as may be necessary for the use of Congress." Over the years, it has expanded to serve all Americans—from the blind, for whom books are recorded on cassette and/or translated into braille, to research scholars and college students. Its first collection of books was destroyed when the British burned the Capitol (where the library was then housed) during the War of 1812. Thomas Jefferson then sold the institution his personal library of 6,487 books as a replacement, and this became the foundation of what would grow to be the world's largest library. Today the collection contains a mind-boggling 104 million items, with new materials being acquired at the rate of 10 items per minute! Its three buildings house, among many other things, 28 million books in all languages, 4 million maps and atlases dating back to the middle of the 14th century; Stradivari violins; the letters of George Washington; more than 15 million prints and photographs; almost 2 million recordings; 694,000 motion picture reels, among them the earliest motion-picture print (made by Thomas Edison in 1893); Thomas Jefferson's rough draft of the Declaration of Independence; the papers of everyone from Freud to Groucho Marx; sketches by Alexander Graham Bell; the magic books of Houdini; and the contents of Lincoln's pockets the night he died. The library also maintains the Dewey decimal system; offers a year-round program of concerts, lectures, and poetry readings; and houses the Copyright Office.

As impressive as the scope of the library's effects and activities is its original home—the ornate Italian Renaissance-style **Thomas Jefferson Building,** erected between 1888 and 1897 to hold the burgeoning collection and establish America as a cultured nation with magnificent institutions equal to anything in Europe. Fifty-two painters and sculptors worked for eight years on its interior, utilizing more than 1,500 fully developed architectural drawings. There are floor mosaics from Italy, allegorical paintings on the overhead vaults, more than 100 murals, and numerous ornamental cornucopias, ribbons, vines and garlands within, as well as 42 granite sculptures and yards of bas-reliefs on the outside. Especially impressive are the exquisite marble Great Hall and the Main Reading Room, the latter under a 160-foot dome. Originally intended to hold the fruits of at least 150 years of collecting, the building was, in fact, filled up in 13. It is now supplemented by the **James Madison Memorial Building** and the **John Adams Building.**

At this writing (see "Note" above) **tours** depart weekdays at 10am and 1 and 3pm from the lobby of the James Madison Building (address above). A prelude to each tour is a 22-minute introductory video shown weekdays every half hour from 9am to a half hour before closing.

Pick up a calendar of events when you visit. The Madison Building offers interesting exhibits and features classic, rare, and unusual films in its Mary Pickford Theater. It also houses a noteworthy restaurant and cafeteria (see "Restaurants at Sightseeing Attractions" in Chapter 6 for details), though picnic tables out front here and at the Thomas Jefferson Building provide a tempting alternative.

Admission: Free.

Open: Mon–Fri 8:30am–9:30pm, Sat 8:30am–6pm. Call ahead for tour information. **Closed:** Sun, Jan 1, and Dec 25. **Metro:** Capitol South.

NATIONAL ARCHIVES, Constitution Ave., between 7th and 9th Sts. NW. Tel. 501-5000 for information on exhibits and films, 501-5400 for research information.

Keeper of America's documentary heritage, the National Archives displays our most cherished treasures in appropriately awe-inspiring surroundings. Housed in the Rotunda of the Exhibition Hall are the Nation's three charter documents—the Declaration of Independence, the Constitution of the United States, and its Bill of Rights—which are on view daily to the public. Every night these three "Charters of Freedom" are lowered 20 feet into a 50-ton vault for safekeeping, and every morning they are once again raised for exhibition. Throughout the day, armed guards stand on duty in the hall.

High above and flanking the documents are two larger-than-life murals painted by Barry Faulkner. One, entitled *The Declaration of Independence,* shows Thomas Jefferson presenting a draft of the Declaration to John Hancock, the presiding officer of the Continental Congress; the other, entitled *The Constitution,* shows James Madison submitting the Constitution to George Washington and the Constitutional Convention. In the display cases on either side of the Declaration of Independence are changing exhibits, most recently, "The Face of War"—documents, photographs, original treaties, and eyewitness accounts relating to World War II, including a description of the D-day invasion by Ernest Hemingway. The 1297 version of the Magna Carta, one of the bases for fundamental English privileges and rights, is on display in the Rotunda indefinitely. And there are temporary exhibits in the Circular Gallery (at this writing, World War II propaganda posters).

The Archives serves as much more than a museum of cherished documents. Most famous as a center of genealogical research—Alex Haley began his work on *Roots* here—it is sometimes called the "nation's memory." This federal institution is charged with sifting through the accumulated papers of a nation's official life—billions of pieces a year—and determining what to save and what to destroy. The Archives' vast accumulation of census figures, military records, naturalization papers, immigrant passenger lists, federal documents, passport applications, ship manifests, maps, charts, photographs, and motion-picture film (and that's not the half of it) spans two centuries. And it's all available for the perusal of anyone 16 or over (call for details). If you're casually thinking about tracing your roots, stop in first at Room 400 where a staff member can tell you whether it's worth the effort and how to go about it.

But the National Archives merits a visit even if you have no research project in mind. The neoclassical building itself, designed by John Russell Pope in the 1930s (also architect of the National Gallery and the Jefferson Memorial) is an impressive example of the beaux arts style. Seventy-two columns create a Corinthian colonnade on each of the four facades. Great bronze doors herald the Constitution Avenue entrance, and allegorical sculpture centered on *The Recorder of the Archives* adorns the pediment. On either side of the steps are male and female figures symbolizing guardianship and heritage, respectively. Guardians of the Portals at the Pennsylvania Avenue entrance represent the past and the future, and the theme of the pediment is destiny.

Free docent **tours** are given weekdays at 10:15am and 1:15pm by appointment only; call 501-5205 for details. Pick up a schedule of events (lectures, films, genealogy workshops) when you visit.

Admission: Free.

Open: Exhibition Hall, Apr–Labor Day, daily 10am–9pm; day after Labor Day–Mar, daily 10am–5:30pm. Call for research hours. **Closed:** Dec 25. **Metro:** Archives.

NATIONAL GALLERY OF ART, on the north side of the Mall between 3rd and 7th Sts. NW (entrances at 6th St. and Constitution Ave. or Madison Dr., also at 4th and 7th Sts. between Madison Dr. and Constitution Ave.). Tel. 737-4215.

Most people don't realize it, but the National Gallery of Art is not really part of the Smithsonian complex (though it is, in some arcane way, related to it); hence its listing here apart from the other Mall museums.

Housing one of the world's foremost collections of Western painting, sculpture, and graphic arts from the Middle Ages through the 20th century, the National Gallery has a dual personality. The original West Building, designed by John Russell Pope (architect of the Jefferson Memorial and the National Archives), is a neoclassic marble masterpiece with a domed rotunda over a colonnaded fountain and high-ceilinged corridors leading to delightful garden courts. It was a gift to the nation from Andrew W. Mellon, who also contributed the nucleus of the collection, including 21 masterpieces from the Hermitage—two Raphaels among them. The ultramodern East Building, designed by I. M. Pei and opened in 1978, is composed of two adjoining triangles with glass walls and lofty tetrahedron skylights. The pink Tennessee marble from which both buildings were constructed was taken from the same quarry; it forms an architectural link between the two structures.

The West Building: On the main floor of the West Building, about 1,000 paintings are always on exhibit. Galleries to the right of the Rotunda (if you've entered from the Mall) feature 17th- to 19th-century French paintings, works of late 19th-century Americans such as Homer and Sargent, and of somewhat earlier British artists such as Constable, Turner, and Gainsborough. To the left are the Italians (Renaissance, 17th and 18th centuries), including the only Leonardo da Vinci outside Europe, *Ginevra de' Benci*. Paintings by El Greco, Goya, and Veláquez highlight the Spanish galleries; Grünewald, Dürer, Holbein, and Cranach can be seen in the German; Van Eyck, Rubens, and Bosch in the Flemish; and an excellent collection of Rembrandts in the Dutch. Room decor reflects the period and country of the art shown: For example, the Italian gallery walls are of travertine marble, while the Dutch galleries are paneled in somber oak. Down a flight are 17th- and 18th-century prints, 19th- and 20th-century sculpture (with many pieces by Daumier, Degas, and Renoir), American naïve 18th- and 19-century paintings, Chinese porcelains, small Renaissance bronzes, 16th-century Flemish tapestries, decorative 18th-century arts, and an immense shop offering art books and prints—one of several.

The East Building: The scene of major changing exhibits, the East Building also houses an important collection of 20th-century art—including a massive aluminum Calder mobile under a four-story skylight and an immense bronze sculpture by Henry Moore.

In addition to its permanent collection, the National Gallery hosts a wide range of important temporary exhibits. Recent shows have ranged from "The Glory of Venice: Art in the 18th Century" to a James McNeill Whistler retrospective.

Pick up a floor plan and calendar of events at an information desk to find out about exhibits, films, tours, lectures, and concerts. Highly recommended are the free highlight **tours** (call for exact times) and audio tours. There are several dining options here (see "Restaurants in Sightseeing Attractions" in Chapter 6 for details).

Admission: Free.

Open: Mon–Sat 10am–5pm, Sun 11am–6pm. **Closed:** Jan 1 and Dec 25. **Metro:** Archives or Judiciary Square.

FEDERAL BUREAU OF INVESTIGATION, J. Edgar Hoover FBI Building, E St. NW, between 9th and 10th Sts. Tel. 324-3447.

More than half a million annual visitors learn why crime doesn't pay by touring the headquarters of the FBI. The attraction is especially popular with kids. To beat the crowds, arrive for the one-hour **tour** before 8:45am or write to a senator or congressperson for a scheduled reservation as far in advance as possible (details in Chapter 2).

IMPRESSIONS

I went to Washington as everybody goes there prepared to see everything done with some furtive intention, but I was disappointed—pleasantly disappointed.
—WALT WHITMAN

The tour begins with a short videotape presentation about the priorities of the bureau—organized crime, white-collar crime, terrorism, foreign counterintelligence, illicit drugs, and violent crimes. En route, you'll learn about this organization's history (it was established in 1908) and its activities over the years. You'll see some of the weapons used by big-time gangsters like Al Capone, Dillinger, Bonnie and Clyde, and "Pretty Boy" Floyd; an exhibit on counterintelligence operation; and photos of the 10 most wanted fugitives—435 of them (including 7 women) have made the list since its inception in 1950; 406 have been captured (127 apprehended through direct citizen cooperation). Two were recognized at this exhibit by people on the tour, and eight have been located via the FBI-assisted TV show, "America's Most Wanted."

Other exhibits deal with white-collar crime, the use of fingerprints for identification, terrorism, and agent training. On display are more than 4,200 weapons, most confiscated from criminals; they're used for reference purposes. An illicit drug exhibit shows paraphernalia and demonstrates how the FBI tries to combat illicit drugs via educational as well as investigational methods.

You'll also visit the DNA lab, the Document Section (where fraudulent checks and holdup notes are examined), the Firearms Unit (where it's determined whether a bullet was fired from a given weapon), the Elemental and Metals Analysis Unit (where from a tiny piece of paint the FBI can determine the approximate make and model of a car), the unit where hairs and fibers are examined, and a Forfeiture and Seizure Exhibit—a display of jewelry, furs, and other proceeds from illegal narcotics operations. The tour ends with a bang—lots of them in fact—when an agent gives a sharpshooting demonstration. He also talks about the FBI's firearms policy and gun safety.

Admission: Free.

Open: Mon–Fri 8:45am–4:15pm. **Closed:** Jan 1, Dec 25, and other federal holidays. **Metro:** Metro Center or Federal Triangle.

JOHN F. KENNEDY CENTER FOR THE PERFORMING ARTS, New Hampshire Ave. NW at Rock Creek Pkwy. Tel. 467-4600, or toll free 800/444-1324 for information or tickets.

Opened in 1971, the Kennedy Center is both our national performing arts center and a memorial to John F. Kennedy, whose administration was quite enthusiastic about its development. Carved into the center's river facade are several Kennedy quotations, including ". . . the New Frontier for which I campaign in public life can also be a New Frontier for American art." Set on 17 acres overlooking the Potomac, the striking $73-million facility, designed by noted architect Edward Durell Stone, houses an opera house, a concert hall, two stage theaters, a theater lab, and a film theater. The best way to see the Kennedy Center—including areas you can't visit on your own—is to take a free 50-minute guided **tour,** given daily between 10am and 1pm. Once again, you can beat the crowds by writing in advance to a senator or congressperson for tickets for a 9:30am VIP tour (details in Chapter 2).

The tour begins in the Hall of States, where flags of the 50 states and four territories are hung in the order they joined the Union. Throughout the center you'll see gifts from more than 40 nations, including all the marble used in the building (3,700 tons), which was donated by Italy. First stop is the Grand Foyer—scene of many free concerts and programs and the reception area for all three theaters on the main level; the 18 crystal chandeliers are a gift from Sweden. You'll also visit the Israeli Lounge (where 40 painted and gilded panels depict scenes mentioned in the Bible); the Concert Hall, home of the National Symphony Orchestra; the Opera House, with its Matisse tapestries; the African room (decorated with beautiful tapestries from African nations); the Eisenhower Theater; the Hall of Nations, where flags of all countries recognized diplomatically by the Unites States are displayed; the Performing Arts Library; and the Terrace Theater, a Bicentennial gift from Japan. Your guide will point out many notable works of art along the way, such as a Barbara Hepworth sculpture (a gift of England), Henri Matisse tapestries (gifts of France), and an alabaster vase from 2600 B.C. found in a pyramid (a gift of Egypt). If rehearsals are going on, visits to the theaters are omitted.

If you'd like to attend performances during your visit, call the toll-free number above and request the current issue of *Kennedy Center News Magazine,* a free publication that describes all Kennedy Center happenings and prices.

After the tour, walk around the building's terrace for a panoramic 360° view of Washington and plan a meal in one of the Kennedy Center restaurants (details in "Restaurants in Sightseeing Attractions" in Chapter 6). See Chapter 9 for specifics on theater, concert, and film offerings. There is parking below the Kennedy Center during the day at $2.50 for the first hour, $1.50 for each additional hour, with a maximum of five hours and $7; nighttime parking (after 5pm) is a flat $5.

Admission: Free.

Open: Daily 10am–midnight. **Metro:** Foggy Bottom. **Bus:** 46 down New Hampshire Avenue from Dupont Circle or 80 from Metro Center.

WASHINGTON NATIONAL CATHEDRAL, Massachusetts and Wisconsin Aves. NW (entrance on Wisconsin Ave.). Tel. 537-6200.

Pierre L'Enfant's 1791 plan for the capital city included "a great church for national purposes," but possibly because of early America's fear of mingling church and state, more than a century elapsed before the foundation for Washington National Cathedral was laid. Its actual name is the Cathedral Church of St. Peter and St. Paul. Though it's Episcopal in denomination, it has no local congregation and seeks to serve the entire nation as a house of prayer for all people. It has been the setting for every kind of religious observance from Jewish to Serbian Orthodox.

A church of this magnitude (it's the sixth largest cathedral in the world!) required a long time to build. Its principal (but not original) architect, Philip Hubert Frohman, worked on the project from 1921 until his death in 1972. The foundation stone (a stone from a field in Bethlehem set into a larger piece of American granite) was laid in 1907 using the mallet with which George Washington set the Capitol cornerstone. Construction was interrupted by both world wars and periods of financial difficulty. It was completed with the placement of periods of financial difficulty. It was completed with the placement of the final stone atop a pinnacle on the west front towers on September 29, 1990—exactly 83 years since its inception.

English Gothic in style (with several distinctly 20th-century innovations, such as a stained-glass window commemorating the flight of *Apollo 11* and containing a piece of moon rock), the cathedral is built in the shape of a cross, complete with flying buttresses and gargoyles. It is, together with the Capitol and the Washington Monument, among the most dominant structures on the Washington skyline. Its 57-acre landscaped grounds have two lovely gardens; four schools, including the College of Preachers; and an herb garden, a greenhouse, and a shop called Herb Cottage (buy seeds and start your own).

Over the years the cathedral has seen a lot of history. Services to celebrate the end of World Wars I and II were held there. It was the scene of President Wilson's funeral (he and his wife are buried here), as well as President Eisenhower's. Helen Keller and her companion, Anne Sullivan, were buried in the cathedral at her request. And during the Iranian crisis, a round-the-clock prayer vigil was held in the Holy Spirit Chapel throughout the hostages' captivity. When they were released, the hostages came to a service here, and tears flowed at Col. Thomas Shaefer's poignant greeting, "Good morning, my fellow Americans. You don't know how long I've been waiting to say those words."

The best way to explore the cathedral and see its abundance of art, architectural carvings, and statuary is to take a one-hour **tour.** They leave continually—from the west end of the nave—Monday to Saturday 10am to 3:15pm and Sunday 12:30 to 2:45pm. Among the highlights are dozens of stained-glass windows with themes ranging from the lives of Civil War Generals Lee and Jackson to the miracles of Christ; three exquisite rose windows; the nave, stretching a tenth of a mile to the high altar; Wilson's tomb; the delightful Children's Chapel; St. John's Chapel, where needlepoint kneelers memorialize great Americans; the Holy Spirit Chapel, painted by Andrew Wyeth's father, N. C. Wyeth; and crypt chambers like the Bethlehem Chapel, first section of the cathedral to be constructed.

Allow time to tour the grounds or "close," and to visit the Observation Gallery where 70 windows provide panoramic views. Tuesday- and Wednesday-afternoon tours are followed by a high tea in the Observation Gallery; reservations are required and a fee is charged. And you can, of course, attend **services** at the cathedral (Monday to Saturday at 7:30am, noon, and 4pm; Sunday at 8, 9, and 11am and 4 and 6:30pm). September to June there's a folk guitar mass on Sunday at 10am.

The cathedral hosts numerous events: organ recitals, choir performances, an annual flower mart, films and slide lectures, calligraphy workshops, and jazz, folk, and classical concerts. Memorable past performances have ranged from Ravi Shankar playing sitar to a Stravinsky Centennial with Leonard Bernstein conducting. The 53-bell carillon is played on Saturday at 5pm during spring and summer, 12:30pm in winter and fall. Organ recitals are usually given on the great organ following Sunday-evening services at 5pm. The Cathedral Choir of Men and Boys can be heard on Sunday at 11am and 4pm; the boys alone (during the school year only), Monday to Wednesday at 4pm.

A large gift shop on the premises sells replicas of cathedral statuary, religious books and art, Christmas cards, and more.

Admission: Suggested donation $2 for adults, $1 for children under 12.

Open: Mon–Sat 10am–4:30pm, Sun 7:30am–4:30pm. **Metro:** Tenleytown; then about a 20-minute walk. **Bus:** Any N bus up Massachusetts Avenue from Dupont Circle.

BUREAU OF ENGRAVING AND PRINTING, 14th and C Sts. SW. Tel. 874-3188.

This is where they make the paper money—$103 *billion* of it each year. A staff of 2,300 work around the clock churning it out at the rate of 22.5 million notes a day. Everyone's eyes pop as they walk past rooms overflowing with money, the kind of rooms that Scrooge McDuck cavorted in. Although the money is the big draw, it's not the whole story. The bureau prints many other products, including 30.5 billion postage stamps per year, Treasury bonds, and White House invitations.

As many as 5,000 people line up each day to get a peek at all that moolah, so early arrival—especially during the peak tourist season—is essential (unless you have secured VIP tickets from your senator or congressperson; details in Chapter 2). From the Monday before Easter to Labor Day (when you must obtain a ticket that specifies a tour time), the ticket booth opens at 8am. Be there! The rest of the year no ticket is needed; you just have to line up.

The 25-minute **self-guided tour** (there are audiovisual aids, and bureau personnel are on hand to answer questions) begins with a short introductory film. Then you'll see, through large windows, all the processes that go into the making of paper money—the inking, stacking (each stack of dollar bills contains $320,000), cutting, and examination for defects. Most printing here is done from engraved steel plates in a process known as "intaglio"—the hardest to counterfeit, because the slightest alteration will cause a noticeable change in the portrait in use. Additional exhibits include bills no longer in use, counterfeit money, and a $100,000 bill designed for official transactions (since 1969, the largest denomination printed for the general public is $100).

After you finish the tour, allow time to explore the **Visitor Center** (open 8:30am to 3:30pm), where the history of money is portrayed from "pieces of eight" to present-day currency. Other exhibits include informative videos, money-related electronic games, and a display of $1 million. Here, too, you can buy unique gifts ranging from bags of shredded money to copies of documents such as the Gettysburg Address.

Admission: Free.

Open: Mon–Fri 9am–2pm. **Closed:** Dec 25–Jan 1 and federal holidays. **Metro:** Smithsonian (Independence Avenue exit).

THE VIETNAM VETERANS MEMORIAL, just across from the Lincoln Memorial, east of Henry Bacon Dr. between 21st and 22nd Sts. NW. Tel. 634-1568.

To my mind, the saddest sight in Washington is the Vietnam Veterans Memorial—two long, black granite walls inscribed with the names of the men and women who gave their lives, or remain missing, in the longest war in our nation's history. Even if no one close to you died in Vietnam, it's emotionally wrenching to watch visitors grimly studying the directories at either end to find out where their husbands, sons, and loved ones are listed. The slow walk along the 492-foot wall of names—close to 60,000 people, many of whom died very young—is a powerful evocation of the tragedy of all wars. And whatever your views on the war, it's also affecting to see how much the monument means to Vietnam vets who visit it. Because of the raging conflict over U.S. involvement in the war, its veterans had received virtually no previous recognition of their service.

The memorial was conceived by Vietnam veteran Jan Scruggs and built by the Vietnam Veterans Memorial Fund, a nonprofit organization that raised $7 million for the project. The VVMF was granted a 2-acre site in tranquil Constitution Gardens to erect a memorial that would make no political statement about the war and would harmonize with neighboring memorials. By separating the issue of the wartime service of individuals from the issue of U.S. policy in Vietnam, VVMF hoped to begin a process of national reconciliation.

Yale senior Maya Ying Lin's design was chosen in a national competition open to all citizens over 18 years of age. It consists of two walls in a quiet, protected park setting, angled at 125 degrees to point to the Washington Monument and the Lincoln Memorial. The walls' mirrorlike surface reflects surrounding trees, lawn, and monuments. The names are inscribed in chronological order, documenting an epoch in American history as a series of individual sacrifices from the date of the first casualty in 1959 to the date of the last death in 1975.

The wall was erected in 1982. In 1984 a life-size sculpture of three Vietnam soldiers by Frederick Hart was installed at the entrance plaza. He describes his work this way: "They wear the uniform and carry the equipment of war; they are young. The contrast between the innocence of their youth and the weapons of war underscores the poignancy of their sacrifice. . . Their strength and their vulnerability are both evident." Near the statue a flag flies from a 60-foot staff. Another sculpture, the Vietnam Veterans Women's Memorial, depicting three nurses tending a wounded soldier was installed on Veterans Day 1993

Admission: Free.
Open: Daily 24 hours, with ranges on duty 8am–midnight.
Metro: Foggy Bottom.

UNITED STATES HOLOCAUST MEMORIAL MUSEUM, 100 Raoul Wallenberg Place (formerly 15th St. SW), near Independence Ave., just off the Mall. Tel. 488-0400.

★ "Out of our memory . . . of the Holocaust we must forge an unshakable oath with all civilized people that never again will the world stand silent, never again will the world . . . fail to act in time to prevent the terrible crime of genocide. . . ." These words of Jimmy Carter are inscribed on a wall outside the museum.

Washington's multitude of museums celebrate the knowledge, the glory, and the creative achievements of human civilization. This museum, mandated by an Act of Congress in 1980 and opened in 1993, reminds us of what can happen when civilization goes awry. It serves the dual purpose of commemorating the dead and educating the living to the dangers of prejudice and fanaticism and the fragility of freedom.

Just over 50 years ago, a seemingly civilized Western nation legalized racism, brutally trampled on human rights, and engaged in the genocide of millions. Here the story is told in full. Even the building housing the museum is designed to reflect the bleakness of the Nazi era—to disorient the visitor with false perspectives and eerily somber spaces. An outer wall is reminiscent of an extermination camp's exterior brickwork, and towers evoke the guard towers of Auschwitz.

Upon entering, you will be issued an identity card of an actual victim of the Holocaust. By 1945, 66% of those whose lives are documented on these cards were dead. As you go up to the fourth floor (where the events of 1933 to 1939 are portrayed), a video in the elevator features an American soldier describing his experiences liberating a camp. The Holocaust story begins with the rise of Nazism—book burnings, the Nuremberg Laws of 1935 that isolated Jews from German society, and the terror of "Kristallnacht" in 1938, when hundreds of Jewish synagogues and businesses were destroyed. A winding path takes you to a border crossing where the near impossibility of escape is dramatized. No countries will admit you; you're forced to return to the horror. Also highlighted are the non-Jewish victims of the Nazis—Gypsies, the physically and mentally handicapped, homosexuals, political and religious dissidents.

On the third floor (documenting the years 1940 to 1944), constricting walls symbolize the narrowing choices of people caught up in the Nazi machine. You'll board a German freightcar of the type used to transport Jews from the Warsaw ghetto to Treblinka and hear recordings of survivors telling what life in the camps was like. A reconstructed Auschwitz barracks, the yellow stars Jews were forced to wear, instruments of genocide, and a gas-chamber door are among the thousands of artifacts bearing silent witness to this grim era. Like your identity card, displays foster identification with individuals who perished. In one of the towers, a montage of 1,500 family photographs documents the beauty and vitality of everyday lives of people in the Jewish town of Ejszyszki, Lithuania, before the Holocaust; later you'll learn that 90% of them were murdered by Nazi death squads during two days in 1941.

On the second floor, the focus turns to a more heartening story: how non-Jews throughout Europe save Jews at great personal risk. In Denmark, 90% of the Jews were hidden and saved. The saga continues with exhibits on the liberation of the camps, life in DP camps, emigration to Israel and America, and the Nuremberg trials. The tour ends in the hexagonal Hall of Remembrance—a place to meditate on what you've experienced and light a candle for the victims.

Dozens of educational interactive videos further enhance understanding, as do films, lectures, cultural events, and temporary exhibits. The exhibits are designed so you can shield children (or yourself) from the most graphic material. This museum is not like any other you've ever visited. It's a deeply affecting encounter with evil—an opportunity to learn the lessons of history and the role of individual responsibility in protecting freedom and preserving human rights.

Allow at least four or five hours to see the exhibits. I would not recommend bringing children under 12 to this museum, and even then, it's advisable to prepare them for what they'll see. There's a cafeteria and museum shop on the premises.

Note: At this writing, because so many people want to visit the museum, tickets specifying a visit time are required. Reserve them via Ticketmaster (tel. 202/432-SEAT, or toll free 800/551-SEAT). There's a small service charge. You can also get them at the museum box office, which opens at 9am daily. However, this advance-ticket policy may change; call ahead for up-to-the-minute details.

Admission: Free.

Open: Daily 10am–5:30pm. **Closed:** Yom Kippur and Dec 25. **Metro:** Smithsonian.

UNION STATION, 40 Massachusetts Ave. NE. Tel. 371-9441.

In Washington, D.C., the very train station where you arrive is itself a noteworthy sightseeing attraction. Union Station, a monument to the great age of rail travel built between 1903 and 1907, was painstakingly restored in the late 1980s to its original grandeur at a cost of $160 million. The station was designed by noted architect Daniel H. Burnham, an enthusiast of French beaux arts neoclassicism and a member of the McMillan Commission—an illustrious task force assembled in 1900 to beautify the Mall and make the city an appropriately imposing world capital. The committee's philosophy was summed up by Burnham, who counseled, "Make no little plans. They have no magic to stir men's blood, and probably themselves will not be realized." The committee's "big plans" included Union Station, modeled after the Baths of Diocletian and Arch of Constantine in Rome.

When it opened in 1907, this was the largest train station in the world. Its Ionic-colonnaded exterior is of white granite, and 100 eagles are portrayed in the facade. Out front are a replica of the Liberty Bell and a monumental statue of Columbus Six carved allegorical fixtures in niches over the entranceway represent Fire, Electricity, Freedom, Imagination, Agriculture, and Mechanics. The station's interior, entered through graceful 50-foot Constantinian arches, is finished with extravagant materials—acres of white marble flooring with red "Champlain dots," bronze grilles, elaborate coffered ceilings (embellished with a half-million dollars' worth of 22-carat gold leaf!), and rich Honduran mahogany. The Main Hall is a massive rectangular room with a 96-foot barrel-vault ceiling, its balcony adorned with 36 Augustus Saint-Gaudens sculptures of Roman legionnaires. Off the Main Hall is the East Hall, one of the most beautiful areas of the station, with scagliola marble walls and columns, a gorgeous hand-stenciled skylight ceiling, and stunning murals of classical scenes inspired by ancient Pompeian art. Today it's the station's plushest shopping venue.

In its heyday, many important events took place at this "temple of transport." President Wilson welcomed General Pershing here in 1918 on his return from France. South Pole explorer Rear Admiral Byrd was also feted at Union Station on his homecoming. Franklin D. Roosevelt's funeral train, bearing his casket, was met by thousands of mourners in 1945. And in the 1960s, the Kennedys greeted King Hassan II of Morocco and Ethiopian Emperor Haile Selassie here.

But soon after, with the decline of rail travel, the station fell on hard times. Rain damage caused parts of the roof to cave in, and the entire building—with floors buckling, rats running about, and mushrooms sprouting in damp rooms—was sealed in 1981. That same year, Congress enacted legislation to preserve and faithfully restore this national treasure.

Today, Union Station is once again a vibrant entity—a transportation/dining/shopping/entertainment center patronized by locals and visitors alike. Every square inch of the facility has been cleaned, repaired, and/or replaced according to original designs. An elliptical mahogany kiosk has been erected in the center of the Main Hall, inspired by a Renaissance baldacchino, to accommodate a bi-level café and a visitor information center. About 100 retail shops on three levels offer a wide array of merchandise. The skylit Main Concourse, extending the entire length of the station, has become the primary shopping area as well as a ticketing and baggage facility. And a nine-screen cinema complex and beautiful food court have been installed on the lower level. The remarkable restoration, which involved hundreds of European and American artisans utilizing historical research, bygone craft techniques, and modern technology, is meticulous in every detail. I'm sure Burnham would be greatly pleased if he could walk the majestic corridors of Union Station today. His own 1907 declaration foretells the spirit of the renovation ". . . . a noble, logical diagram once recorded will never die, but long after we are gone will be a living thing, asserting itself with ever-growing insistency. . . . Let your watchword be order and your beacon beauty."

For information on Union Station restaurants and shops, see Chapter 6 ("Restaurants in Sightseeing Attractions") and Chapter 8.

Admission: Free.
Open: Daily 24 hours. Shops, Mon–Sat 10am–9pm, Sun noon–6pm. **Metro:** Union Station.

FORD'S THEATRE AND LINCOLN MUSEUM, 511 10th St. NW, between E and F Sts. Tel. 426-6924.

On April 14, 1865, President Lincoln was in the audience of Ford's Theatre, one of the most popular playhouses in Washington. Everyone was laughing at a funny line from Tom Taylor's celebrated comedy, *Our American Cousin,* when actor John Wilkes Booth grabbed center stage by shooting the president. Booth escaped by jumping to the stage, mounting his horse in the back alley, and galloping off. Doctors carried Lincoln to the house of William Petersen, across the street, and the president died there the next morning. (See below for details.)

After Lincoln's assassination, the theater was closed by order of Secretary of War Stanton. For many years afterward it was used by the War Department for clerical work. In 1893, 22 clerks were killed when three floors of the building collapsed. It remained in disuse until the 1960s, when it was remodeled and restored to its appearance on the night of the tragedy. Except when rehearsals or matinees are in progress (call before you go), visitors can see the theater and trace Booth's movements on that fateful night. Free 15-minute talks on the history of the theater and the story of the assassination are given throughout the day (call for exact times). Be sure to visit the **Lincoln Museum** in the basement, which has exhibits on Lincoln's life and times. In addition to Lincoln memorabilia, exhibits depict the clothes Lincoln was wearing the night he was killed, the Derringer pistol used by Booth, the killer's diary outlining his rationalization for the deed, and other artifacts. See Chapter 9 for information on theatrical presentations here.

Admission: Free.
Open: Daily 9am–5pm. **Closed:** Dec 25. **Metro:** Metro Center.

THE HOUSE WHERE LINCOLN DIED, 156 10th St. NW. Tel. 426-6830.

This is where Lincoln was carried after the shooting. Furnished with period pieces, it looks much as it did on that fateful April night. You'll see the front parlor where an anguished Mary Todd Lincoln spent the night with her son, Robert. Her emotional state was such that she was banned from the bedroom because she was creating havoc. In the back parlor Secretary of War Edwin M. Stanton held a Cabinet meeting and began questioning witnesses. The room where Lincoln died contains a bed of the same design as the original, complete with the actual bloodstained pillow on which he rested. From this room, Stanton announced at 7:22am on April 15, 1865, "Now he belongs to the ages."

Six years after Lincoln's death, the house was sold to Louis Schade, who published a newspaper called the *Washington Sentinel* in its basement for many years. In 1896 the government bought the house for $30,000, and it is now maintained by the National Park Service.

Admission: Free.
Open: Daily 9am–5pm. **Closed:** Dec 25. **Metro:** Metro Center.

---

2. MORE ATTRACTIONS

PHILLIPS COLLECTION, 1600 21st St. NW, at Q St. Tel. 387-0961.

⭐ Conceived as "a museum of modern art and its sources," this intimate establishment houses—in an elegant 1890s Georgian Revival mansion plus an added wing—the exquisite collection of Duncan and Marjorie Phillips, avid collectors and proselytizers of modernism. Carpeted rooms, with leaded- and stained-glass windows, oak paneling, plush chairs and sofas, and frequently, fireplaces create a comfortable, homelike setting for viewing art. The original building was once the Phillipses' elegant abode, though always doubling as a museum. When their collection totaled 600 paintings, they moved out and had it renovated entirely as a museum. Today the collection includes more than 2,500 works. Among the highlights are superb examples of Daumier, Dove, and Bonnard paintings; some splendid small Vuillards; three van Goghs; Renoir's *Luncheon of the Boating Party*; five Cézannes; and five works by Georgia O'Keeffe. Ingres, Delacroix, Manet, El Greco, Goya, Corot, Constable, Courbet, Giorgione, and Chardin are among the "sources" or forerunners of modernism represented. Modern notables include Rothko, Hopper, Kandinsky, Matisse, Klee, Degas, Rouault, Picasso, and many others. It's a collection no art lover should miss. An ongoing series of temporary shows is presented, with works from the Phillips supplemented by loans from other museums and private collections.

Free **tours** are given on Wednesday and Saturday at 2pm, and a full schedule of events includes gallery talks, lectures, and free concerts in the ornate music room (every Sunday at 5pm, September to May; early arrival is advised at these popular performances).

On the lower level are a charming little restaurant serving light fare and a comprehensive museum shop.

Admission: Sat–Sun, $6.50 adults, $3.25 seniors and students, free for children under 18; Mon–Fri, contribution suggested.

Open: Mon–Sat 10am–5pm, Sun noon–7pm. *Note:* Evening hours are being considered at this writing; call for details. **Closed:** Jan 1, July 4, Thanksgiving Day, and Dec 25. **Metro:** Dupont Circle (Q Street exit).

CORCORAN GALLERY OF ART, 17th St., NW, between E St. and New York Ave. Tel. 638-3211 or 638-1439.

The first art museum in Washington, and one of the first in the country, the Corcoran Gallery was housed from 1874 to 1896 in the red-brick and brownstone building that is now the Renwick. The collection outgrew its quarters and was transferred in 1897 to its present beaux arts building, designed by Ernest Flagg. It features a double atrium with two levels of fluted columns and a grand staircase.

The collection itself—shown in rotating exhibits—focuses chiefly on American art. A prominent Washington banker, William Wilson Corcoran was among the first wealthy American collectors to realize the importance of encouraging and supporting this country's artists. Enhanced by further gifts and bequests, the collectio comprehensively spans American art from 18th-century portraiture to 20th-century moderns like Nevelson, Warhol, and Rothko. Nineteenth-century works include Bierstadt's and Remington's imagery of the American West; Hudson River School artists like Cole, Church, and Durand; genre paintings; expatriates like Whistler, Sargent, and Mary Cassatt; and two giants of the late 19th century—Homer and Eakins. Displayed on the second floor is the white marble female nude, *The Greek Slave*, by Hiram Powers, considered so daring in its day that it was shown on alternate days to men and women.

The Corcoran is not, however, an exclusively American art museum. On the first floor is the collection from the estate of Sen. William Andrews Clark—an eclectic grouping of Dutch and Flemish masters, European painters, French impressionists, Barbizon landscapes, Delft porcelains, a Louis XVI salon doré transported in toto from Paris, and more. Clark's will stated that his diverse collection—which any curator would undoubtedly want to disperse among various museum departments—must be shown as a unit. He left money for a wing to house it which opened in 1928. Other non-American aspects of the museum's collection include a room of exquisite Corot landscapes, another of medieval Renaissance tapestries, and numerous Daumier lithographs donated by Dr. Armand Hammer.

Free 30-minute **tours** are given at 12:30pm (and on Thursday also at 7pm). The museum shop has a terrific selection of art reproductions, books, jewelry, and art nouveau glassware, among other things. And do pick up a schedule of events—temporary exhibits, gallery talks, concerts, art auctions, and more. There's a charming restaurant on the premises (details in "Restaurants at Sightseeing Attractions" in Chapter 6).

Admission: Free.

Open: Wed and Fri–Mon 10am–5pm, Thurs 10am–9pm. **Closed:** Tues, Jan 1, and Dec 25. **Metro:** Farragut West or Farragut North.

NATIONAL MUSEUM OF WOMEN IN THE ARTS, 1250 New York Ave. NW, at 13th St. Tel. 783-5000.

Celebrating "the contribution of women to the history of art," this relatively new museum (opened 1987) is Washington's 72nd but a national first. Founders Wilhelmina and Wallace Holladay, who donated the core of the permanent collection—more than 200 works by women spanning the 16th through the 20th century—became interested in women's art in the 1960s. After discovering that no women were included in H. W. Janson's *History of Art*, a standard text (this, by the way, did not change until 1986!), the

Holladays began collecting women's art, and the concept of a women's art museum (to begin correcting the inequities of underrepresentation) soon evolved. (Though women comprise nearly 50% of the working artists in the United States, more than 95% of the works hanging in museums are by men!)

Since its opening, the collection has grown to 1,500 works by artists including Rosa Bonheur, Frida Kahlo, Helen Frankenthaler, Barbara Hepworth, Georgia O'Keeffe, Lee Krasner, Nancy Graves, Mary Cassatt, Elaine de Kooning, and Käthe Kollwitz, along with many other lesser known but notable artists from earlier centuries. I was interested to discover here, for instance, that the famed Peale family of 19th-century portrait painters included a very talented sister, Sarah Miriam Peale. The collection is complemented by an ongoing series of changing exhibits.

The museum is housed in a magnificent Renaissance Revival landmark building designed in 1907 as a Masonic temple by noted architect Waddy Wood. It's entered via an opulent Great Hall with Turkish white marble floors, silk-brocaded walls, gilded moldings, and Belgian crystal chandeliers suspended from an ornately detailed ceiling. A recently purchased adjoining building will expand the exhibit space and include a rooftop sculpture garden. The museum's library has more than 15,000 volumes. The charming and sunny Mezzanine Cafe serves light lunches Monday through Saturday—soups, salads, and sandwiches.

Admission: Suggested contribution, $3 adults, $2 children.

Open: Mon–Sat 10am–5pm, Sun noon–5pm. **Closed:** Jan 1, Thanksgiving Day, and Dec 25. **Metro:** Metro Center.

UNITED STATES BOTANIC GARDEN, 100 Maryland Ave., at the east end of the Mall. Tel. 225-8333.

Originally conceived by Washington, Jefferson, and Madison, and opened in 1820, the Botanic Garden is a lovely oasis—a series of connected glass-and-stone buildings and greenhouses (they call it a "living museum under glass") filled with pots of brightly colored flowers, rock beds of ferns, Spanish moss, palms, and shrubs. Tropical, subtropical, and desert plants highlight this collection. There's a section filled with cactus, while other areas suggest a lush tropical jungle with tranquil pools. Benches in shady corners create the illusion of a carefully tended woods. Poinsettias bloom at Christmas, chrysanthemums in fall; spring is heralded by lilies, tulips, hyacinths, and daffodils; and a large collection of orchids is on display year-round. The complex also includes Bartholdi Park, centering on a stunning cast-iron fountain created by Frédéric Auguste Bartholdi, designer of the Statue of Liberty. The park encompasses a rose garden and other themed areas. Of topical interest is the Dinosaur Garden of cycads (primitive conifers that resemble palms), mosses, and liverworts that existed in the Jurassic era—an age that predated flowering plants. The Summer Terrace, with umbrella tables amid plants and flower beds overlooking the Capitol's reflecting pool, is a lovely spot for a picnic lunch. For information on special shows (perhaps a rose show or a Japanese flower-arrangement display), tours, lectures, and classes such as "Growing Begonias and African Violets," call the above number. You can also call 225-7099 for a recording of events and to find out what's in bloom.

Admission: Free.

Open: Daily 9am–5pm. **Metro:** Federal Center SW.

DUMBARTON OAKS, 1703 32nd St. NW. (entrance to the collections on 32nd St., between R and S Sts.; garden entrance at 31st and R Sts.). Tel. 338-8278 or 342-3200.

Many people associate Dumbarton Oaks, a 19th-century Georgetown mansion named for a Scottish castle, with the 1944 international conference that led to the formation of the United Nations. Today the 16-acre estate is a research center for studies in Byzantine and pre-Columbian art and history, as well as landscape architecture. Its yards, which wind gently down to Rock Creek Ravine, are magical, modeled after European gardens. The pre-Columbian museum, designed by Philip Johnson, is a small gem, and the Byzantine collection is a rich one.

This unusual collection originated with Robert Woods Bliss and his wife, Mildred. In 1940 they turned over the estate, their extensive Byzantine collection, a library of works on Byzantine civilization, and 16 acres (including 10 acres of exquisite formal gardens) to Mr. Bliss's alma mater, Harvard, and provided endowment funds for continuing research in Byzantine studies. In the early 1960s they also donated their pre-Columbian collection and financed the building of a wing to house it, as well as a second wing for Mrs. Bliss's collection of rare books on landscape gardening. The Byzantine collection includes illuminated manuscripts, a 13th-century icon of St. Peter, mosaics, ivory carvings, a 4th-century sarcophagus, jewelry, and more. The pre-Columbian works, displayed chronologically in eight marble- and oak-floored glass pavilions, feature Olmec jade and serpentine figures. Mayan relief panels, textiles from 900 B.C. to the Spanish Conquest, funerary pottery, gold necklaces made by the lost-wax process, and sculptures of Aztec gods and goddesses.

The history music room, furnished in French, Italian, and Spanish antiques, was the setting for the 1944 Dumbarton Oaks Conversations about the United Nations. It has a beamed, painted 16th-century French-style ceiling and an immense 16th-century stone fireplace. Among its notable artworks is El Greco's *The Visitation*.

Don't miss the formal gardens, which include an Orangery, a Rose Garden (final resting place of the Blisses amid 1,000 rose bushes), wisteria-covered arbors, herbaceous borders, groves of cherry trees, and magnolias. You can picnic nearby in Montrose Park.

Admission: Garden $3 adults, $2 children under 12 and senior citizens; collections, free.

Open: Garden (weather permitting), Nov–Mar, daily 2–5pm; Apr–Oct, daily 2–6pm. Collections, Tues–Sun 2–5pm. **Closed:** Federal holidays and Dec 24.

NATIONAL GEOGRAPHIC SOCIETY'S EXPLORERS HALL, 17th and M Sts. NW, Tel. 857-7588.

The National Geographic Society was formed in 1888 to further "the increase and diffusion of geographic knowledge." At Explorers Hall, dozens of fascinating displays—most of them utilizing interactive videos—put that knowledge literally at your fingertips. In Geographica, on the north side of the hall, you can touch a tornado, find out what it's like inside the earth, explore the vast Martian landscape, and study the origin of humankind. A seven-minute video presentation narrated by Leonard Nimoy introduces visitors to the National Geographic Society. After hearing "Spock" speak, you can test your geographic knowledge at computer trivia games. The major exhibit here is Earth Station One, an interactive amphitheater (centered on an immense free-floating globe) that simulates an orbital flight. My favorite exhibit is a video microscope that zooms in clearly on slides showing such specimens as a hydra (a simple multicellular animal) or mosquito larva. Many of the video exhibits have overtones of environmental awareness.

Also on display: a scale model of Jacques Cousteau's diving saucer in which he descended to 25,000 feet; the flag and dog sledge, among other equipment, of Adm. Robert E. Peary, first man to reach the North Pole, along with a recording he made (his 1909 expedition was funded by the National Geographic Society); an *Aepyornis maximus* egg, from Madagascar's extinct 1,000-pound flightless "elephant bird"; and the world's largest freestand globe (34 feet around the equator, with a scale of 1 inch per 60 miles). There's a full-size replica of a giant Olmec stone head dating to 32 B.C. from La Venta, Mexico. A 3.9-billion-year-old moon rock is on view in a small planetarium, and video excerpts from the society's TV specials are shown in the National Geographic Television Room. In addition, there's an ongoing program of temporary exhibits, and an display of oversize photographs from the magazine is backlit, so it can be viewed even after museum hours.

The National Geographic Store sells a wide array of publications, maps, globes, games, and videos. Within walking distance of the White House, this is a great place to take the kids, but they should be at least 9 or 10 years old. Younger children will not understand most of the exhibits.

Admission: Free.

Open: Mon–Sat 9am–5pm, Sun 10am–5pm. **Closed:** Dec 25. **Metro:** Farragut North (Connecticut Avenue and L Street exit) or Farragut West.

THE FOLGER SHAKESPEARE LIBRARY, 201 E. Capitol St. SE. Tel. 544-7077.

"Shakespeare taught us that the little world of the heart is vaster, deeper, and richer than the spaces of astronomy," wrote Ralph Waldo Emerson in 1864. A decade later, Amherst student Henry Clay Folger was profoundly affected upon hearing a lecture by Emerson similarly extolling the Bard. Folger purchased an inexpensive set of Shakespeare's plays and went on to amass the world's largest collection of his printed works, today housed in the Folger Shakespeare Library. By 1930, when Folger and his wife,

Emily (whose literary enthusiasms matched his own), laid the cornerstone of a building to house the collection, it comprised 93,000 books, 50,000 prints and engravings, and thousands of manuscripts. The Folgers made it all a gift to the American people.

The building itself is classical in style, its Georgian marble facade decorated with nine bas-relief scenes from Shakespeare's plays. A statue of Puck stands in the west garden, and quotations from the Bard and from contemporaries such as Ben Jonson adorn the exterior walls. An Elizabethan garden on the east side of the building is planted with flowers and herbs of the period, many of them mentioned in the plays.

The facility, today housing some 250,000 books, 100,000 of which are rare, is an important research center not only for Shakespearean scholars, but for those studying any aspect of the English and continental Renaissance. And the oak-paneled Great Hall, reminiscent of a Tudor long gallery, is a popular attraction for the general public. It has an intricate plaster ceiling decorated with Shakespeare's coat of arms, fleurs-de-lis, and other motifs. On display are rotating exhibits from the permanent collection—books, paintings, playbills, Renaissance musical instruments, and more.

At the end of the Great Hall is a theater designed to suggest an Elizabethan innyard theater where plays, concerts, readings, and Shakespeare-related events take place (see Chapter 9 for details). The timber and plaster walls are adorned with painted decorations; the gallery is triple-tiered and supported by oak columns with hand-carved satyrs.

Free walk-in **tours** are given at 11am.
Admission: Free.
Open: Mon–Sat 10am–4pm. **Closed:** Federal holidays. **Metro:** Capitol South.

UNITED STATES NAVY MEMORIAL, 701 Pennsylvania Ave. NW. Tel. 737-2300, or toll free 800/831-8892.

Authorized by congress in 1980 to honor the men and women of the United States Navy, this memorial centers on a 100-foot-diameter circular plaza bearing a granite world map flanked by fountains and waterfalls salted with waters from the seven seas. In summer, military bands perform on the plaza. A statue of *The Lone Sailor* watching over the map represents all who have served in the navy. And two sculpture walls adorned with bronze bas-reliefs commemorate navy history and related maritime serviceds.

The building adjoining the memorial houses a naval heritage center. In its "Quarterdeck" entrance area, a wall frieze commemorates battles from Yorktown to Operation Desert Storm, and a statue called *The Homecoming* depicts the joyous reunion of a navy family. Along a spiral staircase, a timeline of ship development spanning 200 years of naval history is etched into a glass wave-motif wall. Museum highlights include interactive video kiosks proffering a wealth of information about navy ships, aircraft, and history; the Navy Memorial Log Room, a computerized record of past and present navy personnel; the Presidents Room, honoring six U.S.

presidents who served in the navy and two who were secretaries of the navy; the Ship's Store, filled with nautical and maritime merchandise; and a wide-screen 70mm Surroundsound film called *At Sea* (by the makers of *To Fly*), which lets viewers experience the grandeur of the ocean and the adventure of going to sea on a navy ship. The 35-minute film plays every hour on the hour between 10am and 4pm; admission is $3.50 for adults, $3 for seniors and students 18 and under.

Guided **tours** are available from the front desk, subject to staff availability. Free concerts take place in spring and summer Tuesday evenings at 8pm and on selected days at noon; call for details.

Admission: Free.

Open: Mon–Sat 9:30am–5pm, Sun noon–5pm. **Closed:** Dec. 25. **Metro:** Archives/Navy Memorial.

3. COOL FOR KIDS

Visiting the capital with parents or classmates is as intrinsic a part of American childhood as baseball, hot dogs, and apple pie. Washington is a great place for family vacations, but how much fun you have depends on your approach and planning. Let the kids help in planning daily itineraries, a project that allows everyone to become acquainted with the sights and build up excitement over what you'll be seeing. The more you know about each place, the easier it is to communicate and create enthusiasm; it's also helpful when taking tours if you can supplement the guide's commentary with child-oriented explanations. Kids tend to stay alert and interested when you discuss with them what you're seeing; leave them to their own devices and boredom—quickly followed by whining—sets in. This might mean doing a wee bit of homework (reading up a bit on the various attractions), but your efforts will enhance everyone's trip.

FAVORITE CHILDREN'S SIGHTS

Check for special children's events at museum information desks when you enter; better yet, call the day before to find out what's available. Here's a rundown of the biggest kid-pleasers in town (for details, see the full entries earlier in this chapter):

National Air and Space Museum: Spectacular IMAX films (don't miss), missiles, rockets, and a walk-through orbital workshop.

National Museum of Natural History: A Discovery Room just for youngsters, an insect zoo, shrunken heads, and dinosaurs.

National Museum of American History: The Foucault Pendulum, locomotives, atom smashers, and an old-fashioned ice-cream parlor.

Federal Bureau of Investigation: Gangster memorabilia, crime-solving methods, espionage devices, and a sharpshooting demonstration. You can't miss.

Bureau of Engraving and Printing: Kids enjoy looking at immense piles of money as much as you do

Capital Children's Museum (see below): All of it is for kids, with sound-and-light shows, hands-on exhibits, and educational computer games.

National Zoological Park: Kids always love a zoo, and this is an especially nice one.

Ford's Theatre and Lincoln Museum and the **House Where Lincoln Died:** Booth's gun and diary, Lincoln's blood-stained pillowcase, the clothes Lincoln was wearing the night he was assassinated; need I say more? Kids adore the whole business.

National Geographic Society's Explorers Hall: A moon rock, the egg of an extinct "elephant bird" (if it hatched it would weigh 1,000 pounds), numerous interactive videos. The magazine comes alive.

Washington Monument: Easy to get them up there, hard to get them down. If only they could use the steps, they'd be in heaven.

Lincoln Memorial: Kids know a lot about Lincoln and enjoy visiting his memorial. A special treat is visiting it after dark (same for the Washington Monument and Jefferson Memorial).

Arts and Industries Building: 19th-century steam engines, ship models, farm machinery, old clocks, and performances just for children in the Discovery Theater.

National Archives: See the original Declaration of Independence, Constitution, and Bill of Rights.

White House, Capitol, and Supreme Court: Kids enjoy learning how our government works.

Call the **Kennedy Center** and **National Theatre** to find out about children's shows; see Chapter 9 for details.

CAPITAL CHILDREN'S MUSEUM, 800 3rd St. NE, at H St. Tel. 543-8600.

Kids are, of necessity, rather restrained at most Washington sightseeing attractions; here's their chance to let loose on three floors of child-oriented hands-on exhibits. They can pet a resident goat, grind Mexican chocolate and prepare tortillas, make slides and film shows, and create shadow art on a wall (one of my favorite activities). A more serious exhibit called "Remember the Children" explores the Holocaust from a child's point of view. At Toona-Vision, an interactive television studio, children can experiment with special-effects equipment, create animation, and broadcast on station WCCM, which is heard in other parts of the museum. Games involving light, shadows, and mirrors teach kids about optics in Science Hall. And a replica of a 30,000-year-old cave, complete with water dripping and the howling of distant beasts, illustrates the use of cave drawings and rituals as Ice Age means of communication. An exhibit about animator Chuck Jones features original cels, drawings, and film of Bugs Bunny, Daffy Duck, and the rest of the gang. Kids can create sound effects and put themselves in cartoons. There's also a maze with optical illusions to wander through.

Inquire about ongoing workshops, demonstrations, and theater presentations for children.

Admission: $6 per person

Open: Daily 10am–5pm. **Closed:** Jan 1, Easter, Thanksgiving Day, and Dec 25. **Metro:** Union Station.

ADDITIONAL TIPS

As to the rest, plan with your children's ages and interests in mind.

An occasional purchase at a museum shop can quickly revive flagging interest, and most of the museums have wonderful toys and children's books, not to mention items like freeze-dried astronaut ice cream.

The Friday "Weekend" section of the *Washington Post* lists numerous activities (mostly free) for kids: special museum events, children's theater, storytelling programs, puppet shows, video-game competitions, and so forth.

A hotel with a swimming pool is the best child-refresher known to man; it also means some time alone for adults. Consider this when making reservations; it may be worth a few extra bucks.

Ride the Metro, and let the kids purchase the tickets and insert their own farecards. It will be a high point, especially if they've never been on a subway before.

Enjoy some of the outdoor attractions listed in "Recreation in the Parks" later in this chapter; go bicycling or rowing; take a guided nature hike or a Potomac boat ride.

Have fun!

4. ORGANIZED TOURS

BY BUS

Even if you have just a few days to spend in Washington, I think you can do better on your own. However, a guided motorcoach tour can provide a good city overview.

The **Gray Line** (tel. 289-1995) offers a variety of tours: "Washington After Dark" (3½ hours), focusing on night-lit national monuments and federal buildings plus Georgetown; the "Washington, D.C., All-Day Combination Tour," which includes major Washington sights plus Arlington National Cemetery, Mount Vernon, and Alexandria; the four-hour "Interiors of Public Buildings," a morning tour visiting Ford's Theatre, the Jefferson Memorial, Museum of American History, and other important edifices, or a similar afternoon tour taking in the Capitol, Library of Congress, Supreme Court, National Air and Space Museum, and National Archives (a nine-hour tour combines both of these); and a "Two-Day Grand Tour." There are also trips as far afield as Colonial Williamsburg, Harper's Ferry, Gettysburg, and Charlottesville. Tours depart from Gray Line's Union Station terminal, with pickups at all major hotels. Headsets and tour tapes in foreign languages are available for afternoon tours. For details, call the above number or inquire at your hotel desk.

A local company, **All About Town, Inc.,** 519 6th St. NW (tel. 393-3696), offers a similar range of tours. Pickup is offered at major hotels. Call for details or, once again, inquire at your hotel desk.

Consider, too, **Tourmobile** and **Old Town Trolley** tours (see "Getting Around" in Chapter 4 for details).

BY BOAT

Since Washington is a river city, why not see it by boat. **Spirit of Washington Cruises,** Pier 4 at 6th and Water Streets SW (tel. 554-8000), offers a variety of such trips daily from early March to December. Lunch and dinner cruises include a 20-minute high-energy musical revue. Call for departure times and make reservations in advance. The following trips are offered at this writing; check when you arrive, because they tend to change with some frequency.

Evening Dinner Cruises (7 to 10pm daily) include dancing to live music and a lavish buffet meal. The fare (including tips) is $45.40 Sunday to Friday, $54.95 on Saturday.

Lunch and Brunch Cruises are two-hour narrated excursions on the Washington Channel. The meal consists of a seafood buffet, dessert, and tea or coffee. The fare (including tips) is $26.35 Tuesday to Friday, $30.20 Saturday and Sunday.

Moonlight Dance Cruises feature dance music, complimentary hors d'oeuvres, cocktails (a cash bar), and dancing under the stars. Music is 1940s to Top 40, geared to adults, not teens (you must be at least 21 to participate). The boat heads to Alexandria. Cost for this 2½-hour late-night cruise is $19.95.

The Mount Vernon Cruise, a popular half-day excursion, takes in D.C. sights en route to Mount Vernon plantation, George Washington's beautiful estate on the Potomac. The trip is about 1½ hours each way. The round-trip fare is $21.50 for adults, $19.25 for seniors, $12.75 for children 6 to 11, free for children 5 and under. Prices include entrance to Mount Vernon. It's a good idea to book in advance.

The *Spirit of Washington* is a luxury ship with climate-controlled, carpeted decks and huge panoramic windows designed for sightseeing. There are three well-stocked bars on board. Mount Vernon cruises are aboard an equally luxurious sister ship, the *Potomac Spirit.*

SCANDAL TOURS

You've seen the Smithsonian and the Lincoln Memorial. Now it's time to bypass the monuments and head right into the gutter. Scandal Tours, the creation of a brilliantly talented D.C. political-comedy group called Gross National Product, is a guided bus tour of Washington's sleaziest sites. ABC News anchor Peter Jennings called it "a worm's-eye view of Washington."

Highlights include the White House, where the focus is on presidential sex scandals; the Old Executive Office Building, where Ollie North and Fawn Hall shredded their way into history; the Tidal

Basin, where Former Congressman Wilbur Mills and "Argentine firecracker" Fanne Foxe cavorted in the moonlight (she fell into the water, he got in hot water); the Capitol steps, scene of a night of passion for John and Rita Jenrette (Congressman Jenrette was later entrapped by Abscam and, still later, caught shoplifting in a department store); the FBI ("Janet Reno" talks about J. Edgar Hoover, "another man in a dress"); the Vista Hotel, where former mayor Marion Barry repeatedly protested the "bitch set me up"; Watergate (of course); and Gary Hart's town house, from which he emerged with Donna Rice one morning to find himself at the evening of his political career. Tour participants are greeted by a GNP troupe member in the guise of a political figure (perhaps "Nancy Reagan" in signature red dress), while other GNP actors aboard the bus portray Clinton, Gennifer Flowers, Sen. Bob Packwood, and other personalities in the forefront of the political arena. Historical figures are not spared—the company even has some dish on George Washington! "The great thing is the constant source of material," says GNP creator John Simmons. "You have power, money, and sex all along the Potomac. It's an unbeatable product—bad things happening to people it's hard to feel sorry for."

The 90-minute tours depart every Saturday at 1pm (call for reservations and departure point). The cost is $27 per person. Or you can buy "Scandal Tour In-A-Box" for $12.95 and take the tour yourself by car. To order or make your reservations, call 301/587-4291. *Note:* You can also see GNP perform Saturday night at the Bayou in Georgetown (details in Chapter 9).

5. RECREATION IN THE PARKS

Like most cities, Washington has manicured pockets of green amid its high-rise office buildings and superhighways. Unlike most cities, it's also extensively endowed with vast natural areas—thousands of parkland acres; two rivers; a 185-mile-long, tree-lined canalside trail; an untamed wilderness area; and a few thousand cherry trees—all centrally located within the District. And there's much more just a stone's throw away. This section explores D.C.'s wealth of outdoor facilities.

ROCK CREEK PARK

Created in 1890, Rock Creek Park was purchased by Congress for its "pleasant valleys and ravines, primeval forests and open fields, its running waters, its rocks clothed with rich ferns and mosses, its repose and tranquillity, its light and shade, its every-varying shrubbery, its beautiful and extensive views." A 1,750-acre valley within the District of Columbia, extending 12 miles from the Potomac River to the Maryland border (another 2,700 acres), it's one of the biggest and finest city parks in the nation. Parts of it are still wild; it's not unusual to see a deer scurrying through the woods in more remote sections.

The park's offerings include the Carter Barron Amphitheatre (see Chapter 9), playgrounds, an extensive system of beautiful wooded hiking trails, and sports facilities.

For full information on the wide range of park programs and activities, visit the **Rock Creek Nature Center,** 5200 Glover Rod. NW (tel. 426-6829), Wednesday to Sunday 9am to 5pm; or **Park Headquarters,** 5000 Glover Rd. (tel. 282-1063), Monday to Friday 7:45am to 4:15pm. The Nature Center itself is the scene of numerous activities—weekend planetarium shows for kids (minimum age 4) and adults, nature films, crafts demonstrations, live animal demonstrations, and guided nature walks, plus a daily mix of lectures, films, and other events. A calendar is available on request. Self-guided nature trials begin here. All activities are free, but for planetarium shows you need to pick up tickets a half hour in advance. There are also nature exhibits on the premises. The Nature Center is closed on federal holidays.

You can see a water-powered 19th-century gristmill (one of more than 20 mills that operated along Rock Creek from 1664 to 1925) grinding corn and wheat into flour at Tilden Street and Beach Drive (tel. 426-6908). It's called **Pierce Mill** (a man named Isaac Pierce built it), and it's open to visitors Wednesday to Sunday 8am to 4:30pm. Pierce's old carriage house is today the **Art Barn** (tel. 244-2482), where works of local artists are exhibited; it's open Wednesday to Saturday 10am to 5pm, and Sunday noon to 5pm (closed federal holidays).

Call 673-7646 or 673-7647 for details, locations, and group reservations at any of the park's 30 **picnic areas,** some with fireplaces. A brochure available at Park Headquarters or the Nature Center also provides details on picnic locations.

There are 15 soft-surface (clay) and 10 hard-surface **tennis courts** (five enclosed for indoor play October to May 1) at 16th and Kennedy Streets NW (tel. 722-5949). April to mid-November you must make a reservation in person at Guest Services on the premises to use them. Fees vary with court surface and time of play; call for details. Six additional clay courts are located off Park Road just east of Pierce Mill.

Poetry readings and workshops are held during the summer at the one-time residence of High Sierra poet Joaquin Miller, Beach Drive north of Military Road. Call 282-1063 for information.

The 18-hole **Rock Creek Golf Course** and clubhouse, 16th and Rittenhouse Streets NW (tel. 723-9832 or 882-7332), are open year-round, daily dawn to dusk. A fee is charged. Clubs, lockers, and carts can be rented.

There are stables at the **Rock Creek Park Horse Center,** near the Nature Center on Glover Road NW (tel. 362-0117). Trail rides are offered Tuesday to Friday 1:30 to 3pm and weekends noon to 3:15pm. Call for rates and information on riding instruction.

You have to rent bikes elsewhere, but there's an 11-mile **bike path** from the Lincoln Memorial through the park into Maryland, all of it paved. On weekends and holidays a large part of it is closed to vehicular traffic.

Joggers will enjoy the 1½-mile **Perrier parcourse** with 18 calisthenics stations en route. It begins near the intersection of Cathedral Avenue and Rock Creek Parkway. There's another Perrier parcourse, with only four stations, at 16th and Kennedy Streets NW.

Finally, 15 miles of **hiking trails,** from easy to strenuous, traverse the park. You can go on your own or participate in guided hikes. Details and maps are available at Park Headquarters or the Nature Center.

There's convenient **free parking** throughout the park. To get to the Nature Center by public transport, take the Metro to Friendship Heights and transfer to an E2 or E4 bus to Military Road and Oregon Avenue/Glover Road.

POTOMAC PARK

West and East Potomac Parks, their 720 riverside acres divided by the Tidal Basin, are most famous for their spring display of **cherry blossoms** and all the hoopla that goes with it.

West Potomac Park has 1,300 trees bordering the Tidal Basin, 10% of them Akebonos with delicate pink blossoms, the rest Yoshinos with white cloudlike flower clusters. It's the focal point of many of the week-long celebrations, which include the lighting of the 300-year-old **Japanese Stone Lantern** near Kutz Bridge, presented to the city by the governor of Tokyo in 1954. The trees bloom for a little less than two weeks beginning somewhere between March 20 and April 17; April 7 is the average date. See the calendar of events in Chapter 2 for further details on cherry blossom events.

Though West Potomac Park gets more cherry blossom publicity, East Potomac Park has more trees (1,800 of them) and more varieties (11). Here, too, are **picnic grounds; 24 tennis courts,** including five indoors and three lit for night play (tel. 554-5962); one 18-hole and two 9-hole **golf courses** (tel. 863-9007); a large **swimming pool** (tel. 727-6523); and **biking** and **hiking** paths by the water.

West Potomac Park encompasses Constitution Gardens; the Vietnam, Lincoln, and Jefferson memorials; a small island where ducks live; and the Reflecting Pool.

CHESAPEAKE & OHIO CANAL NATIONAL HISTORICAL PARK [C&O CANAL]

One of the great joys of living in Washington is the C&O Canal and its unspoiled 184½-mile towpath. One leaves urban cares and stresses behind while hiking, strolling, jogging, cycling, or boating in this lush, natural setting of ancient oaks and red maples, giant sycamores, willows, and wildflowers. I've never walked the canal without making an exciting discovery—a proud mother duck with a new family in tow; raspberries suddenly abundantly in season; a brilliant flowering tree amid the greenery; a quaint canalside home; a sudden appreciation of light shimmering on the water. The canal is a happy place. However, it wasn't always just a leisure spot for city people. It was built in the 1800s, when water routes were considered vital to transportation. Even before it was completed, however, the B&O Railroad, which was constructed at about the same time and along the same route, had begun to render it obsolete. Today, perhaps, it serves an even more important purpose as a cherished urban refuge.

Canal Activities Headquarters for canal activities is the **Office of the Superintendent,** C&O Canal National Historical Park, P.O. Box 4, Sharpsburg, MD 21782 (tel. 301/739-4200). Also knowledgeable is the National Park Service office at **Great Falls Tavern Visitor Center,** 11710 MacArthur Blvd., Potomac, MD 20854 (tel. 301/299-3613). At this 1831 tavern you can see museum exhibits and a film about the canal; there's also a bookstore on the premises. And April to November, Wednesday to Sunday, the **Georgetown Information Center,** 1057 Thomas Jefferson St. NW (tel. 653-5844), can also provide maps and information. Call ahead for hours at all the above.

Hiking any section of the flat dirt towpath—or its more rugged side paths—is a pleasure. There are **picnic tables** (at **camping areas**), some with fire grills, about every 5 miles from Fletcher's Boat House (about 3.2 miles out of Georgetown) to Cumberland. Use of campsites is on a first-come, first-served basis. Enter the towpath in Georgetown below M Street via Thomas Jefferson Street. If you hike 14 miles, you'll reach **Great Falls,** a point where the Potomac becomes a stunning waterfall plunging 76 feet. Or drive to Great Falls Park on the Virginia side of the Potomac.

Stop at **Fletcher's Boat House,** described in "Sports," below (tel. 244-0461), to rent **bikes** or **boats** or purchase bait and tackle (or a license) for **fishing.** A snack bar and picnic area are on the premises. It's also accessible by car.

Much less strenuous than hiking is a **mule-drawn 19th-century canal boat trip** led by Park Service rangers in period dress. They regale passengers with canal legend and lore and sing period songs. These boats depart Wednesday through Sunday from mid-April to early November; call 202/653-5844 or 301/299-3613 for departure times. Tickets are available at the Georgetown Information Center or the Great Falls Tavern (address and phone for both above). The fare is $5 for adults, $3.50 for children under 12 and seniors over 62.

Call any of the above information numbers for details on riding, rock climbing, fishing, birdwatching, concerts, ranger-guided tours, ice skating, camping, and other canal activities.

UNITED STATES NATIONAL ARBORETUM

A research and educational center focusing on trees and shrubs, the U.S. National Arboretum, 3501 New York Ave. NE (tel. 475-4815), is one of the great joys of Washington. Its 9½ miles of paved roads meander through 444 hilly acres of rhododendrons, azaleas (the most extensive plantings in the nation), crab apples, magnolias, hollies, peonies, irises, dogwoods, day lilies, boxwoods, cherry trees, aquatic plants, and dwarf conifers. The highlight for me is the **National Bonsai and Penjing Museum**— a $4.5-million Bicentennial gift from Japan of 53 beautiful miniature trees, some of them more than three centuries old. Each one is an exquisite work of art. The exhibit was augmented by a gift of 35 Chinese Penjing trees in 1986, and again in 1990 by the American Bonsai Collection of 56 North American plants; in 1993 a conservatory for tropical bonsai was erected. This area also includes a **Japanese Garden** and a garden of plants of American origin. The **Herbarium** contains 600,000 dried plants for reference purposes. The **Herb Garden,** another highlight, includes a historic rose garden (100 old-fashioned fragrant varieties), a contemporary interpretation of a 16th-century English-style "knot" garden, and 10 specialty gardens—a dye garden, a medicinal garden, and a culinary garden among them. The **National Bird Garden** features berrying shrubs that attract feathered friends. Along Fern Valley Trail is the Franklin Tree—a species now extinct in the wild—discovered in 1765 by a botanist friend of Benjamin Franklin. And a magnificent sight is the arboretum's **acropolis**—22 of the original U.S. Capitol columns designed by Benjamin Latrobe in a setting created by the noted English landscape artist Russell Page. The **New American Garden,** opened in 1990, is a collection of ornamental grasses— reminiscent of prairie landscapes—and perennials, with brick walkways, terraces, and a statue of Demeter, the Greek goddess of agriculture. Its colorful spring bulb plants comprise a wide variety of narcissi, tulips, irises, and crocuses enhanced by small flowering and fruiting trees and interesting shrubs. Carefully placed teak benches provide a place for quiet contemplation. The **American Friendship Garden** also features an extensive collection of perennials and bulb plants. Magnolias and early bulbs bloom in late March or early April; rhododendrons, daffodils, and flowering cherry trees in mid-April; azaleas and peonies in May; lilies and hibiscus in summer. In autumn the arboretum is ablaze in reds and oranges as the leaves change color. And the **Asian Collections** in a landscaped valley include rare plants from China and Korea.

The arboretum is open Monday to Friday 8am to 5pm, and Saturday, Sunday, and holidays 10am to 5pm; the bonsai collection, 10am to 3:30pm daily. Everything is closed December 25, Take bus B2, B4, or B5 from the Stadium Armory Metro station to Bladensburg Road and R Street NE. Or hop in a taxi; it's only a few dollars. If you drive, **parking** is free (you can drive through if you wish). Frequent tours, lectures, and workshops (including bonsai classes) are offered, and a comprehensive guidebook is available in the gift shop.

THEODORE ROOSEVELT ISLAND

A serene 88-acre wilderness preserve, Theodore Roosevelt Island is a memorial to our 26th president, in recognition of his contributions to conservation. An outdoor enthusiast and expert field naturalist,

Roosevelt once threw away a prepared speech and roared, "I hate a man who would skin the land!" During his administration 150 national forests, 19 national parks, 51 bird refuges, and four game refuges were created.

Theodore Roosevelt Island was inhabited as far back as the 1600s by Native Americans. Over the years it passed through many owners before becoming what it is today—an island preserve of swamp, marsh, and upland forest that's a haven for rabbits, chipmunks, great owls, fox, muskrat, turtles, and groundhogs. It's a complex ecosystem in which cattails, arrowarum, and pickerelweed growing in the marshes create a hospitable habitat for abundant bird life. And willow, ash, and maple trees rooted on the mudflats create the swamp environment favored by the raccoon in its search for crayfish. You can observe these flora and fauna in their natural environs on 2½ miles of foot trails.

In the northern center of the island, overlooking an oval terrace encircled by a water-filled moat, stands a 17-foot bronze statue of Roosevelt. From the terrace rise four 21-foot granite tablets inscribed with the tenets of his philosophy: "There are no words that can tell the hidden spirit of the wilderness, that can reveal its mystery, it melancholy, and its charm. The Nation behaves well if it treats the natural resources as assets which it must turn over to the next generation increased and not impaired in value."

To get to the island, take the George Washington Memorial Parkway exit north from the Theodore Roosevelt Bridge. The **parking** area is accessible only from the northbound lane; from there, a pedestrian bridge connects the island with the Virginia shore. You can also rent a canoe at Thompson's Boat Center (see "Boating" in "Active Sports," in "Sports," below) and paddle over, or walk across the pedestrian bridge at Rosslyn Circle, two blocks from the Rosslyn **Metro** station. **Picnicking** is permitted on the grounds near the memorial.

Fur further information, contact the District Ranger, Theodore Roosevelt Island, George Washington Memorial Parkway, c/o Turkey Run Park, McLean, VA 22101 (tel. 703/285-2598)

6. SPORTS

Too much museum-going and sightseeing can do you in. A change of pace is the answer and Washington has a lot to offer here, too. Catch a Redskins, Hoyas, or Baltimore Orioles games. Or get out there and bike, hike, ride horseback, swim, or play tennis. All this and more is described below. Also check the Friday "Weekend" section of the *Washington Post* for information on these and other activities from volleyball to river rafting.

SPECTATOR SPORTS

USAIR ARENA The **Washington Bullets** (NBA) and the **Washington Capitals** (NHL) play home games at the USAir

Arena, Exit 15A or 17A off the Capital Beltway in Landover, Maryland (tel. 301/350-3400). The 19,000-seat arena is also used for Georgetown University basketball games (the Hoyas), Washington Warthogs (CISL) indoor soccer games, monster truck shows, wrestling, and annual events like the Washington International Horse Show, Campbell's Olympic Figure-Skating Championships, and World Professional Figure Skating Championships. Also big-name concerts. For tickets, call 202/432-SEAT, or toll free 800/551-SEAT.

ROBERT F. KENNEDY MEMORIAL STADIUM/D.C. ARMORY The 55,000-seat Robert F. Kennedy Memorial Stadium (and the 10,000-seat D.C. Armory complex), East Capitol Street between 19th and 20th Streets SE (tel. 547-9077 or 546-3337), is the D.C. home of the **Washington Redskins** (NFL). Events here also include wrestling, nationally televised boxing, roller derby, the circus, soccer games, and rodeos. To charge tickets call 200/432-SEAT, or toll free 800/551-SEAT.

ORIOLE PARK AT CAMDEN YARDS The 48,000-seat Oriole Park at Camden Yards, 333 W. Camden St., between Howard and Conway Streets, in Baltimore, Maryland (tel. 410/685-9800), opened in 1992. It's the home of baseball's **Baltimore Orioles.** Unlike recent ultramodern sports stadiums, Oriole Park incorporates features of its urban environment, such as the old B&O Railroad yards near downtown Baltimore. A renovated brick warehouse serves as a striking visual backdrop beyond the right-field fence. For tickets, call 410/481-SEAT, or toll free 800/551-SEAT. From Union Station in Washington, take a MARC train to Baltimore, which lets you off right at the ballpark. By car, take I-95 north to Exit 53.

BALTIMORE ARENA The 13,500-seat Baltimore Arena, 210 W. Baltimore St., a few blocks from the Inner Harbor in Baltimore (tel. 410/347-2020), is home to the **Baltimore Thunder** (indoor lacrosse) and the **Baltimore Spirit** (NPSL, indoor soccer). The **Washington Bullets** (NBA) play at least four games here each year, and the facility also hosts the Ice Capades every February, Harlem Globetrotters games, tractor pulls, and more. For tickets, call 410/481-SEAT, or toll free 800/551-SEAT Once again, take the MARC train from Union Station. To get here by car, take I-95 north to I-395 (stay in left lane) to the Inner Harbor exit and follow Howard Street to the arena.

THE PATRIOT CENTER The Patriot Center, 4400 University Dr. in Fairfax, Virginia (tel. 703/993-3000), opened in late 1985 on the campus of nearby George Mason University. A 10,000-seat facility, it's used for college basketball games, Harlem Globetrotters games, gymnastic competitions, horse shows, and other events. To get here, take the Wilson Bridge to Braddock Road West (Route 623) and proceed about 8 miles to University Drive. For tickets, call 703/573-SEAT or toll free 800/551-SEAT.

ACTIVE SPORTS

BICYCLING Both **Fletcher's Boat House** and **Thompson's Boat Center** (see "Boating," below for addresses and hours) rent bikes, as does **Big Wheel Bikes,** 1034 33rd St. NW, right near the C&O Canal just below M Street (tel. 337-0254). Hours are 10am to 6pm daily, and till 8pm weekdays from April to September. There's another Big Wheel shop on Capitol Hill at 315 7th St. SE (tel. 543-1600); call for hours. Photo ID and a major credit card are required to rent bicycles.

The *Washington Post* Friday "Weekend" section lists cycling trips. See also Rock Creek Park, the C&O Canal, and the Potomac Parks in "Recreation in the Parks," earlier in his chapter, for details on their biking facilities.

BOATING **Thompson's Boat Center,** 2900 Virginia Ave. at Rock Creek Parkway NW (tel. 333-4861 or 333-9543), rents canoes, sailboats, rowing shells, and rowboats. They also offer sculling and sweep-rowing lessons. Photo ID and a $20 deposit are required. They're open mid-April to early October, daily 8am to 5pm. You can't rent a boat after 5pm. For bike rentals ($10 deposit required) the shop is open March to mid-November, same hours.

April to mid-October you can rent paddleboats on the north end of the Tidal Basin off Independence Avenue.

Fletcher's Boat House, Reservoir and Canal Roads (tel. 244-0461), is right on the C&O Canal, about a 3.2-mile wonderfully scenic walk from Georgetown. Open March to mid-November, daily 7:30am to dusk, Fletcher's rents canoes and rowboats and sells fishing licenses, bait, and tackle. ID is required (a driver's license or major credit card). A snack bar and restrooms here are welcome after that hike. And there are picnic tables (with barbecue grills) overlooking the Potomac. You don't have to walk to Fletcher's; it's accessible by car (west on M Street to Canal Road) and has plenty of free parking.

CAMPING See the C&O Canal in "Recreation in the Parks," earlier in this chapter.

FISHING The Potomac River around Washington provides an abundant variety of fish—some 40 species, all perfectly safe to eat. Good fishing is possible from late February to November, but mid-March to June (spawning season) is peak. Perch and catfish are the most common catch, but during bass season a haul of 20 to 40 is not unusual. The Washington Channel offers good bass and carp fishing year-round.

A **fishing license** is required. You can obtain one at various locations around the city, among them **Fletcher's Boat House** (address and telephone number above) and the **Chinatown Coffee House,** 616 H St. NW (tel. 783-6212). Cost for nonresidents is $7.50 for a year, $3 for a 14-day permit.

GOLF There are dozens of public courses within easy driving distance of the D.C. area, but within the District itself East Potomac Park and Rock Creek Park have the only public courses. The 18-hole **Rock Creek Golf Course** and clubhouse, at 16th and Rittenhouse Streets NW (tel. 882-7332 or 723-9832), are open to the public daily year-round from dawn to dusk. You will find a snack bar and lockers on the premises, and you can rent clubs and carts A fee is charged.

East Potomac Park has one 18-hole, par-72 and two 9-hole courses. For details, call 863-9007.

HIKING If you prefer group hikes, the **Sierra Club** (tel. 547-2326 or 547-5551) organizes guided hikes of varying length and ruggedness just about every weekend. These include backpack trips to local wilderness areas, day hikes to nearby national parks and forests, also bike trips and white-water and flat-water canoe trips. There's an optional charge of $1 per person for each hiking trip, and people sharing rides chip in for gas. A calendar of events is available for $5 a year; call the above phone number for information, or write to Sierra Club Calendar, 1863 Kalorama Rd. NW, Apt. 1B, Washington, DC 20009.

Also check the *Washington Post* Friday "Weekend" section for listings of hiking clubs; almost all are open to the public for a small fee. Be sure to inquire about the difficulty of any hike you plan to join and the speed with which the group proceeds; some hikes are fast-paced, allowing no time to smell the flowers.

On your own, there are numerous hiking paths. The **C&O Canal** offers 184½ miles alone; it would be hard to find a more scenic setting than the 9½ miles of road at the **arboretum** (see "Recreation in the Parks," earlier in this chapter); **Theodore Roosevelt Island** has 88 wilderness acres to explore, including a 2½-mile nature trail (short but rugged); and in **Rock Creek Park** there are 15 miles of hiking tails for which maps are available at the Visitor Information Center or Park Headquarters.

HORSEBACK RIDING The **Rock Creek Park Horse Center,** near the Nature Center on Glover Road NW (tel. 362-0117), offers rental horses for trail rides and riding instruction. there are 14 miles of woodland bridle paths to explore. Call for ride times. No riding experience is required.

ICE SKATING My favorite place for winter skating is on the **C&O Canal,** its banks dotted with cozy fires at which one can warm frozen extremities. Call 301/299-3613 for information on ice conditions. You might find it inspiring to skate on the **Reflecting Pool** between the Lincoln Memorial and the Washington Monument, especially by night when it's dramatically lit. Guest Services, Inc., operates the **National Sculpture Garden Ice Rink** on the Mall at 7th Street and Constitution Avenue NW (tel. 371-5342), the **Pershing Park** outdoor rink at 14th Street and Pennsylvania Avenue NW (tel. 737-6938), and a huge hockey-size indoor facility, the **Fort Dupont Ice Arena,** at 3779 Ely Place SE, at Minnesota Avenue in the Fort Dupont Park (tel. 581-0911). All three offer skate rentals. The Sculpture Garden and Pershing Park rinks are open approximately from December (some years earlier) to February, weather permitting; Fort Dupont, from Labor Day to the end of April. Call for hours and admission prices.

Note: The Pershing Park rink may be closed for repairs this year; call ahead.

JOGGING A **parcourse jogging path,** a gift from Perrier, opened in Rock Creek Park in 1978. Its 1½-mile oval route, beginning near the intersection of Cathedral Avenue and Rock Creek

Parkway, includes 18 calisthenics stations with instructions on pre-scribed exercises. There's another Perrier parcourse, with only four stations, at 16th and Kennedy Streets NW. Other popular jogging areas are the **C&O Canal** and **Mall.**

SWIMMING   There are 45 swimming pools in the District run by the **D.C. Department of Recreation Aquatic Program** (tel. 576-6436). They include the Capitol East Natatorium, an indoor/outdoor pool with sun deck and adjoining baby pool at 635 North Carolina Ave. SE (tel. 724-4495 or 724-4496); the outdoor pool in East Potomac Park (tel. 727-0347); a large outdoor pool at 25th and N Street NW (tel. 727-3825); and the Georgetown outdoor pool at 34th Street and Volta Place NW (tel. 282-2366). Indoor pools are open year-round; outdoor pools, from Memorial Day to Labor Day. Call for hours and details on other locations.

TENNIS   There are 144 outdoor courts in the District (60 of them lighted for night play) at 45 locations. Court uses is on a first-come, first-served basis. For a list of locations, call or write the **D.C. Department of Recreation,** 3149 16th St. NW, Washington, DC 20010 (tel. 202/673-7646). Most courts are open year-round, weather permitting. In addition, there are courts in **Rock Creek** and **East Potomac Parks** (see "Recreation in the Parks," earlier in this chapter, for details).

CHAPTER 8

SHOPPING IN WASHINGTON, D.C.

1. SHOPPING A TO Z
• WALKING TOUR—
   GEORGETOWN
   SHOPPING

The city's most delightful shopping area is historic Georgetown, with hundreds of boutiques, antique shops, and a neo-Victorian mall that provides excellent browsing. Its highlights are detailed in a walking tour. But first I've covered the most interesting and/or budget-oriented shops throughout the District, malls (in D.C. and the suburbs), and major department stores. Check the Georgetown shopping tour for additional shops in each category.

You could also spend a very pleasant shopping day poking about Alexandria's charming boutiques and antique shops. And there are marvelous high-quality selections at all the Smithsonian museum shops—unique toys, craft items, educational games for children, posters, art reproductions, books, jewelry, and so forth, as well as at many other museums and attractions.

1. SHOPPING A TO Z

ART REPRODUCTIONS, PRINTS & ENGRAVINGS

All the art museums detailed in Chapter 7 have noteworthy shops. Of special interest are the following:

BUREAU OF ENGRAVING AND PRINTING, 14th and C Sts. SW. Tel. 874-3188.

Good engravings here, including portraits of presidents and Supreme Court justices, scenes of Washington landmarks, and government seals, plus prints of the Gettysburg Address; the list goes on and on. The bureau also sells sheets of uncut currency. Write for a free catalog or stop by the on-premises store. It's open Monday to Friday 8:30am to 3:30pm. **Metro:** Smithsonian.

NATIONAL GALLERY OF ART, north side of the Mall, between 3rd and 7th Sts. NW. Tel. 737-4215.

The shops here feature a wide choice of prints, posters, art reproductions, Christmas cards, and art books. The West Building shop is the largest; the special exhibition desk in the East Building has current exhibit-related books and art; and a large shop in the concourse specializes in art and children's books. All are open Monday to Saturday 10am to 5pm, Sunday 11am to 6pm. **Metro:** Archives or Judiciary Square.

BOOKS/RECORDS/CDS/AUDIO-
/VIDEOCASSETTES

Besides the stores listed here, you'll find others mentioned in "Malls" (below) and described in the Georgetown shopping tour later in this chapter.

BORDERS BOOKS & MUSIC, at the corner of 18th and L Sts. NW. Tel. 466-4999 for books, 466-6999 for music.

This fabulous 30,000-square-foot two-level bookstore-cum-cultural center sells hardcover books at 10% off and discounts *New York Times* and *Washington Post* best-sellers and staff selections 30%. It also sells CDs, video- and audiotapes, and a wide selection of periodicals and out-of-state newspapers. And there are large remainder and children's book sections. Borders also schedules celebrity book signings, Saturday-morning storytelling for children ages 2 to 7 (at 10:30am), entertainment by local musicians, films, lectures, poetry readings, and showings of local artists. The store has a pleasant café that offers yummy desserts (including Proustian madeleines), salads, sandwiches, cappuccino/espresso, and European sodas. You can borrow a book from the store to read while you eat. Open Monday to Friday 8am to 10pm, Saturday 9am to 10pm, Sunday 11am to 8pm. **Metro:** Farragut North.

GOVERNMENT PRINTING OFFICE BOOKSTORE, 710 N. Capitol St. NW, between G and H Sts. Tel. 512-0132.

The GPO, founded in 1861, is now the world's largest printer, with close to 16,000 titles (books and pamphlets) in print. Every conceivable area is covered, from *Starting and Managing a Small Business on Your Own* to the *Everglades Wildguide.* If you're probing any new hobby, interest, or activity—or writing a term paper, trying to understand a medical problem, looking for a new career, or considering a major purchase—you'll probably find some helpful literature here. The collection makes for fascinating browsing. The GPO bookstore also sells books of photographs (such as *A Century of Photographs: 1846–1946,* selections from the Library of Congress) and sets of actual photographs (for example, a set of seven photos portraying marines in combat situations, suitable for framing); also prints, lithographs, and posters. It's open Monday to Friday 8am to 4pm. **Metro:** Union Station.

The GPO has another bookstore at 1510 H St. NW (tel. 653-5075), open Monday to Friday 9am to 5pm. **Metro:** Farragut West.

KRAMERBOOKS & AFTERWORDS, 1517 Connecticut Ave. NW, between Q St. and Dupont Circle. Tel. 387-1400.

Ask 100 Washingtonians to name their favorite bookstore, and at least half will say Kramerbooks. This San Francisco–style bookstore combines with a popular restaurant (see Chapter 6 for details), so you can buy a book and read it over lunch. Employees here are all avid readers who display their current favorites on the counter and discuss literature with customers. It's also one of the few places anywhere you can buy a book at 8am—or at midnight for that matter. Kramerbooks carries quality paperbacks—fiction

Better Buys ④
Borders Books & Music ⑫
Bureau of Engraving & Printing ⑮
Central Liquor ㉕
For Eyes Optical ⑨
Ginns ⑬
Government Printing Office
  Bookstore ㉗
Hecht's ⑳
Indian Crafts Shop ⑭

Kramerbooks & Afterwords ⑦
Lane Bryant ㉒
Mazza Gallerie ①
Melody Record Shop ⑤
National Gallery of Art ㉖
Olsson's Books & Records ⑥
Once Is Not Enough ②
Pavilion at the Old Post Office ㉓
Penn Camera Exchange ㉔
Red Sage General Store ⑰

WASHINGTON, D.C., SHOPPING

and nonfiction—as well as European and other foreign works of major importance. The store recently expanded, adding 50% more space and large children's, gardening, and travel-book sections. "I look for books of real and substantial quality," says owner David Tenney. Quality books must have an audience because Kramerbooks is one of the highest-grossing bookstores per square foot in the country. It's open Monday to Thursday 7:30am to 1am, and around the clock from Friday at 7:30am to Sunday at 1am. **Metro:** Dupont Circle.

MELODY RECORD SHOP, 1623 Connecticut Ave. NW. Tel. 232-4002.

CDs, cassettes, and tapes are discounted 10% to 20% here, new releases 20% to 40%. There's a wide variety of rock, classical, jazz, pop, show, and folk music, as well as a vast number of international selections. This is also a good place to shop for discounted electronic equipment such as cassette and CD players, as well as blank tapes and cassettes. A knowledgeable staff is a plus. Open Monday to Thursday 10am to 10pm, Friday and Saturday 10am to 11pm, Sunday noon to 8pm. **Metro:** Dupont Circle (Q Street exit).

OLSSON'S BOOKS & RECORDS, 1239 Wisconsin Ave. NW, between M and N Sts. Tel. 338-6712 for recordings, 338-9544 for books.

This independent quality bookstore chain offers discounts of 10% to 20% on many tapes and CDs (of which they stock an immense variety) and has about 60,000 to 70,000 books on its shelves covering almost every area except romance and porn. *Washington Post* hardcover best-sellers are reduced 25%; other books are sold at regular prices. However, if you buy three Penguin books here at one time, you get 20% off any other Penguin paperback forever. At all Olsson's stores (especially the Metro Center location), book signings are frequent events (past ones have included P. D. James, Garrison Keillor, and Anthony Burgess), and there are even occasional signings of recordings.

Additional locations include 1200 F St. at Metro Center (tel. 393-1853 for recordings, 347-3686 for books), and 1307 19th St. NW, just off Dupont Circle (tel. 785-2662 for recordings, 785-1133 for books). All locations are open daily; call for hours.

SIDNEY KRAMER BOOKS, 1825 I St. NW. Tel. 293-2685.

This unique and attractive bookstore specializes "in the business of Washington"—politics, economics, defense, area studies, and business management. Its clientele includes foreign ambassadors, generals, congresspeople, White House staffers, and other major governmental players. The people-watching is almost as good as the browsing. Kramer also offers comprehensive travel-book, fiction, and children's-book sections. Open Monday to Friday 9am to 6:30pm, Saturday 10am to 5pm. **Metro:** Farragut West.

SUPER CROWN, 11 Dupont Circle NW, between New Hampshire Ave. and P St., on the northeast side of the Circle. Tel. 319-1374.

With locations throughout the District and in suburbia, Crown Books offers 40% off *New York Times* hardcover best-sellers and

25% off paperbacks. Other books and magazines are discounted 10% to 20%. Its largest D.C. outlet is this 12,000-square-foot "super" store, which has expanded sections for biographies, audio (books on tape), remaindered books, new authors, magazines (including many foreign periodicals), and children's books. Super Crown can special-order titles for you at its usual discounts. It has wide aisles with benches where people can sit and read. It's open Monday to Saturday 9am to midnight, Sunday 10am to midnight. Check the phone book for other Crown Book store locations. **Metro:** Dupont Circle.

TOWER RECORDS, 2000 Pennsylvania Ave. NW, at the corner of 21st and I Sts. Tel. 331-2400.

Without a doubt, this 18,000-square-foot store houses the largest selection of cassettes and CDs in town. There are large departments for jazz, rock, soul, classical, and any other type of music you might favor, plus a vast inventory of videocassettes (for sale and rental). The store also functions as a **Ticketmaster** outlet. A trendy ambience is created by flashing lights, ultramodern decor, and about 20 monitors showing rock videos, cartoons, and movies. All merchandise is sold below list, with substantial discounts on sale items. Ongoing contests—drawings for trips to reggae festivals in Jamaica, stereo equipment, concert tickets—add to the fun. It's open daily 9am to midnight. **Metro:** Foggy Bottom.

CLOTHING

Don't forget to check out "Department Stores" and "Malls" (below) for more places to shop for clothes.

LANE BRYANT, 10th and F Sts. NW. Tel. 347-1500.

This branch of Lane Bryant carries large sizes (14 to 28) in women's clothing. It's open Monday to Friday 10am to 7pm, Saturday 10am to 6pm, Sunday noon to 5pm. **Metro:** Metro Center.

SUNNY'S SURPLUS, 1416 H St. NW. Tel. 347-2774.

If you like the "M*A*S*H" look, this is the place. They carry a full line of military surplus (mostly new, some used), including jeans, T-shirts, work shoes and clothing, insulated underwear, heavy thermal socks, rainwear and winter garments, pea coats, camouflage fatigues, army blankets, navy wool insignia middy blouses, all camping accessories (tents, sleeping bags, mess kits, rubber rafts, canteens), even World War I Snoopy helmets. It's open Monday to Saturday 8:30am to 6:30pm. **Metro:** McPherson Square.

Other branches are at 912 F St. NW (tel. 737-2032) and 3342 M St. NW (tel. 333-8550). Call for hours.

CRAFTS

INDIAN CRAFTS SHOP, Department of the Interior, 18th and C Sts. NW. Tel. 208-4056.

This shop's wares are of a very high quality, and the price range is wide: I found many lovely small Navajo weavings for $16 to $18 (larger rugs can go up to $3,000), squash-blossom necklaces for $300 to $3,000, and many attractive pieces of jewelry—Navajo,

Zuni, and Hopi—in varied price ranges. The store also offers Navajo sand paintings, a large selection of Eskimo walrus-ivory carvings, and an outstanding selection of Hopi, Santa Clara, San Ildefonso, Jemez, Acoma, Taos, Cochiti, and Navajo pottery. *Note:* You need a photo ID to enter the building. It's open Monday to Friday 8:30am to 4:30pm. **Metro:** Farragut West.

There's another location in Georgetown Park Mall, 3222 M St. NW, at Wisconsin (tel. 342-3918), open Monday to Saturday 10am to 9pm, Sunday noon to 6pm.

DEPARTMENT STORES

In addition to the below-listed, Washington boasts branches of prestigious New York and West Coast stores. **Lord & Taylor** is at 5255 Western Ave. NW (tel. 362-9600); **Saks Fifth Avenue** can be found at 5555 Wisconsin Ave. NW in Chevy Chase, Maryland (tel. 301/657-9000); and **Neiman-Marcus** is located in Mazza Gallerie on upper Wisconsin Avenue (tel. 966-9700). You'll find a branch of **Bloomingdale's** at Tysons Corner Center in McLean, Virginia (tel. 703/556-4600). Also check the stores listed under "Malls" (below).

HECHT'S, 12th and G Sts. NW. Tel. 628-6661.

Hecht's stores have been in Washington for almost a century. But this much newer branch (built in 1985) is anything but fusty. It's a fun store with five floors of moderate- to higher-priced merchandise and lots going on. You might happen upon cooking and merchandise demonstrations here, a contest (win a trip to Paris or a Jaguar XJ6), or an in-store personality appearance; in the past these have included Fabio (for his fragrance), Martin Yan (of "Yan Can Cook"), Jason Priestley (promoting Pepe Jeans), Oscar de la Renta (for Volupté), even Bart Simpson. It's a full-service department store, featuring brand names in clothing and footwear for the whole family and contemporary and traditional home furnishings. Furthermore, all Hecht's store have **Ticketmaster** outlets selling tickets to most major shows, concerts, and sports events in town; you get the best available seats for the price at the time you buy. There are 16 Hecht's stores in the D.C. area; check the phone book for additional locations. This branch is open Monday to Saturday 10am to 8pm, Sunday noon to 6pm. **Metro:** Metro Center.

WOODWARD & LOTHROP, 11th and F Sts. NW. Tel. 347-5300.

This store specializes in clothing for the whole family, plus gifts, shoes, housewares, and furniture. There's a large bridal department on the fifth floor. Woodies—as it's familiarly known to Washington families, who have been coming here for several generations—has an excellent reputation for fine service and quality merchandise at reasonable prices. There are several eating places, including the archetypical department store tearoom, on the premises. Designer showrooms here include Calvin Klein, Donna Karan, Anne Klein, Anne Klein II, Ellen Tracy, and Ralph Lauren/Polo for men. Celebrity promotions—such as Fabio or Baryshnikov for their fragrances,

Greg Louganis for Speedo, and Paloma Picasso for her handbag line—are part of the fun. Altogether, there are 16 Woodward & Lothrop department stores (and two home-furnishing stores) in the D.C. area; check the phone book for additional locations. This branch is open Monday to Saturday 10am to 7:30pm, Sunday noon to 5pm, with extended hours during the Christmas season. Ask about their complimentary personal shopping service. **Metro:** Metro Center.

DRUGSTORES

Washington's major drugstore chain, carrying diversified merchandise that ranges from frozen foods to charcoal briquettes to appliances, is **Peoples** (with about 40 stores). Check the phone book for the most convenient locations.

EYEGLASSES

FOR EYES OPTICAL, 2021 L St. NW. Tel. 659-0077.
    This company offers hefty discounts on lenses, designer frames (Pierre Cardin, Elizabeth Arden, Armani, Gucci, Ralph Lauren/Polo, Dior), and designer sunglasses (Bausch & Lomb and others).
    There are additional locations at 1725 K St. NW (tel. 463-8860) and 700 13th St. NW (tel. 737-2222). All stores are open Monday to Friday 9:30am to 6pm, Saturday 10am to 6pm.

FISH & SEAFOOD

SOUTHWEST WATERFRONT FISH MARKET, between 11th and 12th Sts. SW, along Maine Ave. No phone.
    The best home-cooked meal I ever had in Washington was fresh-caught red snapper from this fabulous fish market. About half a dozen merchants offer a wide selection of just-off-the-boat fish and seafood—shrimp, soft-shell crabs, crabmeat, lobster, red snapper, bluefish, and whatever else the day's catch brings. It's a picturesque outdoor market, and there's usually a boat selling produce as well. The market is open daily 7:30am to 9:30pm. **Metro:** Waterfront.

GOURMET GROCERIES & UPSCALE GIFTS

RED SAGE GENERAL STORE, at 14th and F Sts. NW. Tel. 638-3276.
    This beautiful retail adjunct to one of Washington's most highly acclaimed restaurants sells a wide range of southwestern and other gourmet grocery items. You can stock up on hard-to-find chilies, salsas, and spices here, along with fancy olive oils, coffees and teas, southwestern cookbooks (including famed Red Sage chef Mark Miller's *Coyote Cafe* and *The Great Chili Book*), and fresh-baked breads and desserts. Also on sale here: great T-shirts and posters. It's a great place to find innovative upscale gifts, including gift baskets. Red Sage is open Monday to Thursday 8am to 7pm, Friday 8am to 9pm, Saturday 10am to 8pm. **Metro:** Metro Center.

MALLS

THE FASHION CENTRE AT PENTAGON CITY, 1100 S. Hayes St., at Army-Navy Dr. and I-395. Tel. 703/415-2400.

This Arlington, Virginia, mall has nothing to do with America's defense establishment. It's a plush four-level shopping complex with more than 160 shops, restaurants, and services adjoining a Ritz-Carlton hotel. Anchored by Macy's and Nordstrom, it also features branches of Ann Taylor, Abercrombie & Fitch, the Museum Company (for museum art reproductions), Banana Republic, Brentano's, Scribner's, Disney Store, Record World, Joan & David (upscale women's clothing), America (U.S. souvenirs), Pucci (shoes for men), Crabtree & Evelyn, Godiva Chocolatier, Laura Ashley, Villeroy & Boch, Victoria's Secret, Nature Company, Lane Bryant, The Limited, Body Shop, Charter Clubs, Sam Goody, Britches, and The Gap (also Gap Kids). There are numerous clothing and shoe stores for the whole family, jewelers, and retailers of photographic equipment, beach wear, maternity clothes, luggage, gifts, toys, eyeglasses, whatever. Dining choices include several restaurants plus 13 food-court eateries. There are six movie theaters, the Metro stops right in the mall, and parking is provided for 4,500 cars. The mall is open Monday to Saturday 10am to 9:30pm, Sunday 11am to 6pm. **Metro:** Pentagon City.

THE GALLERIA AT TYSONS II, 2001 International Dr. in McLean, Va. Tel. 703/827-7700.

This plush three-level mall, adjoining a Ritz-Carlton hotel, offers 110 shops, galleries, restaurants, and services. Its lushly planted interior is an indoor park setting, with skylights, gleaming-white Carrara marble, and cascading multilevel fountains. Anchored by three fine department stores—Macy's, Saks, and Neiman-Marcus—the Galleria also houses The Sharper Image, Victoria's Secret, The Limited and Limited Express, Godiva Chocolatier, Pottery Barn, H_2O (exquisite bath/beauty products), Ann Taylor, and Liljenquist & Beckstead (very upscale jewelry). Your whole shopping spectrum is well covered here. There are five full-service restaurants, as well as a lovely Garden Food Court complete with trellises and ivy plantings. There's parking for 3,200 cars. By the way, Tysons Corner Center (see below) is right across the street. The Galleria is open Monday to Saturday from 10am to 9pm, Sunday noon to 6pm. **Metro:** West Falls Church; from there you can catch a shuttle that runs every half hour in both directions.

MAZZA GALLERIE, 5300 Wisconsin Ave. NW, between Western Ave. and Jenifer St. Tel. 686-9515.

Billing itself as "Washington's answer to Rodeo Drive," this *très chic,* four-level mall has 48 boutiques under a skylit atrium, including a branch of Neiman-Marcus, a multilevel Ann Taylor, and Filene's Basement (discount designer labels). Other classy boutiques here are Stephane Kélian (very upscale women's shoes), Laura Ashley (home furnishings), the Forgotten Woman (elegant clothes in large sizes), Pea in the Pod (gorgeous maternity wear), Pampillonia Jewelers (estate jewelry and one-of-a-kind creations) Krön

Chocolatier, and Williams-Sonoma (gourmet cookware and foods). There's an excellent on-premises restaurant called Pleasant Peasant, a Brentano's bookstore, numerous other clothing and shoe stores, jewelers, gourmet food shops, home furnishing stores, and an American Express travel agency/currency exchange. The mall, located at the D.C./Maryland border, is open Monday to Friday 10am to 8pm, Saturday 10am to 6pm, Sunday noon to 5pm. There's two-hour free indoor parking. **Metro:** Friendship Heights.

THE PAVILION AT THE OLD POST OFFICE, 1100 Pennsylvania Ave. NW. Tel. 289-4224.

This is as much of a tourist attraction as a retail complex. Opened in 1983 in one of the capital's oldest federal buildings—an actual 1899 government postal department—it's a vital part of the renovation of the entire Pennsylvania Avenue area. The tallest structure in the city, after the Washington Monument, its 10 floors soar 196 feet to a skylight ceiling and are crowned by a 315-foot clock tower. The atrium is lined with balconied corridors reminiscent of an Italian palazzo, while the exterior stonework, turrets, and massive arches were inspired by the Romanesque cathedrals of 12th-century France. In the tower are 10 great bells, a Bicentennial gift from England; they duplicate those at Westminster Abbey.

Today the building—along with an adjoining three-level, 100,000-square-foot addition of commercial and retail space—houses about 90 boutiques and restaurants, and its hub is a performing-arts stage, the scene of daily lunchtime, afternoon, and early-evening free entertainment. (Call the phone number above to find out the entertainment on a given day.) While you're here, ride the glass elevator to the tower observation deck for a lofty 360° vista. You can climb down a flight and see the bells themselves. If you'd like to hear them, the bellringers practice on Thursday evenings between 6:30 and 9:30pm.

Most of the shops carry whimsical merchandise, ranging from Stars and Stripes (all red, white, and blue items) to Juggling Capitol for juggler's paraphernalia. Others offer African fashions for men and women, jewelry, souvenirs, and accessories.

Plan a meal here, too. Options include a large food court for international and American fare. Blossoms features a gorgeous brick-terraced café and immense salads, among other American/continental entrées. And the brass-railed Enrico's Trattoria offers noteworthy Italian food. Some restaurants have outdoor cafés.

The Pavilion is open March to September, Monday to Saturday 10am to 8pm (the restaurants stay open to 9pm), Sunday noon to 6pm; the rest of the year, Monday to Saturday 10am to 6pm (the restaurants stay open to 8pm) and Sunday noon to 6pm. **Metro:** Federal Triangle.

THE SHOPS AT NATIONAL PLACE, entrance on F St. NW, between 13th and 14th Sts., or via the J. W. Marriott at 1331 Pennsylvania Ave. NW. Tel. 783-9090.

A Rouse Company project (like Baltimore Harborplace and New York's South Street Seaport), this four-tiered, 125,000-square-foot retail complex houses more than 100 stores and eateries in the renovated National Press Building. With its terra-cotta floors, balconies, columns, and fountains, it's a most attractive setting for serious shopping. All the mall regulars are here—B. Dalton, The Sharper Image, The Limited, Banana Republic, and Victoria's Secret—to name a few. You can also shop for candy, leather goods, lingerie, clothing and shoes for the entire family, gifts, and records and tapes. You will find Au Bon Pain (croissant sandwiches and homemade desserts) and two branches of the American Café (see Chapter 6). And if you really want to get down to some serious eating, there are excellent restaurants in the adjoining Marriott (see Chapter 5). The mall is open Monday to Saturday 10am to 7pm, Sunday noon to 5pm. **Metro:** Metro Center.

SPRINGFIELD MALL, just off I-95 at Exit 169A (Franconia Rd.). Tel. 703/971-3000.

This major shopping complex is about 10 miles from the downtown D.C. area in Springfield, Virginia. It has 240 shops and restaurants (including a food court) and 10 movie theaters. Major stores here include branches of Macy's, J. C. Penney, and Montgomery Ward. Ann Taylor, Britches of Georgetown, The Limited, The Gap, Disney Store, Sports Authority, and Victoria's Secret are also represented. There are more than a dozen shoe stores; other shops and boutiques carry clothing for the entire family, athletic footwear, audio equipment, telephones, bicycles, books, toys, jewelry, health foods, gourmet foods, sporting goods, maternity wear, records and tapes, and just about anything else you might need or desire. While you're here you can have your hair done (several salons vie for your patronage) or even have your eyes examined. There's free parking. And you can park the kids either at the movies or at one of two video-game arcades while you shop. The mall is open Monday to Saturday 10am to 9:30pm, Sunday noon to 5pm. **Metro:** Huntington Station; then take bus no. 109 or 110.

TYSONS CORNER CENTER, 1961 Chain Bridge Rd., at Rte. 7. Tel. 703/893-9400.

This well-known mall is about 15 minutes from town in McLean, Virginia (take the Beltway, I-495, to Exit 11B and follow the signs). Among the 220-plus shops here are five major department stores—Bloomingdale's, Nordstrom, Lord & Taylor, Hecht's, and Woodward & Lothrop. Other notable emporia include Laura Ashley, Nature Company, Williams-Sonoma (kitchenware), The Limited, Disney Store, Banana Republic, Brooks Brothers, F. A. O. Schwarz, A/X Armani Exchange, Abercrombie & Fitch, Britches of Georgetown, Ann Taylor, Crabtree & Evelyn, Woolworth's, and The Gap. Once again, there are more than a dozen shoe stores, hair salons, a spa, and a bank. More than 30 eateries include the Magic Pan, America, and California Pizza Kitchen, and eight movie theaters make this a good choice for an afternoon shopping spree followed by a relaxing dinner and a film. There's free parking. The mall is open Monday to Saturday 10am to 9:30pm, Sunday noon to 6pm. **Metro:** West Falls Church; from there you can catch a shuttle that runs every half hour in both directions.

UNION STATION, 40 Massachusetts Ave. Tel. 371-9441.

Union Station, with about 100 high-quality shops, has become one of Washington's most frequented retail complexes. The setting is magnificent; there are lots of great on-premises eateries (details in Chapter 6); and the stores here offer a wide array of unique and high-quality merchandise.

The plushest emporia are in the **East Hall,** with wares displayed in handsome brass-trimmed mahogany kiosks amid tall palm trees, or in alcoves flanked by scagliola marble columns. Here you'll find, among others, Pacifica (handcrafted jewelry and wood carvings from Bali), Aurea (pre-Columbian jewelry and pottery, African amber necklaces, jewelry from India, and more, including museum replicas), Treasures (international art, antiques, crafts, and jewelry), Christmas Spirit (upscale holiday merchandise), Post Impressions (collector stamps—everything from Civil War to Elvis stamps), Appalachian Spring (for items handcrafted in America—patchwork quilts, pottery, exquisite jewelry, and an incredible collection of kaleidoscopes), Initial Impressions (an engraver), and Washington Pen (fine pens and accessories).

Notable **West Hall** shops include Tavros Leatherwear, Made in America (American-made and U.S.-related items, from military accessories to western sculpture), Political Americana (historic and political memorabilia), and, one of my favorite shops in the complex, the Nature Company, carrying all nature-environmental-themed items, including books, cassettes, artwork, toys, kites, leaf-collecting kits, bird feeders, backpacks, telescopes, and more.

The **Main Floor Level** of the Concourse is home to branches of B. Dalton, Victoria's Secret, Crabtree & Evelyn, and The Limited. Also here: The Great Train Store (model trains, books, cassettes, and numerous other railroad-motif items); a toy store called Flights of Fancy; Brookstone, a kind of adult toy store selling upscale gadgetry; and Parfumerie Douglas, for international fragrances.

Women's clothing boutiques predominate on the **Concourse Mezzanine Level,** among them Pendleton, Jones of New York, Ann Taylor, and an interesting shop called White House, which specializes in all-white clothing and accessory items. There are men's clothing stores here, too. And don't miss Imposters for fine jewelry reproductions (most are between $30 and $95, and it all looks real!).

There's quite a bit more, including electronics stores, a branch of Sam Goody, additional jewelry shops, accessory stores, nine movie theaters, and a variety of services (car and limousine rental, tour desks, post office, shoe repair, shoeshine, currency exchange, and so on).

Union Station is open Monday to Saturday 10am to 9pm, Sunday noon to 6pm. **Metro:** Union Station.

OFFICE SUPPLIES/STATIONERY

GINNS, 1208 18th St. NW, at M St. Tel. 833-6112.

Ginns offers an extensive selection of supplies—all you'd expect, plus office furniture, lamps, globes, leather portfolios, photo albums, reference books, maps, magazines, calendars, datebooks, and greeting cards. In addition, there's a large giftware section stocked with malachite boxes, elegant bird cages, fine crystal, and more. Check the phone book for other locations. This Ginns is open Monday to Friday 8:30am to 6pm, Saturday 9am to 6pm. **Metro:** Dupont Circle.

STAPLES, 3307 M St. NW. Tel. 337-8179.

This marvelous "super store" offers discounts of 40% to 70% on a wide selection of office supplies, business machines (computers, answering machines, copiers, fax machines, and more), and office furniture. The staff is well informed, and you can return anything within 30 days if not satisfied. It's open Monday to Saturday 7am to 9pm, Sunday 10am to 6pm.

There are other locations at 1133 20th St. NW (between L and M Streets; tel. 331-8844) and 1250 H St. NW (tel. 638-3907). Call for hours.

PHOTOGRAPHIC EQUIPMENT

PENN CAMERA EXCHANGE, 915 E St. NW. Tel. 347-5777, or toll free 800/347-5770.

Penn offers big discounts (up to 40%) on all major brand-name equipment—such as Olympus, Canon, Minolta, Pentax, Leica, Vivitar, and Nikon. The store has been owned and operated by the camera-buff Zweig family since 1953; their staff is quite knowledgeable, their inventory wide-ranging. Many professional Washington photographers shop at Penn. Most of the merchandise is new and comes with a U.S. warranty, but you'll also find good buys on used equipment here. Check the Friday *Washington Post* ("Weekend" section) for announcements of special sales. Penn is open Monday to Friday 9am to 60m, Saturday 10am to 5pm. **Metro:** Metro Center.

RESALE & THRIFT SHOPS

In addition to the below-listed, stop by **Christ Child Opportunity Shop** and **Secondhand Rose,** detailed in the Georgetown shopping tour later in this chapter.

ONCE IS NOT ENOUGH, 4830 MacArthur Blvd. NW, near Reservoir Rd. Tel. 337-3072.

Washington society women must change their wardrobes frequently: What do they do with the lovely clothes they've worn only once or twice? Some of their garments find their way to this resale shop, which specializes in top-quality women's clothing. I've seen names here like Gloria Sachs, Ellen Tracy, Nippon, Fendi, Louis Feraud, Anne Klein, and Calvin Klein, to mention just a few. On my last visit I saw a black voile Chanel gown for $150 (it had retailed for $2,500), a Perry Ellis sweater for $40, and a four-piece Valentino outfit worth thousands for $450. Many items were much less. The store sometimes scoops up brand-new clothing too, and sells it at unfancy prices, averaging 40% off regular store tabs. You'll also find new clothing from top stores for children here at

30% to 60% off. And there are terrific bargains in used men's clothing; some examples: a $400 camel's-hair coat for $75, an $800 sheepskin coat for $150, and a Polo raw-silk blazer for $75. Brooks Brothers and Armani suits, Sulka shirts, tuxedos, and Liberty ties are other frequent finds. Open Monday to Wednesday and Friday and Saturday 10am to 4:30pm, Thursday 10am to 8pm.

WINES & LIQUORS

CENTRAL LIQUOR, 726 9th St. NW, between G and H Sts. Tel. 737-2800.

Central Liquor abounds in bottled booze—more than 35,000 items on display, including thousands of wines ranging from Gallo to Château Mouton Rothschild. Not just wines, but liquors, cordials, and other alcoholic potables are all discounted 10% to 25%, with special sales on loss leaders. Good deals are also offered when you buy by the case. It's open Monday to Thursday 9am to 9pm, Friday 9am to 10pm, Saturday 9am to midnight. **Metro:** Gallery Place.

WALKING TOUR — Georgetown Shopping

Start: M and 29th Streets NW.
Finish: Wisconsin Avenue NW, between Q Street and Reservoir Road.
Time: Allow one to three hours, depending on how much time you spend browsing—or actually shopping.
Best Times: During store hours.

In Georgetown you can combine shopping and browsing (there are hundreds of stores) with a meal at a good restaurant, crowd-watching over cappuccino at a café, even a little sightseeing. The hub is at Wisconsin Avenue and M Street, and most of the stores are on those two arteries. In addition to shops, you'll encounter street vendors hawking T-shirts and handmade jewelry.

If you drive into Georgetown—definitely not advised because parking is almost impossible—check out the side streets off Wisconsin Avenue above M Street for possible spots. The Georgetown Park Mall (see below) offers validated parking. There's also public transportation (by bus) to Georgetown.

About Refreshment Stops Most of the Georgetown restaurants recommended in this book are along the shopping route described below. See Chapter 6 for additional dining suggestions.

Along M Street NW For the first part of this Shopping Tour, we'll head generally along M Street from 29th to 33rd Streets. Start at the:

  1. **Spectrum Gallery,** 1132 29th St. NW, just below M Street (tel. 333-0954), a cooperative venture (since 1968) in which 28 professional Washington-area artists—painters, potters, sculptors, collagists, and printmakers—share in shaping gallery

policy, maintenance, and operation. The art is reasonably priced. Open Tuesday to Saturday 11am to 6pm, Sunday noon to 5pm.

Walk around the corner onto M Street to:

2. **Grafix,** 2904 M St. NW (tel. 342-0610), which carries a noteworthy collection of vintage posters (from 1895 on), 16th- to 20th-century maps, 19th-century prints, and other collectibles. Open Monday to Friday 11am to 6pm, Saturday 11am to 5pm.

3. **American Hand Plus,** 2906 M St. NW (tel. 965-3273), features exquisite contemporary handcrafted American ceramics and jewelry, plus international objets d'art. Open Monday to Saturday 11am to 6pm, Sunday 1 to 5pm.

4. **Animation Sensations,** 2914 M St. NW (tel. 337-5024). It's fun to peruse this collection of original animation cels and drawings, comic book/strip art, vintage movie posters, movie star autographs, Disney/Warner Brothers/Hanna-Barbera character figurines and toys, Betty Boop lamps, and movie memorabilia. There are paint-a-cel kits for kids. Open Monday to Saturday 11am to 7pm, Sunday noon to 5pm.

5. **Georgetown Antiques Center,** 2918 M St. NW, houses the **Cherub Antiques Gallery** (tel. 337-2224; art nouveau, art deco, art glass, Louis Icart etchings) and **Michael Getz Antiques** (tel. 338-3111), offering American English silver and a vast selection of fireplace accessories. Open Monday to Saturday 11am to 6pm, Sunday noon to 5pm; closed July and August.

6. **Ashburner Beargie Antiques,** just next door at 2920 M St. NW (tel. 337-4513), specializes in 17th-, 18th-, and early 19th-century European antiques and old master paintings. Open Monday to Saturday 11am to 6pm.

7. **Junior League Shop of Washington,** at 3066 M St. NW (tel. 337-6120), is a secondhand clothing shop that sells goods donated or consigned by upper-crust Washingtonians. You can buy designer gowns, furs, formal wear, preppy wear, and good costume jewelry for a song. I've seen designer wear by Victor Costa, Oscar de la Renta, Chanel, Chloë, and Ungaro here. Children's and men's clothing, too. The proceeds all go to charity. Open Monday to Saturday 11am to 6pm.

Turn left on 31st Street NW, and continue past the canal; on your left is the:

8. **Yes! Bookshop,** 1035 31st St. NW (tel. 338-7874, or toll free 800/YES-1516 for a free catalog). A wealth of literature (both books and books on tape) on personal growth and personal-transformation subjects can be found on the shelves of this rather unique store, along with books on health, natural medicine, men's and women's studies, mythology, creative writing, Jungian psychology, how to save the planet, ancient history, and Native American traditions. CDs and cassettes include non-Western music, instrumental music, new-age music, and instruction in everything from quitting smoking to astral projection

- **1** Spectrum Gallery
- **2** Grafix
- **3** American Hand Plus
- **4** Animation Sensations
- **5** Georgetown Antiques Center
- **6** Ashburner Beargle Antiques
- **7** Junior League Shop of Washington
- **8** YesI Bookshop
- **9** Irish Corner at the Threepenny Bit
- **10** Crown Books
- **11** Georgetown Park
- **12** Laura Ashley
- **13** Olsson's Books & Records
- **14** Martin's of Georgetown
- **15** Betsey Johnson
- **16** The Nature Company
- **17** Georgetown Coffee, Tea & Spice
- **18** Santa Fe Style
- **19** Appalachian Spring
- **20** Little Caledonia
- **21** Christ Child Opportunity Shop
- **22** Secondhand Rose
- **23** The French Market

and hypnosis. They also sell a large number of instructional videocassettes here. Open Monday to Saturday 10am to 8pm, Sunday noon to 7pm (later hours spring through fall).

9. Irish Corner at the Threepenny Bit, 3122 M St. NW (tel. 338-1338), sells Irish imports—beautiful mohair scarves, linen clothing, ladies' wood tweeds, Irish records and tapes, shamrock-motif clothing, hand-knit fishermen's sweaters, delicate hand-painted Belleek china, Galway crystal, hand-painted coats-of-arms on parchment, Claddagh rings, 100% wool tartan blankets, and Irish jams, jellies, biscuits, and fruitcakes. It's worth stopping in just to hear the wonderful Irish music that's always playing. Open Monday to Saturday 10am to 6pm, Sunday noon to 5pm; St. Patrick's Day to September and during the Christmas season, it's open Thursday to Saturday until 9pm.

10. Crown Books, 3131 M St. NW (tel. 333-4493), is a sizable link in this bookstore chain. It offers 40% off *New York Times* hardcover best-sellers, 25% off paperbacks. Other books and magazines are discounted 10% to 20%. Stop in and browse. Open Monday to Thursday 10am to 9pm, Friday and Saturday 10am to 11pm, Sunday 11am to 6pm.

11. Georgetown Park, 3222 M St. NW, at Wisconsin Avenue (tel. 298-5577). This four-story complex of about 100 shops belongs, architecturally, to two worlds: outside, quietly Federal, in keeping with the character of the neighborhood; inside, flamboyantly Victorian, with a huge skylight, fountains, and ornate chandeliers. You could spend hours here exploring branches of the nation's most exclusive specialty stores. Represented are Ann Taylor, Caché, J. Crew, Polo/Ralph Lauren, and Abercrombie & Fitch. Also featured are many gift/lifestyle boutiques such as Circuit City Express, Dapy, The Sharper Image, Crabtree & Evelyn, and the fascinating Gallery of History (framed collector historical documents). If you have kids take them to see the adorable stuffed animals at Georgetown Zoo, F. A. O. Schwarz, and Learningsmith (billing itself as "the general store for the curious mind," it has many interactive facilities for children). And an exciting new addition is VOR for virtual-reality games and experiences. An Old Town Trolley ticket booth (see Chapter 4) is on the premises. There are several restaurants, including Clyde's and a branch of the gourmet emporium/café Dean & Deluca (details in Chapter 6). An archaeological exhibit of artifacts found during the complex's excavation can be viewed on Level 2. And Georgetown Park maintains a full-service Concierge Center offering gift wrapping, worldwide shipping, postal/fax/photocopy services, gift certificates, even sightseeing information. Validated parking is available at an underground garage on Wisconsin Avenue. Open Monday to Saturday 10am to 9pm, Sunday noon to 6pm.

12. Laura Ashley, 3213 M St. NW. (tel. 338-5481). You probably need no introduction to Laura Ashley's romantic-look 100% cotton clothing and very feminine lingerie; luggage, china, stationery, perfume, and floral-design fabrics and wallpapers here, too. Open Monday to Saturday 10am to 6pm, Sunday noon to 6pm.

Now go back to Wisconsin Avenue to continue shopping or for a:

REFRESHMENT STOP Stop in for croissants and cappuccino, a Camembert sandwich on baguette, or afternoon tea with sumptuous desserts at **Patisserie Café Didier,** 3206

Grace St. NW, off Wisconsin Avenue just below M Street. (See details in Chapter 6.)

Along Wisconsin Avenue NW Walk back up Wisconsin Avenue crossing M Street en route to:

13. **Olsson's Books & Records,** 1239 Wisconsin Ave. NW, between M and N Streets (tel. 338-6712). Open Monday to Thursday 10am to 10:45pm, Friday and Saturday 10am to midnight, Sunday noon to 7pm. See details in Section 1 under "Books."

14. **Martin's of Georgetown,** 1304 Wisconsin Ave. NW (tel. 338-6144). This shop has been proffering exquisite wares since 1929. Come in and feast your eyes on Martin's selection of Lalique vases, Christofle silver, fine linens, hand-painted Herend china, and Limoges boxes, along with other fine lines of china, silver, crystal, flatware, and dinnerware. Martin's is a prestigious bridal registry (both the Nixon and Johnson daughters were registered here). Stuffed animals, baby gifts, picture frames, and other quality gift items here, too. Open Monday to Saturday 10am to 6pm.

REFRESHMENT STOP **Paolo's,** for California-style Italian cuisine in a simpatico setting, is just down the street at 1303 Wisconsin Ave. NW, at N Street. (See details in Chapter 6.)

---

15. **Betsey Johnson,** 1319 Wisconsin Ave. NW (tel. 338-4090). New York's flamboyant flower-child designer has a Georgetown shop. She personally decorated the bubble-gum pink walls. Her sexy, offbeat play-dress-up styles are great party and club clothes for the young and the still-skinny young at heart. Open Monday to Friday 11am to 7pm, Saturday 11am to 8pm, Sunday noon to 6pm.

16. **The Nature Company,** 1323 Wisconsin Ave. NW (tel. 333-4100), my favorite mall emporium, has a branch here. These ecologically themed stores sell bird feeders, chimes, craft kits, decorative mineral specimens, cassettes of whale songs, beautiful T-shirts, wonderful books (many for kids) and toys, sundials, delightful novelties, and much more. Open Monday to Thursday 11am to 7pm, Friday and Saturday 10am to 9pm, Sunday noon to 6pm.

17. **Georgetown Coffee, Tea & Spice,** 1330 Wisconsin Ave. NW, between N and O Streets (tel. 338-3801), features a collection of more than 80 different coffees—everything from Jamaican Peaberry to Ethiopian Harrar, plus a choice of about 20 decafs. Then there are some 85 varieties of tea—plum from Sri Lanka, Japanese basket-fired green, Kenyan broken-leaf orange pekoe, and many less exotic varieties. Also decaffeinated teas. The spice selection is equally wide-ranging, and this gourmet emporium also sells fancy chocolates, candies, and tea and coffee pots. They mail purchases all over the world. Open Monday to Saturday 10am to 8pm, Sunday 11am to 7pm.

18. **Sante Fe Style,** 1413 Wisconsin Ave. NW (tel. 333-3747). Here you'll find high-quality southwest merchandise, most of it handmade items from New Mexico and Arizona. The inventory includes silver and turquoise jewelry, picture frames, oxidized-iron animal decorations, barbed-wire art, antique Mexican and iron furniture, pottery, Zapotec blankets and pillows from Oaxaca, rugs, colorful painted sculptures made from barn-roof tin, T-shirts, birdhouses, southwest cookbooks, and more. Open Monday to Saturday 10am to 6m, Sunday noon to 5pm.

19. **Appalachian Spring,** 1415 Wisconsin Ave. NW, at P Street (tel. 337-5780), brings country crafts to citified Georgetown. They sell pottery, jewelry, newly made pieced and appliqué quilts in traditional and contemporary patterns, stuffed dolls and animals, candles, rag rugs, hand-blown glassware, an incredible collection of kaleidoscopes, glorious weavings, and simple country toys. Everything in the store is made by hand in the U.S.A. There's another branch in Union Station. Open Monday to Friday 10am to 8pm, Saturday 10am to 6pm, Sunday noon to 6pm.

20. **Little Caledonia,** 1419 Wisconsin Ave. NW (tel. 333-4700), is a rabbit warren of tiny rooms filled with indoor and outdoor furnishings (18th- and 19th-century mahogany reproductions are featured), dolls, Beatrix Potter ceramic figures, stuffed animals, children's books and toys, exquisite fabrics, housewares (copperware, cookbooks, cookie jars, baking molds, and so forth), candles, fancy gift wrappings, Indian dhurrie rugs, tablecloths, wallpapers, lamps, and much, much more. A delight. Open Monday to Saturday 10am to 6pm, and Thanksgiving to Christmas Sunday noon to 5pm.

21. **Christ Child Opportunity Shop,** 1427 Wisconsin Ave. NW (tel. 333-6635). Proceeds from merchandise bought here go to various children's charities. Among the first-floor items (donations all), I saw a wicker trunk for $5 and the usual thriftshop jumble of jewelry, clothes, shoes, hats, and odds and ends. Upstairs, higher quality merchandise is left on consignment; it's considerably more expensive, but if you know antiques you might find bargains in jewelry, silver, china, quilts, paintings, and other items. Good browsing. Open Monday to Saturday 10am to 3:45pm; closed in August.

22. **Secondhand Rose,** 1516 Wisconsin Ave. NW, at P Street (tel. 337-3378). This upscale second-floor consignment shop specializes in designer merchandise. Creations by Norma Kamali, Armani, Donna Karan, Calvin Klein, Yves Saint-Laurent, Ungaro, Ralph Lauren, and others are sold at about a third of the original price. Everything is in style, in season, and in excellent condition. On a recent visit I saw a gorgeous Scaasi black velvet and yellow satin ball gown for $400 (it was $1,200 new) and Yves Saint-Laurent pumps in perfect condition for $45. Secondhand Rose is also a great place to shop for gorgeous furs, designer shoes and bags, and costume jewelry. Open Monday to Saturday 10am to 6pm.

REFRESHMENT STOP   Sample totally authentic Persian fare at the charming **Nekeysa,** 1564 Wisconsin Ave., just below Q Street. It's scrumptious, and you can bring your own wine. (See details in Chapter 6.)

23. **The French Market,** at 1626–32 Wisconsin Ave. NW, between Q Street and Reservoir Road (tel. 338-4828), has been supplying Washingtonians with French fare for more than half a century—long before most Americans knew pâtés from potatoes. Run by three French brothers, Georges, Robert, and Jean-Jacob, the market has a *boucheri* carrying game (pheasant, quail, partridge, guinea hens, and mallards) in addition to less exotic European-cut meats. Other departments include a *charcuterie* (homemade pâtés en croûte and in loaf, superb salads, escargots); a *boulangerie* for baguettes, croissants, and pastries; and a *fromagerie* offering more than 50 French cheeses. You can also get imported oils and vinegars, mustards, crème de marrons, canned pâtés, and other fine French groceries here as well as wines, champagnes, and French-roast coffees. *C'est merveilleux!* There's free parking behind the store on 33rd Street, and there are a few tables inside where you can enjoy a light meal. Open Monday, Tuesday, Thursday, and Friday 8:30am to 6pm; Wednesday 8:30am to 1:30pm; Saturday 7:30am to 6pm.

CHAPTER 9

NIGHTS IN WASHINGTON, D.C.

Not so many years ago, Washington rolled up the sidewalks at an early hour. But today the city offers a wealth of nighttime activities. Don't go to bed early just because you're worn out from traipsing around museums and monuments all day. Take a nap before dinner and catch your second wind. In addition to the listings below, check the Friday "Weekend" section of the *Washington Post*, which will also tell you about children's theater, sports events, flower shows, and all else. *Washingtonian* magazine and *The City Paper* are other good sources.

TICKETS

TICKETplace, in the *Washington Post* building on L Street NW between 15th and 16th Streets (tel: TICKETS) is a service of the Cultural Alliance of Greater Washington. Here—on the day of performance only (except Sunday and Monday, see below)—you can pick up half-price tickets (for cash only) to productions at most major Washington-area theaters and concert halls, not only for dramatic productions, but for opera, ballet, and other performances as well. This place also serves as a **Ticketmaster** outlet. TICKETplace is open Tuesday to Friday noon to 4pm and Saturday 11am to 5pm; half-price tickets to Sunday and Monday shows are sold on Saturday. Closest **Metro:** Farragut North.

Full-price tickets for most performances in town can also be bought through **Ticketmaster** (tel. 432-SEAT) at **Hecht's Department Store,** 12th and G Streets NW. You can purchase tickets to Washington entertainments before you leave home by calling toll free 800/551-SEAT.

1. THEATER

Except for New York, I can't think of another U.S. city that offers more first-rate theatrical productions than D.C. Almost anything on Broadway will eventually come to—or have previewed in—

Washington. There are also several nationally acclaimed repertory companies here and an excellent theater specializing in Shakespearean productions. Additional theater offerings, including those at the **Kennedy Center,** are listed under "Accent on Entertainment," later in this chapter.

ARENA STAGE, 6th St. and Maine Ave. SW. Tel. 488-3300.

Founded by the brilliant Zelda Fichandler, the Arena Stage, now in its fifth decade, is the home of one of the longest standing acting ensembles in the nation. Several works nurtured here have moved to Broadway, and many graduates—among them "L.A. Law"'s Jill Eikenberry and Michael Tucker, Ned Beatty, James Earl Jones, Robert Prosky, Jane Alexander, and George Grizzard—have gone on to commercial stardom.

The Arena's subscription-season productions (there are eight annually) are presented on two stages—the **Fichandler** (a theater-in-the-round), and the smaller, fan-shaped **Kreeger.** In addition, the Arena houses the **Old Vat,** a space used for new play readings and productions.

A recent September-to-June season (sometimes shows are extended into summer) included productions of *Twelfth Night,* Arthur Miller's *The Price, A Room of One's Own* (a one-woman show about Virginia Woolf), *The Revenger's Comedies* Parts I and II (a farce by Alan Ayckbourn), Brian Friel's *Dancing at Lughnasa,* and *A Community Carol,* an adaptation of the famous Dickens story set in present-day Anacostia. The theater has always championed new plays and playwrights and is committed to producing works of playwrights from diverse cultures. Douglas Wagner is the Arena Stage's artistic director. **Metro:** Waterfront.

Admission: Tickets $22–$39; discounts available for students, the disabled, groups, and senior citizens. And HOTTIX, a limited number of half-price tickets, are available 90 minutes before most performances (call for details).

NATIONAL THEATRE, 1321 Pennsylvania Ave. NW. Tel. 628-6161, or toll free 800/447-7400.

The luxurious, Federal-style National Theatre, elegantly renovated to the tune of $6.5 million in 1983, is the oldest continuously

---

MAJOR CONCERT & PERFORMANCE HALL BOX OFFICES

Arena Stage tel. 488-3300
Constitution Hall tel. 638-2661
Ford's Theatre tel. 347-4833
John F. Kennedy Center for the Performing Arts
   tel. 467-4600
National Theatre tel. 628-6161
Shakespeare Theatre tel. 393-2700
Wolf Trap Farm for the Performing Arts
   tel. 703/255-1900

operating theater in Washington (since 1835) and the third-oldest in the nation. It's exciting just to see this stage on which Sarah Bernhardt, John Barrymore, Helen Hayes, and so many other notables have performed. The National is the closest thing Washington has to a Broadway-style playhouse. Managed by New York's Shubert Organization, the National presents star-studded hits—often pre- or post-Broadway—all year round. A recent season included productions of *Annie Get Your Gun* starring Kathy Rigby, *My Fair Lady* starring Richard Chamberlain, *A Chorus Line, Six Degrees of Separation* starring Marlo Thomas, and *Grease* with Rosie O'Donnell.

The National also offers free public-service programs: Saturday-morning children's theater (puppets, clowns, magicians, dancers, and singers), free summer films, and Monday-night showcases of local groups and performers. Call 783-3370 for details. **Metro:** Metro Center.

Admission: Tickets, $22.50–$60; discounts available for students, senior citizens, military personnel, and the handicapped.

FORD'S THEATRE, 511 10th St. NW, between E and F Sts. Tel. 347-4833 for listings. 432-SEAT to charge tickets.

This is the actual theater where, on the evening of April 14, 1865, actor John Wilkes Booth shot President Lincoln. The assassination marked the end of what had been John T. Ford's very popular theater—it remained closed for more than a century. In 1968 Ford's reopened, completely restored to its 1865 appearance, based on photographs, sketches, newspaper articles, and samples of wallpaper and curtain material from museum collections. The presidential box is decorated and furnished as it was on that fateful night, including the original crimson damask sofa and framed engraving of George Washington.

Ford's season is more or less year-round (except for August and September). Past productions have included several shows that went on to Broadway and off-Broadway. Some recent shows here were *Five Guys Named Moe, Hot Mikado,* and Lynn Redgrave's one-woman show, *Shakespeare for My Father.*

A big event here is the nationally televised A Festival at Ford's, always a celebrity-studded bash. **Metro:** Metro Center or Gallery Place.

Admission: Tickets $23–$34; discounts available for families, also for senior citizens at matinee performances; both seniors and students with ID can get "rush" tickets a half hour before performances.

SOURCE THEATRE COMPANY, 1835 14th St. NW, between S and T Sts. Tel. 462-1073.

Washington's major producer of new plays, the Source also mounts works of established playwrights—for instance, David Mamet's *The Woods.* It presents top local artists in a year-round schedule of dramatic and comedy plays, both at the above address and during the summer, at various spaces around town. The theater is also used for an OFF HOURS series of productions geared to a contemporary urban audience Annual events here include the

Washington Theatre Festival each July, a four-week showcase of 50 or so new plays. The Source produces many African-American works and welcomes original scripts from unknowns.

Admission: Tickets $16–$18, OFF HOURS shows $10, July Festival shows $5–$10.

STUDIO THEATRE, 1333 P St. NW. Tel. 332-3300.

Under artistic director Joy Zinoman, the Studio had consistently produced interesting contemporary plays, nurtured Washington acting talent, and garnered numerous Helen Hayes Awards for outstanding achievement. Many plays come here from off-Broadway. Recent productions have included Ariel Dorfman's *Death and the Maiden,* Harold Pinter's *The Caretaker,* Tom Stoppard's *Rosencranz and Guildenstern Are Dead,* and Terrence McNally's *Lips Together, Teeth Apart.* The Studio also houses **Secondstage,** a 50-seat space on the third floor where emerging artists, directors, and actors can showcase their work. The season runs from September through June (some productions run longer). Street parking is easy to find. **Metro:** Dupont Circle or McPherson Square.

Admission: Tickets $16.50–$28.50, Secondstage shows $12. Discounts available for students and senior citizens.

SHAKESPEARE THEATRE, 450 7th St. NW, between D and E Sts. Tel. 393-2700.

This internationally renowned classical ensemble company, which for two decades performed at the Folger Shakespeare Library, moved to larger quarters at the above address in 1992. Under the direction of Michael Kahn, it offers three Shakespearean productions and one other classical work (last year it was *The Doctor's Dilemma* by George Bernard Shaw) each September-to-June season. Well-known actors such as Stacy Keach, Jean Stapleton, Tom Hulce, Richard Thomas, and Pat Carroll have joined the company for specific productions. This is top-level theater. Furthermore, the company offers admission-free summer Shakespearean productions at the Carter Barron Amphitheatre in Rock Creek Park, usually for two to three weeks in June. Tickets are available the day of performance only, on a first-come, first-served basis. Call for details. **Metro:** Archives or Gallery Place.

Admission: Tickets $20–$45, $10 for standing-room tickets sold two hours prior to sold-out performances; discounts available for students and senior citizens.

WOOLLY MAMMOTH THEATRE COMPANY, 1401 Church St. NW. Tel. 393-3939.

Established in 1980, the Woolly Mammoth offers four or five productions each year-long season, specializing, according to a publicist, in "new, offbeat, and quirky plays." "I'm not interested in theater where people sit back and say, 'That was nice. I enjoyed that,'" says artistic director Howard Shalwitz. "I only look for plays that directly challenge the audience in some important way." Hence shows here have included Wallace Shawn's *The Fever,* which radically confronted America's materialist lifestyle in the face of massive suffering throughout the world (audience discussion followed); *Kvetch* by Steven Borkoff (a wild comedy about anxiety, sex, and the nagging inner voices that plague us all); and Obie-winning play-wright Harry Kondoleon's *Half Off* (two alcoholic aunts arrive to care for two adolescents whose bohemian parents have just died in a car crash). This company has garnered nine Helen Hayes Awards, among other accolades.

Metro: Dupont Circle, about five blocks away. You might prefer to take a cab from there, since the neighborhood is rather deserted and spooky at night; on request, they'll call a cab for you after the show. There's free parking across the street.

Admission: Tickets $16.50–$24.50. They offer a range of ticket discounts, from two-for-the-price-of-one admissions to pay-what-you-can nights; inquire at the box office. An hour prior to perfor-mances, a limited number of "stampede seats" are offered for $10.

2. ACCENT ON ENTERTAINMENT

The following listings are a potpourri of places offering a mixed bag of theater, opera, classical music, headliners, jazz, rock, dance, and comedy. Here you'll find some of the top entertainment choices in the District.

WASHINGTON'S MAJOR PERFORMANCE FACILITY

JOHN F. KENNEDY CENTER FOR THE PERFORMING ARTS, at the southern end of New Hampshire Ave. NW and Rock Creek Pkwy. Tel. 467-4600, or toll free 800/444-1324.

Our national performing arts center, the hub of Washington's cultural and entertainment scene, is actually made up of five differ-ent theaters. You can find out what will be on during your stay be-fore leaving home (and charge tickets) by calling the above toll-free number. Half-price tickets are available for full-time students, senior citizens, enlisted personnel, and the disabled (call 416-8340 for de-tails).

Opera House This plush red-and-gilt 2,300-seat theater is designed for ballet, modern dance, and musical comedy, as well as opera, and it's also the setting for occasional gala events such as the Kennedy Center Honors, which you've probably seen on TV (Lillian Gish, Cary Grant, Katharine Hepburn, and Gregory Peck have been honorees). Other offerings have included performances by the Joffrey Ballet, the Bolshoi Ballet, the Kirov Ballet, the Royal Ballet, the American Ballet Theatre, and the Metropolitan Opera. Recent theater productions here have included *Miss Saigon, Phantom of the Opera, The Who's Tommy, How to Succeed in Business Without Really Trying* (starring Matthew Broderick), and *Crazy for You.*

Concert Hall The National Symphony Orchestra has its home here and presents concerts from September to June. Tickets are available by subscription and single sales. Guest artists have included Itzhak Perlman, Vladimir Ashkenazy, Zubin Mehta, Pinchas Zuckerman, André Previn, Jean-Pierre Rampal, and Isaac Stern. In addition, chamber music societies, orchestras, and choral groups from all over the world have performed in this space; there's an annual free Christmas concert, the *Messiah* sing-along; and rounding things out are headliner entertainers such as Johnny Mathis, Joel Grey, Dionne Warwick, Marvin Hamlisch, and Harry Belafonte.

Terrace Theater　Small chamber works, choral recitals, musicals, comedy revues, cabarets, and theatrical and modern-dance performances are among the varied provinces of the 500-seat Terrace Theater, a Bicentennial gift from Japan. It's been the setting for solo performances by violinist Eugene Fodor, pianists Santiago Rodriguez and Peter Serkin, soprano Dawn Upshaw, and jazz singer Barbara Cook. Performance artists Laurie Anderson and Michael Moschen have performed here, and jazz evenings have included tributes to Count Basie, Louis Armstrong, and Duke Ellington. Every spring the Terrace (along with the Theater Lab) hosts productions of six finalists in the American College Theatre Festival competition.

Eisenhower Theater　A wide range of dramatic productions can be seen here. Some recent examples: *Angels in America* (parts I and II), David Mamet's controversial *Oleanna,* and Wendy Wasserstein's *The Sisters Rosensweig.* The Eisenhower is also the setting for smaller productions of the **Washington Opera** from December to February. Tickets for most theatrical productions are in the $18 to $40 range. Opera seats soar higher.

Theater Lab and More　By day, the Theater Lab is Washington's premier stage for children's theater. Evenings it becomes a cabaret, now in a long run of *Shear Madness,* a comedy whodunit (tickets are $19 to $23). Elsewhere at the center, there are family concerts by the National Symphony Orchestra several times each year, not to mention clowns, jugglers, dance troupes, improvisational theater, storytellers, and films. Many events are scheduled for Christmas, Easter, and the annual Kennedy Center Open House Arts Festival (September).

See also "Cinema," below, for details on the **American Film Institute,** yet another Kennedy Center facility.

Underground parking at the Kennedy Center is $5 for the entire evening after 5pm. **Metro:** Foggy Bottom. **Bus:** 46 from Dupont Circle.

OTHER MULTICULTURAL FACILITIES

THE FOLGER, 201 E. Capitol St. SE. Tel. 544-7077.

The **Folger Consort,** a medieval and Renaissance music ensemble, performs secular and sacred music, troubadour songs, madrigals, and court ensembles in 30 concerts given over seven weekends between October and May. Tickets are $14 to $28.

The Folger also presents a full October-to-June season of **theatrical programs** annually relating to Shakespeare and other literary greats. Some recent examples: Irish actor Donal Donnelly in *My Astonishing Self* (a one-man show as George Bernard Shaw), *Stand-up*

Shakespeare (a musical revue), a production of *Macbeth* by the Traveling Shakespeare Company, and *Shenandoah Shakespeare Express* (the Bard's plays performed as they were in his time). Tickets are $12 to $23.

In addition, there are periodic **evening lectures** on Renaissance-related subjects (tickets $6). On selected evenings, **readings** (tickets $6 to $12) feature poets such as Joseph Brodsky, Octavio Paz, Czeslaw Milosz, Adrienne Rich, and Allen Ginsberg. Another exciting program is the Friday-night PEN/Faulkner series of fiction readings by noted authors; Arthur Miller, Nadine Gordimer, Margaret Atwood, J. P. Donleavy, Pat Conroy, and John Irving have participated. And September to May, the Folger offers Saturday morning **programs for children** ranging from medieval treasure hunts to preparing an Elizabethan feast. Admission is $7.50 per child. **Metro:** Capitol South.

WARNER THEATRE, 1299 Pennsylvania Ave. NW (entrance on 13th St., between E and F Sts.). Tel. 783-4000; 432-SEAT to charge tickets.

Opened in 1924 as the Earle Theatre (a movie/vaudeville palace)—and restored to its original appearance in 1992 at a cost of $10 million—this stunning neoclassical-style theater features a gold-leafed grand lobby and auditorium. Everything is plush and magnificent, from the glittering crystal chandeliers to the gold-tasseled swagged-velvet draperies. It's worth coming by just to see its ornately detailed interior. The Warner offers year-round entertainment, alternating dance performances (Twyla Tharp, Baryshnikov, Alvin Ailey, the Washington Ballet's Christmas performance of *The Nutcracker*) and Broadway shows (Robert Goulet in *Camelot, The Sound of Music* starring Marie Osmond, *Hair*) with headliner entertainment (Liza Minnelli, Frank Sinatra, Shirley MacLaine, Charles Aznavour, Tony Bennett). Call to find out what's on during your visit. **Metro:** Metro Center.

Admission: Play tickets $32.50–$60; concert prices vary according to the performer.

WOLF TRAP FARM PARK FOR THE PERFORMING ARTS, 1551 Trap Rd., Vienna, Va. Tel. 703/255-1900; call PROTIX (703/218-6500) to charge tickets.

The country's only national park devoted to the performing arts, Wolf Trap, just 30 minutes by car from downtown D.C., offers a star-studded **Summer Festival Season** from late May to mid-September. Recent seasons have featured performances by the National Symphony Orchestra (it's their summer home), jazz trumpeter Wynton Marsalis, Ray Charles, Mary Chapin Carpenter, Emmylou Harris, John Denver, Bill Cosby, the Joffrey Ballet, Willie Nelson, Sonny Rollins, Marilyn Horne, tenor José Carreras, and Penn & Teller. Talk about eclectic! There's also an Irish music festival every May. Performances take place in the 7,000-seat **Filene Center,** about half of which is under the open sky. You can also buy cheaper lawn seats on the hill, which is sometimes the nicest way to go. If you do, arrive early (the lawn opens 90 minutes before the performance), and bring a blanket and a picnic dinner; it's a tradition.

October to May is Wolf Trap's **Barn Season,** featuring the Wolf Trap Opera Company, jazz, pop, country, folk, and bluegrass performers, chamber music, and more in the pre-Revolutionary, 350-seat German Barn at 1635 Trap Rd. Call 703/938-2404 for information.

Metro: West Falls Church; in summer only, the Wolf Trap Express Shuttle ($3.50 round-trip) runs from the Metro every 20 minutes starting two hours before the performance time and (return trip) 20 minutes after the performance ends or 11pm (whichever comes first). By car, take I-495 to Exit 12W (Dulles Toll Road); stay on the local exit road (you'll see a sign) until you come to Wolf Trap.

Admission: Summer Festival $18–$39 seats, $7–$17 lawn; Barn season tickets average $10–$18.

MOSTLY HEADLINERS

The following facilities offer primarily big-name entertainers—they're large spaces only headliners can fill.

BALTIMORE ARENA, 201 W. Baltimore St., Baltimore, Md. Tel. 410/347-2020; 410/481-SEAT or toll free 800/551-SEAT for tickets.

This 13,500-seat arena, a few blocks from Baltimore's Inner Harbor, is home to several local sports teams. When they're not playing, there are big-name concerts and family entertainment shows here. The Arena hosted the Beatles back in the 1960s. More recently, they've presented *Nickelodeon Double Dare Live,* Ringling Brothers and Barnum & Bailey Circus, *Disney on Ice,* and headliners such as Neil Diamond, Randy Travis, Paul Simon, Liza Minnelli, Luther Vandross, Alan Jackson, and George Jones.

To get here by car, take I-95 north to I-395 (stay in the left lane) to the Inner Harbor exit and follow Howard Street to the Arena. You can also take a MARC train from Union Station.

Admission: Ticket prices vary according to the performer or show.

USAIR ARENA, Exit 15A or 17A off the Capital Beltway in Landover, Md. Tel. 301/350-3400.

This 19,000-seat arena hosts a variety of concerts and headliner entertainment in between sporting events. Pavarotti, Michael Jackson, Janet Jackson, Van Halen, Madonna, Elton John, Eric Clapton, Neil Diamond, Garth Brooks, Barbra Streisand, Aerosmith, and the Rolling Stones have all played here.

Admission: Ticket prices vary according to the performer.

CONSTITUTION HALL, 18th and D Sts. NW. Tel. 638-2661 or 628-4780; 432-SEAT to charge tickets.

Somehow I don't associate such people as Richard Pryor and Eddie Murphy with the Daughters of the American Revolution. Nevertheless, they've both appeared at this beautiful 3,746-seat Federal-style auditorium at the DAR's national headquarters. Others who've headlined here include Lee Greenwood, the Washington

Civic Symphony, Patti LaBelle, Diana Ross, Jay Leno, Ray Charles, and Marilyn Horne. **Metro:** Farragut West.

Admission: Tickets $15–$50 depending on the performer.

MERRIWEATHER POST PAVILION, 10475 Little Patuxent Pkwy., Just off Rte. 29 in Columbia, Md. Tel. 410/730-2424; 432-SEAT to charge tickets.

During the summer there's celebrity entertainment almost nightly at the Merriweather Post Pavilion, about 40 minutes by car from downtown D.C. There's reserved seating in the open-air pavilion (overhead protection provided in case of rain) and general-admission seating on the lawn (no refunds for rain) to see such performers as James Taylor, Tina Turner, Van Halen, the Beach Boys, Frank Sinatra, Liza Minnelli, Sting, John Mellencamp, Julio Iglesias, Joan Rivers, Willie Nelson, Jimmy Buffett, Elton John, Al Jarreau, and Barry Manilow. If you choose the lawn seating, bring blankets and picnic fare (beverages must be bought on the premises).

Admission: Tickets $17–$50 pavilion, $13.50–$20 lawn.

THE PATRIOT CENTER, George Mason University, 4400 University Dr., Fairfax, Va. Tel. 703/993-3000; 703/573-SEAT to charge tickets.

This 10,000-seat facility hosts major headliners. Performers here have included Prince, Randy Travis, David Copperfield, Gloria Estefan, Tom Petty, Natalie Cole, Sting, Billy Idol, and Kenny Rogers. There are family events such as *Sesame Street Live* here, too. To get here by car, take the Wilson Bridge to Braddock Road West, and continue about 8 miles to University Drive.

Admission: Ticket prices vary according to the performer.

ROBERT F. KENNEDY MEMORIAL STADIUM, 2400 E. Capitol St. SE. Tel. 547-9077 or 546-3337; 432-SEAT to charge tickets.

It takes superstars to pack this 55,000-plus-seat facility. Michael Jackson, Bruce Springsteen, the Rolling Stones, U-2, Pink Floyd, Paul McCartney, the Grateful Dead, New Kids on the Block, and Bob Dylan are among those who've played here. **Metro:** Stadium-Armory.

Admission: Ticket prices vary according to the performer.

3. THE MUSIC, BAR & CLUB SCENE

In addition to the big concert spaces detailed in "Accent on Entertainment," above, and the free concerts listed in "Free Shows," below, Washington has many more intimate places where great rock and jazz artists play. There are also lively bars, dance clubs (the latter offering some of the best singles action), and comedy clubs. there's even big-band music, square and folk dancing, and more, in a park. What else could you ask for?

By the way, some of these places could also fit under another category on occasion, so read all sections and then call the ones that interest you to see what's happening that night before setting out.

ROCK & JAZZ

THE BAYOU, 3135 K St. NW, under the Whitehurst Fwy. near Wisconsin Ave. Tel. 333-2897.

This lively nightclub, located on the Georgetown waterfront, features a mixed bag of live musical entertainment—mostly progressive, reggae, and alternative sounds. Performers are up-and-coming national groups, with occasional big names playing the club for old time's sake. Show times vary.

Every Saturday night at 7:30pm (doors open at 6:30pm), an extremely funny comedy group called **Gross National Product** takes the stage. Their satirical show targets the foibles and frailties of the present administration—its pundits, policymakers, and hangers-on. Part of the show includes a mock town meeting in which the audience bombards "President Clinton" with irreverent questions on topics ranging from health care to Whitewatergate. This ever changing show (today's scandal is tomorrow's skit) is so popular that advance reservations are required (call 783-7212).

The Bayou is a funky, cavelike club, with exposed brick and stone walls and seating on two levels. Sandwiches and pizza are available during the show. Drinks average $3; most food items are $5 or less. Except at special all-age shows, no one under 18 is admitted.

Admission: $5–$17, $15 for Gross National Product.

BLUES ALLEY, 1073 Wisconsin Ave. NW, in an alley below M St. Tel. 337-4141.

Blues Alley, in Georgetown, has been Washington's top jazz club since 1965, featuring such artists as Nancy Wilson, McCoy Tyner, Phyllis Hyman, Sonny Rollins, Flora Purim, Herbie Mann, Wynton Marsalis, Charlie Byrd, Ramsey Lewis, Dr. John, and Maynard Ferguson. There are usually two shows nightly. Reservations are essential (call after noon); since seating is on a first-come, first-served basis it's best to arrive no later than 7pm and have dinner. Entrées on the steak and Créole-seafood menu (for example, jambalaya, chicken Créole, and crabcakes) are in the $14 to $19 range, snacks and sandwiches are $5.25 to $9, and drinks are $4.50 to $6. The decor is of the classic jazz club genre—exposed brick walls, beamed ceiling, and small candlelit tables. Sometimes well-known visiting musicians get up and jam with performers, and one night, when Jerry Lewis was in the audience, he got up on stage and told a few jokes.

Blues Alley will open a new adjoining club offering a wider spectrum of entertainers in the near future.

Admission: $13–$40, depending on the performer, plus $7 food or drink minimum.

PUBS & BARS

BOTTOM LINE, 1716 I St. NW. Tel. 298-8488.

The Bottom Line is a popular sports bar, owned by Dick Heidenberger and Jack Million, both former PAC rugby team players. Consequently, lots of ruggers and other athletes hang out here. Monday night, sporting events are televised at the bar, and free hot dogs are offered to customers. Tuesday to Saturday, there's dancing to music (Top-40 tunes, progressive rock, reggae) provided by a DJ from 9pm to closing. Some people describe the Bottom Line as a place to come and go nuts. There's a definite anything-goes attitude, enhanced by frequent zany promotions. One night, anyone who could sit on a block of ice for an hour had $100 donated to the charity of his or her choice—plus unlimited free drinks while ice-sitting. And, of course, there's a big holiday bash on Christmas, New Year's, Valentine's Day, St. Patrick's Day, and so forth—let's just say the party never stops. A reasonably priced menu—salads, omelets, pita sandwiches, deli sandwiches, and burgers—is offered until 10 or 11pm. Drinks run $2.50 to $3.50. Open Monday to Thursday until 1:30am, to 2:30am Friday and Saturday. **Metro:** Farragut West.

CHAMPIONS, 1206 Wisconsin Ave. NW, just north of M St. Tel. 965-4005.

This Georgetown spot is D.C.'s premier hangout for athletes and sports groupies. The heaviest singles action takes place at the first-floor bar; the upstairs bar and glassed-in deck are more laid-back. The attractive interior is chockablock with autographed sports photos, posters, and artifacts such as Carl Lewis's running shoes, Sugar Ray Leonard's boxing gloves, Joe Louis's headgear, and O. J. Simpson's football jersey. And many TV monitors air nonstop sporting events. Of course, you're likely to see your favorite sports stars (particularly of Washington area teams) at the bars or tables, and entertainment world celebrities also drop by with some frequency. I once glimpsed Ryan O'Neal at the bar cheering the Celtics. Champions is always packed, and they don't take reservations, so unless you arrive early, you'll probably have to wait for a table. If you do get a seat, you might order such fare as nachos, burgers, a steak-and-cheese sandwich, or buffalo wings. And should you make your way through the crowd to the bar, you'll see that it's pasted over with $15,000 worth of baseball cards. Drinks average $3. A DJ is on hand nightly playing oldies and Top-40 tunes. Open Sunday to Thursday until 2am, Friday and Saturday until 3am.

CLYDE'S, 3236 M St. NW. Tel. 333-9180.

Located in Georgetown, this New York–style bar complete with checkered tablecloths, gaslight sconces, and white tile floors is mobbed every evening with an upscale crowd of young professionals, college students, political types, and Old Line Washingtonians. If you should want solid rather than liquid refreshment, there are several dining areas—my favorite is the candlelit patio with numerous plants and a skylight ceiling. Or you can adjourn to the Omelette Room where a chef working in an open copper-canopied kitchen turns out such omelets as the Bonne Femme—stuffed with bacon, sautéed potatoes, onions, sour cream, and chives—until the wee hours. (See further details on the food here in Chapter 6.) Clyde's opens at 11:30am and drinks are served until 2am Sunday to Thursday, 3am Friday and Saturday. Drinks average $3.20.

OLD EBBITT GRILL, 675 15th St. NW, between F and G Sts. Tel. 347-4801.

While I'm on the subject of simpatico hangouts, the Old Ebbitt, described in detail in Chapter 6, offers a good bit of glamour in its sumptuous turn-of-the-century bars and dining areas. A scene from Clint Eastwood's movie *In the Line of Fire* was shot here. Drinks average $3.20. **Metro:** McPherson Square or Metro Center.

DANCE CLUBS

DEJA VU, 2119 M St. NW. Tel. 452-1966.

This 10-room Victorian extravaganza, with two dance floors, eight bars, and two restaurants on the premises, is one of the liveliest places in D.C. Both dance floors have wood-burning fireplaces, which, along with stained-glass paneling, tropical plants, fountains, and plush furnishings, make for a warm setting. A DJ plays the "greatest hits of yesterday and today." Every Thursday, there's a dance contest at midnight, and there are frequent theme parties such as Christmas in July. You can dine here (reservations advised) at Blackie's House of Beef (steaks, prime rib, fresh seafood) or Lulu's New Orleans Cafe, offering Créole-Cajun and seafood entrées as well as indoor and outdoor seating. Drinks average $3.25. Open Sunday to Thursday to 2am, Friday and Saturday to 3am. **Metro:** Dupont Circle or Foggy Bottom.

Admission: $2 cover Fri–Sat, no cover or drink minimum Sun–Thurs.

FIFTH COLUMN, 915 F St. NW. Tel. 393-3632.

Fronted by massive neoclassical columns, the Fifth Column isn't decorator fancy but does have a rather grand interior—a former Equitable Bank with a soaring 45-foot arched ceiling over the dance floor. Especially plush is the upstairs VIP room with comfortable sofas, a working fireplace, aquariums, and water bubbling through blue neon-lit mirrored walls. Guests are admitted to the latter at the discretion of the man behind the velvet rope; bar prices are higher in this elevated precinct, but it's a cozy setting for sipping champagne. Also simpatico is the open-air patio out back. The music (mostly DJ/occasional live entertainment, till 2am Monday to Thursday, to 3am Friday and Saturday) is a mix of progressive house, European house, acid jazz, techno, and underground. The club stays on top of trends, keeps an ear to New York and London, and often plays prerelease recordings. There are changing art shows on the walls. The crowd is 25 to 30 years old, upwardly mobile with a sprinkling of Arab princes and the occasional visiting celeb (Cher,

Prince, Julia Roberts, Sylvester Stallone). You must be 21 to get in (18 Monday and Wednesday nights). No drink minimum; the average drink is about $3.75. **Metro:** Metro Center.

Admission: $5–$10.

KILIMANJARO, 1724 California St. NW, between 18th St. and Florida Ave. Tel. 328-3838 or 328-3839.

This popular reggae/calypso/African-music club, owned by a Kenyan and a Bajan, is the hub of Washington's Caribbean music scene. The setting is fittingly exotic—dimly lit, with candles aglow in red-glass holders and zebra skins adorning the walls. There are two separate dance areas; on weekends, a different band plays in each (good acoustics here; there's no cacophony). Some of the artists who've played Kilimanjaro are Shabba Ranks (from Jamaica), Hugh Masekela (South Africa), Arrow (Trinidad), and Gregory Isaacs (Jamaica). There's usually a live band Thursday, Friday, and Saturday nights, a DJ the rest of the week. You can dine here on such menu items as nyama ya mbuzi—East African–style charcoal-grilled goat. Drinks average $3.75. Open till 2am Sunday to Thursday, till 4am Friday and Saturday. Best way to get here is by taxi. You must be 21 to get in.

Admission: Free Mon–Wed, $5 Thurs and Sun, $10 Fri–Sat; there's always a two-drink minimum.

NIGHTCLUB 9:30, 930 F St. NW. Tel. 638-2008 or 393-0930.

This funky club features live bands—punk, metal, house/industrial, reggae, rockabilly, and rap—including some well-known performers like Ice T, Run DMC, Nine Inch Nails, Helmet, and the Screaming Trees. Occasionally jazz artists—such as Sun Ra and Sonny Sharrock—play here as well. It's all very un-Washington, not just the music and the crowd but the grotty, black-walled interior with exposed pipes overhead. There are themed dance parties to introduce new artists and releases. The club is open five or six nights a week (it depends on bookings), until 12:30 to 1:30am Sunday to Thursday, until 3am Friday and Saturday; there's no minimum age for admission—a boom to young teens looking for trouble. No drink minimum; drinks average $3.75. Pizza and snack items are available. **Metro:** Metro Center.

Admission: $3–$25 depending on the performer.

RIVER CLUB, 3223 K St. NW. Tel. 333-8118.

Isn't it romantic? This elegant art deco Georgetown nightspot evokes the sophisticated dine-and-dance clubs that flourished in the 1920s and 1930s, bringing unprecedented champagne-and-caviar glamour to the Washington nightlife scene. The clientele is glittery and gorgeous (wear your best), many with limos waiting out front. One often sees local and visiting celebrities here. I've spotted Redskins owner Jack Kent Cooke, Ted Kennedy, Ryan O'Neal, Jesse Jackson, Cher, Lynda Carter, Sen. John Warner, and Sylvester Stallone on various visits. You can hang out at the large bar up front or have dinner (the food's superb) at the tables surrounding the circular dance floor. It's a great place to dance. Weekends from 7 to 10pm a pianist plays light jazz and show tunes. The rest of the night (and weeknights—except Thursday, big band night—there's a DJ, and the music is a mix of Sinatra, Cole Porter, big band and swing, Motown, contemporary sounds, even a bit of European music. If you can't manage sparkling repartee or kindle the spark of romance in this setting, you never will. Open for dinner Monday to Thursday 5:30 to 11:30pm, for dancing until 2am; Friday and Saturday for dinner until midnight, for dancing until 3am. See Chapter 6 for a detailed description of the River Club and its culinary offerings. Drinks average $5.

SPY CLUB, 805 15th St. NW, between H and I Sts., in Zei Alley. Tel. 289-1779.

The Spy Club's dance floor is punctuated by columns designed to evoke skyscrapers, complete with lighted windows. There are cozy nooks off the dance floor, including the Den (with overstuffed sofas, shaded table lamps, and a working fireplace), the Cubana Room (with palm trees and a roulette wheel), and the Billiards Room (set up with a pool table and backgammon boards). Every Wednesday the club hosts an upscale Latin night, when men in jackets and ties twirl ladies in high heels to sounds of salsa. Friday and Saturday feature cutting-edge mixes of high-energy, house, techno, and European music. The dress code prohibits sneakers or T-shirts. The crowd is early 20s to 35. If you'd like to dine sometime during the evening, Notte Luna, a fine northern Italian restaurant, is right upstairs. Hours vary, but the club is generally open Wednesday, Friday, and Saturday 10pm to 2:30am. Drinks average $4. **Metro:** McPherson Square. Valet parking is $5.

Admission: $5–$8.

COMEDY CLUBS & CABARET

Although big-name comedians perform around town at such places as **Constitution Hall,** and lesser known comedians and groups at such places as **D.C. Space,** there are two clubs in town totally devoted to comedy:

COMEDY CAFE, 1520 K St. NW. Tel. 638-JOKE.

The Comedy Cafe features both local talent and nationally known comics you might have seen in movies or on TV (for example, Larry Miller, David Brenner, Brett Butler, Chris Rock, Judy Tenuta, David Alan Grier, and Jeff Foxworthy). Reservations are recommended, and it's a good idea to arrive early to get a good seat. There are two shows every Friday night (at 8:30 and 10:30pm) and three every Saturday night (at 7, 9, and 11pm). There's no minimum, but you can order food; a reasonably priced menu offers full entrées (such as chicken teriyaki and prime rib), as well as sandwiches, burgers, hors d'oeuvres, desserts, and, of course, drinks. Wednesday (from 8:30pm) is open-mike night; that means people are auditioning or, occasionally, pros are working out new material ($4.95 cover, no minimum). And on Thursday (same hours) four comics take the stage ($4.95 cover, no minimum).

The Comedy Cafe is on the second floor. Below, under the same ownership, is **Fanatics,** a sports-themed club where there's a DJ and karaoke weekend nights. Sporting events are aired on at least a dozen TV monitors, and there are games (pinball, darts, computerized bowling, and so forth). Open until 2am Sunday to Thursday, until 3am on Friday and Saturday. **Metro:** McPherson Square or Farragut North.

Admission: Comedy Cafe $10–$25; Fanatics no cover or minimum.

THE IMPROV, 1140 Connecticut Ave. NW, between L and M Sts. Tel. 296-7008.

Offering a similar format to the above, the Improv features top performers on the national comedy club circuit. "Saturday Night Live" regulars Ellen Cleghorne (Queen Shenequa), David Spade, and Adam Sandler have all played here. Shows are about 1½ hours long and include three comics (an emcee, feature act, and headliner). Show times are 8:30pm Sunday to Thursday, 8:30 and 10:30pm Friday and Saturday. Best way to snag a good seat is to have dinner here (make reservations), which allows you to enter the club as early as 7pm. Dinner entrées ($8.95 to $12.95) include prime rib, chicken Cordon Bleu, and pasta and seafood selections. Drinks average $3.25. You must be 18 to get in. **Metro:** Farragut North.

Admission: $8 Sun–Thurs, $10 Fri–Sat, plus a two-item minimum (waived if you dine).

MARQUEE CABARET, in the Omni Shoreham Hotel, 2500 Calvert St. NW, at Connecticut Ave. Tel. 234-0700.

A hotel with a long history of providing great entertainment, the Shoreham today features talented ensembles in its plush art deco nightclub. In the 1930s, Lena Horne, Frank Sinatra, Marlene Dietrich, and Judy Garland performed at the hotel. And political satirist Mark Russell played the room for 20 years. For the last six years, a politically oriented and extremely funny musical comedy revue called *Mrs. Foggybottom & Friends* has been playing Thursday to Saturday at 9pm. On Monday at 8pm an improvisational comedy group called Now This takes the stage. Singers and comics fill in other nights. There's almost always something on. Reservations suggested. **Metro:** Woodley Park–Zoo.

Admission: $7–$21 depending on the entertainment.

4. CINEMA

With the advent of VCRs, classic film theaters have almost become extinct. In addition to the **Mary Pickford Theater,** in the John Adams Building of the Library of Congress (see Chapter 7), there are only two choices in this category, but they're both good:

AMERICAN FILM INSTITUTE, at the Kennedy Center, New Hampshire Ave. NW and Rock Creek Pkwy. Tel. 828-4000 or 785-4600.

This marvelous facility features classic films, cult movies, themed film festivals, and the like in a 224-seat theater designed to offer the highest standard of projection, picture, and sound quality. There's something on almost every evening and weekend afternoon. The AFI also sponsors audience-participation discussions with major directors, film stars, and screenwriters, for example, Linda Yellin, Sigourney Weaver, Gore Vidal, Nora Ephron, Jonathan Demme, and Ivan Reitman.

Underground parking at the Kennedy Center is $5 for the entire evening after 5pm. **Metro:** Foggy Bottom.

Admission: $6; $5 for members (AFI memberships are $15 a year), senior citizens, and students under 18 with ID.

BIOGRAPH, 2819 M St. NW. Tel. 333-2696.

The Biograph, in Georgetown, specializes in small, independent first-run and foreign films, documentaries, and other cinematographic efforts of interest to serious filmgoers. It shows many notable (often award-winning) foreign films and independent-filmmaker productions. Recent offerings have ranged from a Garbo retrospective to the 24th International Tourney of Animation. Stop by and pick up a calendar if you're going to be in town for a while.

Admission: $6. A discount ticket book good for 10 admissions Monday to Thursday evenings and at all matinee shows is $25.

5. FREE SHOWS

In D.C. some of the best things at night are free—or so cheap they might as well be free.

MILITARY BAND CONCERTS

The **U.S. Army Band, "Pershing's Own"** (tel. 703/696-3399), presents a mix of country, blues, Bach, choral music, jazz, pop, and show tunes every summer, all of it outdoors. There are performances at 8pm every Friday on the east steps of the Capitol and every Tuesday at the Sylvan Theatre on the grounds of the Washington Monument. Every June there's a major American history–themed pageant at the USAir Arena called *Spirit of America* (call 202/475-0685 to obtain free tickets). And beginning early in July (until mid- to late August) the band joins with the Third U.S. Infantry, "The Old Guard," on Wednesday at 7pm to present *Twilight Tattoo,* a military pageant, on the Ellipse; it features the Old Guard Fife and Drum Corps, rifle drills, flag presentations, and a musical salute to America's heritage. Arrive early to get a good seat at any of the above, and bring a picnic dinner and blanket to outdoor concerts. The season's highlight is a performance in August of Tchaikovsky's *1812* Overture with real roaring cannons. There are additional performances in winter at Brucker Hall in Arlington, Virginia. Call for details.

The **U.S. Navy Band, "The World's Finest"** (tel. 433-2525 for a 24-hour recording, or 433-6090), performs a similar variety of music, alternately at 8pm Monday on the east steps of the Capitol and at 8pm Thursday at the Sylvan Theatre, June to August. There are also summer U.S. Navy Band concerts Tuesday nights at 8pm at the U.S. Navy Memorial, 701 Pennsylvania Ave. NW. The navy band highlight: the *Children's Lollipop Concert* of child-oriented music, the third Thursday in August, with elaborate sets, costumes, balloons, clowns, and free lollipops for the audience. And the band also features the *Navy Summer Pageant,* a multimedia presentation tracing the history of the U.S. Navy, every Wednesday June to August at 9pm at the Washington Navy Yard Waterfront, 901 M St. SE. Advance reservations are required; call 433-2218.

The **U.S. Marine Band, "The President's Own"** (tel. 433-4011 for a 24-hour recording, or 433-5809), alternates performances June to August on the east steps of the Capitol on Wednesday at 8pm and at the Sylvan Theatre on Sunday at 8pm. It offers additional free concerts January and February at the Marine Barracks, 8th and I Streets SE, including a chamber music series at 2pm every Sunday (no tickets required). Call for details.

Finally, there's the **U.S. Air Force Band, "America's International Musical Ambassadors"** (tel. 767-5658 for a 24-hour recording, or 767-4310). June through August they (or their jazz ensemble, **The Airmen of Note**) can be seen on the east steps of the Capitol on Tuesday at 8pm and at the Sylvan Theatre on Friday at the same time. And the Friday closest to August 25 is set aside for Christmas in August (carols and other Christmas music).

HEADLINERS—MOSTLY JAZZ

Anheuser-Busch, together with local radio stations, sponsors two fabulous outdoor summer concert series in conjunction with the National Park Service.

Big names in jazz, pop, rock, Latin, and avant-garde music perform in the 4,200-seat **Carter Barron Amphitheatre,** Colorado Avenue and 16th Street NW, in Rock Creek Park (tel. 426-6837 or 619-7222) from mid-June to the end of August on Friday and Saturday nights at 8:30pm. Tickets are relatively inexpensive—about $15. They go on sale at Ticketmaster outlets (tel. 432-SEAT) at the beginning of the season and sell out fast. Seating is on a first-come, first-served basis, so arrive early and get in line. Who might you see here? Nancy Wilson, Phoebe Snow, Roberta Flack, Gladys Knight, Phyllis Hyman, or B. B. King, among other stars. In addition, the National Symphony Orchestra presents several free summer concerts here, and the *Washington Post* also sponsors free Carter Barron concerts. Call for details.

Under the same sponsorship is a series of jazz concerts on the lawn in the **Fort Dupont Summer Theatre,** Randle Circle and Minnesota Avenue SE, in Fort Dupont Park (tel. 426-7723 or 619-7222), every Friday or Saturday at 8:30pm from sometime in June to the end of August. Bring a blanket and a picnic dinner; arrive early (by 6pm) to get a good spot on the lawn. Past performers here have included Stanley Turrentine, Roy Ayres, Herbie Mann, McCoy Tyner, Betty Carter, the Motown Revue, Flora Purim, and Ahmad Jamal. Admission is free.

MORE OUTDOOR CONCERTS

Concerts at the Capitol, an American Festival, is sponsored jointly by the National Park Service and Congress. It's a series of free summer concerts with the National Symphony Orchestra that take place at 8pm on the west side of the Capitol on Memorial Day, July 4, and Labor Day. Seating is on the lawn, so bring a picnic. Major guest stars in past years have included E. G. Marshall (a narrator and host), Leontyne Price, Johnny Cash, Rita Moreno, Mary Chapin Carpenter, and Mstislav Rostropovich. The music ranges from light classical to country to show tunes of the Gershwin/Rodgers and Hammerstein genre. For further information call 619-7222.

The Corporate Community Family (which is made up of such organizations as Exxon and the *Washington Post*) sponsors free **Music Under the Stars Concerts** on Wednesday nights in summer at the Sylvan Theatre on the lawn south of the Washington Monument (tel. 619-7222). The series offers a variety of big band, jazz, and international music; in the latter category, I once attended a fabulous Polynesian show, complete with fire dancers. Be sure to arrive early in order to snag a good spot, and bring a picnic dinner. Concerts begin at 7pm.

Concerts on the Canal, sponsored by the Mobil Corporation, are free afternoon concerts right on the C&O Canal between 30th and Thomas Jefferson Streets NW, just below M Street (tel. 653-5844). Featuring jazz, folk, Dixieland, bluegrass, country, and classical artists, they take place every other Sunday afternoon (1:30 to 4pm) from early June to Late August or early September.

CHAPTER 10

EASY EXCURSIONS FROM WASHINGTON, D.C.

1. ARLINGTON NATIONAL CEMETERY
2. MOUNT VERNON
3. ALEXANDRIA

If possible, consider spending a few days away from Washington, visiting pre-Revolutionary America and other close-to-the-capital attractions. All of the destinations discussed below can be visited on day trips, while you keep your Washington, D.C., hotel base.

1. ARLINGTON NATIONAL CEMETERY

The land that today comprises Arlington County was originally carved out of Virginia as part of the territory ceded to form the nation's new capital district. In 1847 the land was returned to the state of Virginia, although it was known as Alexandria County until 1920, when the name was changed to avoid confusion with the city of Alexandria.

The county was named to honor Arlington House, built by George Washington Parke Custis (see below), whose daughter, Mary Ann Randolph Custis, married a young army officer named Robert E. Lee. The Lees lived in Arlington House until the onset of the Civil War in 1861. After the first Battle of Bull Run, at Manassas, several Union soldiers were buried here, and the beginnings of the national cemetery date from that time. The Arlington Memorial Bridge at the base of the Lincoln Memorial symbolizes the reunion of North and South after the Civil War.

Note: Keep in mind that this is still an active cemetery and observe the proper decorum.

GETTING THERE Arlington National Cemetery is just across the Potomac River from Washington, D.C. **By car,** from the Lincoln Memorial, drive across the Arlington Memorial Bridge. You can park in the huge lots (you're not allowed to drive around the cemetery). Or you can take the **Metro** to the Arlington National Cemetery stop on the Blue Line. If you're sightseeing on the **Tourmobile,** see "Getting Around" in Chapter 4.

GETTING AROUND   Upon your arrival, head over to the **Visitor Center,** where you can purchase a Tourmobile ticket allowing you to stop at all major sights and then reboard whenever you like. Service is continuous, and the narrated commentary is informative. (See "Getting Around" in Chapter 4 for details.) However, if you've lots of stamina, consider doing the tour on foot (a free map is available at the Visitor Center). Riding the Tourmobile with crowds of tourists (usually in a holiday mood) usually makes me feel like I'm at Universal Studios. Walking provides a more contemplative experience. You could compromise by walking some and riding some. On hot and humid summer days, walking requires an almost Spartan determination.

Arlington National Cemetery is open to visitors daily April to September 8am to 7pm, until 5pm the rest of the year. Call 703/692-0931 for further information.

WHAT TO SEE

This famous cemetery occupies 612 acres on the high hills overlooking the capital from the west side of the Memorial Bridge. One of America's most famous national shrines, it honors many national heroes and more than 230,000 war dead, veterans, and dependents. Many graves of the famous at Arlington bear nothing more than simple markers. Five-star Gen. John J. Pershing's is one of those. Secretary of State John Foster Dulles is buried here. So are Pres. William Howard Taft and Supreme Court Justice Thurgood Marshall.

The **Tomb of the Unknowns,** containing the unidentified remains of soldiers from both world wars through the Vietnam War, is located here. It's an unembellished 79-ton white-marble block, moving in its simplicity. Inscribed are the words: "Here rests in honored glory an American Soldier known but to God." Soldiers stationed at Fort Myer guard the tomb day and night. Changing of the guard is performed every half hour April to September and every hour on the hour October to March.

Arlington House (tel. 703/557-0613) was for 30 years (1831–61) the residence of Gen. Robert E. Lee. Lee married the great-granddaughter of Martha Washington, Mary Ann Randolph Custis, who inherited the estate upon the death of her father. It was at Arlington House that Lee received the news of Virginia's secession from the Union and decided to resign his commission in the U.S. Army. During the Civil War the estate was taken over by Union forces, and troops were buried there. Shortly after the defeat of the Confederate forces at Gettysburg, the estate was bought by the government. A fine example of Greek Revival architecture combined with many features of the grand plantation houses of the early 1800s, it has been administered by the National Park Service since 1933.

You can take a self-guided tour of the house; hosts in pre–Civil War dress give an orientation talk, hand out brochures, and answer questions. About 30% of the furnishings are original. Servants' quarters and a small museum adjoin. Admission is free. It's open daily: 9:30am to 4:30pm October to March, until 6pm April to September; closed January 1 and December 25.

Pierre Charles L'Enfant's Grave was placed near Arlington House at a spot that is believed to offer the best view of Washington, the city he designed.

Below Arlington House is the **Gravesite of John Fitzgerald Kennedy.** Simplicity is the key to grandeur here, too. John Carl Warnecke designed a low crescent wall embracing a marble terrace, inscribed with memorable words of the 35th U.S. president, including his famous utterance, "And so my fellow Americans, ask not what your country can do for you, ask what you can do for your country. . . ." Jacqueline Kennedy Onassis, and Sen. Robert Kennedy, are buried close by. The Kennedy graves attract streams of visitors. Arrive as close to 8am as possible to experience the mood of quiet contemplation the site evokes when it's not mobbed with tourists. Looking north, there's a spectacular view of Washington.

Close by, the famous statue of the marines raising the flag on Iwo Jima—the **Marine Corps Memorial**—stands near the north (or Orde-Weitzel Gate) entrance to the cemetery as a tribute to marines who died in all wars. In summer there are military parades on the grounds on Tuesday evenings at 7pm.

Close to the Iwo Jima statue is the **Netherlands Carillon,** a gift from the people of the Netherlands, with 49 bells. Every spring more than 18,000 tulip bulbs are planted on the surrounding grounds. Carillon concerts take place from 2 to 4pm on Saturday during April, May, and September; from 6 to 8pm on Saturday from June to August. (Sometimes the hours change; call 703/285-2598 before you go.) Visitors are permitted to enter the tower to watch the carillonneur perform and enjoy panoramic views of Washington

2. MOUNT VERNON

No visit to Washington is complete without a trip to Mount Vernon, the estate of George Washington. Only 16 miles south of the capital, this southern plantation dates back to a 1674 land grant to Washington's great-grandfather.

GETTING THERE If you're going **by car,** take any of the bridges over the Potomac into Virginia to the George Washington Memorial Parkway (Va. 400) going south; the parkway ends at Mount Vernon. **Tourmobile** buses (tel. 554-7950) depart daily, April to October, from Arlington National Cemetery, the White House, and the Washington Monument. The round-trip fare is $17 for adults, $8.25 for children 3 to 11 (free for children under 3), and includes the admission fee to Mount Vernon (for details on the Tourmobile, see "Getting Around" in Chapter 4) You can also get

EXCURSIONS FROM WASHINGTON, D.C.

Great Falls Park

MacArthur Blvd.

Bethesda

Silver Spring

University of Maryland

Goddard Space Flight Center

Rock Creek

George Washington Mem. Pkwy.

Connecticut Ave.

Wisconsin Ave.

16th St.

Rock Creek Park National Zoo

Anacostia River

Baltimore - Washington Pkwy.

WASHINGTON

New York Ave.

Arlington

Constitution Ave.
Independence Ave.

Arlington National Cemetery ❶

The Pentagon

Washington National Airport

❷ **Alexandria**

Andrews Air Force Base

Geo. Wash. Mem. Pkwy.

❸ **Mount Vernon**

Potomac River

❶ Arlington National Cemetery

❷ Alexandria

❸ Mount Vernon

there on a **Spirit of Washington Cruises** riverboat, which from early March to December travels down the Potomac from Pier 4, at 6th and Water Streets SW (tel. 554-8000 for departure times). Round-trip fares—including the admission fee to Mount Vernon—are $21.50 for adults, $19.25 for seniors, $12.75 for children 6 to 11, and free for children under 6. Book in advance.

TOURING THE ESTATE

Mount Vernon (tel. 703/780-2000) was purchased for $200,000 in 1858 by the Mount Vernon Ladies' Association from John Augustine Washington, great-grandnephew of the first president. Without the group's purchase, the estate might have crumbled and disappeared, for the federal government and the Commonwealth of Virginia both refused to buy the property when it was offered for sale earlier. The restoration is an unmarred beauty; many of the furnishings are original pieces acquired by Washington, and the rooms have been repainted in the original colors favored by George and Martha.

Mount Vernon's mansion and grounds are stunning. Some 500 of the original 8,000 acres (divided into five farms) owned by Washington are still intact. Washington delighted in riding horseback around his property, directing planting and other activities; the Bowling Green entrance is still graced by some of the trees he planted. The American Revolution and his years as president took Washington away from his beloved estate most of the time. He finally retired to Mount Vernon in 1797, just two years before his death, to "view the solitary walk and tread the paths of private life with heartfelt satisfaction." He is buried on the estate. Martha was buried next to him in May 1802. Public memorial services are held at the estate every year on the third Monday in February, the date commemorating Washington's birthday; admission is free that day.

Mount Vernon has been one of the nation's most-visited shrines since the mid-19th century. Today more than a million people tour the property annually. There's no formal tour, but attendants stationed throughout the house and grounds provide brief orientations and answer questions. Best time to visit is off-season; during the heavy tourist months, avoid weekends and holidays if possible, and year-round, arrive early to beat the crowds. Late afternoon is usually also a good time to visit.

The house itself is interesting as an outstanding example of colonial architecture, as an example of the aristocratic lifestyle in the 18th century, and of course, as the home of our first president. There are a number of family portraits, and the rooms are appointed as if actually in day-to-day use.

After leaving the house, you can tour the outbuildings—the kitchen, slave quarters, storeroom, smokehouse, overseer's quarters, coachhouse, and stables. A 4-acre exhibit area called "George Washington, Pioneer Farmer" includes a replica of Washington's 16-sided barn and fields of crops that he grew (corn, wheat, oats, and so forth). Docents in period costumes demonstrate 18th-century farming methods. A museum on the property exhibits Washington memorabilia, and details of the restoration are explained in the museum's annex; there's also a gift shop on the premises. You'll want to walk around the grounds (most pleasant in nice weather), see the wharf, the slave burial ground, the greenhouse, the tomb containing George and Martha Washington's sarcophagi (24 other family members are also interred here), the lawns, and the gardens

The house and grounds are open to the public daily 8am to 5pm April to August; 9am to 5pm in March, September, and October; and 9am to 4pm November to February. Allow at least two hours to see everything. Adults pay $7; senior citizens, $6; children 6 to 11, $3; under 6, free. A map is provided at the entrance.

WHERE TO DINE

At the entrance to Mount Vernon you'll find a **snack bar** serving light fare, and there are picnic tables outside. However, if a picnic is what you have in mind, drive a mile north on the parkway to **Riverside Park,** where you can lunch at tables overlooking the Potomac.

MOUNT VERNON INN, near the entrance to Mount Vernon. Tel. 703/780-0011.

Cuisine: AMERICAN. **Reservations:** Recommended at dinner.

$ Prices: Appetizers $1.75–$2.50 at lunch, $3.50–$5 at dinner; main courses $4.50–$7.50 at lunch, $12–$23 at dinner; fixed-price dinner $14. AE, DISC, MC, V.

Open: Lunch Mon–Sat 11am–3:30pm, Sun 11am–4pm; dinner Mon–Sat 5–9pm.

Lunch or dinner at the inn is an intrinsic part of the Mount Vernon experience. It's a quaintly charming colonial-style restaurant, complete with period furnishings and three working fireplaces. Waiters and waitresses are in colonial costume. Lunch here is quite reasonable. Be sure to begin your meal with an order of homemade peanut and chestnut soup. Entrées range from colonial pye (a crock of meat or fowl and garden vegetables with a puffed pastry top) to a 20th-century-style burger and fries. There's a full bar, and premium wines are offered by the glass. At dinner, tablecloths and candlelight make this a plusher choice. Happily, a fixed-price dinner means that it is also affordable. The meal includes soup (perhaps broccoli Cheddar) or salad, an entrée such as Maryland crabcakes or roast venison with peppercorn sauce, homemade breads, and dessert (like Bavarian parfait or English trifle).

3. ALEXANDRIA

Founded by a group of Scottish tobacco merchants, the seaport town of Alexandria came into being in 1749 when a 60-acre tract of land was auctioned off in half-acre lots. Colonists came from miles around, in ramshackle wagons and stately carriages, in sloops, brigantines, and lesser craft, to bid on land that would be "commodious for trade and navigation and tend greatly to the ease and advantage of the frontier inhabitants. . . ." The auction took place in **Market Square** (still intact today), and the surveyor's assistant was a capable lad of 17 named George Washington.

Today the original 60 acres of lots in George Washington's

hometown (also Robert E. Lee's) are the heart of **Old Town,** a multimillion-dollar urban-renewal historic district. As you stroll Old Town's brick sidewalks and cobblestone streets, you'll see more than 2,000 18th- and 19th-century buildings. You'll visit **Gadsby's Tavern,** where two centuries ago the men who created this nation discussed politics, freedom, and revolution over tankards of ale. You'll stand in the tavern doorway where Washington reviewed his troops for the last time (he trained them in Market Square), visit Lee's boyhood home, and sit in the pews of **Christ Church** where both men worshiped.

Many Alexandria streets still bear their original colonial names (King, Queen, Prince, Princess, Royal—you get the drift), while others like Jefferson, Franklin, Lee, Patrick, and Henry are obviously post-Revolutionary.

In this "mother lode of Americana," the past is being increasingly restored in an ongoing archeological and historical research program. And though the present can be seen in the abundance of quaint shops, boutiques, art galleries, and restaurants capitalizing on the volume of tourism, it's still easy to imagine yourself in colonial times—to smell the fragrant tobacco; hear the rumbling of horse-drawn vehicles over cobblestone; envision the oxcarts piled with crates of chickens, country-cured ham, and casks of cheese and butter; and picture the bustling waterfront where fishermen brought in the daily catch and foreign vessels unloaded exotic cargo.

GETTING THERE If you're traveling **by car,** take the Arlington Memorial or the 14th Street Bridge to the George Washington Memorial Parkway (Va. 400) south; it leads right to King Street, Alexandria's main thoroughfare. Parking permits are available from the Alexandria Convention & Visitors Bureau (see below). The easiest way to make the trip is on the **Metro,** and the Old Town is so compact that you won't need a car once you arrive. Take the Metro Yellow Line to the King Street station, but be sure to get a transfer from your departure station. From King Street, take a blue-and-gold DASH bus (75¢) to the Visitors Bureau.

ORIENTATION

INFORMATION Before you do anything else, visit the **Alexandria Convention & Visitors Bureau** at Ramsay House, 221 King St., at Fairfax Street (tel. 703/838-4200, 703/838-5005 for a 24-hour Alexandria events recording), which is open daily from 9am to 5pm (closed January 1, Thanksgiving, and December 25). Here you can obtain a map/self-guided walking tour and brochures about the area; learn about special events that might be scheduled during your visit and get tickets for them; see a 13-minute video about Alexandria history; and receive answers to any questions you might have about accommodations, restaurants, sights, shopping, and whatever else. The bureau has materials in 20 languages.

If you came by car, get a free **one-day parking permit** here for gratis parking at any two-hour meter for up to 24 hours. It can be renewed for a second day

ALEXANDRIA

↑ To National Airport and Washington, D.C.

Potomac River

To I-95 and U.S. 1 →
From I-95 and U.S. 1 →
To Mount Vernon, Woodlawn, Gunston Hall ↓

Alexandria Archeology/Torpedo
Factory Art Center ❶
Alexandria Black History Resource Center ❸
Alexandria Waterfront Museum ❷
Boyhood Home of Robert E. Lee ❹
Carlyle House ⓯
Christ Church ❻
Friendship Firehouse ❼

Gadsby's Tavern Museum ⓮
Lee-Fendall House ❺
The Lyceum ❽
Market Square ⓭
Old Presbyterian Meeting House ❾
Ramsay House Visitors Bureau ⓬
The Schooner *Alexandria* ❿
Stabler-Leadbeater Apothecary Shop ⓫

Also available at Ramsay House: a **block ticket** for admission to four historic Alexandria properties—Gadsby's Tavern, Lee's Boyhood Home, the Carlyle House, and the Lee-Fendall House. The ticket, which can also be purchased at any of the four buildings, costs $8 to see all four sights, $5 for any two—a saving over purchasing the tickets separately. Children 11 to 17 are charged $3 for all four sights, $2 for two; children under 11 enter free.

You'll find the staff friendly and knowledgeable; they'll even be happy to book your hotel room or make restaurant reservations.

TOURS Though it's easy to see Alexandria on your own by putting yourself in the hands of guides at the various attractions, your experience may be enhanced by taking a comprehensive walking tour. **Doorways to Old Virginia** (tel. 703/548-0100) has tours leaving from the Visitors Bureau at Ramsay House at 11am Monday through Saturday, and at 2pm Sunday (all weather permitting); tours cost $3 for adults and $1.50 for students 7 to 17.

CITY LAYOUT Old Town is contained within several blocks. Park your car for the day, don comfortable shoes, and start walking—it's the easiest way. It's helpful to know, when looking for addresses, that Alexandria is laid out in a simple grid system. Union to Lee Street is the 100 block, Lee to Fairfax the 200 block, and so on up. The cross streets (more or less going north and south) are divided north and south by King Street. King to Cameron is the 100 block north, Cameron to Queen the 200 block north, and so on. King to Prince is the 100 block south and so forth.

SPECIAL EVENTS The below-listed are only the *major* events. If you're planning to participate in any of them, book your accommodations far ahead and contact the Visitors Bureau for details and necessary advance tickets. Whenever you come, you're sure to run into some activity or other—a jazz festival, tea garden or tavern gambol, quilt exhibit, wine tasting, or organ recital. It's all part of Alexandria's *ceád mile failte* (100,000 welcomes) to visitors.

January The **birthdays of Robert E. Lee** and his father, Revolutionary War Col. **"Light Horse Harry" Lee,** are celebrated together at the Lee-Fendall House and Lee's Boyhood Home the fourth Sunday of the month. The party features period music, refreshments, and house tours.

February Throughout the month Alexandria celebrates **George Washington's Birthday.** Festivities typically include a colonial–costume or black-tie banquet followed by a ball at Gadsby's, a 10-kilometer race, special tours, a Revolutionary War encampment at Fort Ward Park (complete with uniformed troops engaging in skirmishes), the nation's largest George Washington Day Parade (75,000 to 100,000 people attend each year), and 18th-century comic opera performances.

April Alexandria celebrates **Historic Garden Week in Virginia** with tours of privately owned local (usually historic) homes and gardens the fourth Saturday of the month.

June The **Red Cross Waterfront Festival,** the second week in June, honors Alexandria's historic importance as a seaport and the vitality of its Potomac shoreline today with a display of historic tall ships, ship tours, boat rides and races, nautical art exhibits, waterfront walking tours, fireworks, children's games, an arts and crafts show, food booths, and entertainment. This is the nation's largest Red Cross outdoor fund-raiser, attended by more than 120,000 people each year. Admission is charged.

There's a **Civil War Living History** program on a selected weekend at Fort Ward, with authentically equipped and costumed military units demonstrating camp life with drills, music, a review of troops, and a torchlight tour. Admission is charged. For details on either of these, call 703/838-4848.

July Gather with the clans for **Virginia Scottish Games,** a two-day Celtic festival the fourth weekend of the month that celebrates Alexandria's Highland heritage. Activities include athletic events (such as the caber toss, in which competitors heave a 140-pound pole in the air), musicians (playing reels, strathspeys, and laments), fiddling and harp competitions, a parade of clan societies in tartans, a Celtic crafts fair, storytelling, Highland dance performances and competitions, booths selling Scottish foods and wares, dog trials featuring Scottish breeds, and a Scottish Country Dance Party. Tickets at the gate are about $9 for one day, $15 for the entire weekend; children 15 and under are admitted free with a paying adult. You can get a small discount on tickets purchased in advance at the Visitors Bureau.

September During the **18th-Century Fair** (usually the second week of the month) colonial life is re-created on Market Square and at Gadsby's (an authentic 18th-century tavern) with period food, music, and entertainment.

October Chili enthusiasts can sample "bowls of red" at the **War Between the States Chili Cookoff** in Waterfront Park. Contestants from almost every U.S. state and territory compete, and for a few dollars admission, you can taste all their culinary creations. Proceeds to go charity. Fiddling contests, jalapeño-eating contests, and country music are part of the fun. For details and exact dates, call 703/683-5340.

Explore the ghosts and graveyards of Alexandria on a **Halloween Walking Tour** with a lantern-carrying guide in 18th-century costume. The tour focuses on eerie Alexandria legend, myth, and folklore. Admission is $4 for adults, $2 for students 7 to 17. For details, call 703/548-0100.

November The **Historic Alexandria Antiques Show,** the third weekend of the month, features several dozen dealers from many states displaying an array of high-quality antiques—jewelry, silver, rare books, rugs, paintings, folk art, furniture, pottery, and decorative objects—in room settings. Admission is about $6 per day, including free parking and a catalog. Proceeds are used for restoration of historic sites. Pricier activities include a gala opening party (about $75 admission) and a champagne brunch with a featured speaker (about $40). Call 703/838-4554 for details.

December There's a **Christmas Tree Lighting** in Market Square the Friday after Thanksgiving; the ceremony—which includes choir singing, puppet shows, dance performances, and an appearance by Santa and his elves—begins at 7pm. The night the tree is lit, thousands of tiny lights adorning King Street trees also go on.

Holiday festivities continue with the **Annual Scottish Christmas Walk,** the first Saturday in December. Activities include kilted bagpipers, Highland dancers, a parade of Scottish clans (with horses and dogs), caroling, fashion shows, storytelling, booths (selling crafts, antiques, food, hot mulled punch, heather, fresh wreaths, and holly), and children's games. Admission is charged to some events.

The **Old Town Christmas Candlelight Tour,** the second week in December, visits seasonally decorated historic Alexandria homes and an 18th-century tavern. There are colonial dancing, string quartets, madrigal and opera singers, and refreshments, too. Tickets—$12 for adults, $5 for students 6 to 17—are available at the Visitors Bureau.

There are so many holiday season activities, the Visitors Bureau issues a special brochure about them each year. Pick one up to learn about decorations, workshops, walking tours, tree lightings, concerts, bazaars, bake sales, crafts fairs, and much more.

WHAT TO SEE & DO

In addition to the annual events mentioned above, there's much to see and do. The attractions on the block ticket are in the not-to-be-missed category.

About Admissions: If you have not purchased the money-saving block ticket described above, individual tickets to these first four attractions cost $3 for adults and $1 for children.

Note: Many Alexandria attractions are closed on Monday.

GADSBY'S TAVERN MUSEUM, 134 N. Royal St., at Cameron St. Tel. 703/838-4242.

Alexandria was at the crossroads of 18th-century America, and its social center was Gadsby's Tavern, which consisted of two buildings (one Georgian, one Federal) dating from 1770 and 1792, respectively. Innkeeper John Gadsby combined them to create "a gentleman's tavern," which he operated from 1796 to 1808; it was considered one of the finest in the country. George Washington was a frequent dinner guest (he and Martha danced in the second-floor ballroom), and the tavern was also visited by Thomas Jefferson, James Madison, and Lafayette. It was the scene of lavish parties, theatrical performances, small circuses, government meetings, and concerts. Itinerant merchants used the tavern to display their wares, and traveling doctors and dentists treated an unfortunate clientele (these were rudimentary professions in the 18th century) on the premises.

The rooms have been restored to their 18th-century appearance with the help of modern excavations and colonial inventories that included such minutiae as lemon squeezers. On the 30-minute tour, you'll get a good look at the Tap Room, a small dining room, the Assembly Room, the ballroom, typical bedrooms, and the underground icehouse, which was filled each winter from the icy river. Tours depart 15 minutes before and after the hour. Inquire about a special "living history" tour called Gadsby's Time Travels; it's given the last Sunday of each month. And cap off the experience with a meal at the restored colonial-style restaurant that occupies three tavern rooms (see "Where to Dine," below).

Admission: $3 adults, $1 children 11–17, free for children under 11; or buy the block ticket.

Open: Tours given Apr–Sept, Tues–Sat 10:15am–4:15pm, Sun 1:15–4:15pm; Oct–Mar, Tues–Sat 11:15am–3:15pm, Sun 1:15–3:15pm. **Closed:** All federal holidays except Veterans Day.

BOYHOOD HOME OF ROBERT E. LEE, 607 Oronoco St., between St. Asaph and Washington Sts. Tel. 703/548-8454.

Revolutionary War cavalry hero Henry "Light Horse Harry" Lee brought his wife, Ann Hill Carter, and five children to this early Federal-style mansion in 1812, when Robert, destined to become a Confederate military leader, was just 5 years old. A tour of the house, built in 1795, provides a glimpse into the gracious lifestyle of Alexandria's gentry. George Washington was an occasional guest of two earlier occupants, John Potts (the builder of the house) and Col. William Fitzhugh. In 1804 the Fitzhughs' daughter, Mary Lee, married Martha Washington's grandson, George Washington Parke Custis, in the drawing room. And the Custises' daughter, Mary Ann Randolph, married Robert E. Lee.

General Lafayette honored Ann Hill Carter Lee with a visit to the house in October 1824 in tribute to her husband, "Light Horse Harry" Lee, who had died in 1818. Lafayette had been a comrade-in-arms with Lee during the American Revolution. The drawing room today is called the Lafayette Room to commemorate that visit.

On a fascinating tour, you'll see the nursery with its little canopied bed and toy box; Mrs. Lee's room; the Lafayette Room, furnished in period antiques with the tea table set up for use; the morning room, where *The Iliad* translated into Latin reposes on a gaming table (both "Light Horse Harry" and Robert were classical scholars), and the winter kitchen. The furnishings are of the Lee period but did not belong to the family. The house was occupied by 17 different owners after the Lees left. It was made into a museum in 1967.

Admission: $3 adults, $1 children 11–17, free for children under 11; or buy the block ticket.

Open: Tours given Mon–Sat 10am–3:30pm, Sun 1–3:30pm. **Closed:** Easter, Thanksgiving, and Dec 15–Jan 31 (except for the Sun closest to Jan 19, Robert E. Lee's birthday).

LEE-FENDALL HOUSE, 614 Oronoco St., at Washington St. Tel. 703/548-1789.

This handsome Greek Revival–style house is a veritable Lee family museum of furniture, heirlooms, and documents. "Light Horse Harry" Lee never actually lived here, though he was a frequent visitor, as was his good friend, George Washington. He did own the original lot, but sold it to Philip Richard Fendall (himself a Lee on his mother's side), who built the house in 1785. Fendall married three Lee wives, including Harry's first mother-in-law and, later, Harry's sister.

Thirty-seven Lees occupied the house over a period of 118 years (1785–1903), and it was from this house that Harry wrote Alexandria's farewell address to Washington, delivered when he passed through town on his way to assume the presidency. (Harry also wrote and delivered, but not at this house, the famous funeral oration to Washington that contained the immortal words: "First in war, first in peace, and first in the hearts of his countrymen.") During the Civil War, the house was seized and used as a Union hospital.

Thirty-minute guided tours interpret the 1850s era of the home and provide insight into Victorian family life. You'll also see the colonial garden with its magnolia and chestnut trees, roses, and boxwood-lined paths. Much of the interior woodwork and glass is original.

Admission: $3 adults, $1 children 11–17, free for children under 11; or buy the block ticket.

Open: Tues–Sat 10am–3:45pm, Sun noon–3:45pm. Tours depart frequently throughout the day. **Closed:** Jan 1, Thanksgiving, and Dec 24–25.

CARLYLE HOUSE, 121 N. Fairfax St., at Cameron St. Tel. 703/549-2997.

Not only is Carlyle House regarded as one of Virginia's most architecturally impressive 18th-century houses, but it also figured prominently in American history. In 1753 Scottish merchant John Carlyle completed the mansion for his bride, Sara Fairfax of Belvoir, a daughter of one of Virginia's most prominent families. It was designed in the style of a Scottish/English manor house and lavishly furnished. Carlyle, a successful merchant, had the means to import the best furnishings and appointments available abroad for his new Alexandria home.

When it was built, Carlyle House was a waterfront property with its own wharf. A social and political center, the house was visited by numerous great men of the time, George Washington among them. But its most important moment in history occurred in April 1755 when Maj. Gen. Edward Braddock, commander-in-chief of His Majesty's forces in North America, met with five colonial governors here and asked them to tax colonists to finance a campaign against the French and Indians. Colonial legislatures refused to comply, one of the first instances of serious friction between America and Britain. Nevertheless, Braddock made Carlyle House his headquarters during the campaign, and Carlyle was less than impressed with him. He called the general "a man of weak understanding . . . very indolent . . . a slave to his passions, women and wine . . . as great an Epicure as could be in his eating, tho a brave man." Possibly these were the reasons his unfinanced campaign met with disaster. Braddock received, as Carlyle described it, "a most remarkable drubbing."

A **tour** of Carlyle House takes about 40 minutes. Two of the original rooms—the large parlor and the adjacent study—have survived intact; the former, where Braddock met the governors, still retains its original fine woodwork, paneling, and pediments. The house is furnished in period pieces; however, only a few of Carlyle's possessions remain. In an upstairs room an architecture exhibit depicts 18th-century construction methods with hand-hewn beams and hand-wrought nails. Tours are given every half hour on the hour and half hour.

Admission: $3 adults, $1 children 11–17, free for children under 11; or buy a block ticket.

Open: Tues–Sat 10am–4:30pm, Sun noon–4:30pm.

CHRIST CHURCH, 118 N. Washington St., at Cameron St. Tel. 703/549-1450.

This sturdy red-brick Georgian-style church would be an important national landmark even if its two most distinguished members had not been Washington and Lee. It has been in continuous use since 1773.

There have, of course, been many changes since Washington's day. The bell tower, church bell, galleries, and organ were added by the early 1800s, the "wineglass" pulpit in 1891. But much of what was changed later has since been restored to its earlier state. The pristine white interior with wood moldings and gold trim is colonially correct, though modern heating has obviated the need for charcoal braziers and hot bricks. For the most part, the original structure remains, including the hand-blown glass in the windows that the first worshipers gazed through when their minds wandered from the service. The town has grown up around the building that was first called the "Church in the Woods" because of its rural setting.

Christ Church has had its historic moments. Washington and other early church members discussed revolution in the churchyard, and Robert E. Lee met here with Richmond representatives to discuss assuming a command of Virginia's military forces at the beginning of the Civil War. You can sit in the pew where George and Martha sat with her two Custis grandchildren, or in the Robert E. Lee family pew.

It's a tradition for U.S. presidents to attend a service here on a Sunday close to Washington's birthday and sit in his pew. One of the most memorable of these visits took place shortly after Pearl Harbor when Franklin Delano Roosevelt attended services with Winston Churchill on the World Day of Prayer, January 1, 1942.

Of course, you're invited to attend a service. There's no admission, but donations are appreciated. A docent gives brief lectures to visitors. The old Parish Hall today houses a gift shop and an exhibit on the history of the church. Walk out to the weathered graveyard after you see the church. It was Alexandria's first and only burial ground until 1805; its oldest marked grave is that of Issac Pearce, who died in 1771. The remains of 34 Confederate soldiers are also interred here.

Admission: Free.

Open: Mon–Fri 9am–4pm, Sat 9am–noon, Sun 2–4:30pm.

STABLER-LEADBEATER APOTHECARY MUSEUM, 105–107
S. Fairfax St., near King St. Tel. 703/836-3713.

When its doors closed in 1933, this landmark drugstore was the second oldest in continuous operation in America. Run for five generations by the same Quaker family (beginning in 1792), its famous early patrons included Robert E. Lee (he purchased the paint for Arlington House here), George Mason, Henry Clay, John C. Calhoun, and George Washington. Gothic Revival decorative elements and Victorian-style doors were added in the 1840s.

Today the apothecary looks much as it did in colonial times, its shelves lined with original hand-blown gold-leaf-labeled bottles (the most valuable collection of antique medicinal bottles in the country, actually), old scales stamped with the royal crown, patent medicines, and equipment for blood-letting. The clock on the rear wall, the porcelain-handled mahogany drawers, and two mortars and pestles all date from about 1790. Among the shop's documentary records is this 1802 order from Mount Vernon: "Mrs. Washington desires Mr. Stabler to send by the bearer a quart bottle of his best Castor Oil and the bill for it."

There's no tour, but a 10-minute recording will guide you around the displays. The adjoining antiques shop uses its proceeds to maintain the apothecary.

Admission: $1; free for children under 12.

Open: Mon–Sat 10am–4pm. **Closed:** Jan 1, Thanksgiving, Dec 25, and occasional days in winter.

OLD PRESBYTERIAN MEETING HOUSE, 321 S. Fairfax
St., between Duke and Wolfe Sts. Tel. 703/549-6670.

Presbyterian congregations have worshiped in Virginia since Jamestown days when the Rev. Alexander Whittaker converted Pocahontas. This brick church was built by Scottish pioneers in 1775. Although it wasn't George Washington's church, the Meeting House bell tolled continuously for four days after his death in December 1799, and memorial services were preached from the pulpit here by Presbyterian, Episcopal, and Methodist ministers. According to the Alexandria paper of the day, "The walking being bad to the Episcopal church for funeral sermon of George Washington will be preached at the Presbyterian Meeting House. . . ." Two months later, on Washington's birthday, Alexandria citizens marched from Market Square to the church to pay their respects to his memory.

Many famous Alexandrians are buried in the church graveyard, including John and Sara Carlyle, Dr. James Craik (the surgeon who treated—some say killed—Washington, dressed Lafayette's wounds at Brandywine, and ministered to the dying Braddock at Monongahela), and William Hunter, Jr., founder of the St. Andrew's Society of Scottish descendants (bagpipers pay homage to him the first Saturday each December). It is also the site of a Tomb of an Unknown Revolutionary War Soldier, and Dr. James Muir, whose distinguished ministry spanned the years 1789 to 1820, is buried beneath the sanctuary in his gown and bands.

The original Meeting House was gutted by a lightning fire in

1835 but restored around the old walls in the style of the day a few years later. The present bell, said to be recast from the metal of the old one, was hung in a newly constructed belfry in 1843, and a new organ was installed in 1849. The Meeting House closed its doors in 1889, and for 60 years it was virtually abandoned. But in 1949 it was reborn as a living Presbyterian U.S.A. church, and today the old Meeting House looks much as it did following the restoration after the fire. The original parsonage, or manse, is still intact. There's no guided tour, but there is a recorded narrative in the graveyard.

Admission: Free.

Open: Mon–Fri 9am–3pm; Sun services at 8:30 and 11am.

LYCEUM, 201 S. Washington St., off Prince St. Tel. 703/838-4994.

This Greek Revival building houses a museum that depicts Alexandria's history from colonial times through the 20th century. It features changing exhibits (many of them focusing on the decorative arts and architecture) and an ongoing series of lectures, concerts, and films. An adjoining nonprofit shop carries 18th-century reproductions, candles, needlepoint patterns, and such.

Information is also available here about Virginia state attractions, especially Alexandria attractions. You can obtain maps and brochures, and a knowledgeable staff will be happy to answer your questions.

But even without its many attractions, the brick and stucco Lyceum (restored in 1993) merits a visit. Built in 1839, it was designed in the Doric temple style to serve as a lecture, meeting, and concert hall. It was an important center of Alexandria's cultural life until the Civil War when Union forces took it over for use as a hospital. After the war it became a private residence, and still later it was subdivided for office space. In 1969, however, the City Council's use of eminent domain alone prevented the Lyceum from being demolished in favor of the proverbial parking lot.

Admission: Free.

Open: Mon–Sat 10am–5pm, Sun 1–5pm. **Closed:** Jan 1, Thanksgiving, and Dec 25.

FORT WARD MUSEUM AND PARK, 4301 W. Braddock Rd., between Rte. 7 (Leesburg Tpk.) and Seminary Rd. Tel. 703/838-4848.

A short drive from Old Town is a 45-acre museum, park, and historic site that takes you on a leap forward in Alexandria history to the Civil War. The action here centers, as it did in the early 1860s, on an actual Union fort that Lincoln ordered erected to defend Washington, D.C. It was part of a system of Civil War forts surrounding Washington. The Northwest Bastion has been restored, and six mounted guns (originally there were 36) face south waiting for trouble that in fact never came; the fort was not attacked. Self-guided tours begin at the Fort Ward ceremonial gate.

Visitors can explore the fort and replicas of the Ceremonial Entrance Gate and an officer's hut. There's a museum of Civil War artifacts on the premises where changing exhibits focus on subjects such as Union arms and equipment, medical care of the wounded, and local war history.

There are picnic areas with barbecue grills in the woods surrounding the fort. Concerts are presented on selected evenings June to mid-September in the outdoor amphitheater. And throughout the summer there are living-history programs on selected weekends (call for details).

Admission: Free.

Open: Park, daily 9am–sunset; museum, Tues–Sat 9am–5pm, Sun noon–5pm. **Closed:** Jan 1, Thanksgiving, and Dec 25. **Directions:** From Old Town, follow King Street west, go right on Kenwood Avenue, then left on West Braddock Road; continue for three-quarters of a mile to the entrance on the right.

TORPEDO FACTORY, 105 N. Union St., near Cameron St. Tel. 703/838-4565.

This block-long, three-story building, once a torpedo shell-case factory, now accommodates some 175 professional artists and craftspeople who create and sell their own works on the premises. Here you can see artists at work in their studios—potters, painters, printmakers, photographers, sculptors, and jewelers, as well as those who make stained-glass windows and fiber art.

On permanent display here are exhibits on Alexandria history provided by **Alexandria Archaeology** (tel. 703/838-4399), which is headquartered here and engages in extensive city research. Their special exhibit area and lab are open to the public during the hours listed below, with a volunteer or staff member on hand to answer questions. An ongoing exhibit, "Archaeologists at Work," highlights current excavation finds and methodology.

Admission: Free.

Open: Daily 10am–5pm; archeology exhibit area, Tues–Fri 10am–3pm, Sat 10am–5pm, Sun 1–5pm.

SCHOONER *ALEXANDRIA,* Waterfront Park, at the foot of Prince St. Tel. 703/549-7078.

The **Alexandria Seaport Foundation,** a nonprofit organization devoted to maritime heritage, acquired the Swedish three-masted, gaff-rigged, topsail schooner *Alexandria* in 1983. When it's in port (sometimes it participates in tall-ship festivals elsewhere), it's docked at Waterfront Park and open to the public. A Baltic trader vessel built in 1929, the ship was remodeled for passenger use in the 1970s. Seaport Traders, a maritime antique store and coffee shop, is next door.

Admission (and tour): Free. Donations requested.

Open: When in port (usually fall–spring), Sat–Sun noon–5pm.

FRIENDSHIP FIREHOUSE, 107 S. Alfred St., between King and Prince Sts. Tel. 703/838-3891 or 838-4994.

In 1774 Alexandria's first firefighting organization, the Friendship Fire Company, was established. In the early days, the company met in taverns and kept its firefighting equipment in a member's barn. Its present Italianate-style brick building dates to 1855; it was erected after an earlier building was, ironically, destroyed by fire. A strong local tradition centers on George Washington's involvement with the firehouse as a founding member, active firefighter, and purchaser of its first fire engine, although extensive research does not bear out these stories. This interesting museum not only houses exhibits of firefighting engines and paraphernalia, but also documents the Friendship Company's efforts to claim Washington as one of their own.

Admission: Free.
Open: Thurs–Sat 10am–4pm, Sun 1–4pm.

ALEXANDRIA BLACK HISTORY RESOURCE CENTER, 638 N. Alfred St., at Wythe St. Tel. 703/838-4356.

In a 1940s building that originally housed the black community's first public library, the center exhibits historical objects, photographs, documents, and memorabilia relating to African-American Alexandrians from the 18th century forward. Besides the permanent collection, the museum presents twice-yearly rotating exhibits, walking tours, and other activities.

Admission: Free.
Open: Tues–Sat 10am–4pm.

SHOPPING

Old Town has hundreds of charming boutiques, antique stores, and gift shops selling everything from souvenir T-shirts to 18th-century reproductions. Some of the most interesting are at the sights (for example, Museum Shop at the Lyceum), but most are clustered on King and Cameron Streets and their connecting cross streets. Plan to spend a fair amount of time browsing in between visits to historic sites. A guide to antique stores is available at the Visitors Bureau.

WHERE TO DINE

There are so many fine restaurants in Alexandria that Washingtonians often drive over just to dine here and stroll the cobblestone streets.

EXPENSIVE

LANDINI BROTHERS, 115 King St., between Lee and Union Sts. Tel. 703/836-8404.

Cuisine: ITALIAN. **Reservations:** Recommended.

$ Prices: Appetizers $4.95–$7.50 at lunch, $5.95–$8.95 at dinner; main courses $8.95–$11.95 at lunch, $11.95–$20.95 at dinner. AE, CB, DC, MC, V.

Open: Mon–Sat 11:30am–11pm. Sun 4–10pm.

The classic, delicate cuisine of Tuscany is featured at this rustic, almost grottolike restaurant with stone walls, a flagstone floor, and rough-hewn beams overhead. Diners sit in wicker-seated chairs at white-linen-covered tables. It's especially charming at night by candlelight. There's additional seating in a lovely dining room upstairs. Everything is homemade—the pasta, the desserts, and the crusty Italian bread. At lunch you might choose a cold seafood salad or spinach and ricotta-stuffed agnolotti in buttery parmesan cheese sauce, followed by a dessert of zuccotto (creamy frozen zabaglione). At dinner, get things under way with prosciutto and melon or shrimp sautéed in garlic with tangy lemon sauce. Then you might proceed to an order of prime aged beef tenderloin médaillons sautéed with garlic, mushrooms, and rosemary in a Barolo wine sauce. Or perhaps linguine with scallops, shrimp, clams, mussels, and squid in a garlic/parsley/red-pepper and white-wine sauce. Dessert choices include tira misu and custard-filled fruit tarts.

MODERATE

EAST WIND, 809 King St., between Columbus and Alfred Sts. Tel. 703/836-1515.
   Cuisine: VIETNAMESE. **Reservations:** Recommended.
$ **Prices:** Appetizers $3.50–$4.95 at lunch, $3.95–$6.95 at dinner; main courses $5.95–$7.95 at lunch, $7.95–$13.95 at dinner; fixed-price lunch $6.95. AE, CB, DC, MC, V.
   Open: Lunch Mon–Fri 11:30am–2:30pm; dinner Mon–Thurs 5:30–10pm. Fri–Sat 5:30–10:30pm. Sun 5:30–9:30pm.

The decor of this Vietnamese restaurant is very appealing: Its sienna stucco and knotty-pine-paneled walls are adorned with works of Vietnamese artist Minh Nguyen, and there are planters of greenery, flowers on each pink-clothed table, and a large floral display up front. The owner personally visits the market each morning to select the freshest fish.

An East Wind meal might begin with an appetizer of cha gio (delicate Vietnamese egg rolls) or a salad of shredded chicken and vegetables mixed with fish sauce. One of my favorite entrées is bo dun—beef tenderloin strips marinated in wine, honey, and spices, rolled in fresh onions, and broiled on bamboo skewers. Also excellent are grilled lemon chicken or charcoal-broiled shrimp and scallops served on rice vermicelli. There's refreshing ginger ice cream for dessert. A good bargain is the fixed-price lunch, which includes soup, an entrée, and coffee or tea.

GADSBY'S TAVERN, 138 N. Royal St., at Cameron St. Tel. 703/548-1288.
   Cuisine: COLONIAL AMERICAN. **Reservations:** Recommended.
$ **Prices:** Appetizers $4.50–$5.25 at lunch, $4.50–$6.25 at dinner; main courses $6.50–$9.95 at lunch/brunch, $14.95–$21.95 at dinner. Half-price portions available on some items for children 12 and under. DC, DISC, MC, V.
   Open: Lunch Mon–Sat 11:30am–3pm, dinner nightly 5:30–10pm, brunch Sun 11am–3pm.

In the spirit of history, pass through the portals where Washington reviewed his troops for the last time and dine at the famous Gadsby's Tavern. The setting authentically evokes the 18th century, with period music, wood-plank floors, hurricane-lamp wall sconces, and a rendition of a Hogarth painting over the fireplace (one of several). Servers are dressed in authentic colonial attire. George Washington dined and danced here often. At night, appropriate entertainment—a strolling minstrel or balladeer—adds to the ambience. A flagstone courtyard edged with flower beds serves as an outdoor dining area in nice weather.

All the fare is homemade, including the sweet Sally Lunn bread baked on the premises daily. You might start off with soup from the stockpot served with homemade sourdough crackers, continue with an entrée of baked ham and cheese pye (a sort of Early American quiche), hot roast turkey with bread/sage stuffing and giblet gravy on Sally Lunn bread, or George Washington's favorite—slow-roasted crisp duckling served with fruit dressing and Madeira sauce. For dessert, try the English trifle or creamy buttermilk-custard pye with a hint of lemon. Colonial "coolers" are also available—scuppernong, Wench's Punch, and such. The Sunday brunch menu adds items like thick slices of toast dipped in a batter of rum and spices, with sausage, hash browns, and hot cinnamon syrup. And a "desserts and libations" menu highlights items like Scottish apple gingerbread and bourbon apple pye, along with a wide selection of beverages. A strolling violinist entertains Sunday and Monday nights and at Sunday brunch. Tuesday to Saturday night an "18th-century gentleman" regales guests with song and tells the news of the day (200 years ago).

RADIO FREE ITALY, 5 Cameron St., right behind the Torpedo Factory. Tel. 703/683-0361.

Cuisine: CALIFORNIA-STYLE ITALIAN. **Reservations:** Accepted for large parties only.

$ Prices: Appetizers $2.95–$6.95, main courses $5.50–$10.95. AE, DC, DISC, MC. V.

Open: Daily 11:30am–11pm.

Anchor of the Food Pavilion, a pleasant waterfront dining complex, Radio Free Italy consists of a downstairs carry-out eatery and a fancier upstairs dining room with wraparound windows providing great views of the boat-filled harbor. The latter, with 62 theatrical halogen lights dramatically spotlighting tables at dinner, has a modernistic Italian black-and-white interior with exposed pipes overhead. Both levels offer outdoor waterfront seating in good weather.

There are marvelous salads such as mixed chilled seafood—mussels, clams, calamari, scallops, and shrimp—marinated in lemon and olive oil. The antipasto sampler is also noteworthy. Oak-fired pizzas have California-style toppings such as grilled chicken, goat cheese, spinach, marinara, and quattro formaggio (romano, fontina, parmesan, and provolone). A bowl of mixed seafood is served on a bed of saffron linguine with three sauces—marinara, cream, and pesto. Yet another good entrée choice is fresh fettuccine tossed with pesto, sun-dried tomatoes, garlic-roasted mushrooms, and paper-thin slices of oak-roasted, peppercorn-studded sirloin. There's a full bar, with Italian wines available by the glass. Desserts include a decadently delicious tira misu.

SOUTH AUSTIN GRILL, 801 King St., at S. Columbus St. Tel. 703/684-8969.

    Cuisine: TEX-MEX. **Reservations:** Not accepted.

$ Prices: Appetizers $3.25–$7.95, main courses mostly $5.25–$10, lunch specials $4.95–$5.75. AE, DC, DISC, MC, V.

    Open: Sun–Thurs 11:30am–11pm, Fri–Sat 11:30am–midnight.

The South Austin Grill opened in 1991 and immediately became one of my favorite Alexandria restaurants. This is great Tex-Mex food, totally authentic and brought to its highest culinary level. The two dining floors are cheerfully decorated with roomy booths painted in bright primary hues. Pastel walls are hung with Austin music club posters and other Texiana, and campy copper sculptures of lizards and snakes are suspended overhead. A corner location lets lots of sunlight stream in.

Start with some delicious chili con queso, flavored with finely minced jalapeño, tomato, and onion and spiked with Dos Equis beer. Also not to be missed are crabmeat quesadillas, stuffed with a mix of lump crabmeat, Monterey jack cheese, green onions, and poblano peppers; they're served with fresh guacamole. For an entrée, South Austin's lime-marinated, mesquite-grilled fajitas (beef or chicken) are out of this world; they come with rice, beans, guacamole, cheese, sour cream, and pico de gallo. Tacos al carbon—pork rubbed with red chilies, garlic, and spices, mesquite grilled, and served up in a tortilla with melted cheese—are also fabulous. Fresh-made iced tea comes with unlimited refills, Texas style, and margaritas are made from scratch. Leave a bit of room for sweet-potato flan—a scrumptious finale. Arrive off-hours to avoid a wait for seating.

BUDGET

THE DELI ON THE STRAND, 211 The Strand, entrance on S. Union St. between Duke and Prince Sts. Tel. 703/ 548-7222.

    Cuisine: DELI.

$ Prices: Sandwiches $1.95–$6.25. AE, MC, V.

    Open: Daily 8am–5pm, with extended hours spring–fall.

Why not a picnic, either combined with a visit to Fort Ward Park (described above), or right in Old Town at Founders Park, bordering the Potomac at the foot of Queen Street? The park doesn't have picnic tables, but there are benches and there's plenty of grass to sit on. Market Square is another possibility. Buy the fixings at the Deli on the Strand. They bake breads on the premises, so the aroma is divine, and you can get reasonably priced cold-cut sandwiches on fresh-baked rye and wheat bread, as well as muffins, and on weekends, bagels. Also available are homemade salads like seafood/pasta, cheeses, yummy desserts, beer, wine, and champagne. There are a few picnic tables outside under an awning.

HARD TIMES CAFE, 1404 King St., near S. West St. Tel. 703/683-5340.

    Cuisine: AMERICAN SOUTHWEST. **Reservations:** Not accepted.

$ Prices: Main courses $3.95–$6.55. MC, V.

Open: Mon–Thurs 11am–10pm, Fri–Sat 11am–11pm, Sun noon–10pm.

⭐ Will Rogers once said he "always judged a town by the quality of its chili." He would have loved Alexandria, where the fabulous Hard Times Cafe serves up top-secret-recipe homemade chilis and fresh-from-the-oven cornbread. It's a laid-back hangout where waiters and waitresses wear jeans and T-shirts; country music is always playing on the jukebox; and the Texas decor features Lone Star flags, a longhorn steer hide overhead, and historic photos of the Old West on the walls. The chili comes in three varieties—Texas, Cincinnati (cooked with sweeter spices, including cinnamon), and vegetarian. I favor the Texas style—coarseground chuck simmered for six hours with special spices in beef sauce. If chili isn't your thing, order grilled chicken breast, a burger, or salad. Side orders of steak fries cooked with the skins, spicy chicken wings, Cheddar-filled jalapeños, and deep-fried onion rings are ample for two. Wash it all down with a bottle of Coors or Lone Star. The menu lists about 30 beers, including a Hard Times label and many selections from western "microbreweries." The Hard Times has garnered many a chili cookoff award, and CHILI-U.S.A.—a resolution before Congress "to make chili the official food of this great nation"—was conceived by Oklahoma lobbyists over a "bowl of red" here. There's additional seating upstairs; the Colorado flag overhead was brought in by a senator from that state.

MURPHY'S, 713 King St., between N. Washington and Columbus Sts. Tel. 703/548-1717.

Cuisine: IRISH/AMERICAN. **Reservations:** Accepted until 7:30pm only.

$ Prices: Appetizers $3.25–$4.95, main courses $5.95–$10.95. AE, CB, DC, MC, V.

Open: Daily 11am–2am; brunch Sun 10am–3pm.

Murphy's is a self-described "grand Irish restaurant and pub," and it couldn't be more cozy and fun-loving. The bar serves up Irish liqueurs and whiskeys and Irish coffee, and has Guinness stout, Murphy's (from County Cork), Mooney's (a local microbrewery stout made especially for this restaurant), and 15 draft beers on tap. Fireplaces are ablaze on both floors during the winter, and Irish bands entertain nightly. This is the kind of bar where you can take the whole family; the kids will love it.

The food is fresh and tasty. Order up a meat-and-potato pie (filled with sage-spiced sausage, ground beef, pork, and mashed potatoes), a platter of fried oysters served with cottage fries (they're great), or hearty Irish stew. There's a low-priced children's menu, and desserts include brown-sugary homemade apple crisp topped with ice cream. At Sunday brunch, Murphy's offers a glass of champagne with a choice of entrées—perhaps bacon, eggs, sausage, home fries, homemade biscuit, and jelly—for $6.95.

THE TEA COSY, 119 S. Royal St., between King and Prince Sts. Tel. 703/836-8181.

Cuisine: BRITISH TEAROOM. **Reservations:** Not accepted.

$ Prices: Tea cakes and sandwiches $1.95–$4.95, full afternoon tea $8.50, main courses $3.50–$8.25. DISC, MC, V.

Open: Sat–Thurs 10am–6pm, Fri 10am–9pm.

This pristine British tearoom is 100% authentic. It's a charming little place, with posters advertising Bovril and Colman's Mustard on whitewashed walls, a beamed ceiling, and a magazine rack stocked with British periodicals and newspapers. Tables are set with pretty floral-patterned place mats. A shop in the back sells archetypically British foodstuffs—digestive biscuits, ginger wine, Irish oatmeal, chutney, and such.

Come in for a full afternoon tea, including assorted tea sandwiches and oven-fresh scones (date/pecan, lemon, raisin, apricot, or cheese) served with jams and Devonshire cream. Assorted tea sandwiches, crumpets, shortbread, and trifle are also à la carte options. For heartier meals, your choices include steak-and-kidney pie, shepherd's pie, Cornish pasty, cheese-and-vegetable pasty, Scottish sausage rolls, and bangers and mash. Everything, including vegetables, is fresh and homemade. There are daily dessert specials such as apple-blackberry pie with custard. Possible libations: British ales and beers, hard cider, and a soft drink called orange quosh.

INDEX

Please Send Me the Books Checked Below:

FROMMER'S COMPREHENSIVE GUIDES
(Guides listing facilities from budget to deluxe,
with emphasis on the medium-priced)

	Retail Price	Code		Retail Price	Code
☐ Acapulco/Ixtapa/Taxco 1993–94	$15.00	C120	☐ Morocco 1992–93	$18.00	C021
☐ Alaska 1994–95	$17.00	C131	☐ Nepal 1994–95	$18.00	C126
☐ Arizona 1993–94	$18.00	C101	☐ New England 1994 (Avail. 1/94)	$16.00	C137
☐ Australia 1992–93	$18.00	C002	☐ New Mexico 1993–94	$15.00	C117
☐ Austria 1993–94	$19.00	C119	☐ New York State 1994–95	$19.00	C133
☐ Bahamas 1994–95	$17.00	C121	☐ Northwest 1994–95 (Avail. 2/94)	$17.00	C140
☐ Belgium/Holland/ Luxembourg 1993–94	$18.00	C106	☐ Portugal 1994–95 (Avail. 2/94)	$17.00	C141
☐ Bermuda 1994–95	$15.00	C122	☐ Puerto Rico 1993–94	$15.00	C103
☐ Brazil 1993–94	$20.00	C111	☐ Puerto Vallarta/ Manzanillo/Guadalajara 1994–95 (Avail. 1/94)	$14.00	C028
☐ California 1994	$15.00	C134	☐ Scandinavia 1993–94	$19.00	C135
☐ Canada 1994–95 (Avail. 4/94)	$19.00	C145	☐ Scotland 1994–95 (Avail. 4/94)	$17.00	C146
☐ Caribbean 1994	$18.00	C123	☐ South Pacific 1994–95 (Avail. 1/94)	$20.00	C138
☐ Carolinas/Georgia 1994–95	$17.00	C128	☐ Spain 1993–94	$19.00	C115
☐ Colorado 1994–95 (Avail. 3/94)	$16.00	C143	☐ Switzerland/ Liechtenstein 1994–95 (Avail. 1/94)	$19.00	C139
☐ Cruises 1993–94	$19.00	C107	☐ Thailand 1992–93	$20.00	C033
☐ Delaware/Maryland 1994–95 (Avail. 1/94)	$15.00	C136	☐ U.S.A. 1993–94	$19.00	C116
☐ England 1994	$18.00	C129	☐ Virgin Islands 1994–95	$13.00	C127
☐ Florida 1994	$18.00	C124	☐ Virginia 1994–95 (Avail. 2/94)	$14.00	C142
☐ France 1994–95	$20.00	C132	☐ Yucatán 1993–94	$18.00	C110
☐ Germany 1994	$19.00	C125			
☐ Italy 1994	$19.00	C130			
☐ Jamaica/Barbados 1993–94	$15.00	C105			
☐ Japan 1994–95 (Avail. 3/94)	$19.00	C144			

FROMMER'S $-A-DAY GUIDES
(Guides to low-cost tourist accommodations and facilities)

	Retail Price	Code		Retail Price	Code
☐ Australia on $45 1993–94	$18.00	D102	☐ Israel on $45 1993–94	$18.00	D101
☐ Costa Rica/Guatemala/ Belize on $35 1993–94	$17.00	D108	☐ Mexico on $45 1994	$19.00	D116
☐ Eastern Europe on $30 1993–94	$18.00	D110	☐ New York on $70 1994–95	$16.00	D120
☐ England on $60 1994	$18.00	D112	☐ New Zealand on $45 1993–94	$18.00	D103
☐ Europe on $50 1994	$19.00	D115	☐ Scotland/Wales on $50 1992–93	$18.00	D019
☐ Greece on $45 1993–94	$19.00	D100	☐ South America on $40 1993–94	$19.00	D109
☐ Hawaii on $75 1994	$19.00	D113	☐ Turkey on $40 1992–93	$22.00	D023
☐ India on $40 1992–93	$20.00	D010	☐ Washington, D.C. on $40 1994–95 (Avail. 2/94)	$17.00	D119
☐ Ireland on $45 1994–95 (Avail. 1/94)	$17.00	D117			

FROMMER'S CITY $-A-DAY GUIDES
(Pocket-size guides to low-cost tourist accommodations
and facilities)

	Retail Price	Code		Retail Price	Code
☐ Berlin on $40 1994–95	$12.00	D111	☐ Madrid on $50 1994–95 (Avail. 1/94)	$13.00	D118
☐ Copenhagen on $50 1992–93	$12.00	D003	☐ Paris on $50 1994–95	$12.00	D117
☐ London on $45 1994–95	$12.00	D114	☐ Stockholm on $50 1992–93	$13.00	D022

FROMMER'S WALKING TOURS
(With routes and detailed maps, these companion guides point out
the places and pleasures that make a city unique)

	Retail Price	Code		Retail Price	Code
☐ Berlin	$12.00	W100	☐ Paris	$12.00	W103
☐ London	$12.00	W101	☐ San Francisco	$12.00	W104
☐ New York	$12.00	W102	☐ Washington, D.C.	$12.00	W105

FROMMER'S TOURING GUIDES
(Color-illustrated guides that include walking tours, cultural and historic
sights, and practical information)

	Retail Price	Code		Retail Price	Code
☐ Amsterdam	$11.00	T001	☐ New York	$11.00	T008
☐ Barcelona	$14.00	T015	☐ Rome	$11.00	T010
☐ Brazil	$11.00	T003	☐ Scotland	$10.00	T011
☐ Florence	$ 9.00	T005	☐ Sicily	$15.00	T017
☐ Hong Kong/Singapore/			☐ Tokyo	$15.00	T016
Macau	$11.00	T006	☐ Turkey	$11.00	T013
☐ Kenya	$14.00	T018	☐ Venice	$ 9.00	T014
☐ London	$13.00	T007			

FROMMER'S FAMILY GUIDES

	Retail Price	Code		Retail Price	Code
☐ California with Kids	$18.00	F100	☐ San Francisco with Kids		
☐ Los Angeles with Kids			(Avail. 4/94)	$17.00	F104
(Avail. 4/94)	$17.00	F103	☐ Washington, D.C. with		
☐ New York City with Kids			Kids (Avail. 2/94)	$17.00	F102
(Avail. 2/94)	$18.00	F101			

FROMMER'S CITY GUIDES
(Pocket-size guides to sightseeing and tourist accommodations and
facilities in all price ranges)

	Retail Price	Code		Retail Price	Code
☐ Amsterdam 1993–94	$13.00	S110	☐ Montréal/Québec		
☐ Athens 1993–94	$13.00	S114	City 1993–94	$13.00	S125
☐ Atlanta 1993–94	$13.00	S112	☐ Nashville/Memphis		
☐ Atlantic City/Cape			1994–95 (Avail. 4/94)	$13.00	S141
May 1993–94	$13.00	S130	☐ New Orleans 1993–		
☐ Bangkok 1992–93	$13.00	S005	94	$13.00	S103
☐ Barcelona/Majorca/			☐ New York 1994 (Avail.		
Minorca/Ibiza 1993–			1/94)	$13.00	S138
94	$13.00	S115	☐ Orlando 1994	$13.00	S135
☐ Berlin 1993–94	$13.00	S116	☐ Paris 1993–94	$13.00	S109
☐ Boston 1993–94	$13.00	S117	☐ Philadelphia 1993–94	$13.00	S113
☐ Budapest 1994–95			☐ San Diego 1993–94	$13.00	S107
(Avail. 2/94)	$13.00	S139	☐ San Francisco 1994	$13.00	S133
☐ Chicago 1993–94	$13.00	S122	☐ Santa Fe/Taos/		
☐ Denver/Boulder/			Albuquerque 1993–94	$13.00	S108
Colorado Springs			☐ Seattle/Portland 1994–		
1993–94	$13.00	S131	95	$13.00	S137
☐ Dublin 1993–94	$13.00	S128	☐ St. Louis/Kansas		
☐ Hong Kong 1994–95			City 1993–94	$13.00	S127
(Avail. 4/94)	$13.00	S140	☐ Sydney 1993–94	$13.00	S129
☐ Honolulu/Oahu 1994	$13.00	S134	☐ Tampa/St.		
☐ Las Vegas 1993–94	$13.00	S121	Petersburg 1993–94	$13.00	S105
☐ London 1994	$13.00	S132	☐ Tokyo 1992–93	$13.00	S039
☐ Los Angeles 1993–94	$13.00	S123	☐ Toronto 1993–94	$13.00	S126
☐ Madrid/Costa del			☐ Vancouver/Victoria		
Sol 1993–94	$13.00	S124	1994–95 (Avail. 1/94)	$13.00	S142
☐ Miami 1993–94	$13.00	S118	☐ Washington,		
☐ Minneapolis/St.			D.C. 1994 (Avail.		
Paul 1993–94	$13.00	S119	1/94)	$13.00	S136

SPECIAL EDITIONS

	Retail Price	Code		Retail Price	Code
☐ Bed & Breakfast Southwest	$16.00	P100	☐ Caribbean Hideaways	$16.00	P103
☐ Bed & Breakfast Great American Cities (Avail. 1/94)	$16.00	P104	☐ National Park Guide 1994 (Avail. 3/94)	$16.00	P105
			☐ Where to Stay U.S.A.	$15.00	P102

Please note: if the availability of a book is several months away, we may have back issues of guides to that particular destination. Call customer service at (815) 734-1104.